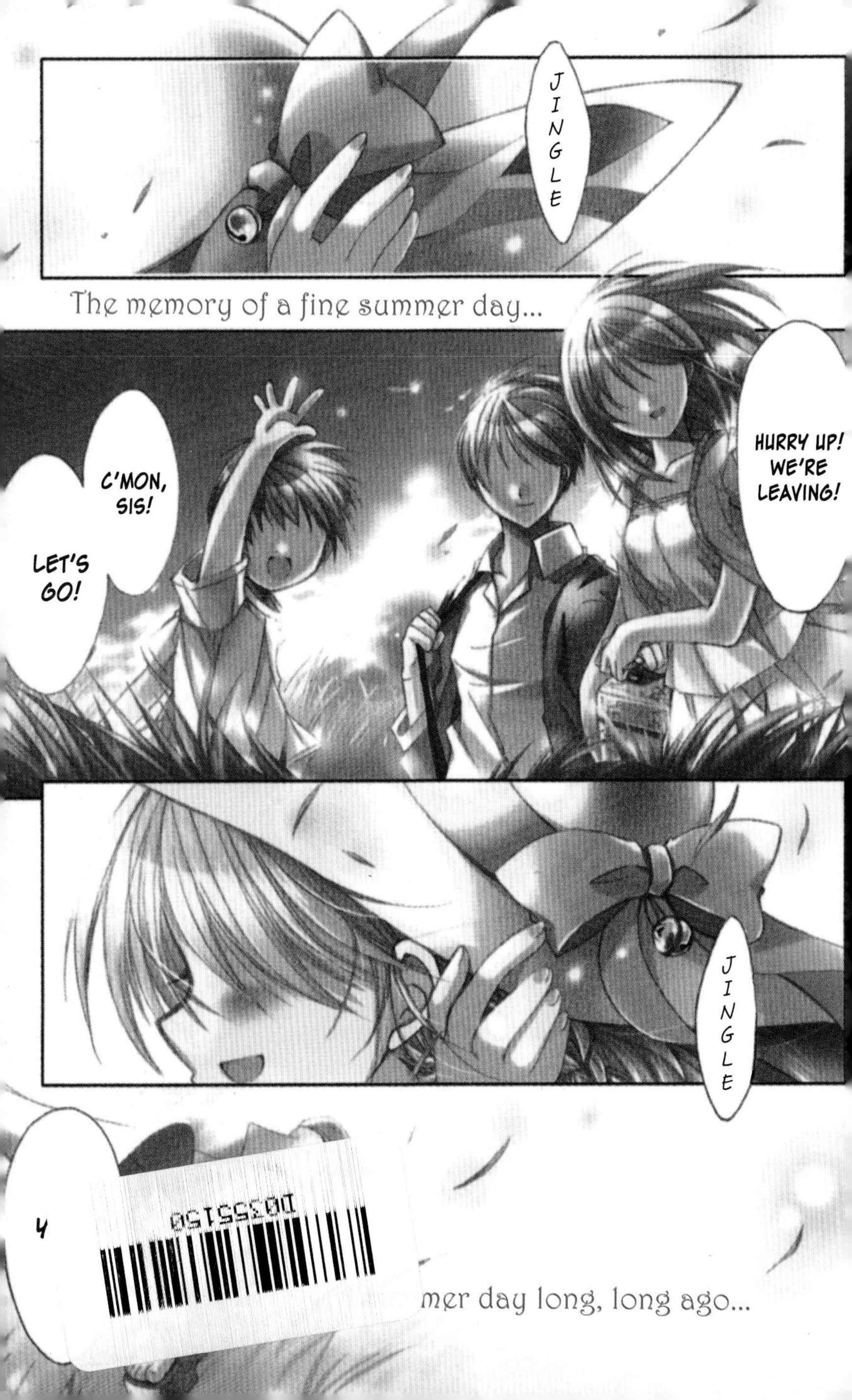
JINGLE
The memory of a fine summer day...
HURRY UP! WE'RE LEAVING!
C'MON, SIS!
LET'S GO!
JINGLE
mer day long, long ago...

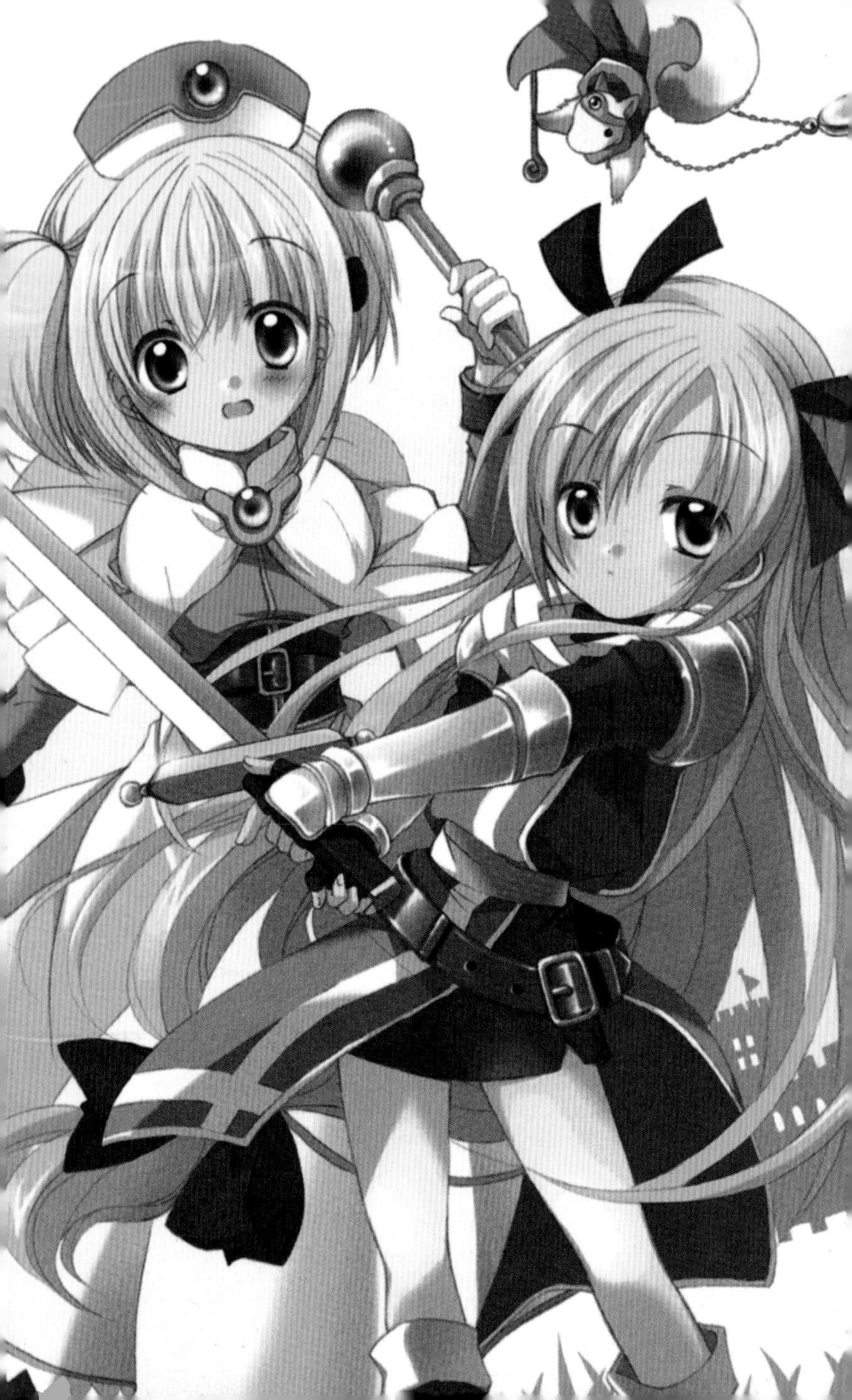

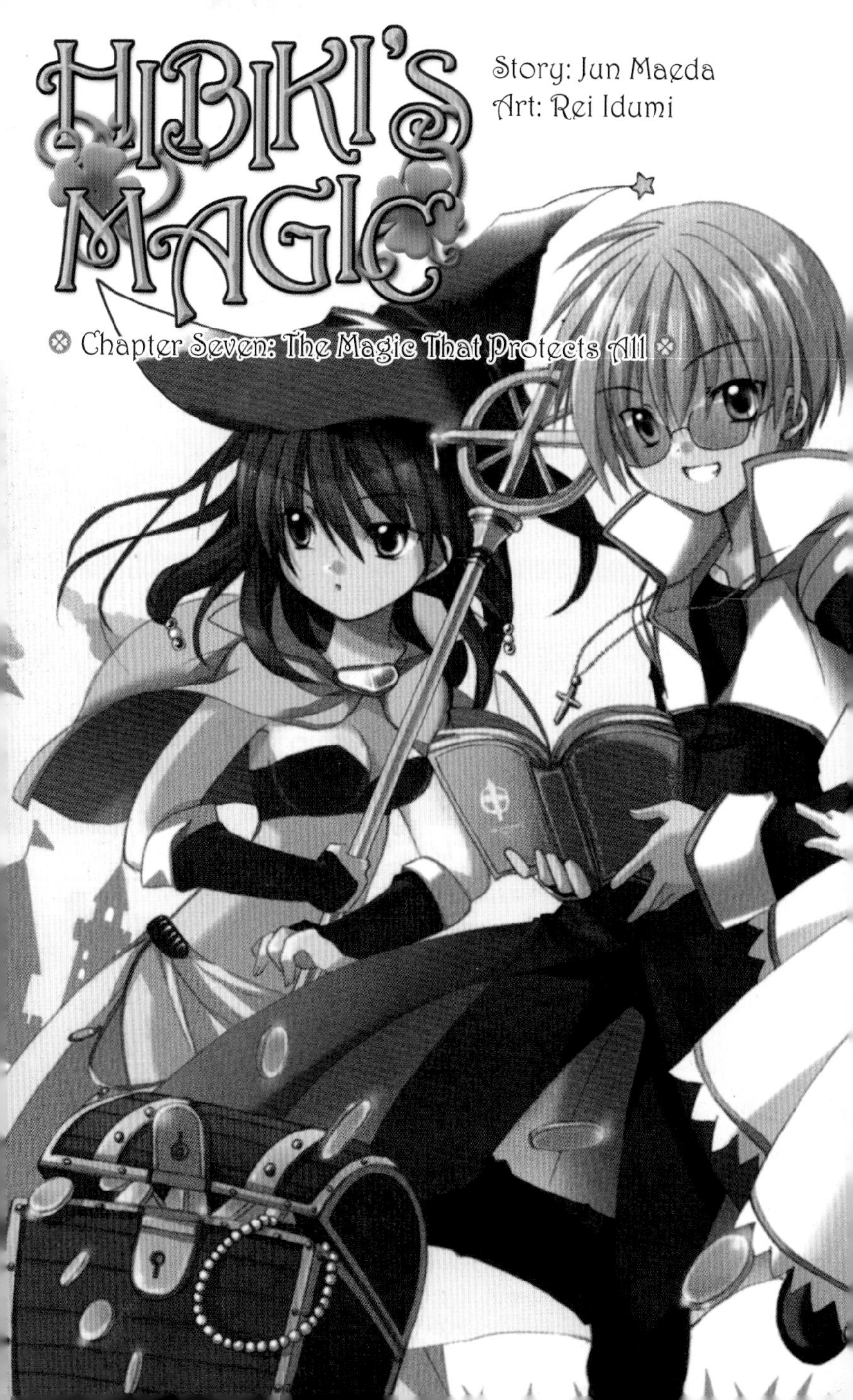
Hibiki's Magic
Story: Jun Maeda
Art: Rei Idumi
Chapter Seven: The Magic That Protects All

HIBIKI'S MAGIC™
Contents

HIBIKI'S MAGIC™

Volume 2

Rei Idumi & Jun Maeda

TOKYOPOP®

HAMBURG // LONDON // LOS ANGELES // TOKYO

Hibiki's Magic Vol. 2
Created by Jun Maeda and Rei Idumi

Translation - Alexis Kirsch
English Adaption - Jamie S. Rich
Copy Editor - Stephanie Duchin
Layout and Lettering - Star Print Brokers
Production Artist - Vicente Rivera, Jr.
Cover Layout - James Lee

Editor - Peter Ahlstrom
Digital Imaging Manager - Chris Buford
Pre-Production Supervisor - Erika Terriquez
Art Director - Anne Marie Horne
Production Manager - Elisabeth Brizzi
Managing Editor - Vy Nguyen
VP of Production - Ron Klamert
Editor-in-Chief - Rob Tokar
Publisher - Mike Kiley
President and C.O.O. - John Parker
C.E.O. and Chief Creative Officer - Stuart Levy

A  Manga

TOKYOPOP Inc.
5900 Wilshire Blvd. Suite 2000
Los Angeles, CA 90036

E-mail: info@TOKYOPOP.com
Come visit us online at www.TOKYOPOP.com

ISBN: 978-1-4278-0458-7

First TOKYOPOP printing: September 2007
10 9 8 7 6 5 4 3 2 1
Printed in the USA

The Story So Far

Magic. It can do marvelous things—but there is always a cost. For the wizard Shirotsuki, an expert in magical circles and researcher into immortality, the price he pays for his magical studies is the random loss of his memory. And so he has told his young assistant that if he ever asks her who she is, she must promptly reply, "I am the wizard Shirotsuki's one and only assistant, Hibiki."

Hibiki tends toward clumsiness and tears, and has very little confidence in her own ability to do anything right beyond making a cup of tea, but Shirotsuki has recognized in her the potential for inner strength and great magical ability. When a fire strikes their home in the middle of a risky magical experiment, destroying Shirotsuki's body and leaving his mind trapped inside a squirrel-like gusk, Hibiki must draw on her potential and face the world alone—well, not quite alone, since her master is still with her in the form of the little gusk perched on her shoulder.

When Hibiki arrives in the nation of Kamisaid's capital, Kamigusk, she is recognized as the famous wizard Shirotsuki's assistant by administrators from Royal Kamisaid Magic Academy. Assuming her to be a great magician in her own right, they invite her to join the faculty, and Hibiki finds herself in the unlikely role of professor to students who are all older than her. They are skeptical at first, especially a youngster named Ahito who has had a bad experience with magic in the past. His eyes have the ability to heal others, to the detriment of his own health, and when he was not strong enough to save a friend of his, he decided to put his faith in technology instead of magic. So he challenges Hibiki to a duel of technology vs. magic, and when Hibiki defeats him by creating a vision of Ahito's past, the sympathy she shows him turns Ahito into one of her biggest supporters.

Hibiki's big heart also reaches out to Yutsuko, a nearby magic researcher whose grief at her daughter's death has led her to attempt to create a homunculus—a magically created artificial being—to replace the daughter she lost, but whose futile experiments have repeatedly failed to create anything more than an amorphous blob lasting no longer than three days. Hibiki plunges headlong into homunculus research, and with her master's help is able to create one in the form of a little girl. The homunculus names herself Lord Shiraasan, after one of the most successful military homunculi of the recent war, but Hibiki calls her Shi-chan. Since homunculi were originally developed as tools of warfare, Shi-chan's instincts are to respond to any annoyance with violence, and she is annoyed that Hibiki is keeping her cooped up indoors—because Hibiki fears that her creation's body will become unstable and dissolve when the three-day limit hits.

Sure enough, Shi-chan falls ill as the deadline approaches, but she is saved by a medicine that came from Yutsuko's daughter's tears. Confident that the homunculus will last indefinitely as long as she doesn't use up her military magic, Hibiki takes her to Yutsuko and announces that Yutsuko will be her new mother, but Shi-chan only feels abandoned. Yutsuko is deeply touched by Hibiki's sacrifice, but she realizes her daughter can never be replaced, and Shi-chan is tearfully reunited with Hibiki.

And so the tale of Hibiki's heartfelt magic continues...

HIBIKI'S MAGIC™

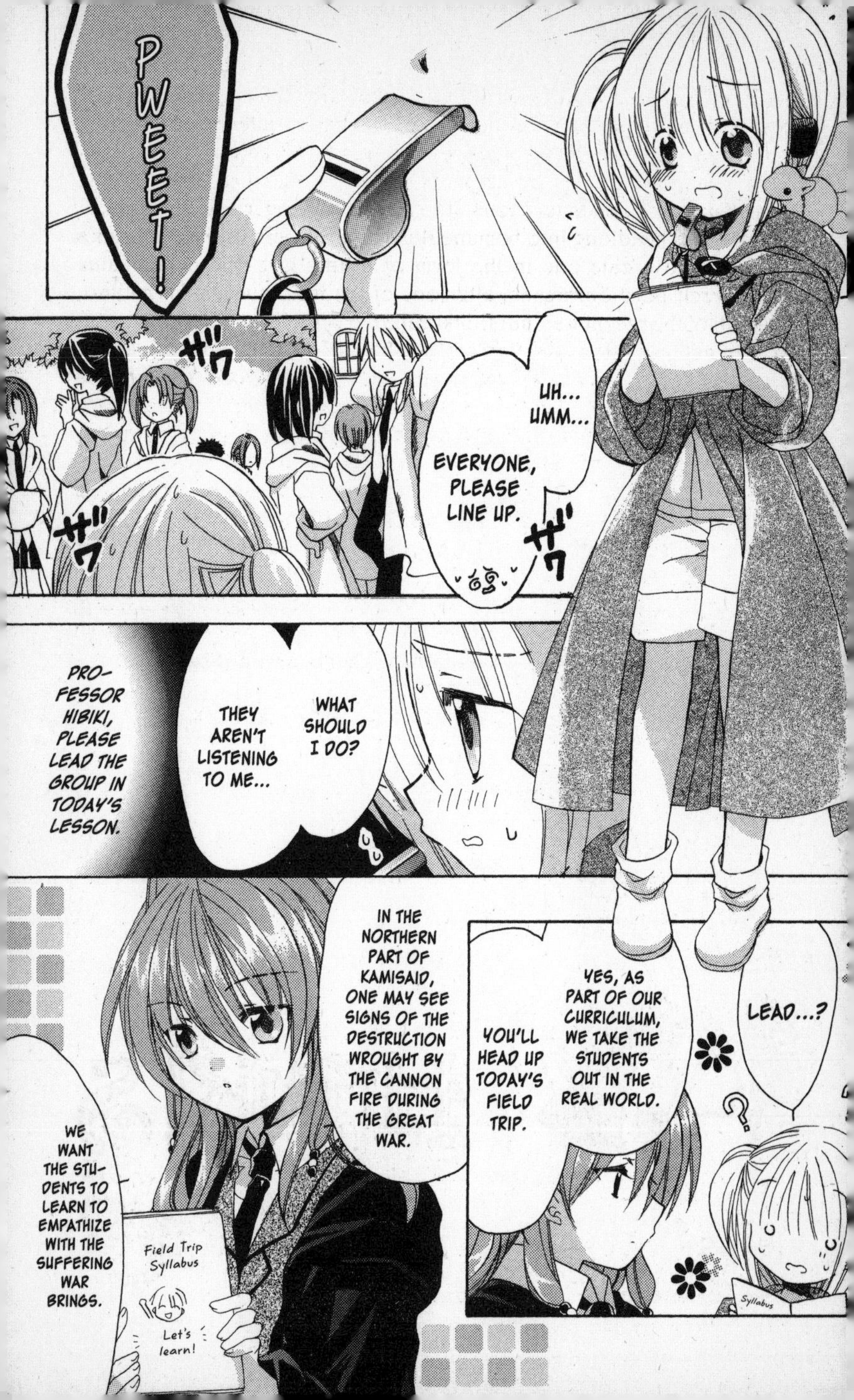
PWEET!
UH... UMM...
EVERYONE, PLEASE LINE UP.
ザワ
ザワ
ザワ
WHAT SHOULD I DO?
THEY AREN'T LISTENING TO ME...
PRO-FESSOR HIBIKI, PLEASE LEAD THE GROUP IN TODAY'S LESSON.
LEAD...?
Syllabus
YES, AS PART OF OUR CURRICULUM, WE TAKE THE STUDENTS OUT IN THE REAL WORLD.
YOU'LL HEAD UP TODAY'S FIELD TRIP.
IN THE NORTHERN PART OF KAMISAID, ONE MAY SEE SIGNS OF THE DESTRUCTION WROUGHT BY THE CANNON FIRE DURING THE GREAT WAR.
WE WANT THE STU-DENTS TO LEARN TO EMPATHIZE WITH THE SUFFERING WAR BRINGS.
Field Trip Syllabus
Let's learn!

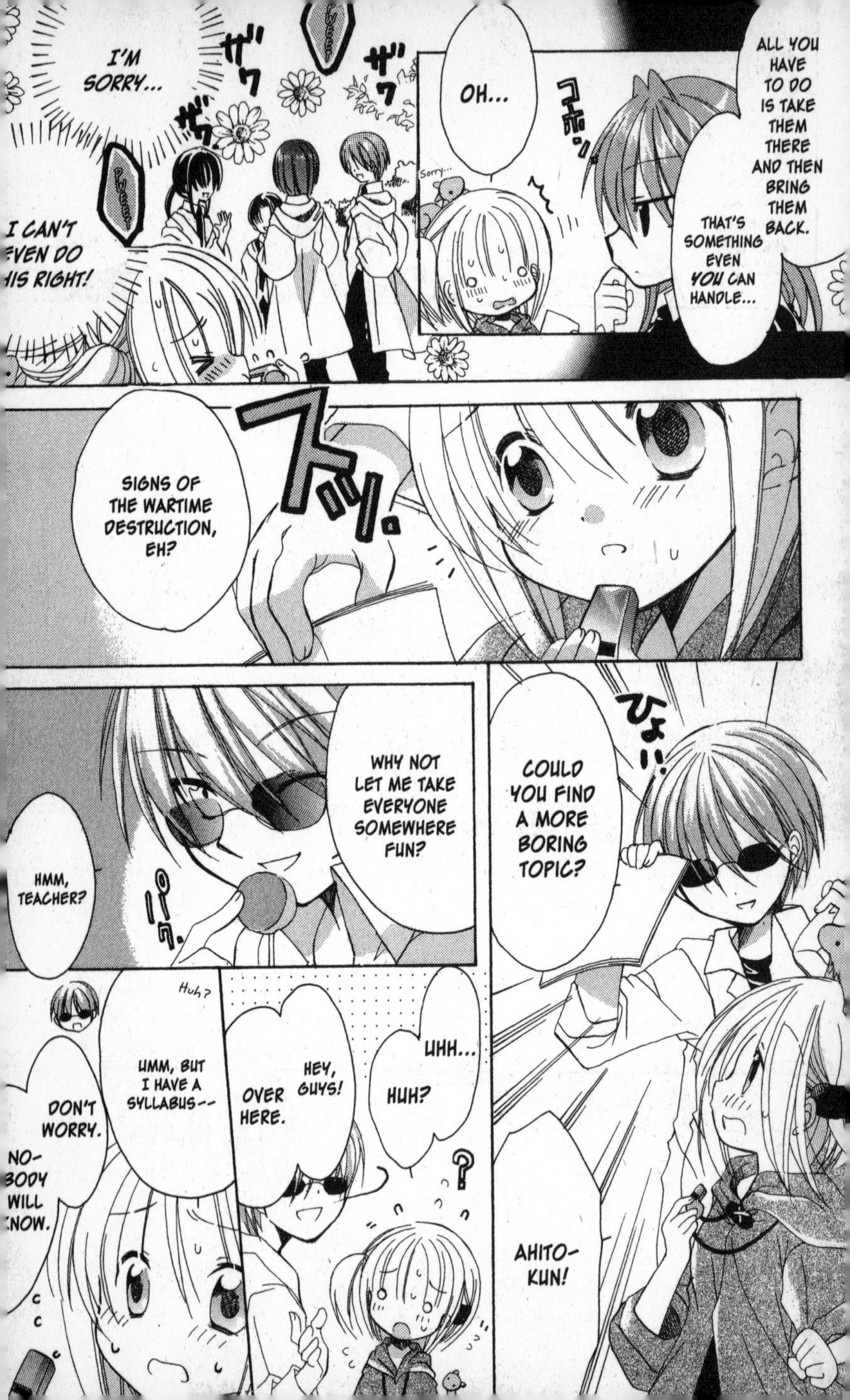
ALL YOU HAVE TO DO IS TAKE THEM THERE AND THEN BRING THEM BACK.
THAT'S SOMETHING EVEN YOU CAN HANDLE...
OH...
Sorry...
PWEET
I'M SORRY...
PWEET
I CAN'T EVEN DO HIS RIGHT!
SIGNS OF THE WARTIME DESTRUCTION, EH?
COULD YOU FIND A MORE BORING TOPIC?
AHITO-KUN!
WHY NOT LET ME TAKE EVERYONE SOMEWHERE FUN?
HMM, TEACHER?
UHH...
HUH?
HEY, GUYS!
OVER HERE.
Huh?
UMM, BUT I HAVE A SYLLABUS--
DON'T WORRY.
NO-BODY WILL KNOW.

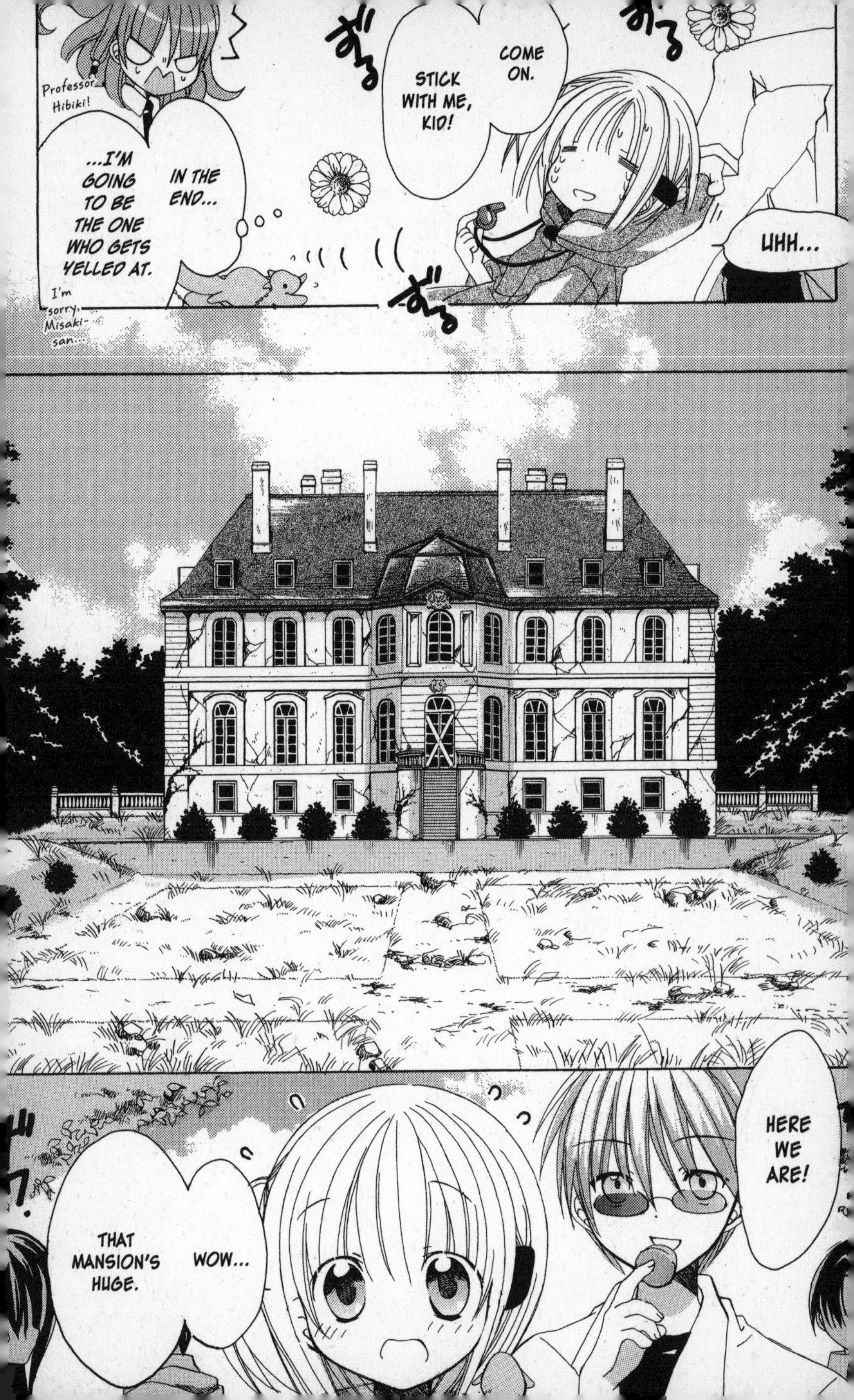
ずる
COME ON. STICK WITH ME, KID!
ずる
UHH...
ずる
Professor Hibiki!
IN THE END... ...I'M GOING TO BE THE ONE WHO GETS YELLED AT.
I'm sorry, Misaki-san...
HERE WE ARE!
WOW... THAT MANSION'S HUGE.

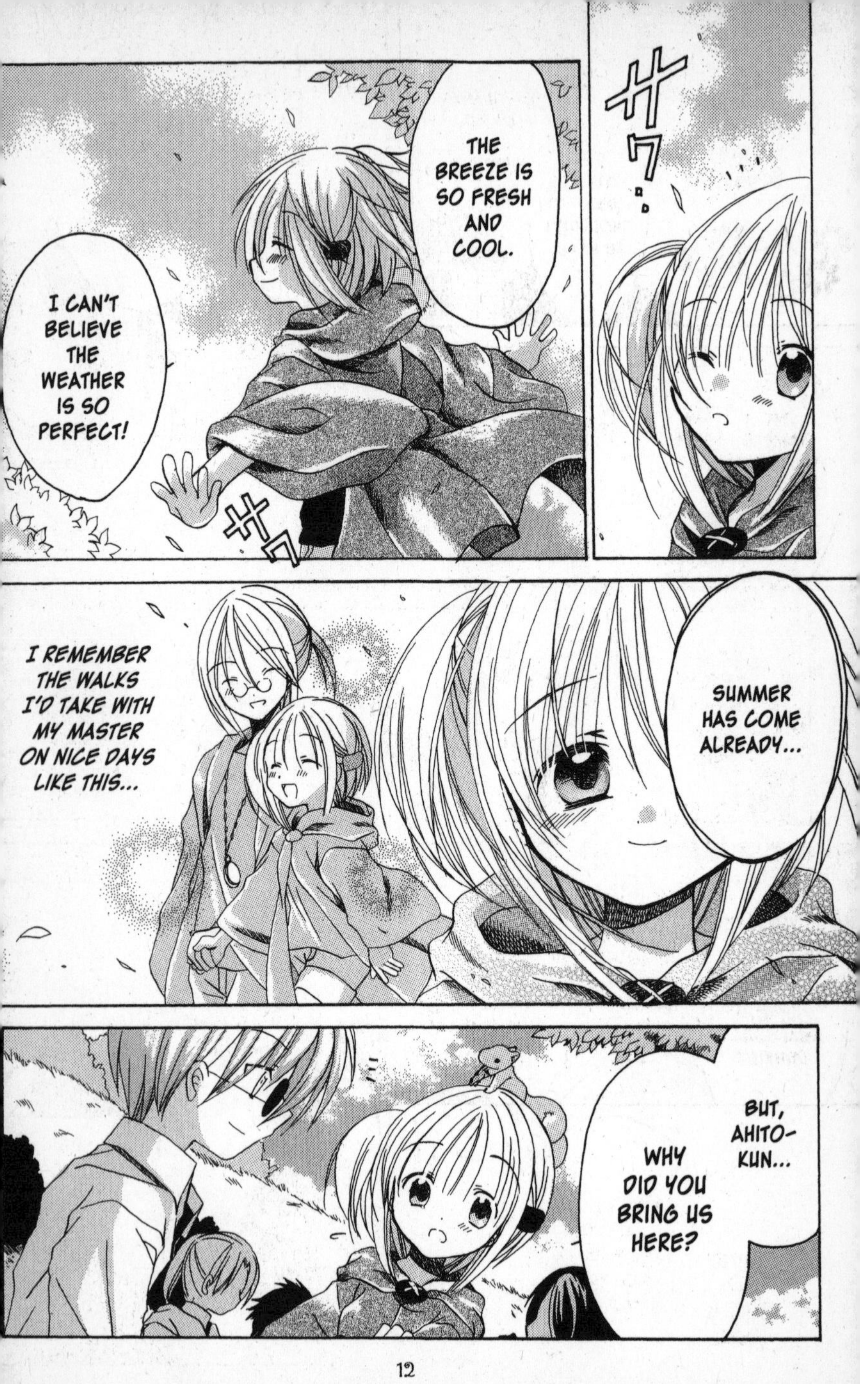
ハッ
THE BREEZE IS SO FRESH AND COOL.
I CAN'T BELIEVE THE WEATHER IS SO PERFECT!
ハッ
SUMMER HAS COME ALREADY...
I REMEMBER THE WALKS I'D TAKE WITH MY MASTER ON NICE DAYS LIKE THIS...
BUT, AHITO-KUN...
WHY DID YOU BRING US HERE?

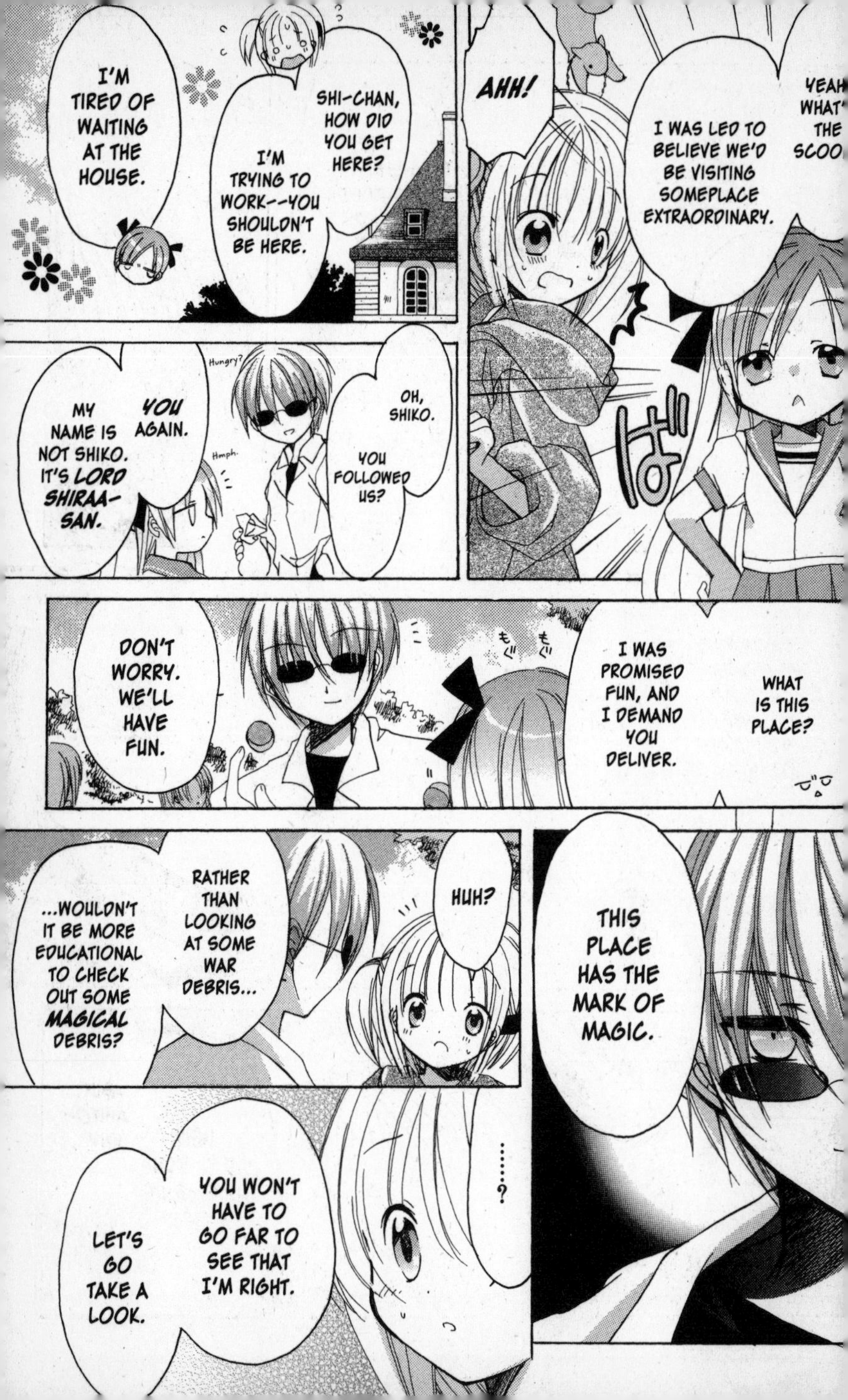
YEAH WHAT' THE SCOO
I WAS LED TO BELIEVE WE'D BE VISITING SOMEPLACE EXTRAORDINARY.
AHH!
ば
SHI-CHAN, HOW DID YOU GET HERE?
I'M TRYING TO WORK--YOU SHOULDN'T BE HERE.
I'M TIRED OF WAITING AT THE HOUSE.
OH, SHIKO.
YOU FOLLOWED US?
Hungry?
YOU AGAIN.
Hmph.
MY NAME IS NOT SHIKO. IT'S LORD SHIRAA-SAN.
WHAT IS THIS PLACE?
I WAS PROMISED FUN, AND I DEMAND YOU DELIVER.
もぐ もぐ
DON'T WORRY. WE'LL HAVE FUN.
THIS PLACE HAS THE MARK OF MAGIC.
HUH?
RATHER THAN LOOKING AT SOME WAR DEBRIS...
...WOULDN'T IT BE MORE EDUCATIONAL TO CHECK OUT SOME MAGICAL DEBRIS?
......?
YOU WON'T HAVE TO GO FAR TO SEE THAT I'M RIGHT.
LET'S GO TAKE A LOOK.

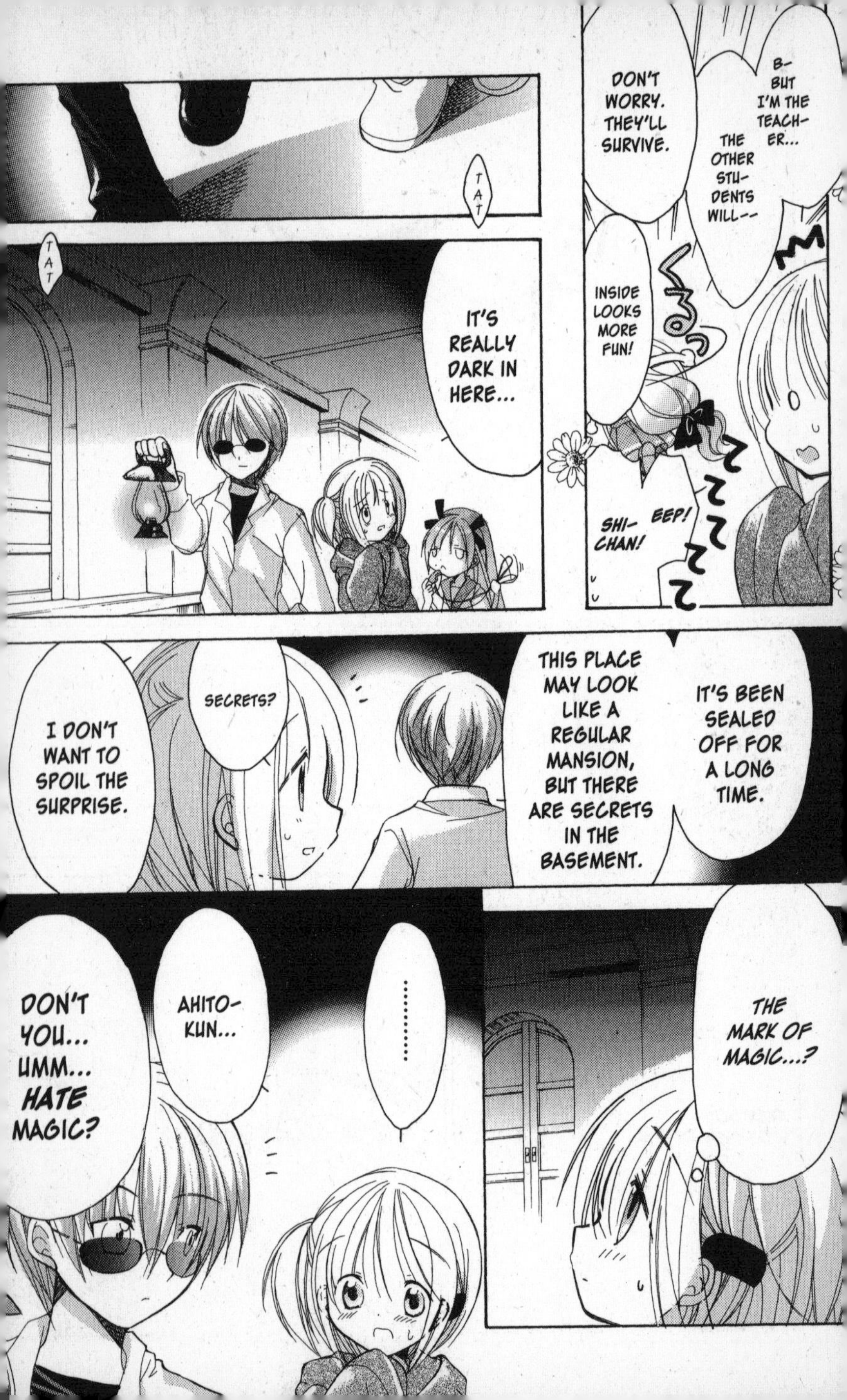

B-BUT I'M THE TEACHER...
THE OTHER STUDENTS WILL--
DON'T WORRY. THEY'LL SURVIVE.
INSIDE LOOKS MORE FUN!
EEP!
SHI-CHAN!
TAT
TAT
IT'S REALLY DARK IN HERE...
IT'S BEEN SEALED OFF FOR A LONG TIME.
THIS PLACE MAY LOOK LIKE A REGULAR MANSION, BUT THERE ARE SECRETS IN THE BASEMENT.
SECRETS?
I DON'T WANT TO SPOIL THE SURPRISE.
THE MARK OF MAGIC...?
....
AHITO-KUN...
DON'T YOU... UMM... HATE MAGIC?

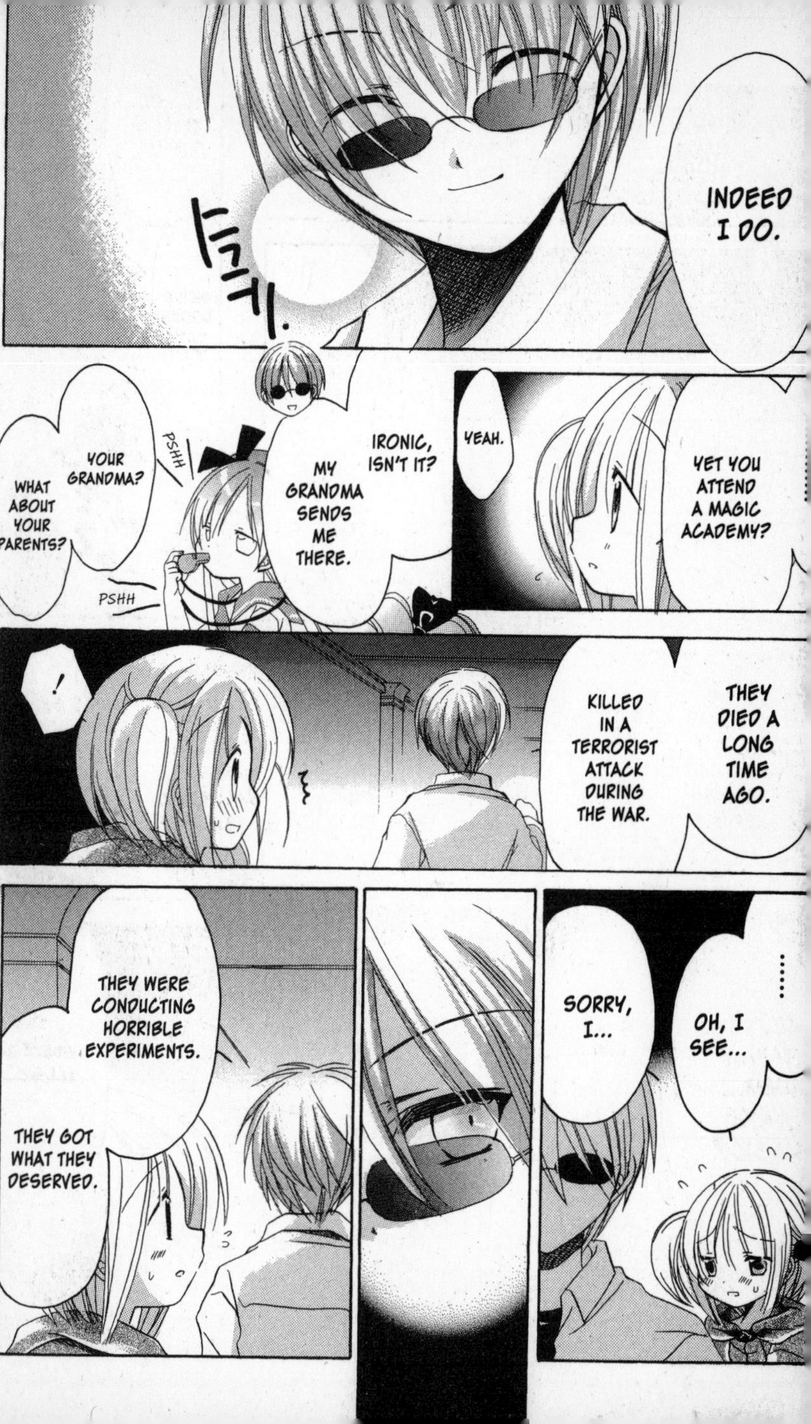
INDEED I DO.
YET YOU ATTEND A MAGIC ACADEMY?
YEAH.
IRONIC, ISN'T IT?
MY GRANDMA SENDS ME THERE.
PSHH
YOUR GRANDMA?
WHAT ABOUT YOUR PARENTS?
PSHH
THEY DIED A LONG TIME AGO.
KILLED IN A TERRORIST ATTACK DURING THE WAR.
!
......
OH, I SEE...
SORRY, I...
THEY WERE CONDUCTING HORRIBLE EXPERIMENTS.
THEY GOT WHAT THEY DESERVED.

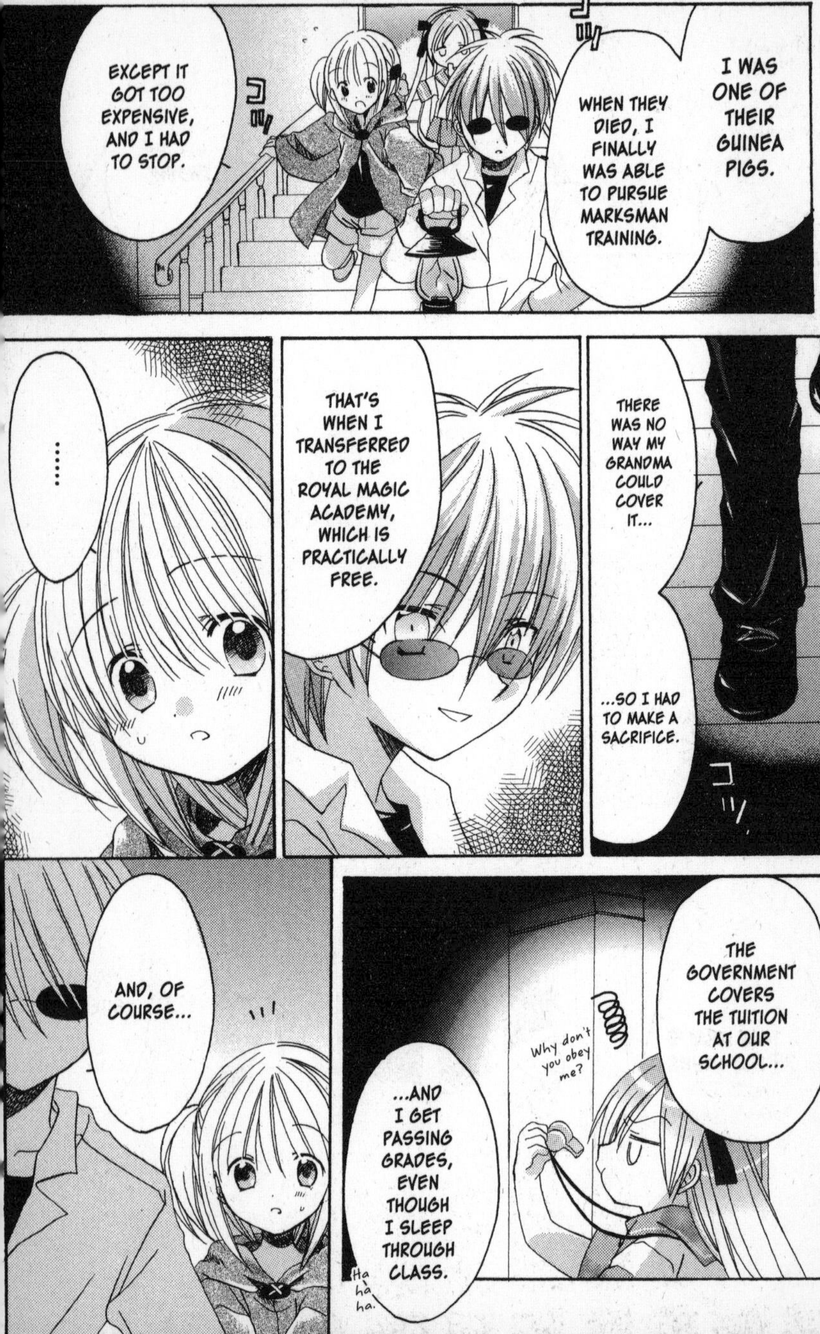
I WAS ONE OF THEIR GUINEA PIGS.
コツ
WHEN THEY DIED, I FINALLY WAS ABLE TO PURSUE MARKSMAN TRAINING.
コツ
EXCEPT IT GOT TOO EXPENSIVE, AND I HAD TO STOP.
THERE WAS NO WAY MY GRANDMA COULD COVER IT...
コツ
...SO I HAD TO MAKE A SACRIFICE.
コツ
THAT'S WHEN I TRANSFERRED TO THE ROYAL MAGIC ACADEMY, WHICH IS PRACTICALLY FREE.
......
THE GOVERNMENT COVERS THE TUITION AT OUR SCHOOL...
Why don't you obey me?
...AND I GET PASSING GRADES, EVEN THOUGH I SLEEP THROUGH CLASS.
Ha ha ha.
AND, OF COURSE...

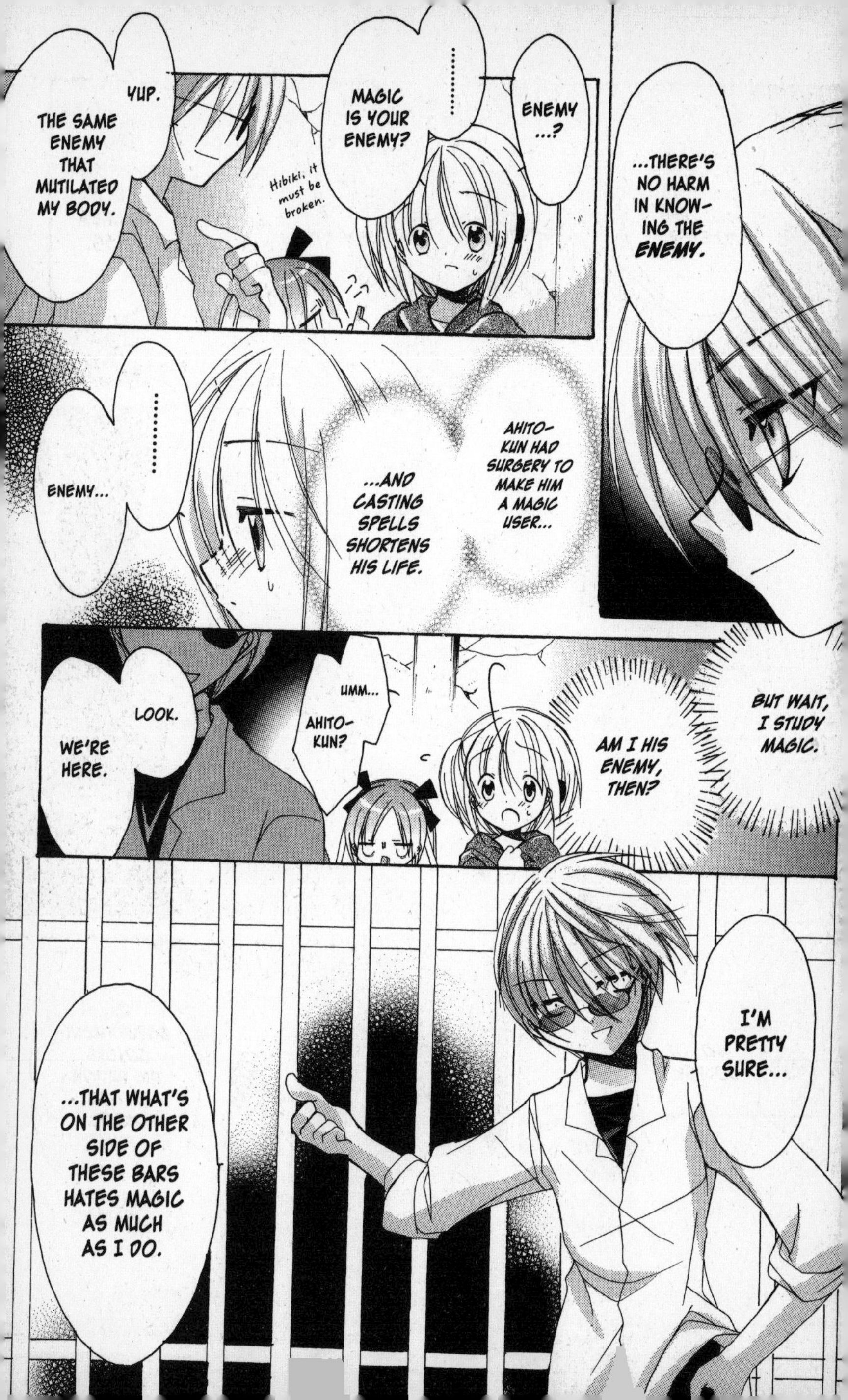
...THERE'S NO HARM IN KNOWING THE ENEMY.
ENEMY ...?
......
MAGIC IS YOUR ENEMY?
Hibiki, it must be broken.
YUP.
THE SAME ENEMY THAT MUTILATED MY BODY.
AHITO-KUN HAD SURGERY TO MAKE HIM A MAGIC USER...
...AND CASTING SPELLS SHORTENS HIS LIFE.
......
ENEMY...
BUT WAIT, I STUDY MAGIC.
AM I HIS ENEMY, THEN?
UMM...
AHITO-KUN?
LOOK.
WE'RE HERE.
I'M PRETTY SURE...
...THAT WHAT'S ON THE OTHER SIDE OF THESE BARS HATES MAGIC AS MUCH AS I DO.

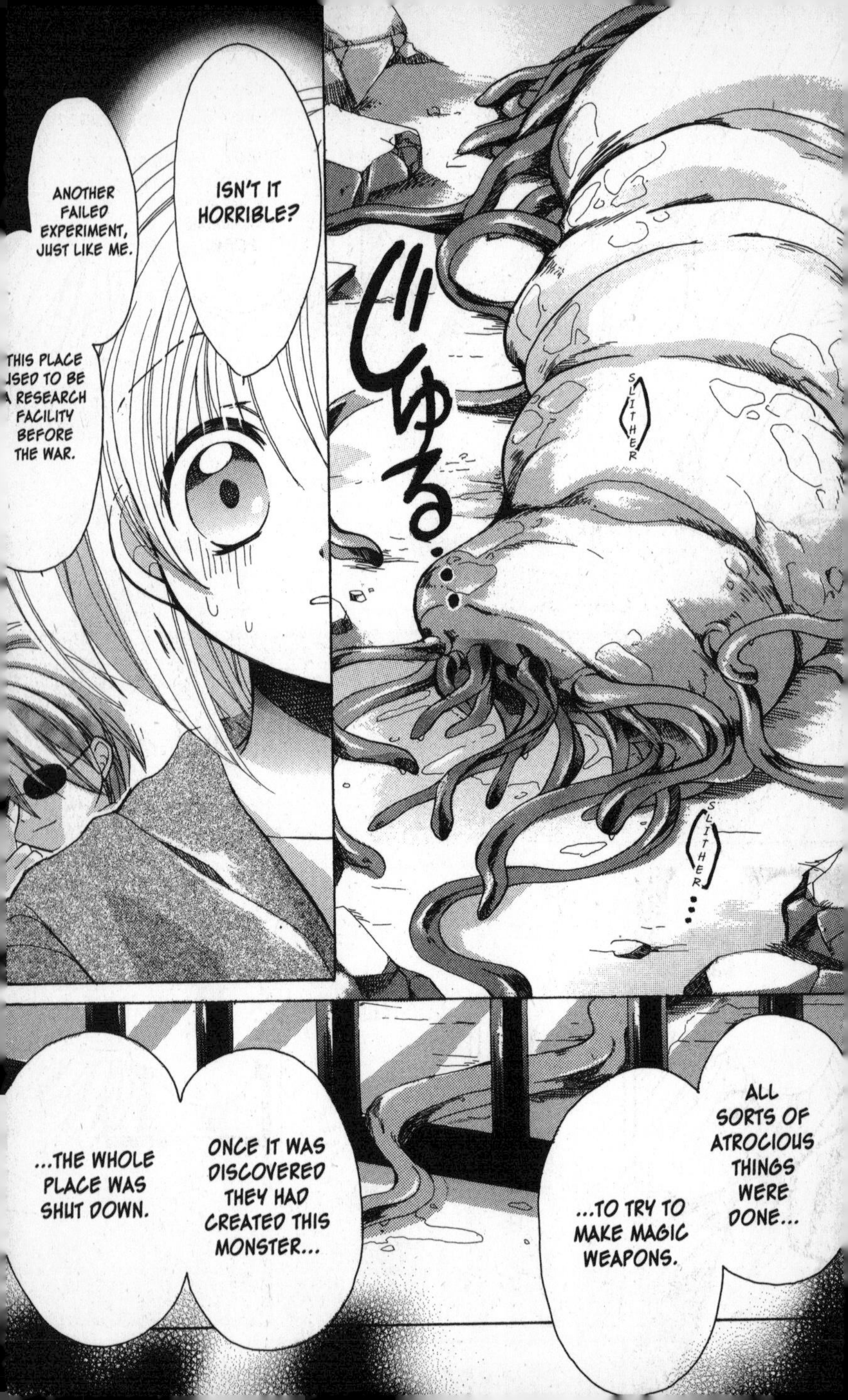
じゅる…
SLITHER
SLITHER…
ISN'T IT HORRIBLE?
ANOTHER FAILED EXPERIMENT, JUST LIKE ME.
THIS PLACE USED TO BE A RESEARCH FACILITY BEFORE THE WAR.
ALL SORTS OF ATROCIOUS THINGS WERE DONE...
...TO TRY TO MAKE MAGIC WEAPONS.
ONCE IT WAS DISCOVERED THEY HAD CREATED THIS MONSTER...
...THE WHOLE PLACE WAS SHUT DOWN.

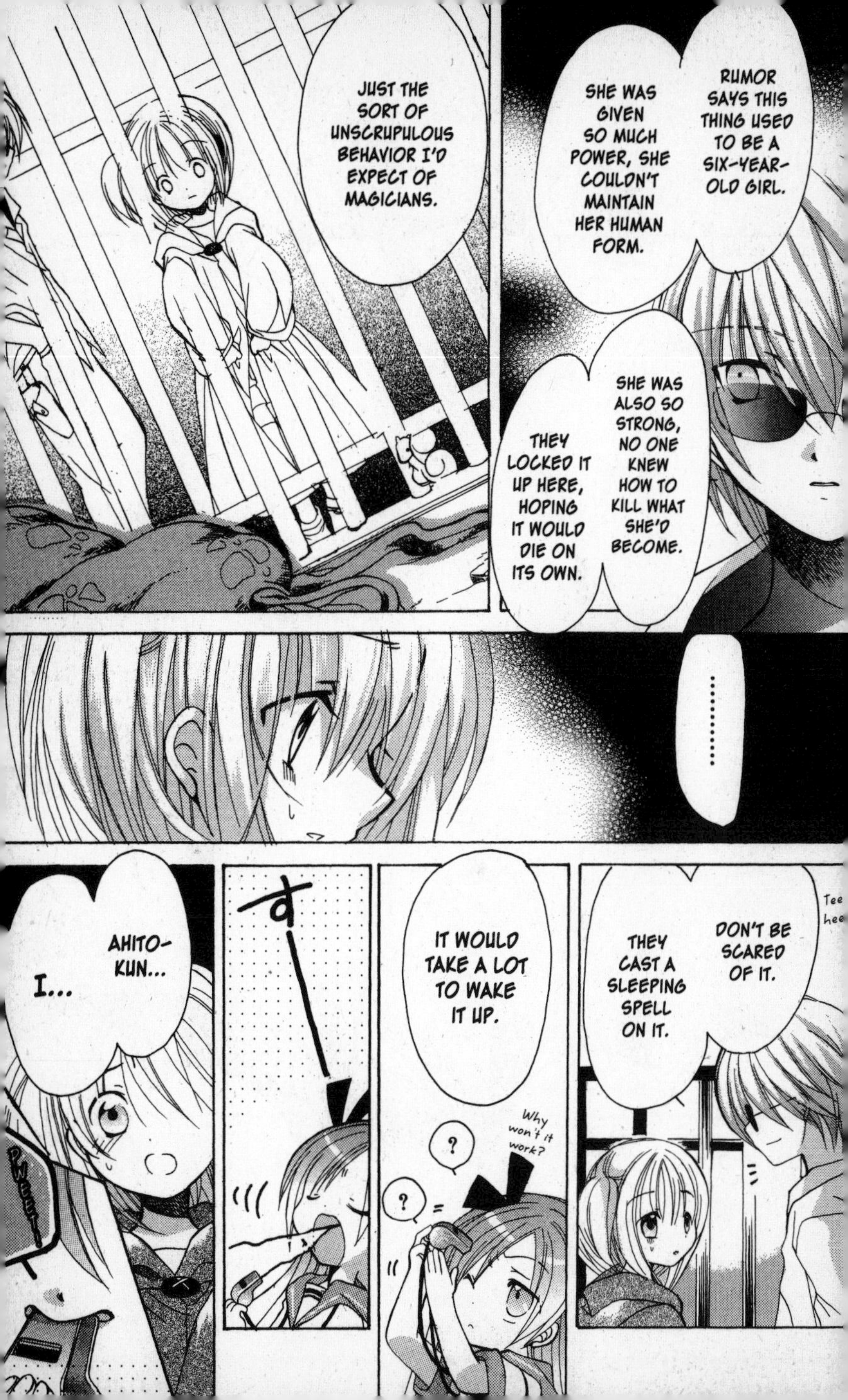
RUMOR SAYS THIS THING USED TO BE A SIX-YEAR-OLD GIRL.
SHE WAS GIVEN SO MUCH POWER, SHE COULDN'T MAINTAIN HER HUMAN FORM.
SHE WAS ALSO SO STRONG, NO ONE KNEW HOW TO KILL WHAT SHE'D BECOME.
THEY LOCKED IT UP HERE, HOPING IT WOULD DIE ON ITS OWN.
JUST THE SORT OF UNSCRUPULOUS BEHAVIOR I'D EXPECT OF MAGICIANS.
......
Tee hee
DON'T BE SCARED OF IT.
THEY CAST A SLEEPING SPELL ON IT.
IT WOULD TAKE A LOT TO WAKE IT UP.
?
?
Why won't it work?
す
AHITO-KUN...
I...
PWEET!

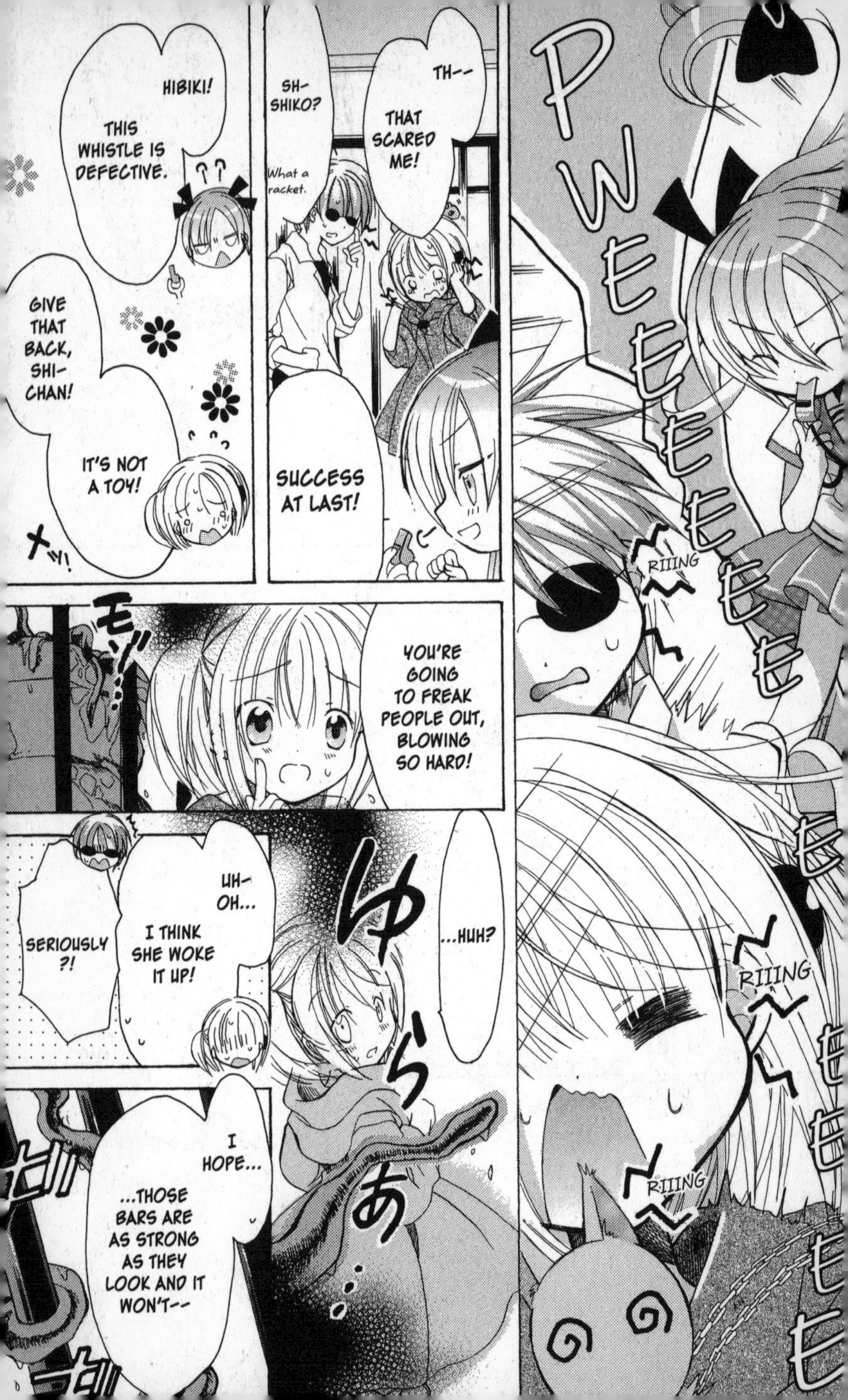
PWEEEEEEEEEEEEEE
RIIING
RIIING
RIIING
TH-- THAT SCARED ME!
SH-SHIKO?
What a racket.
SUCCESS AT LAST!
HIBIKI! THIS WHISTLE IS DEFECTIVE.
GIVE THAT BACK, SHI-CHAN!
IT'S NOT A TOY!
YOU'RE GOING TO FREAK PEOPLE OUT, BLOWING SO HARD!
...HUH?
UH-OH...
I THINK SHE WOKE IT UP!
SERIOUSLY?!
I HOPE...
...THOSE BARS ARE AS STRONG AS THEY LOOK AND IT WON'T--

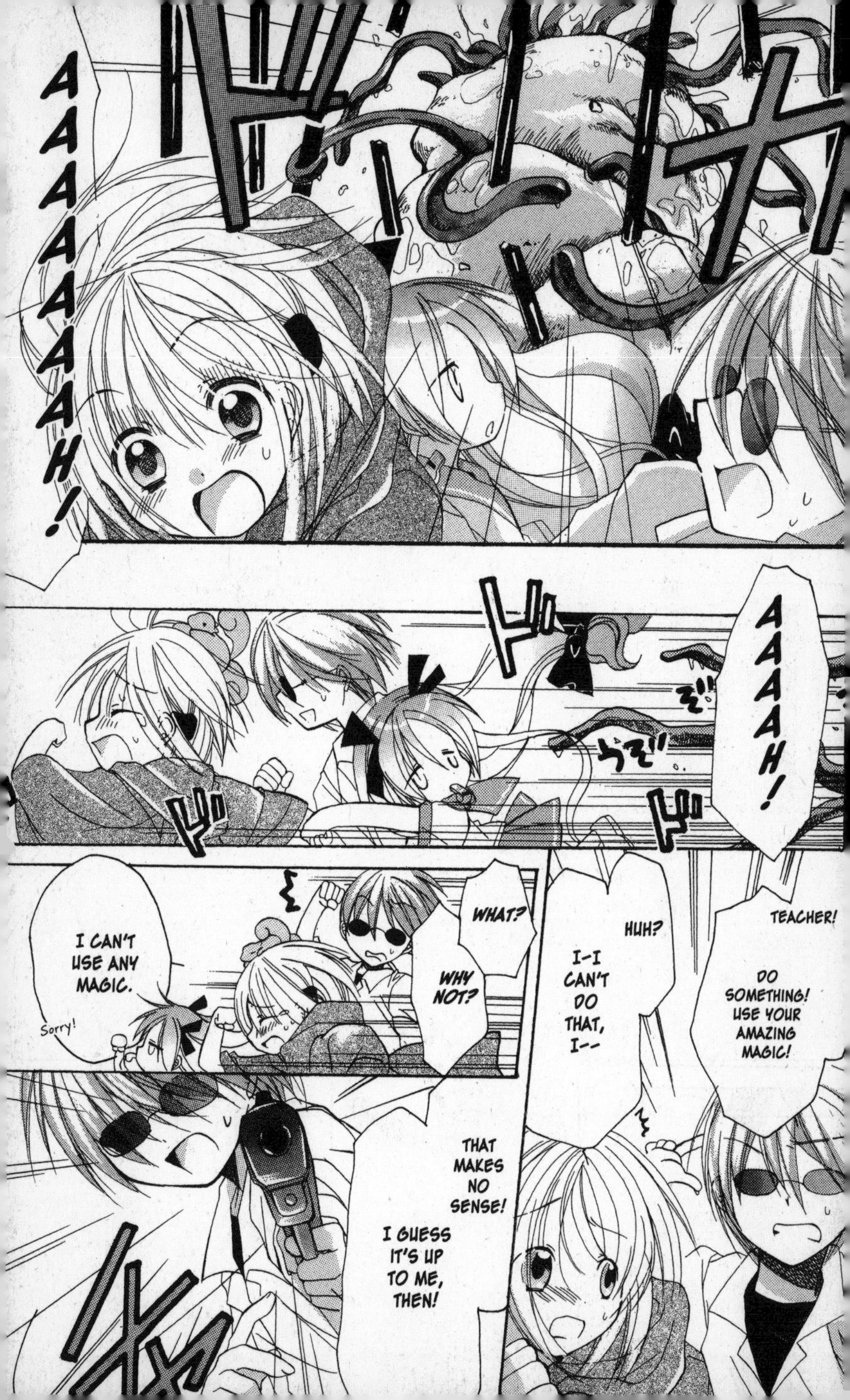
AAAAAAAH!
AAAAH!
TEACHER!
DO SOMETHING! USE YOUR AMAZING MAGIC!
HUH?
I-I CAN'T DO THAT, I--
WHAT?
WHY NOT?
I CAN'T USE ANY MAGIC.
Sorry!
THAT MAKES NO SENSE!
I GUESS IT'S UP TO ME, THEN!

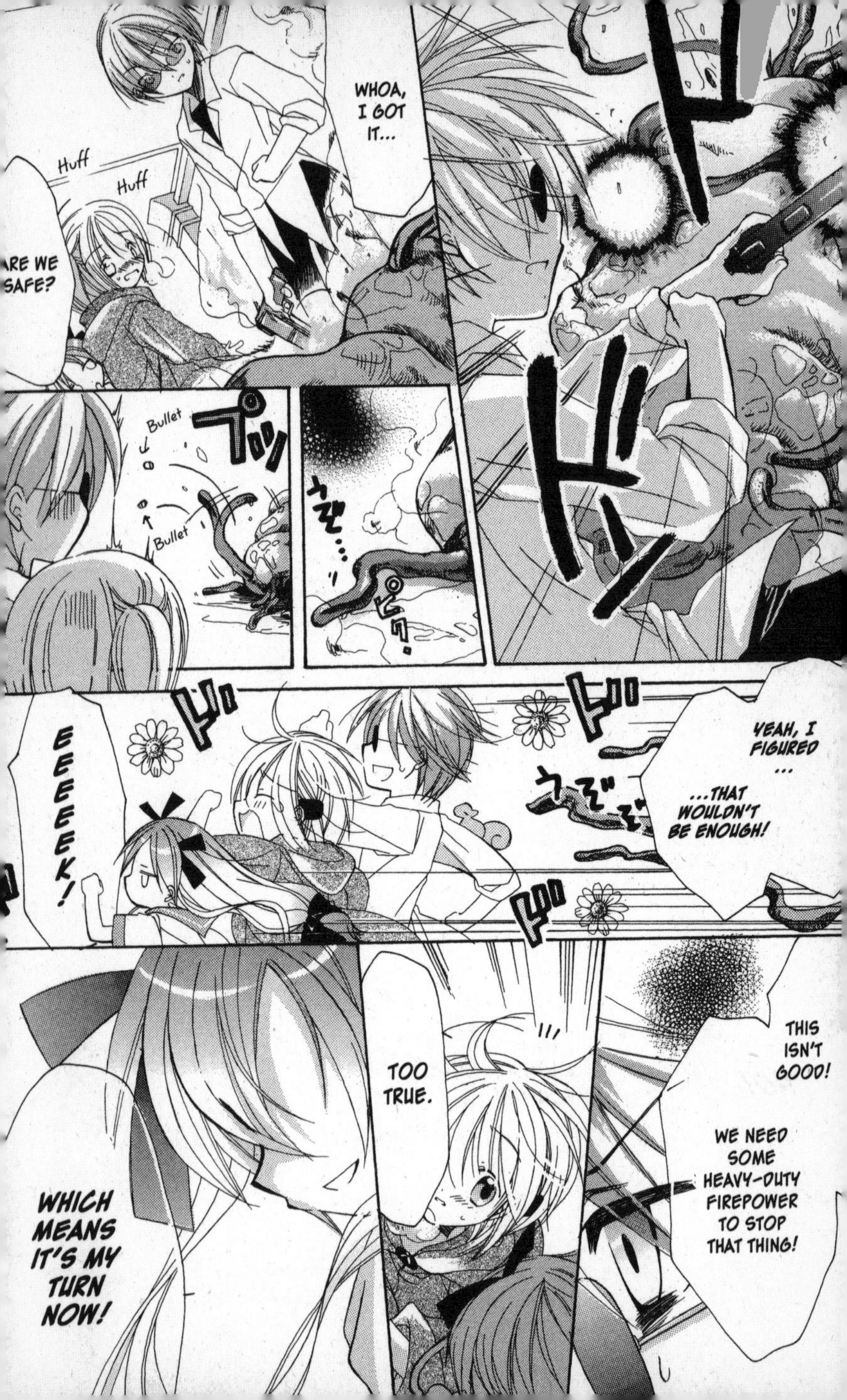
WHOA, I GOT IT...
Huff
Huff
ARE WE SAFE?
Bullet
Bullet
YEAH, I FIGURED...
...THAT WOULDN'T BE ENOUGH!
EEEEEEK!
THIS ISN'T GOOD!
WE NEED SOME HEAVY-DUTY FIREPOWER TO STOP THAT THING!
TOO TRUE.
WHICH MEANS IT'S MY TURN NOW!

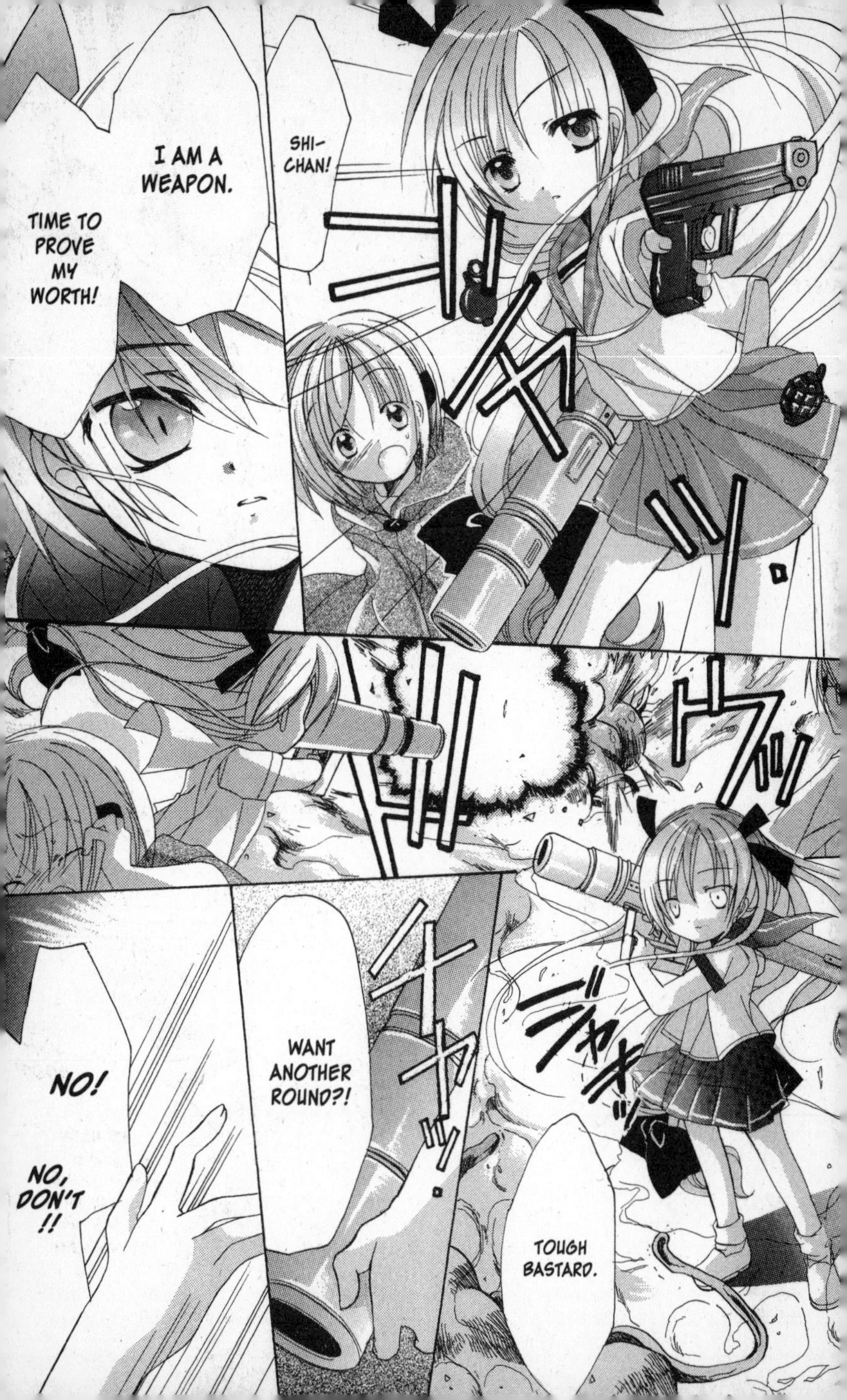
SHI-CHAN!
I AM A WEAPON.
TIME TO PROVE MY WORTH!
TOUGH BASTARD.
WANT ANOTHER ROUND?!
NO!
NO, DON'T !!

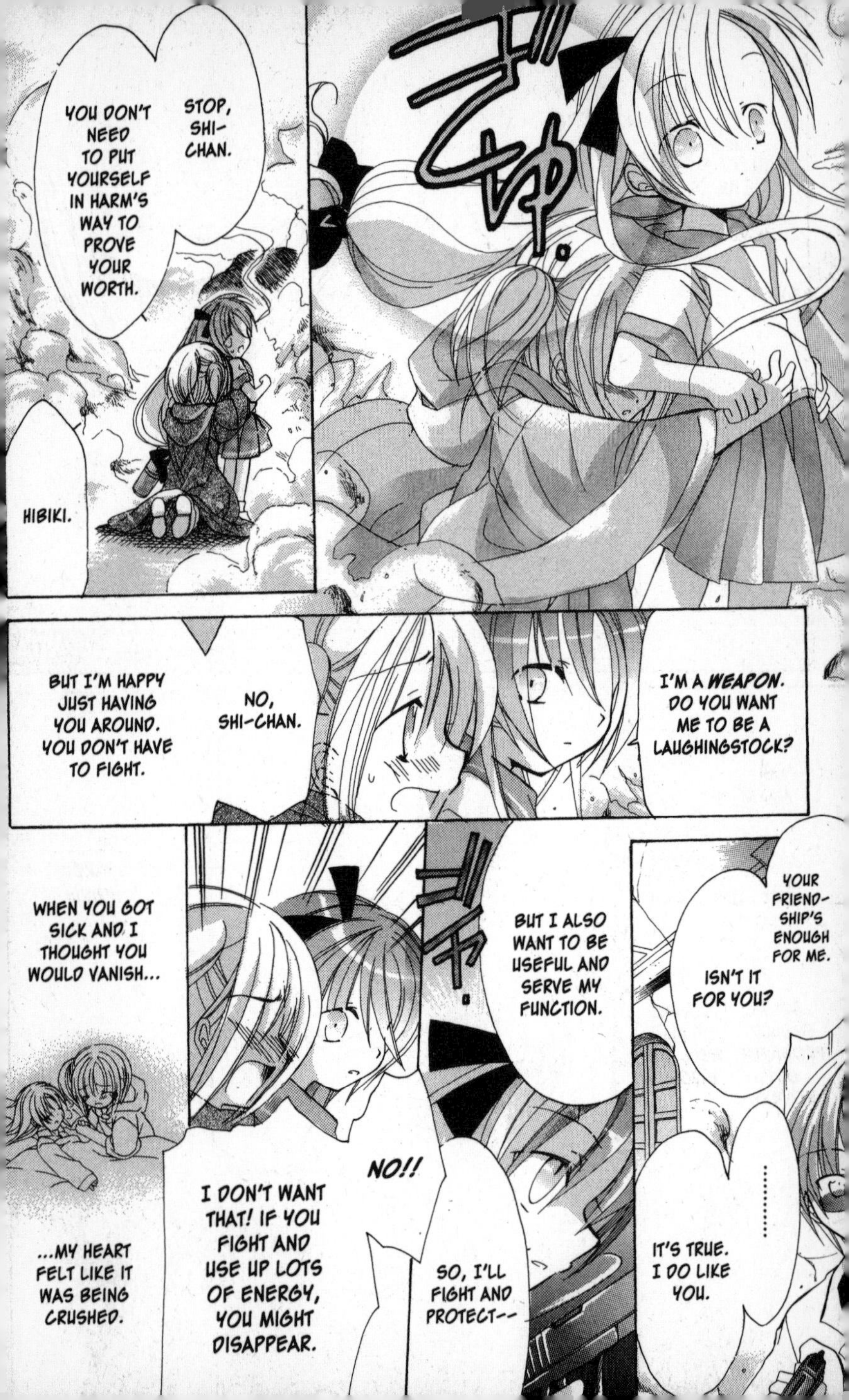
STOP, SHI-CHAN.
YOU DON'T NEED TO PUT YOURSELF IN HARM'S WAY TO PROVE YOUR WORTH.
HIBIKI.
I'M A *WEAPON*. DO YOU WANT ME TO BE A LAUGHINGSTOCK?
NO, SHI-CHAN.
BUT I'M HAPPY JUST HAVING YOU AROUND. YOU DON'T HAVE TO FIGHT.
YOUR FRIENDSHIP'S ENOUGH FOR ME.
ISN'T IT FOR YOU?
......
IT'S TRUE. I DO LIKE YOU.
BUT I ALSO WANT TO BE USEFUL AND SERVE MY FUNCTION.
SO, I'LL FIGHT AND PROTECT--
NO!!
I DON'T WANT THAT! IF YOU FIGHT AND USE UP LOTS OF ENERGY, YOU MIGHT DISAPPEAR.
WHEN YOU GOT SICK AND I THOUGHT YOU WOULD VANISH...
...MY HEART FELT LIKE IT WAS BEING CRUSHED.

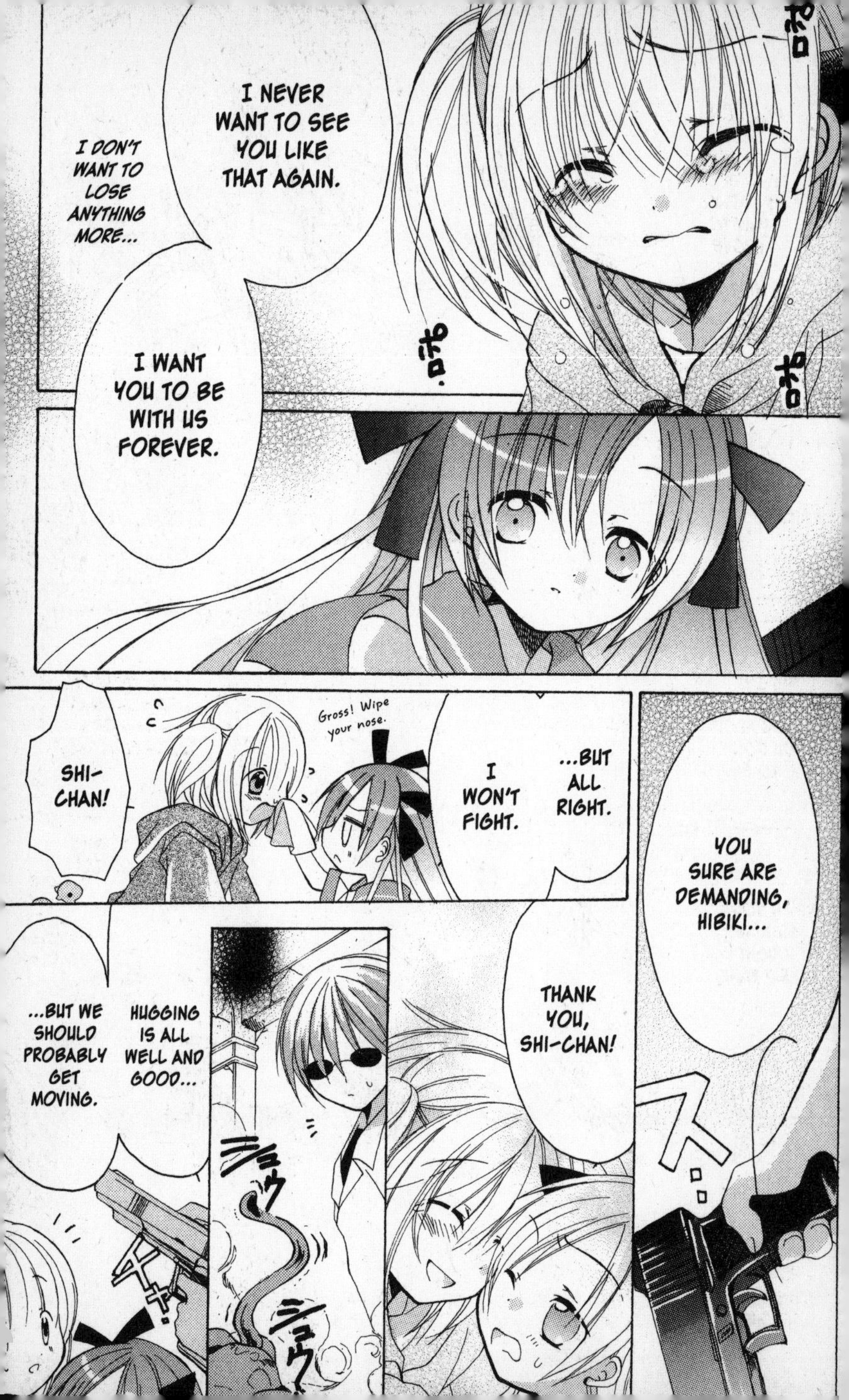
ポロ
I NEVER WANT TO SEE YOU LIKE THAT AGAIN.
I DON'T WANT TO LOSE ANYTHING MORE...
ポロ
ポロ
I WANT YOU TO BE WITH US FOREVER.
YOU SURE ARE DEMANDING, HIBIKI...
...BUT ALL RIGHT.
I WON'T FIGHT.
Gross! Wipe your nose.
SHI-CHAN!
THANK YOU, SHI-CHAN!
HUGGING IS ALL WELL AND GOOD...
...BUT WE SHOULD PROBABLY GET MOVING.

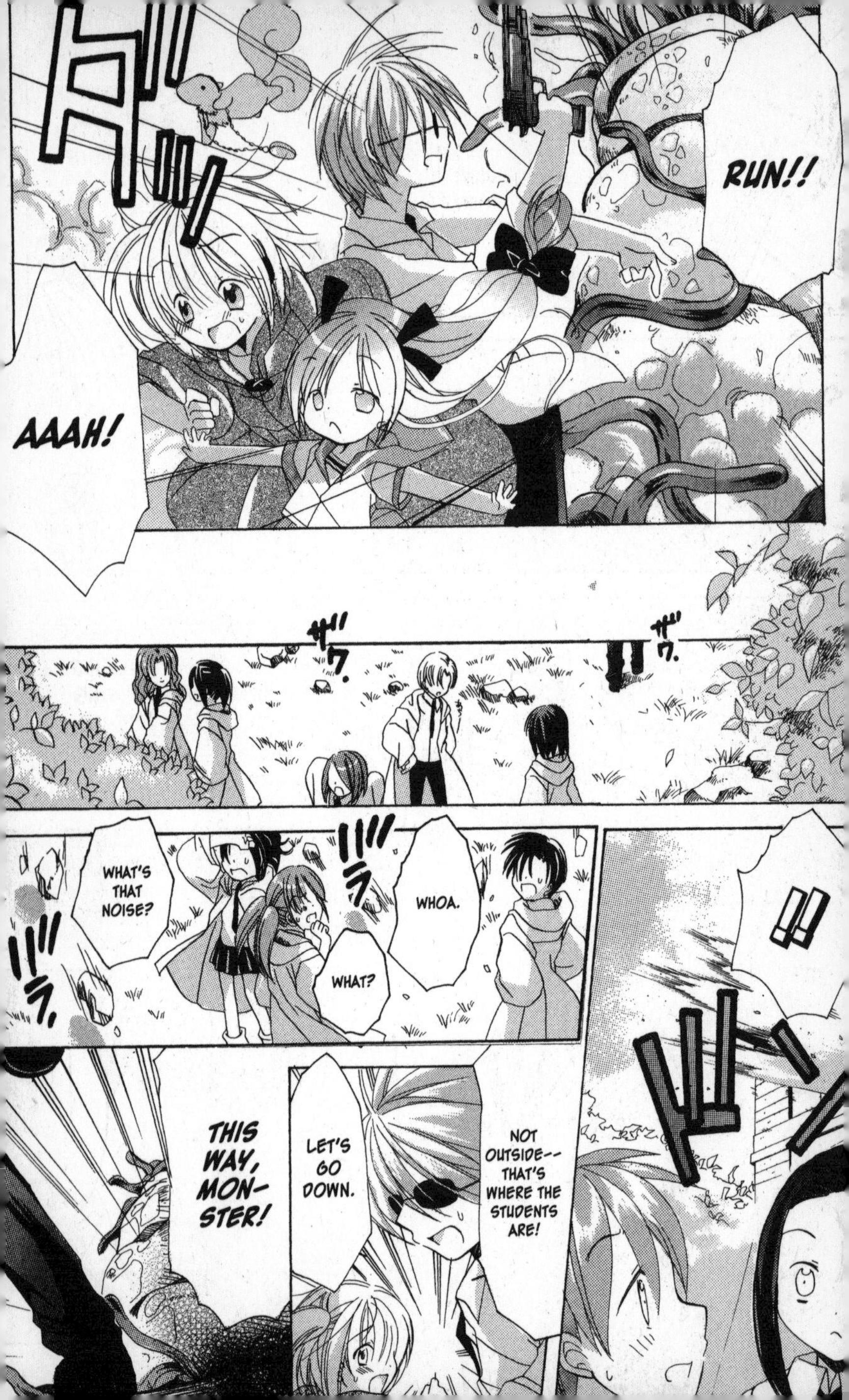
RUN!!
AAAH!
!!
WHOA.
WHAT?
WHAT'S THAT NOISE?
NOT OUTSIDE--THAT'S WHERE THE STUDENTS ARE!
LET'S GO DOWN.
THIS WAY, MONSTER!

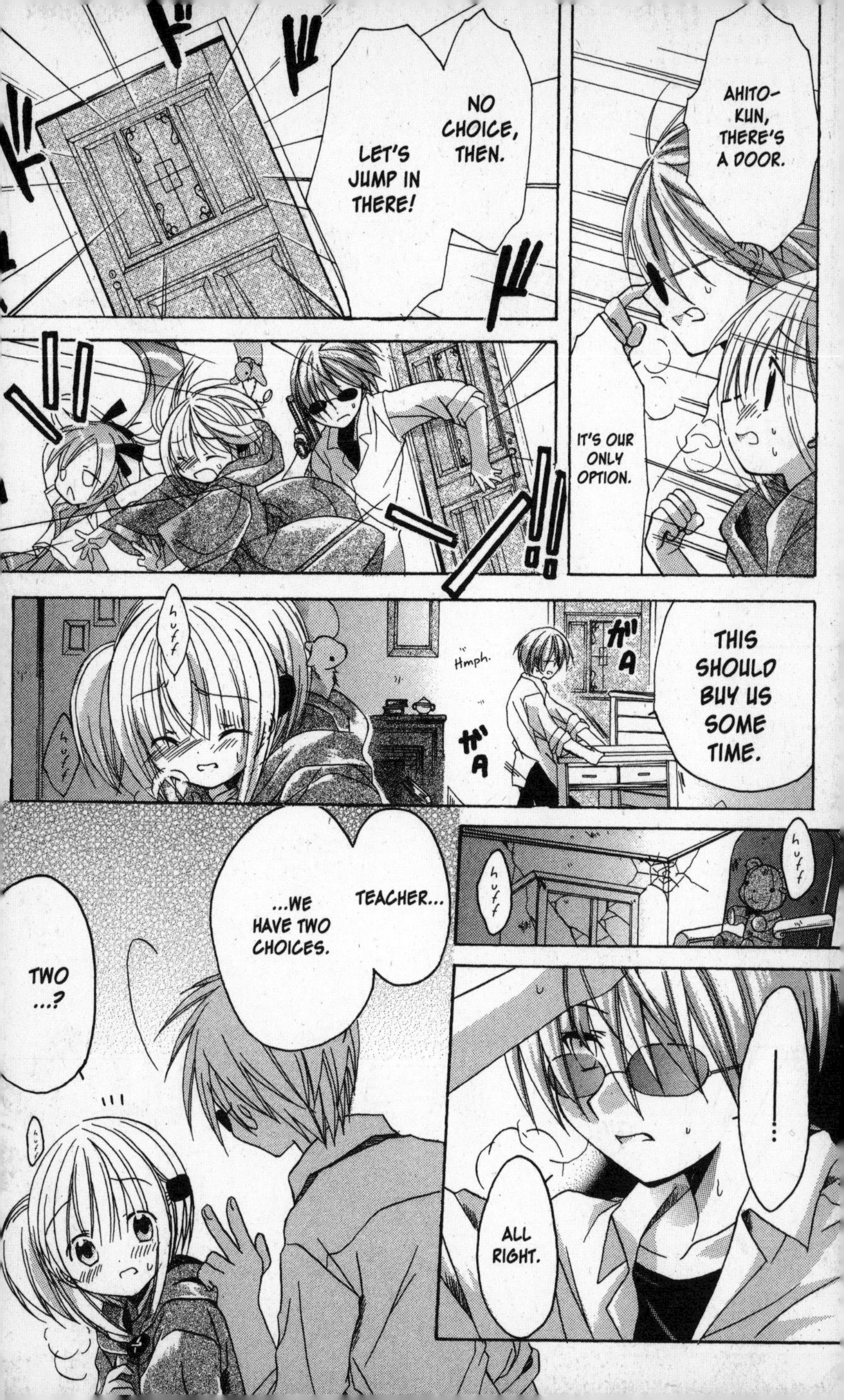
AHITO-KUN, THERE'S A DOOR.
IT'S OUR ONLY OPTION.
NO CHOICE, THEN.
LET'S JUMP IN THERE!
THIS SHOULD BUY US SOME TIME.
Hmph.
huff
huff
huff
huff
...!
ALL RIGHT.
TEACHER...
...WE HAVE TWO CHOICES.
TWO ...?

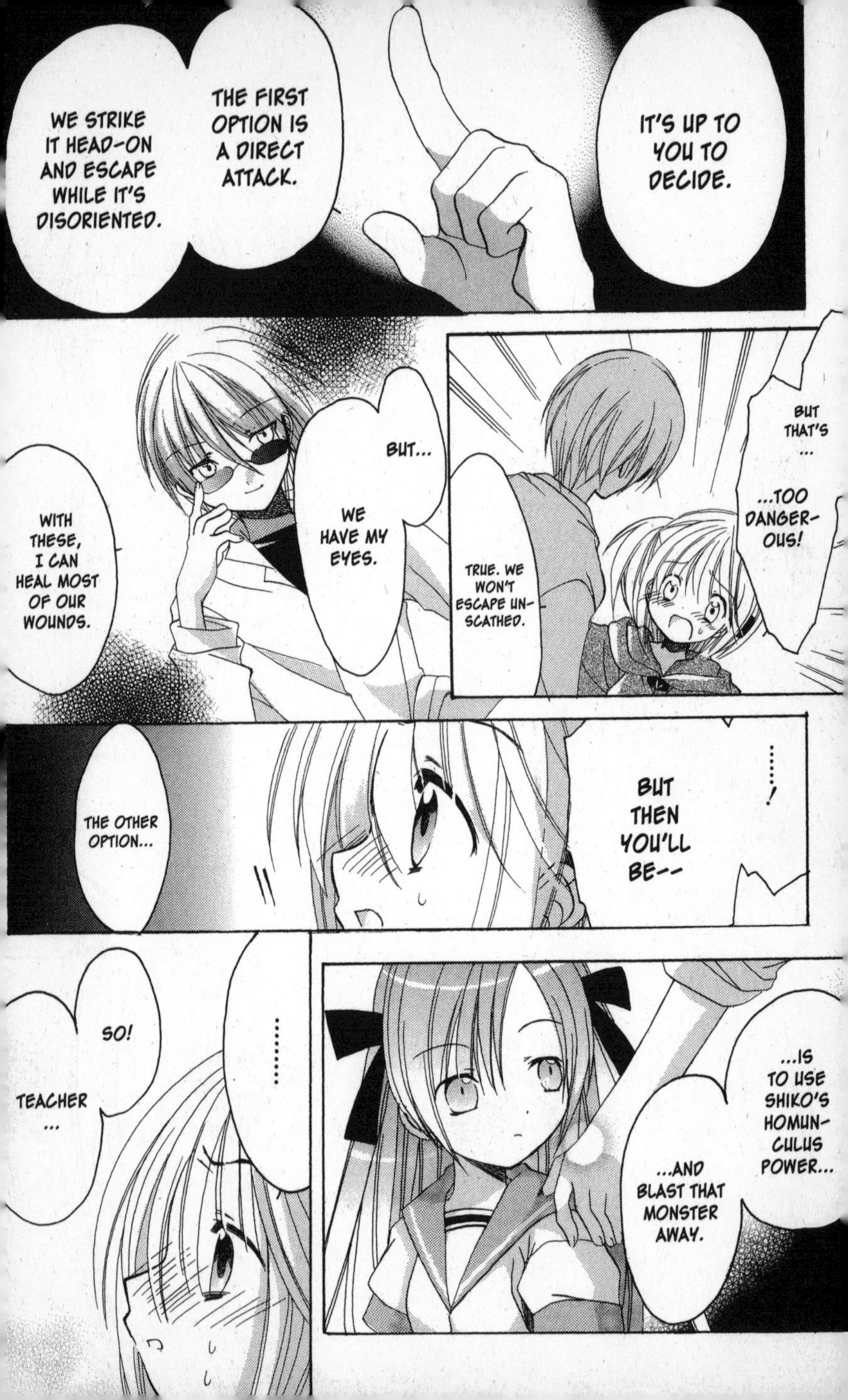
IT'S UP TO YOU TO DECIDE.
THE FIRST OPTION IS A DIRECT ATTACK.
WE STRIKE IT HEAD-ON AND ESCAPE WHILE IT'S DISORIENTED.
BUT THAT'S ...
...TOO DANGER-OUS!
TRUE. WE WON'T ESCAPE UN-SCATHED.
BUT...
WE HAVE MY EYES.
WITH THESE, I CAN HEAL MOST OF OUR WOUNDS.
......!
BUT THEN YOU'LL BE--
THE OTHER OPTION...
...IS TO USE SHIKO'S HOMUN-CULUS POWER...
...AND BLAST THAT MONSTER AWAY.
......
SO!
TEACHER ...

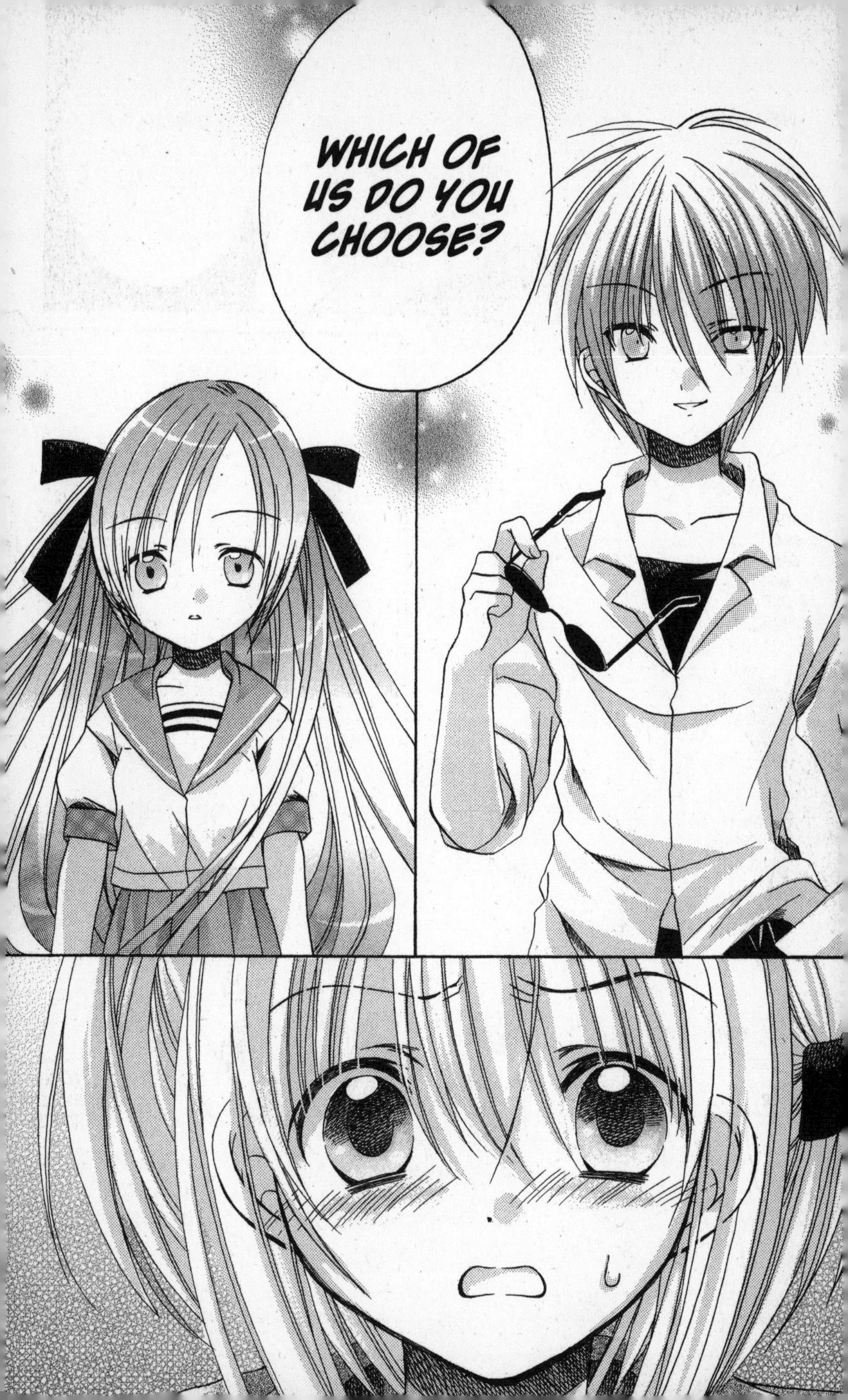
WHICH OF US DO YOU CHOOSE?

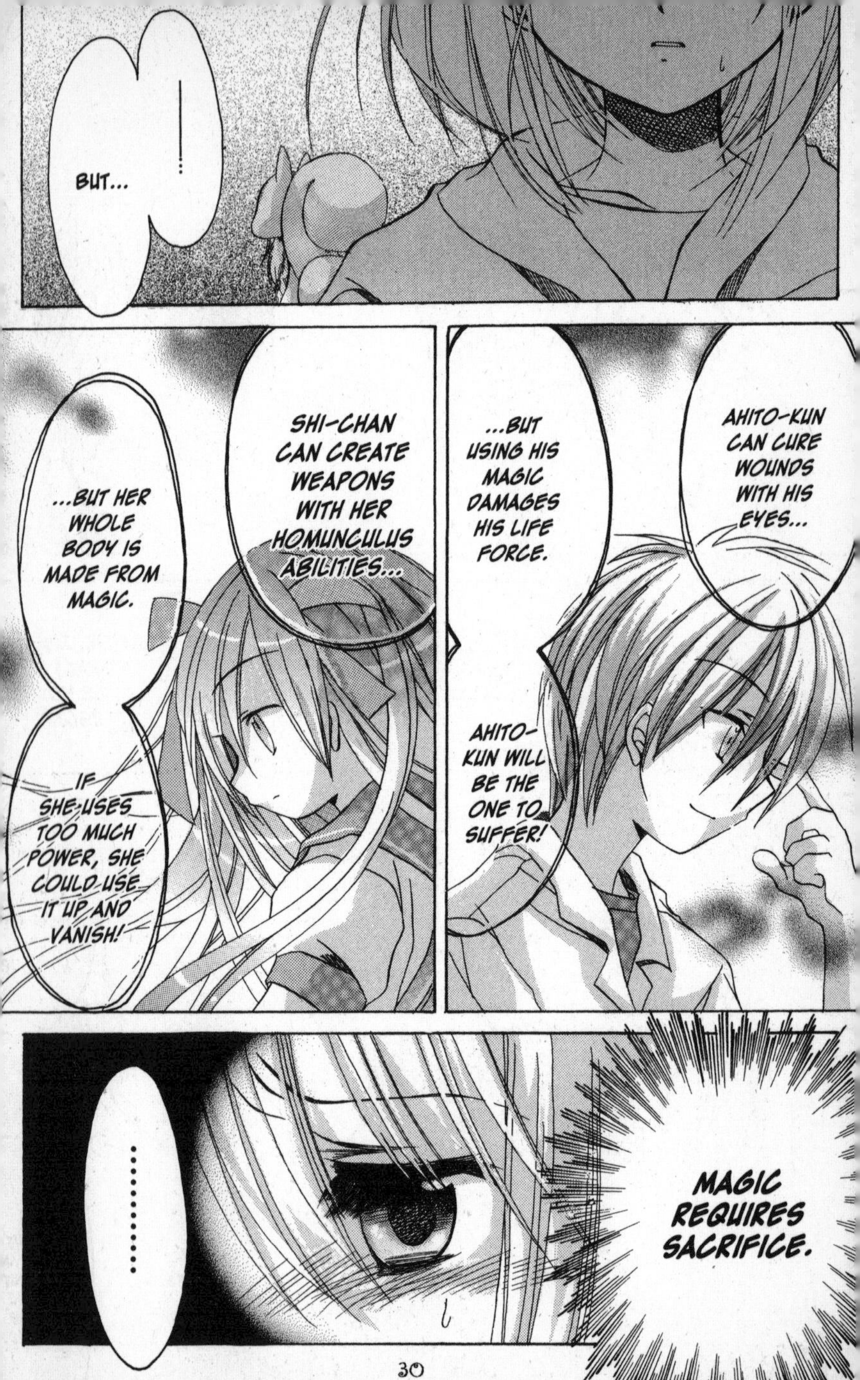
BUT...
AHITO-KUN CAN CURE WOUNDS WITH HIS EYES...
...BUT USING HIS MAGIC DAMAGES HIS LIFE FORCE.
AHITO-KUN WILL BE THE ONE TO SUFFER!
SHI-CHAN CAN CREATE WEAPONS WITH HER HOMUNCULUS ABILITIES...
...BUT HER WHOLE BODY IS MADE FROM MAGIC.
IF SHE USES TOO MUCH POWER, SHE COULD USE IT UP AND VANISH!
MAGIC REQUIRES SACRIFICE.
....

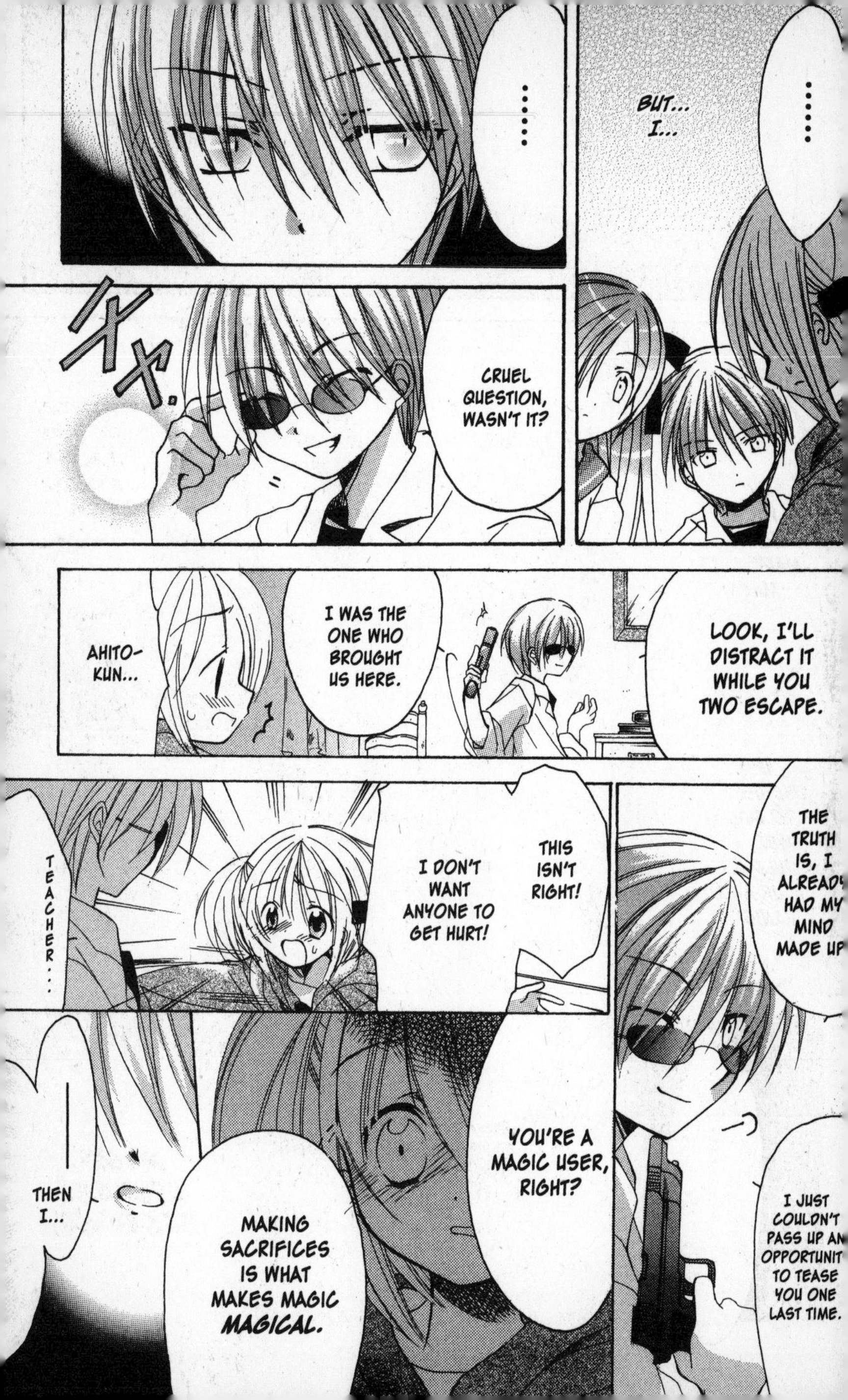
......
BUT... I...
......
CRUEL QUESTION, WASN'T IT?
LOOK, I'LL DISTRACT IT WHILE YOU TWO ESCAPE.
I WAS THE ONE WHO BROUGHT US HERE.
AHITO-KUN...
THE TRUTH IS, I ALREADY HAD MY MIND MADE UP
THIS ISN'T RIGHT!
I DON'T WANT ANYONE TO GET HURT!
TEACHER...
I JUST COULDN'T PASS UP AN OPPORTUNIT TO TEASE YOU ONE LAST TIME.
YOU'RE A MAGIC USER, RIGHT?
MAKING SACRIFICES IS WHAT MAKES MAGIC MAGICAL.
THEN I...

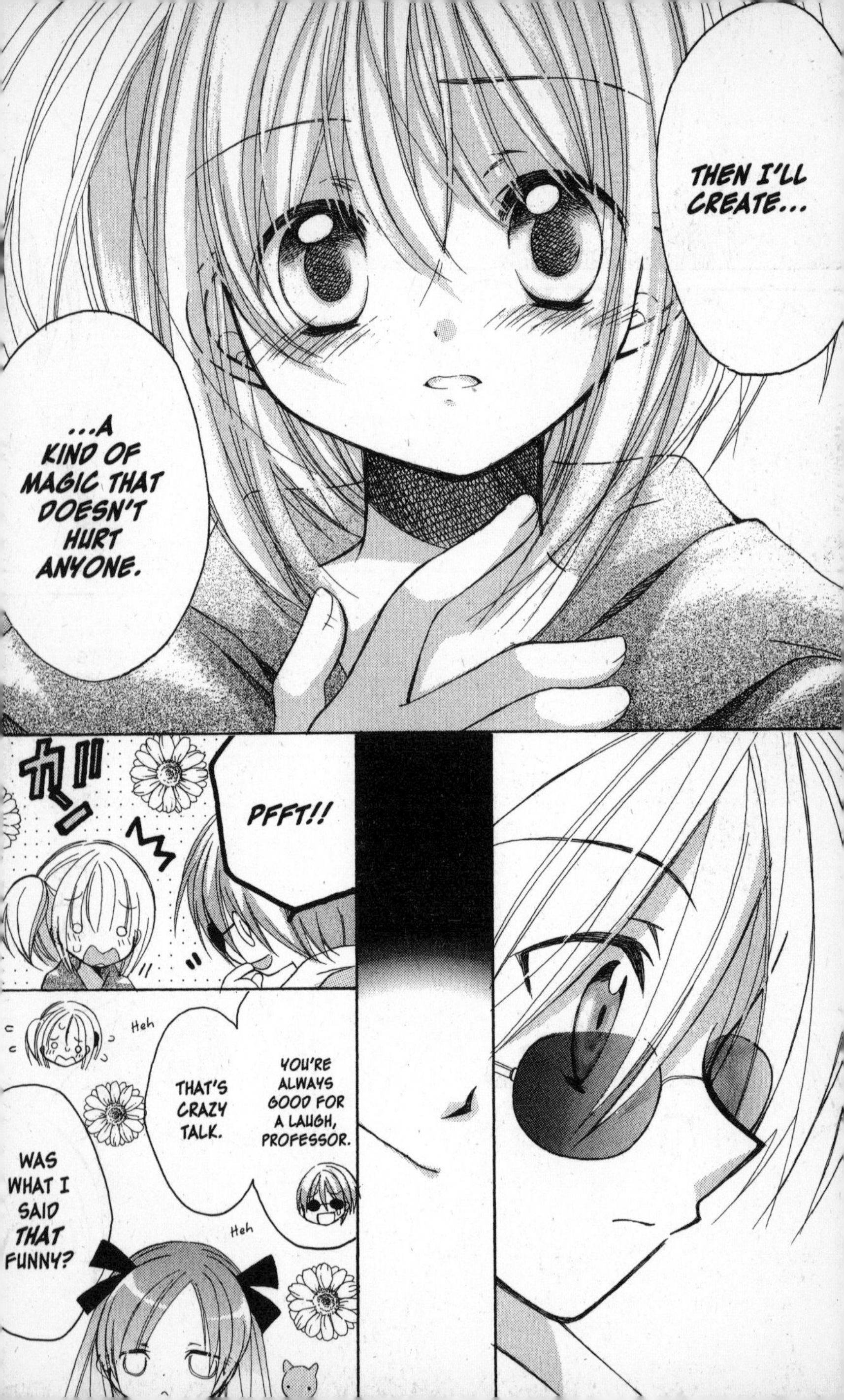
THEN I'LL CREATE...
...A KIND OF MAGIC THAT DOESN'T HURT ANYONE.
PFFT!!
YOU'RE ALWAYS GOOD FOR A LAUGH, PROFESSOR.
THAT'S CRAZY TALK.
Heh
Heh
WAS WHAT I SAID THAT FUNNY?

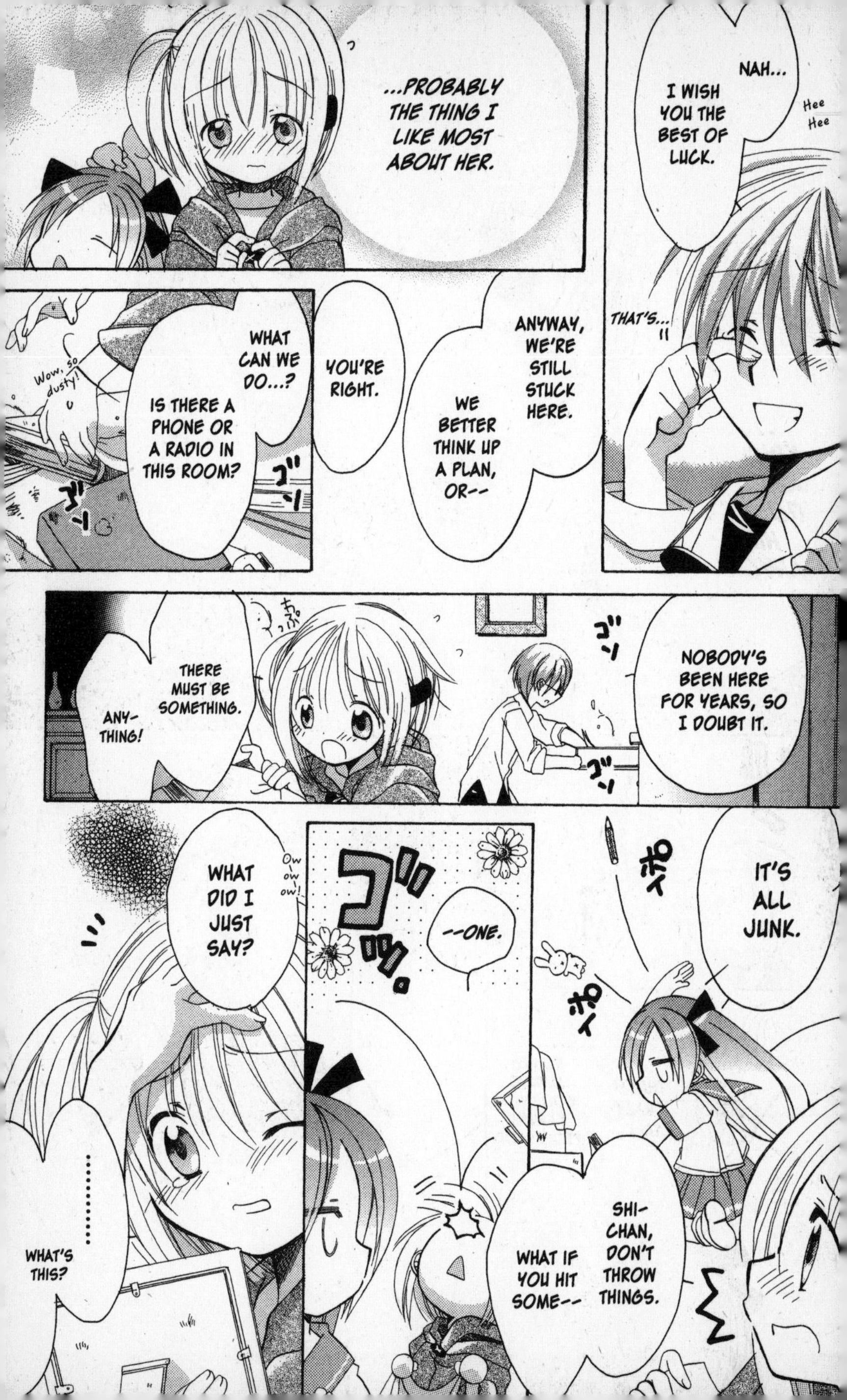
NAH... I WISH YOU THE BEST OF LUCK.
Hee Hee
...PROBABLY THE THING I LIKE MOST ABOUT HER.
THAT'S...
ANYWAY, WE'RE STILL STUCK HERE.
WE BETTER THINK UP A PLAN, OR--
YOU'RE RIGHT.
WHAT CAN WE DO...?
IS THERE A PHONE OR A RADIO IN THIS ROOM?
Wow, so dusty!
NOBODY'S BEEN HERE FOR YEARS, SO I DOUBT IT.
THERE MUST BE SOMETHING.
ANY-THING!
IT'S ALL JUNK.
SHI-CHAN, DON'T THROW THINGS.
WHAT IF YOU HIT SOME--
--ONE.
WHAT DID I JUST SAY?
Ow ow ow!
......
WHAT'S THIS?

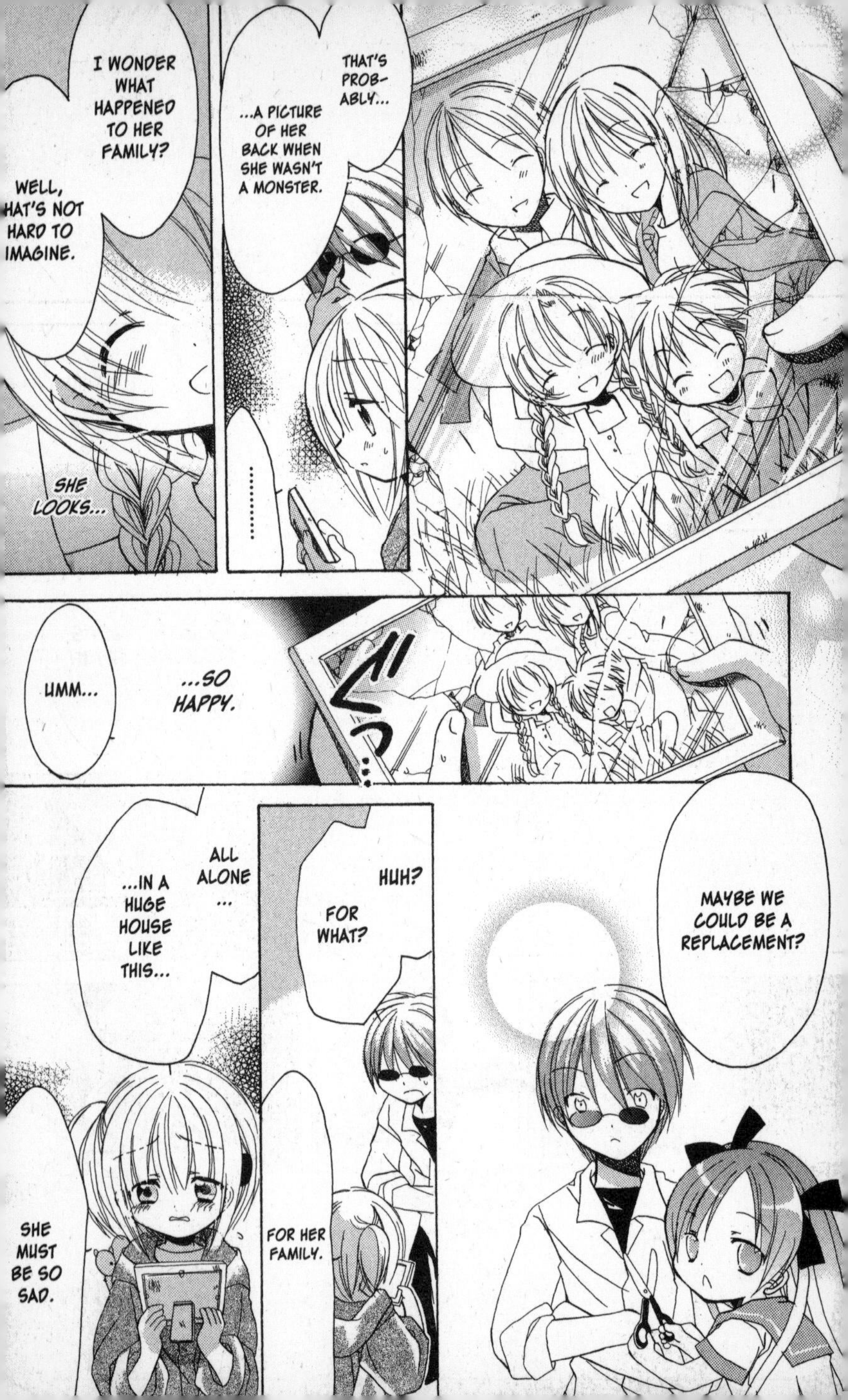
THAT'S PROBABLY...
...A PICTURE OF HER BACK WHEN SHE WASN'T A MONSTER.
......
I WONDER WHAT HAPPENED TO HER FAMILY?
WELL, HAT'S NOT HARD TO IMAGINE.
SHE LOOKS...
...SO HAPPY.
UMM...
MAYBE WE COULD BE A REPLACEMENT?
HUH?
FOR WHAT?
FOR HER FAMILY.
ALL ALONE...
...IN A HUGE HOUSE LIKE THIS...
SHE MUST BE SO SAD.

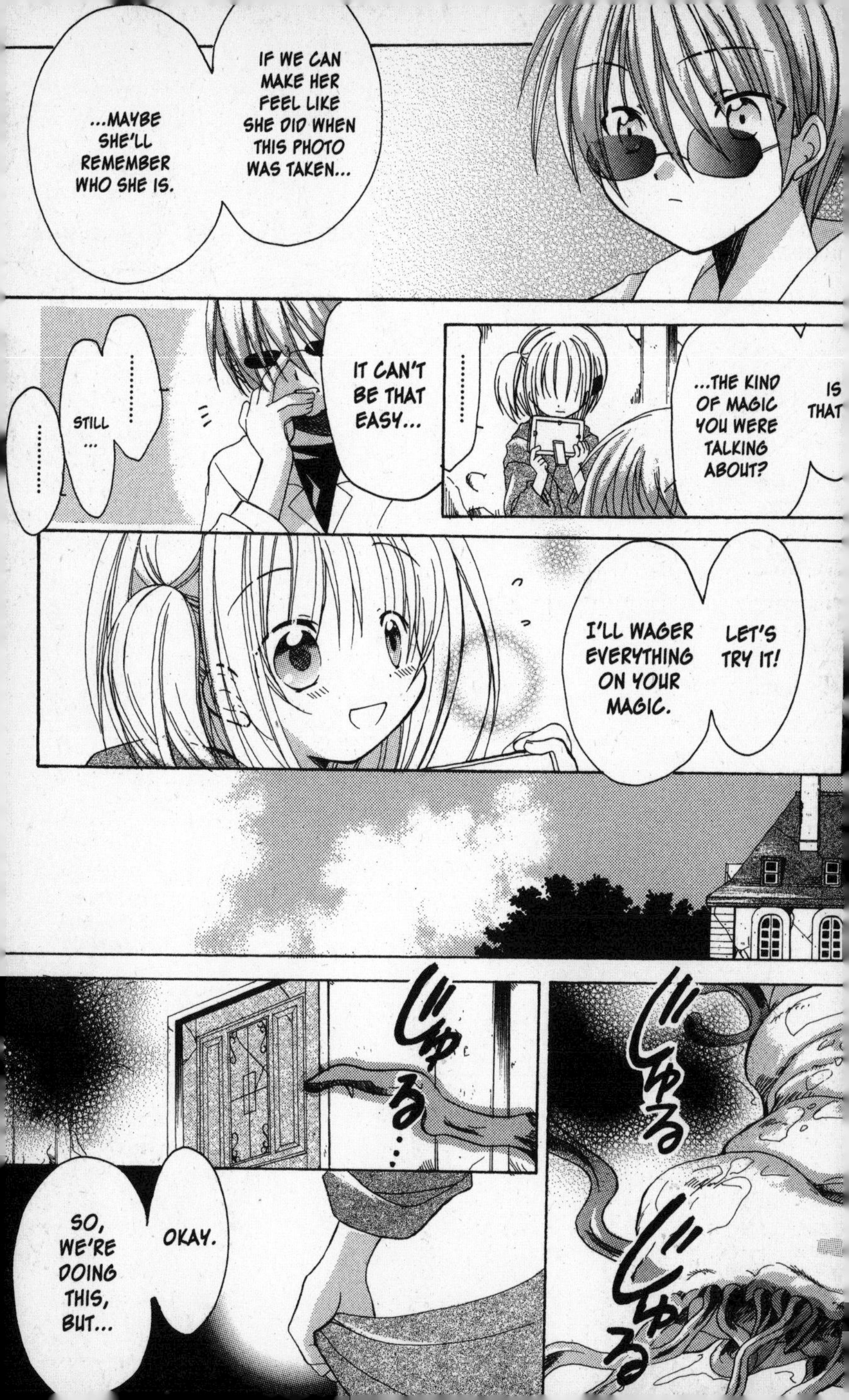
IF WE CAN MAKE HER FEEL LIKE SHE DID WHEN THIS PHOTO WAS TAKEN...
...MAYBE SHE'LL REMEMBER WHO SHE IS.
...THE KIND OF MAGIC YOU WERE TALKING ABOUT?
IS THAT
....
IT CAN'T BE THAT EASY...
....
STILL ...
....
LET'S TRY IT!
I'LL WAGER EVERYTHING ON YOUR MAGIC.
じゅる
じゅる
じゅる…
OKAY.
SO, WE'RE DOING THIS, BUT...

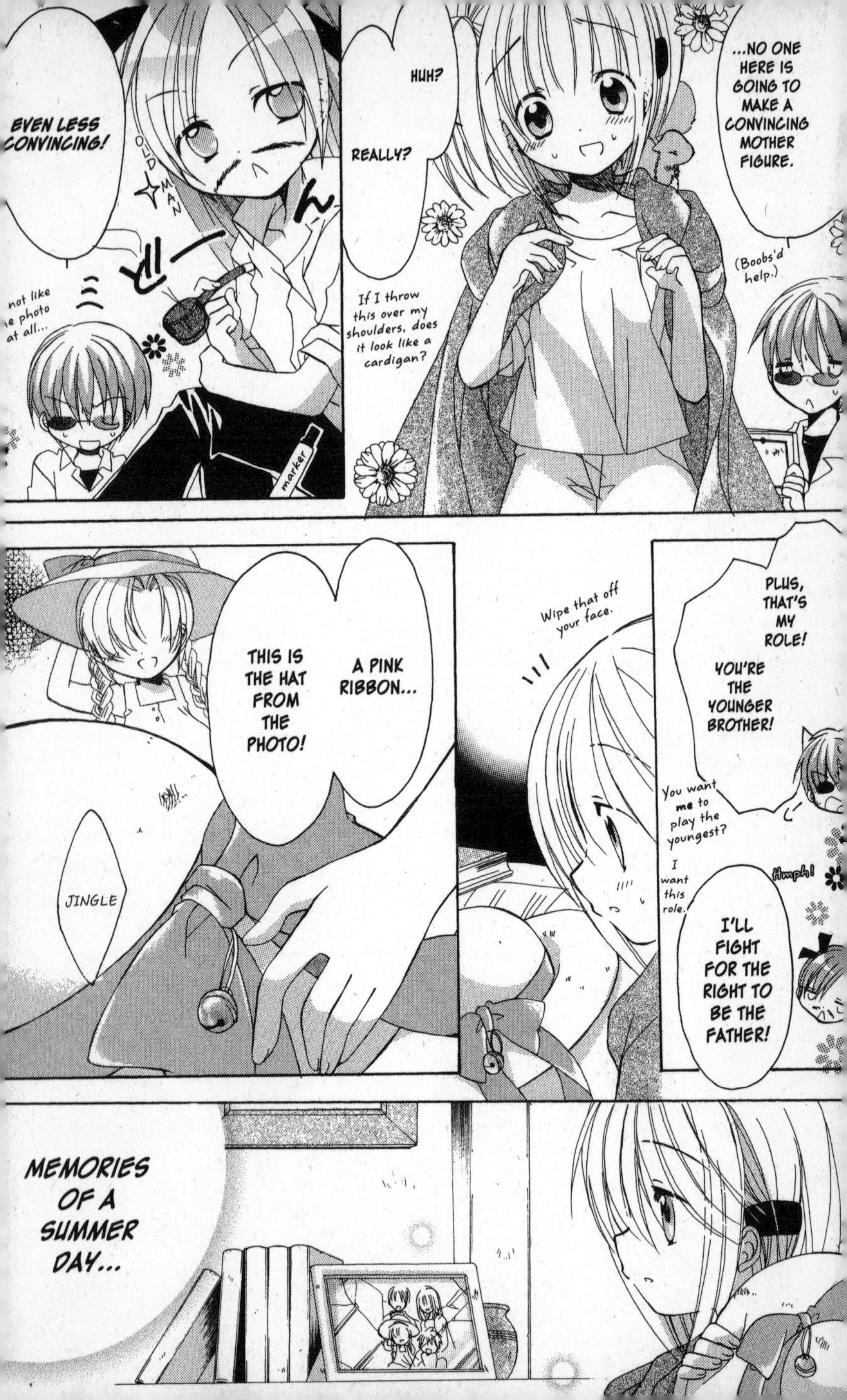
...NO ONE HERE IS GOING TO MAKE A CONVINCING MOTHER FIGURE.
HUH?
REALLY?
(Boobs'd help.)
If I throw this over my shoulders, does it look like a cardigan?
EVEN LESS CONVINCING!
OLD MAN
not like he photo at all...
marker
PLUS, THAT'S MY ROLE!
YOU'RE THE YOUNGER BROTHER!
You want me to play the youngest?
I want this role.
Hmph!
I'LL FIGHT FOR THE RIGHT TO BE THE FATHER!
Wipe that off your face.
A PINK RIBBON...
THIS IS THE HAT FROM THE PHOTO!
JINGLE
MEMORIES OF A SUMMER DAY...

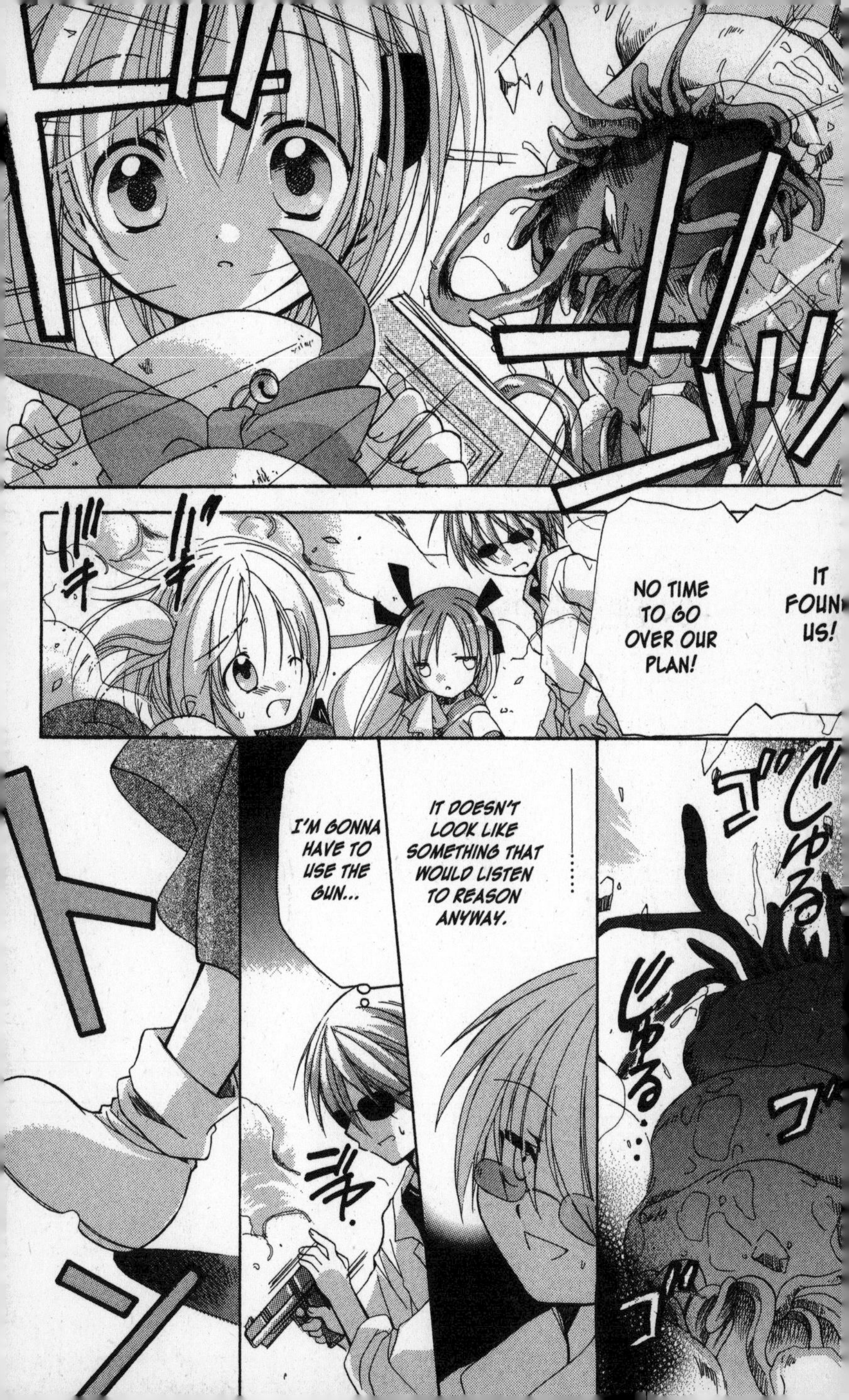
IT FOUN US!
NO TIME TO GO OVER OUR PLAN!
......
IT DOESN'T LOOK LIKE SOMETHING THAT WOULD LISTEN TO REASON ANYWAY.
I'M GONNA HAVE TO USE THE GUN...

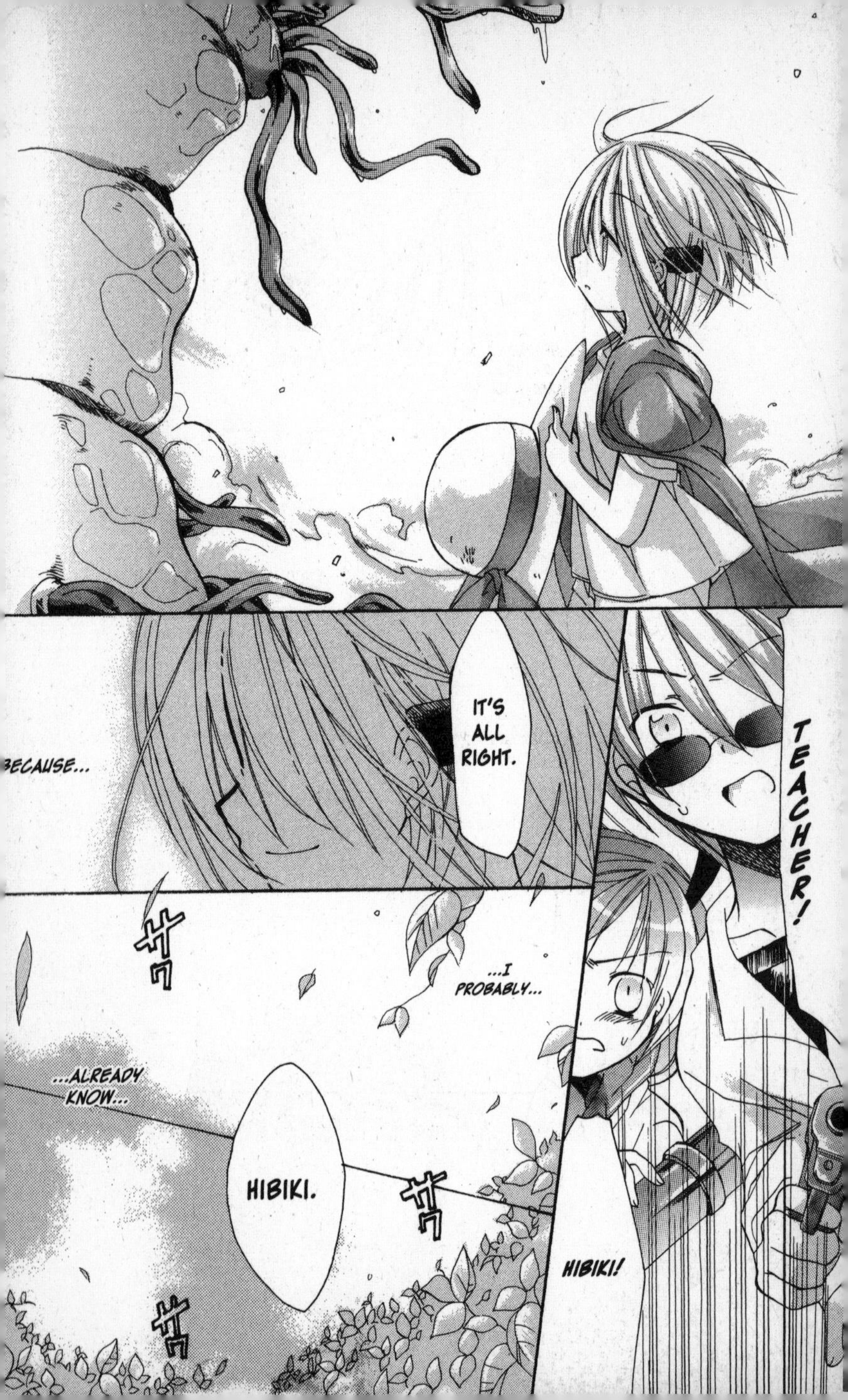
TEACHER!
IT'S ALL RIGHT.
BECAUSE...
HIBIKI!
...I PROBABLY...
...ALREADY KNOW...
HIBIKI.

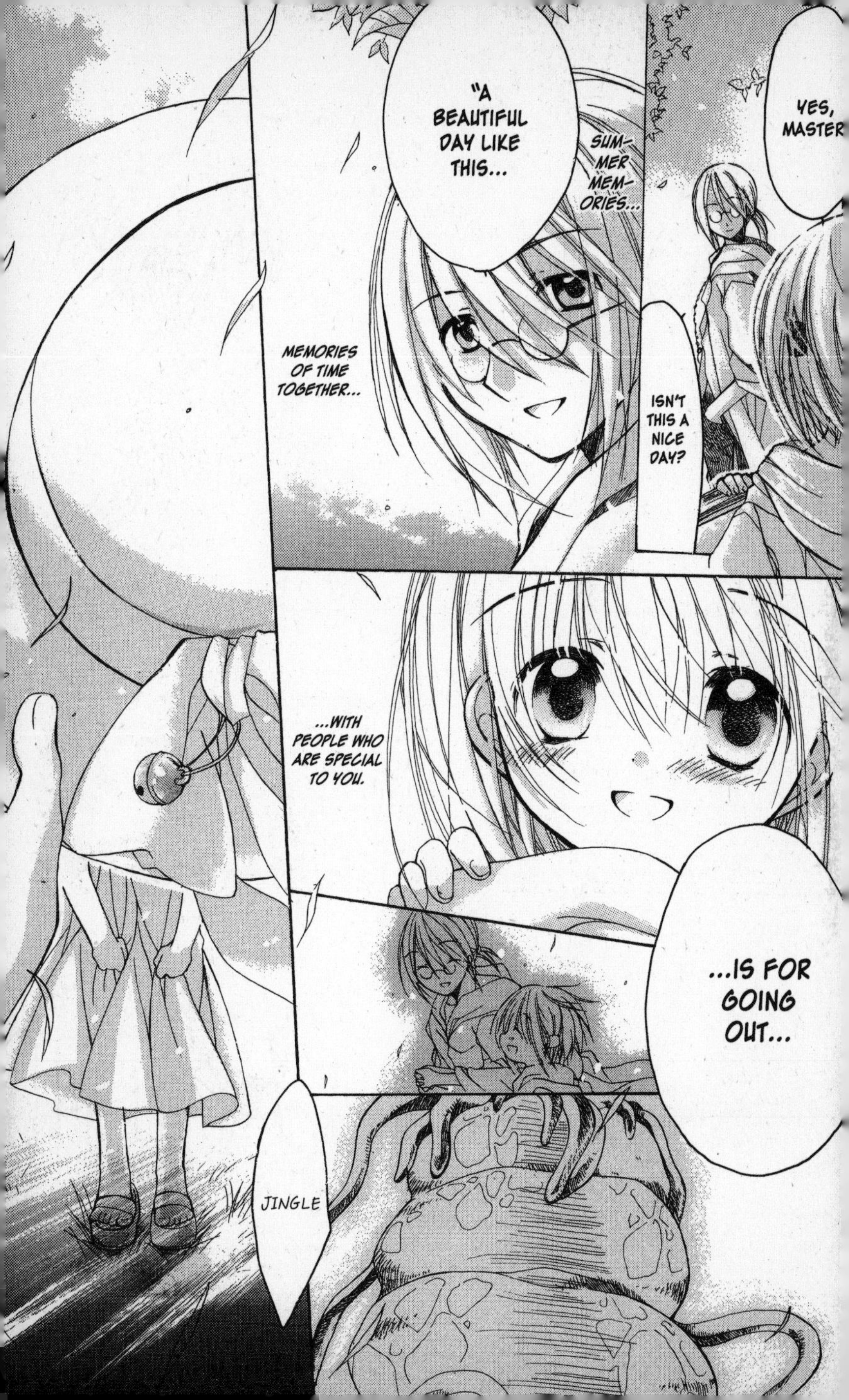
YES, MASTER
ISN'T THIS A NICE DAY?
"A BEAUTIFUL DAY LIKE THIS...
SUM-MER MEM-ORIES...
MEMORIES OF TIME TOGETHER...
...WITH PEOPLE WHO ARE SPECIAL TO YOU.
...IS FOR GOING OUT...
JINGLE

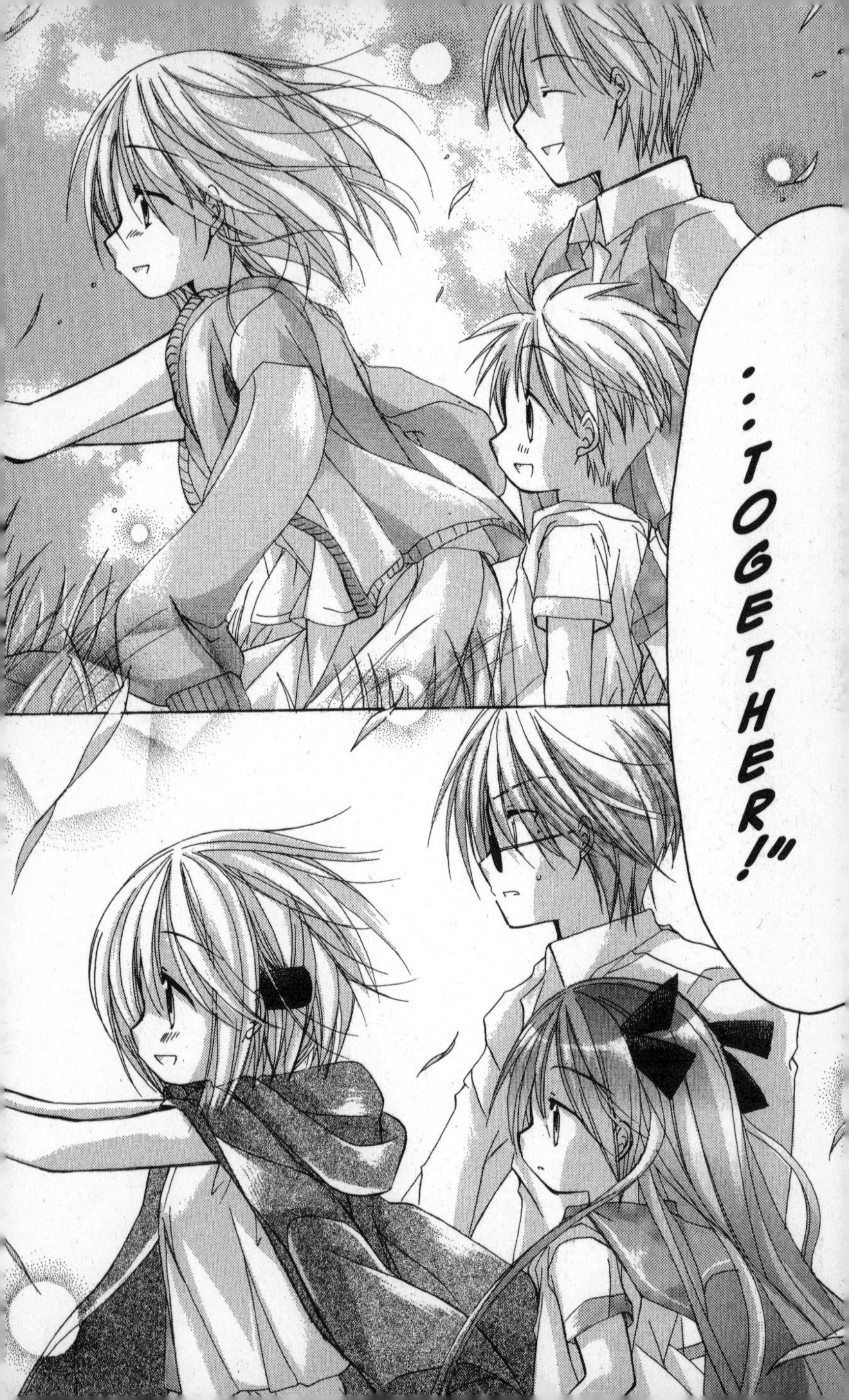
...TOGETHER!"

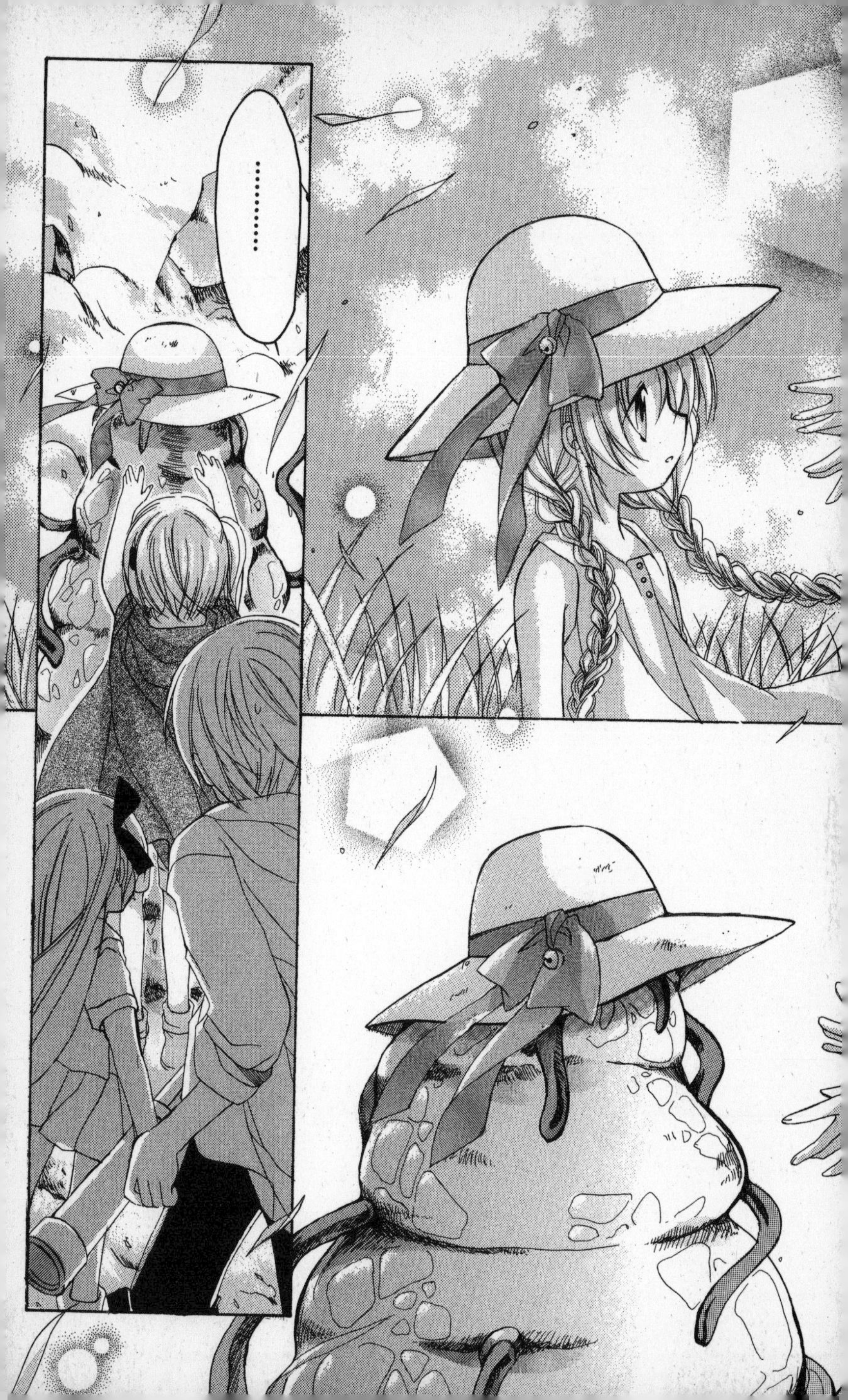
……

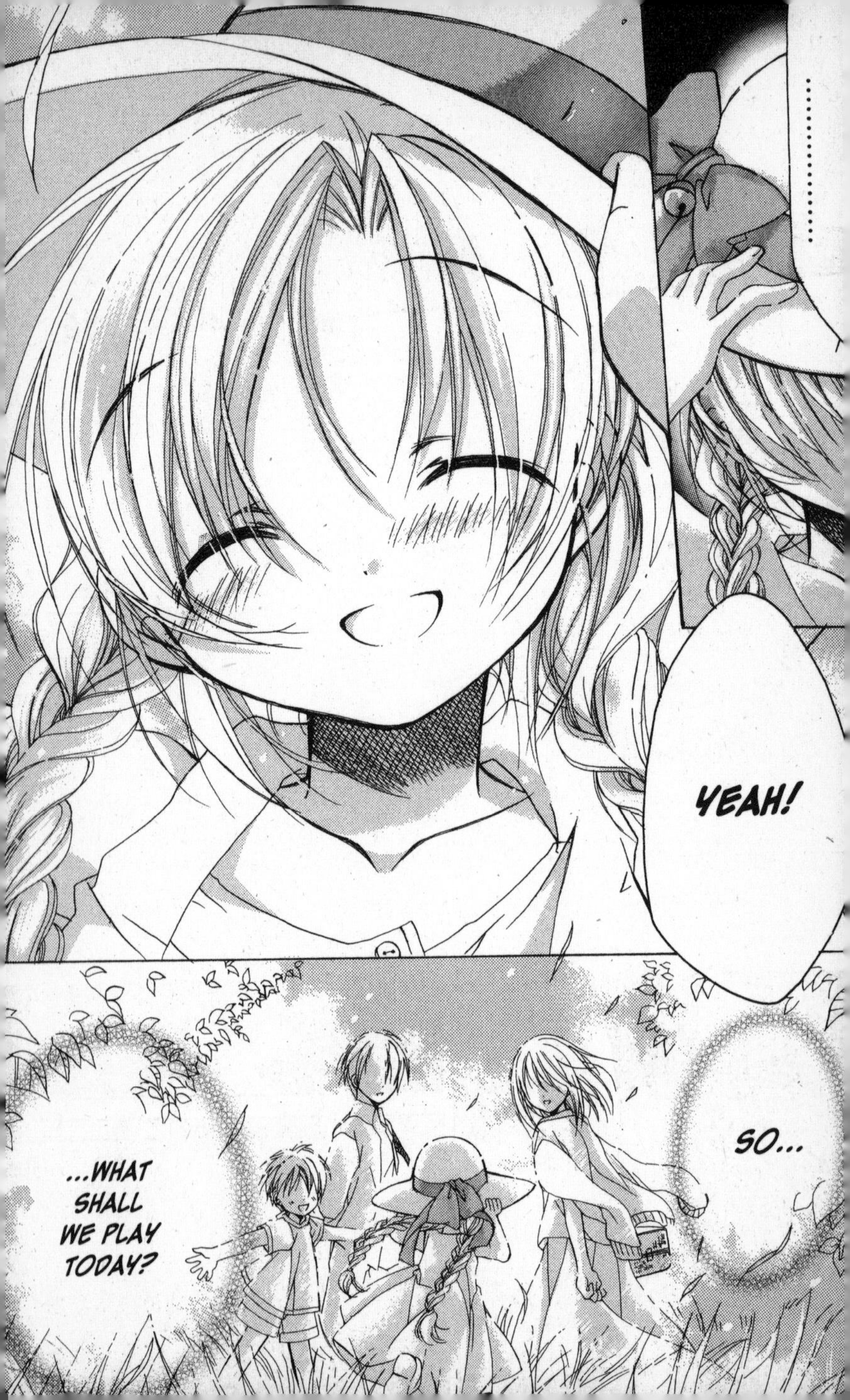
......
YEAH!
SO...
...WHAT SHALL WE PLAY TODAY?

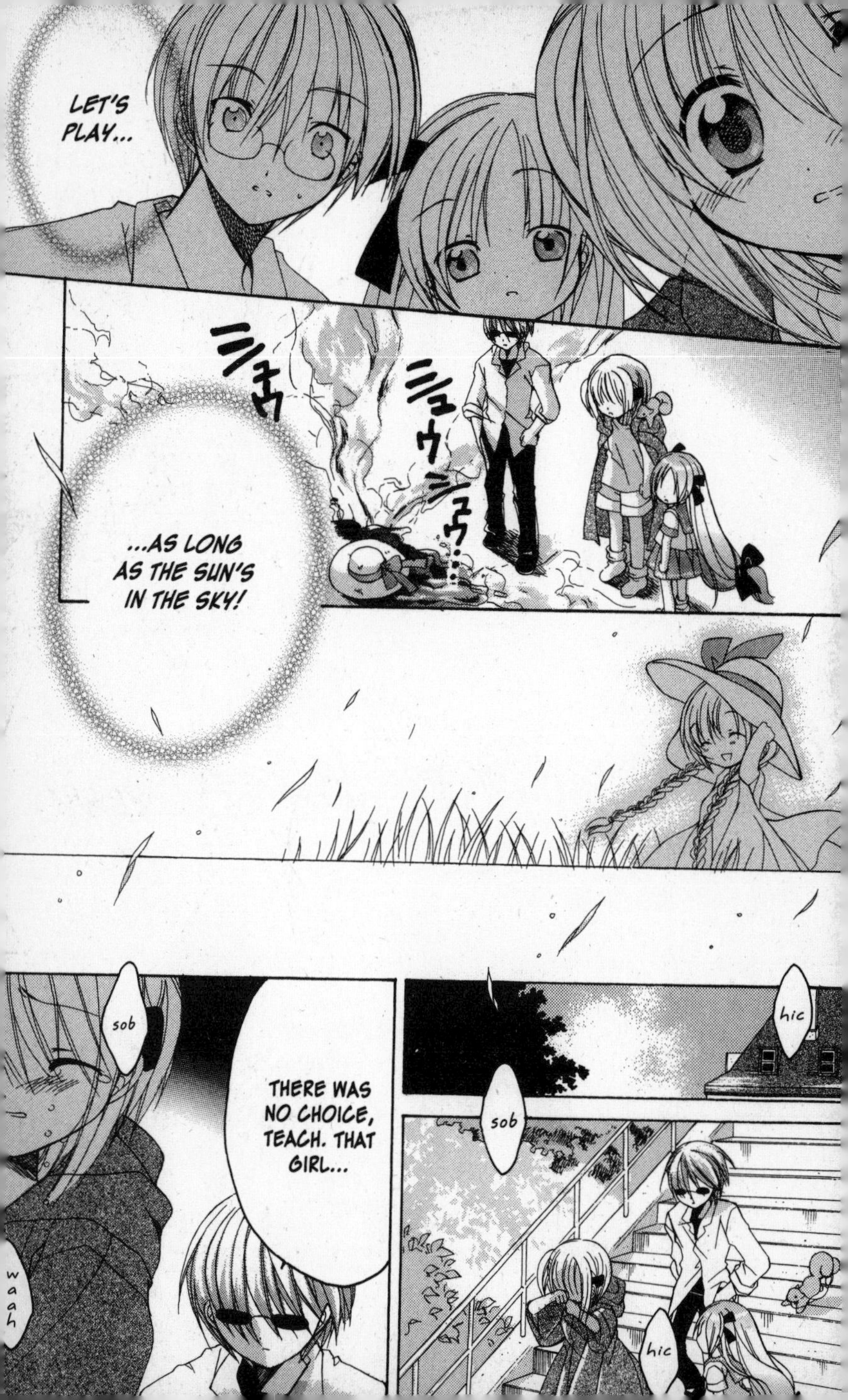
LET'S PLAY...
シュウシュウ…
シュウ
...AS LONG AS THE SUN'S IN THE SKY!
hic
sob
hic
THERE WAS NO CHOICE, TEACH. THAT GIRL...
sob
waah

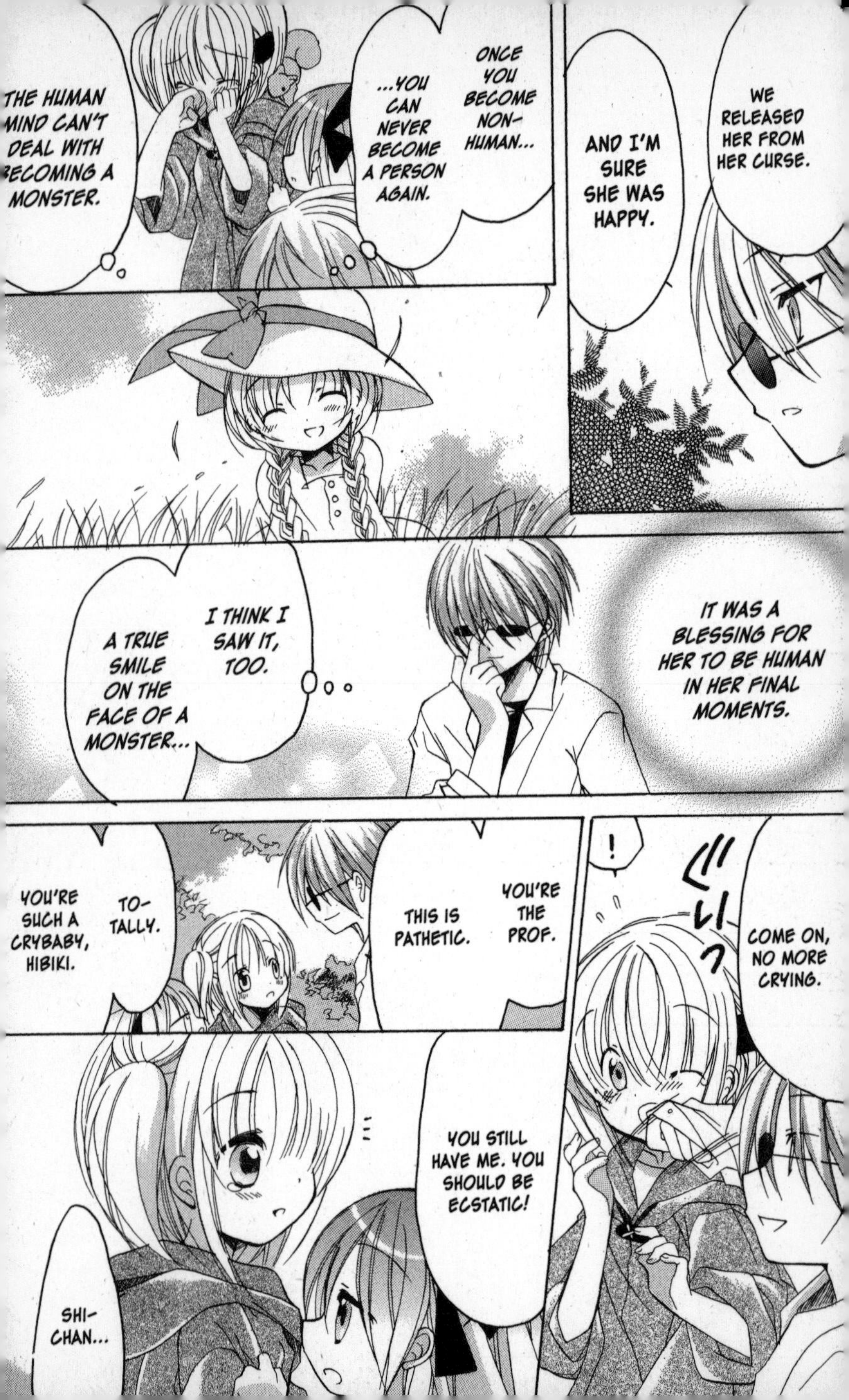
WE RELEASED HER FROM HER CURSE.
AND I'M SURE SHE WAS HAPPY.
ONCE YOU BECOME NON-HUMAN...
...YOU CAN NEVER BECOME A PERSON AGAIN.
THE HUMAN MIND CAN'T DEAL WITH BECOMING A MONSTER.
IT WAS A BLESSING FOR HER TO BE HUMAN IN HER FINAL MOMENTS.
I THINK I SAW IT, TOO.
A TRUE SMILE ON THE FACE OF A MONSTER...
ぐしっ
COME ON, NO MORE CRYING.
!
YOU'RE THE PROF.
THIS IS PATHETIC.
TO-TALLY.
YOU'RE SUCH A CRYBABY, HIBIKI.
YOU STILL HAVE ME. YOU SHOULD BE ECSTATIC!
SHI-CHAN...

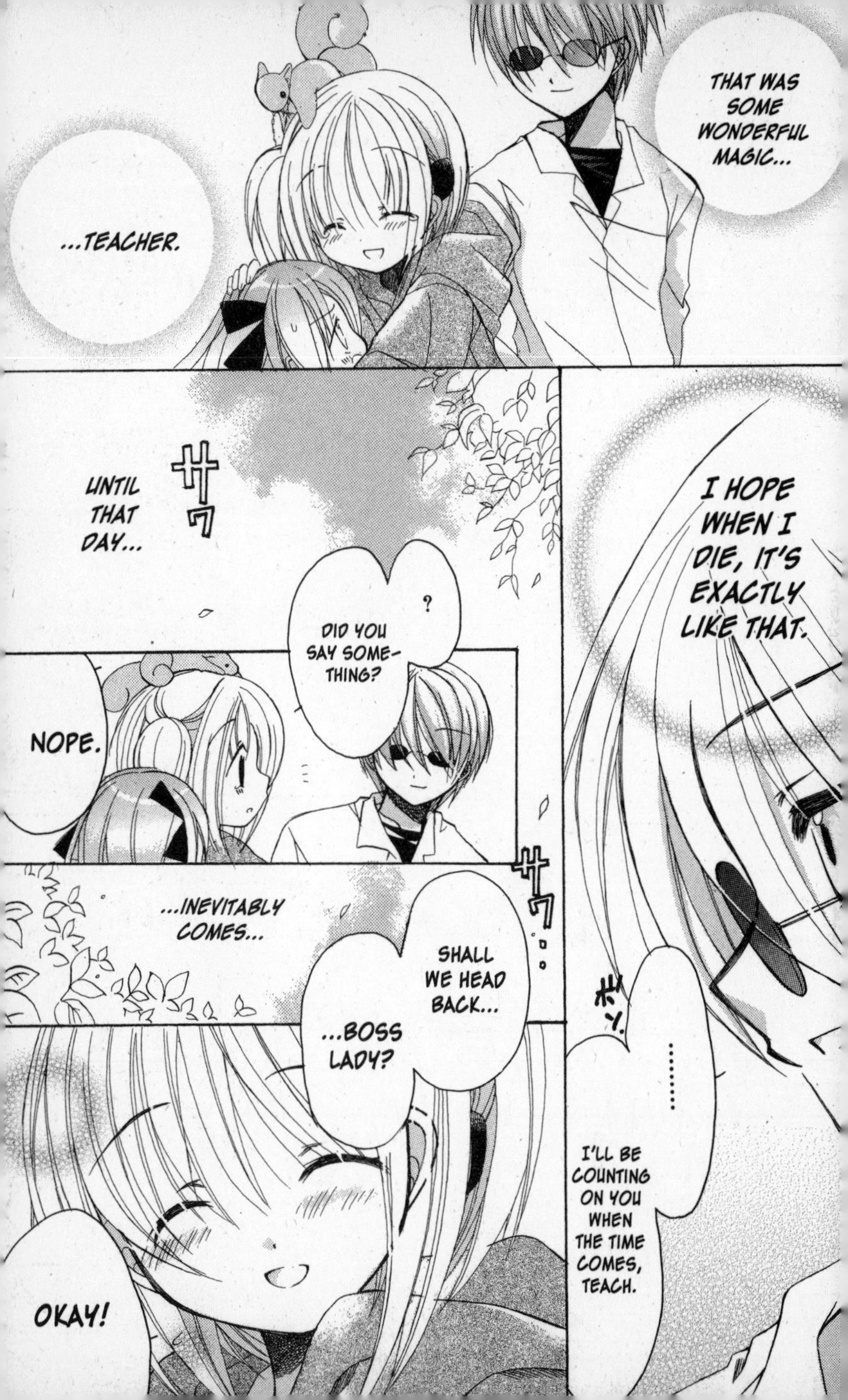
THAT WAS SOME WONDERFUL MAGIC...
...TEACHER.
I HOPE WHEN I DIE, IT'S EXACTLY LIKE THAT.
......
I'LL BE COUNTING ON YOU WHEN THE TIME COMES, TEACH.
UNTIL THAT DAY...
サァ
DID YOU SAY SOME-THING?
?
NOPE.
...INEVITABLY COMES...
サァ...
SHALL WE HEAD BACK...
...BOSS LADY?
OKAY!

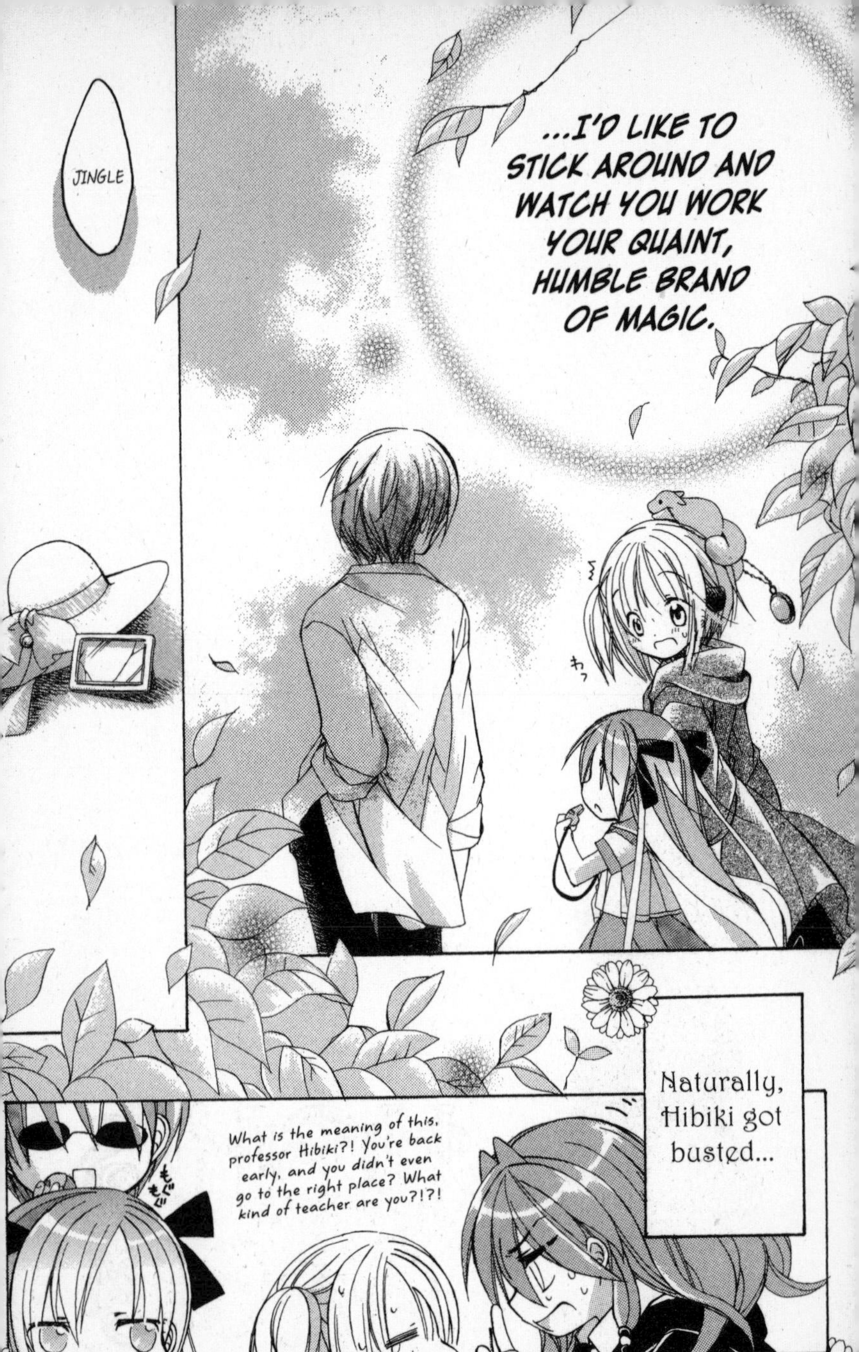
...I'D LIKE TO STICK AROUND AND WATCH YOU WORK YOUR QUAINT, HUMBLE BRAND OF MAGIC.
JINGLE
Naturally, Hibiki got busted...
What is the meaning of this, professor Hibiki?! You're back early, and you didn't even go to the right place? What kind of teacher are you?!?!

HIBIKI'S MAGIC™

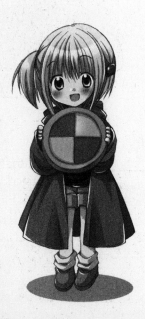

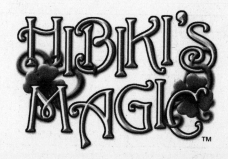

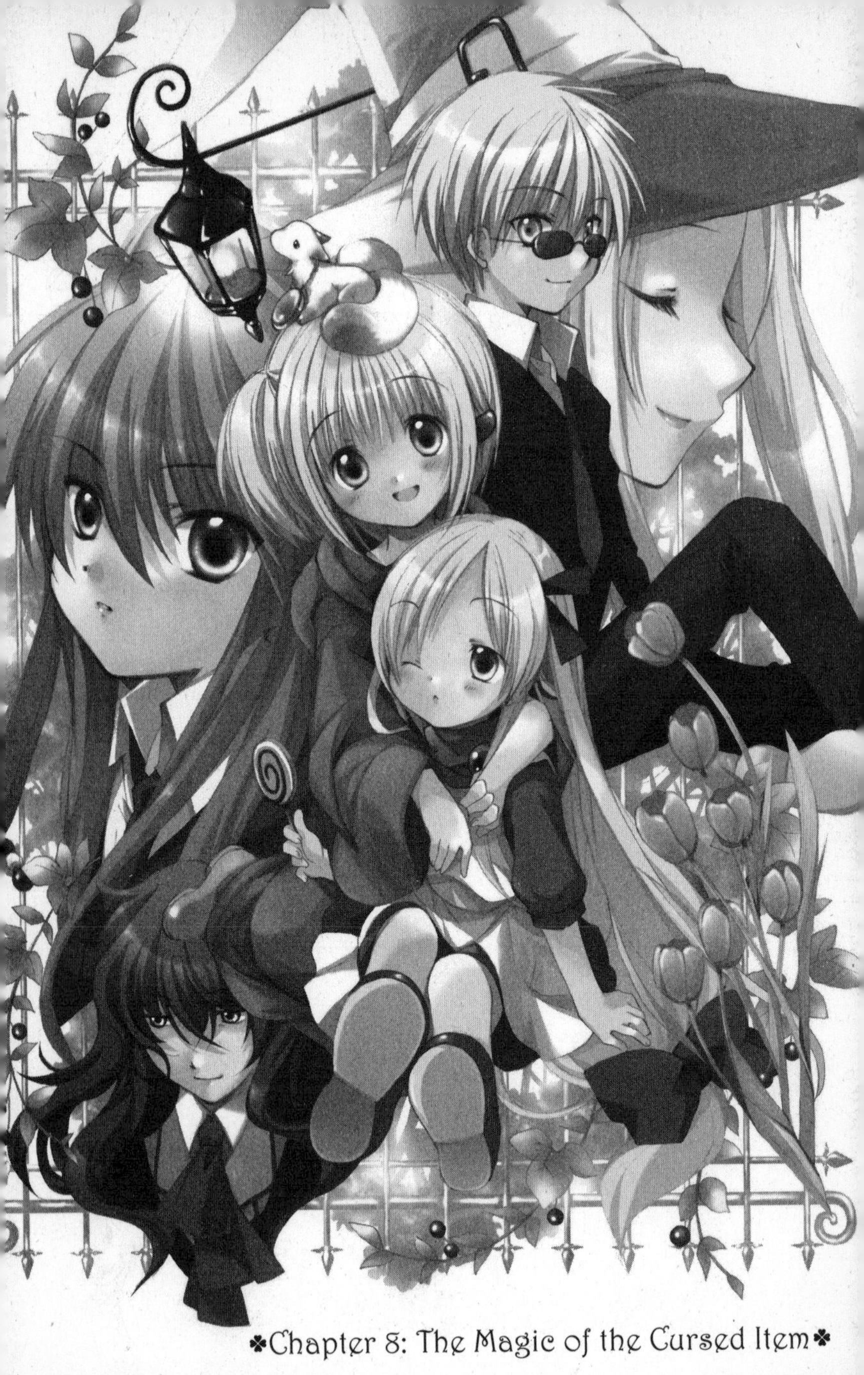

✤Chapter 8: The Magic of the Cursed Item✤

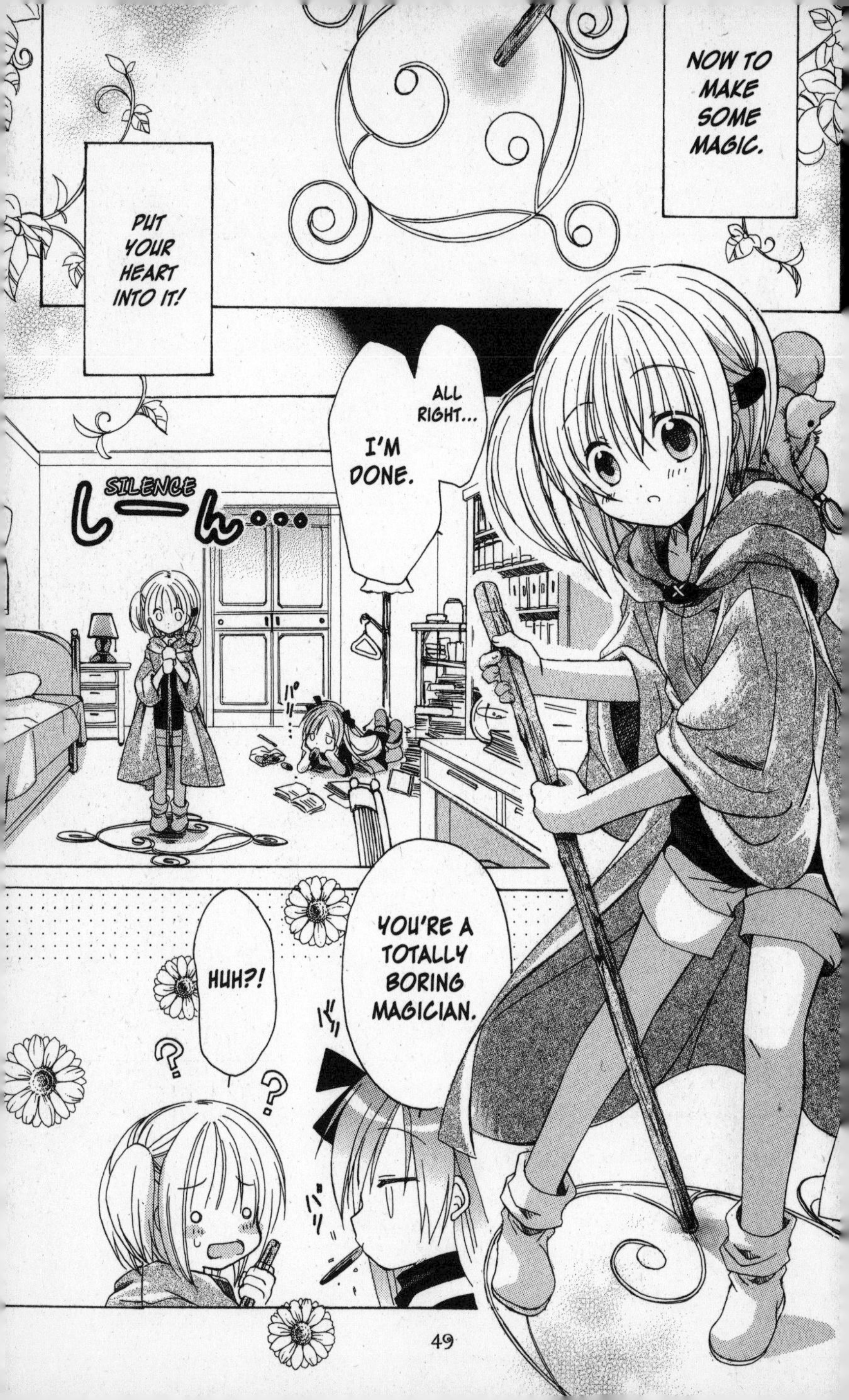
NOW TO MAKE SOME MAGIC.
PUT YOUR HEART INTO IT!
ALL RIGHT... I'M DONE.
SILENCE
YOU'RE A TOTALLY BORING MAGICIAN.
HUH?!

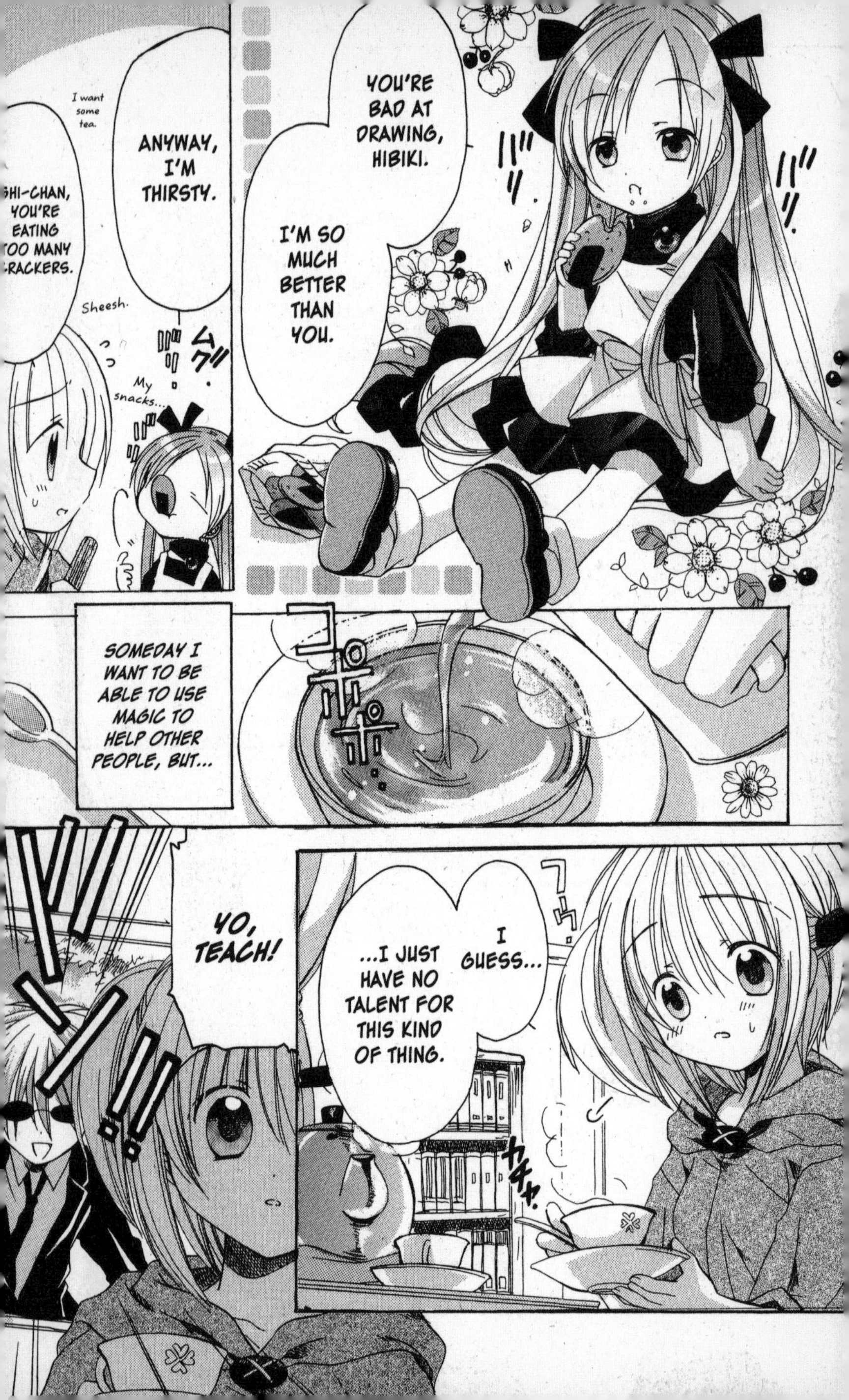
YOU'RE BAD AT DRAWING, HIBIKI.
I'M SO MUCH BETTER THAN YOU.
ANYWAY, I'M THIRSTY.
I want some tea.
HI-CHAN, YOU'RE EATING TOO MANY CRACKERS.
Sheesh.
My snacks...
SOMEDAY I WANT TO BE ABLE TO USE MAGIC TO HELP OTHER PEOPLE, BUT...
I GUESS...
...I JUST HAVE NO TALENT FOR THIS KIND OF THING.
YO, TEACH!

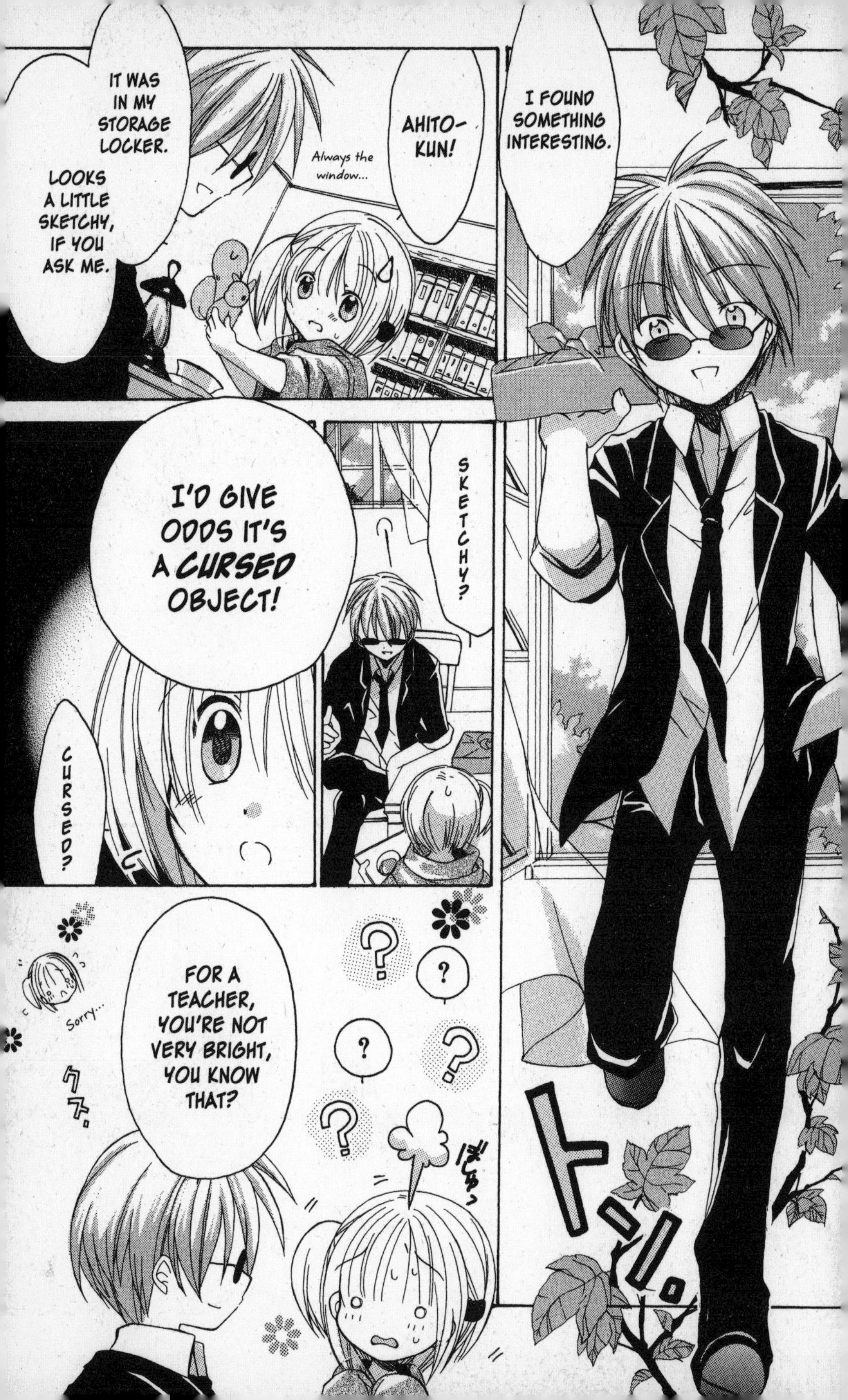

I FOUND SOMETHING INTERESTING.
トーン。
AHITO-KUN!
Always the window...
IT WAS IN MY STORAGE LOCKER.
LOOKS A LITTLE SKETCHY, IF YOU ASK ME.
SKETCHY?
I'D GIVE ODDS IT'S A CURSED OBJECT!
CURSED?
FOR A TEACHER, YOU'RE NOT VERY BRIGHT, YOU KNOW THAT?
Sorry...
クス。

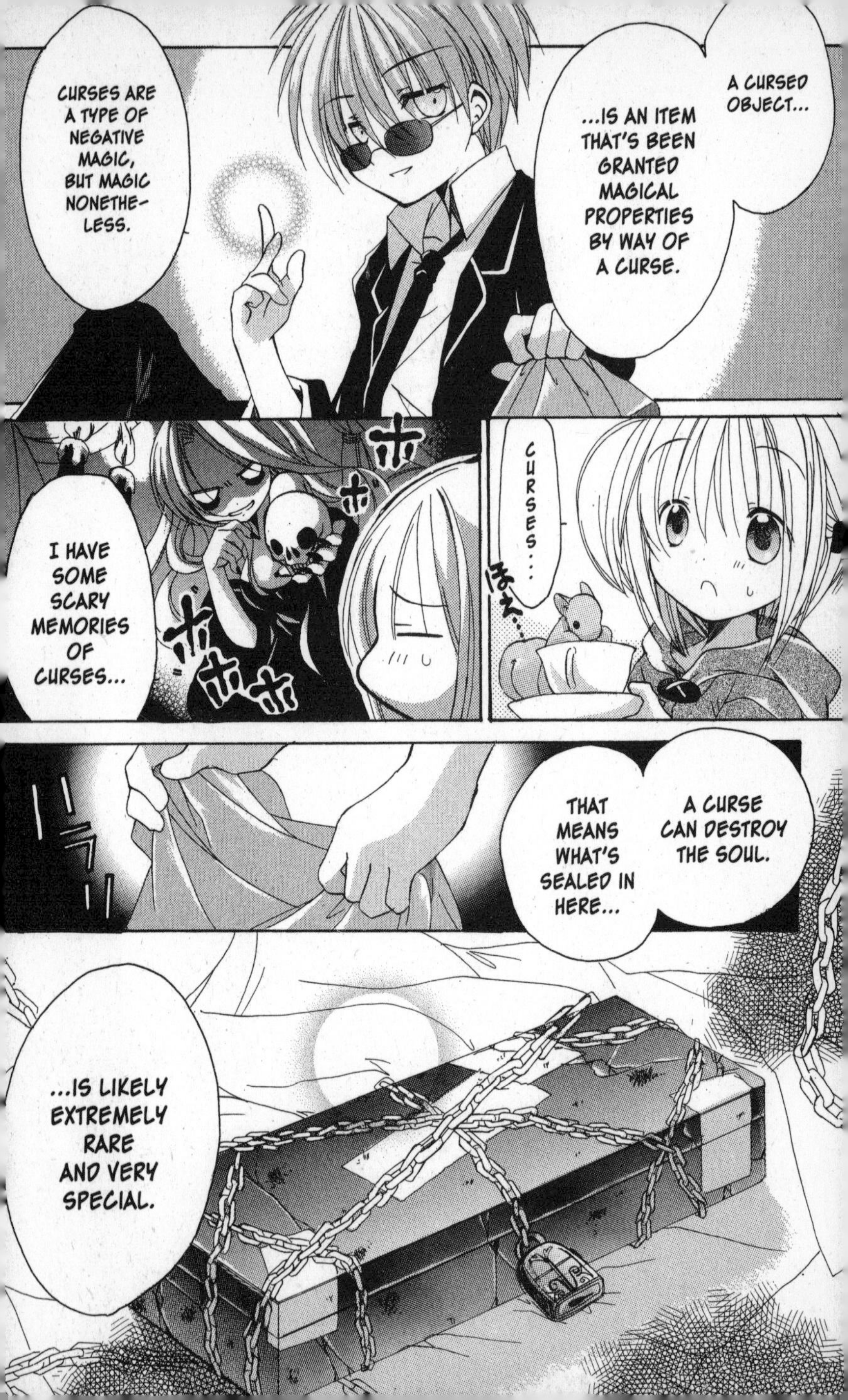
A CURSED OBJECT...
...IS AN ITEM THAT'S BEEN GRANTED MAGICAL PROPERTIES BY WAY OF A CURSE.
CURSES ARE A TYPE OF NEGATIVE MAGIC, BUT MAGIC NONETHELESS.
CURSES...
ほえ…
I HAVE SOME SCARY MEMORIES OF CURSES...
A CURSE CAN DESTROY THE SOUL.
THAT MEANS WHAT'S SEALED IN HERE...
...IS LIKELY EXTREMELY RARE AND VERY SPECIAL.

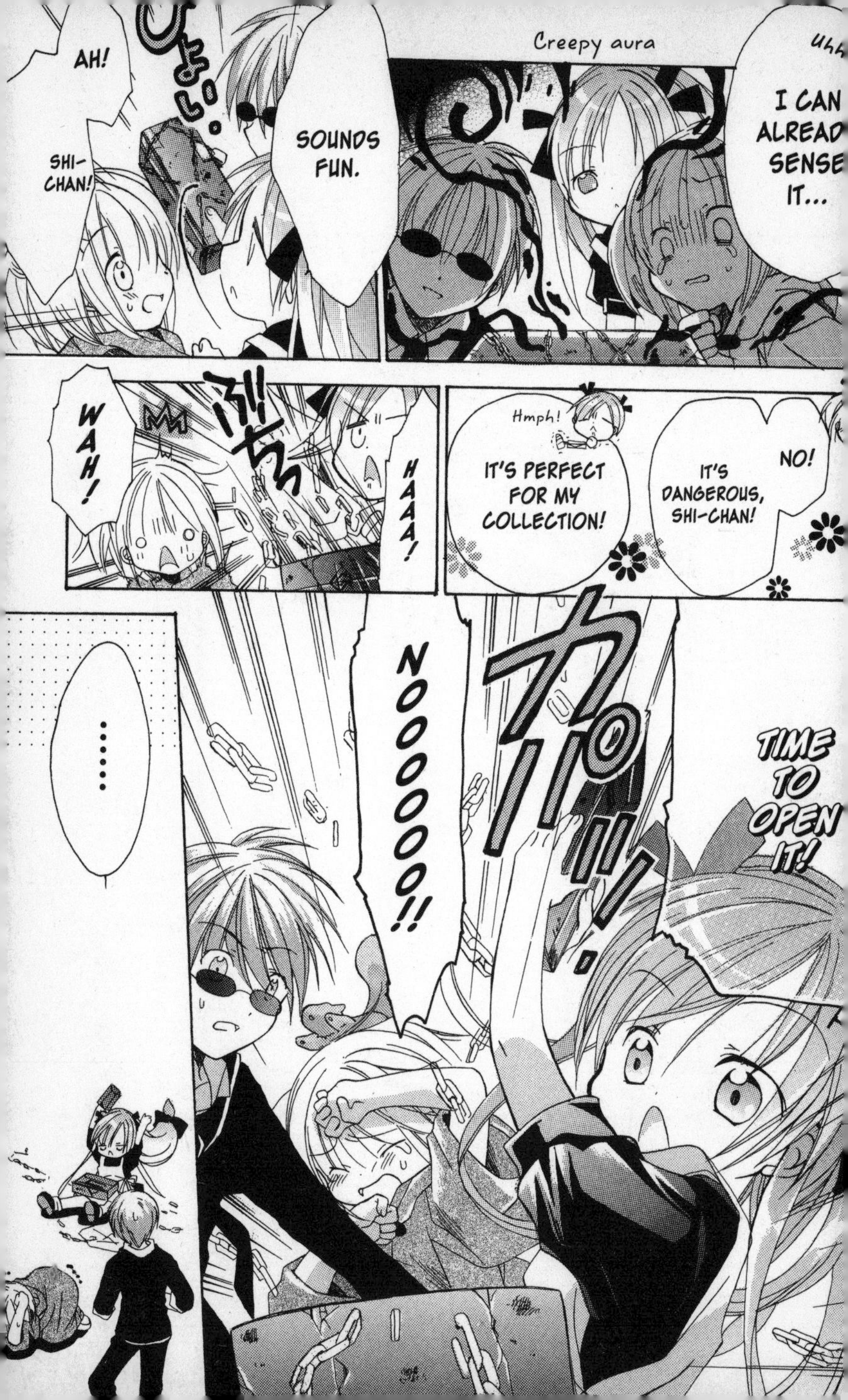
Creepy aura
Uhh
I CAN ALREAD SENSE IT...
SOUNDS FUN.
AH!
SHI-CHAN!
NO!
IT'S DANGEROUS, SHI-CHAN!
Hmph!
IT'S PERFECT FOR MY COLLECTION!
HAAAA!
WAH!
TIME TO OPEN IT!
NOOOOOOOO!!
......

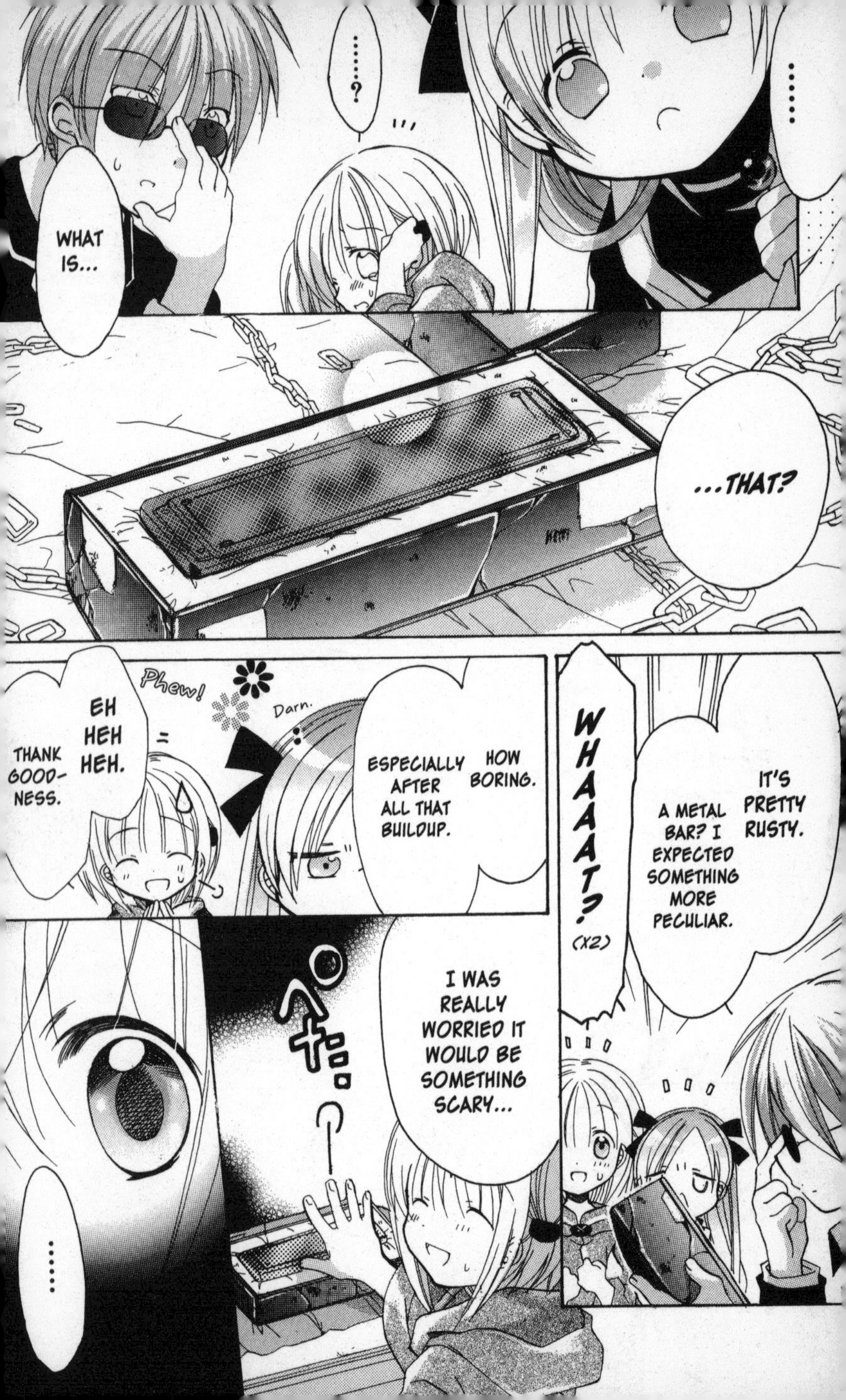
......
......?
WHAT IS...
...THAT?
WHAAAAT?! (X2)
IT'S PRETTY RUSTY.
A METAL BAR? I EXPECTED SOMETHING MORE PECULIAR.
HOW BORING.
ESPECIALLY AFTER ALL THAT BUILDUP.
Darn.
Phew!
EH HEH HEH.
THANK GOODNESS.
I WAS REALLY WORRIED IT WOULD BE SOMETHING SCARY...
......

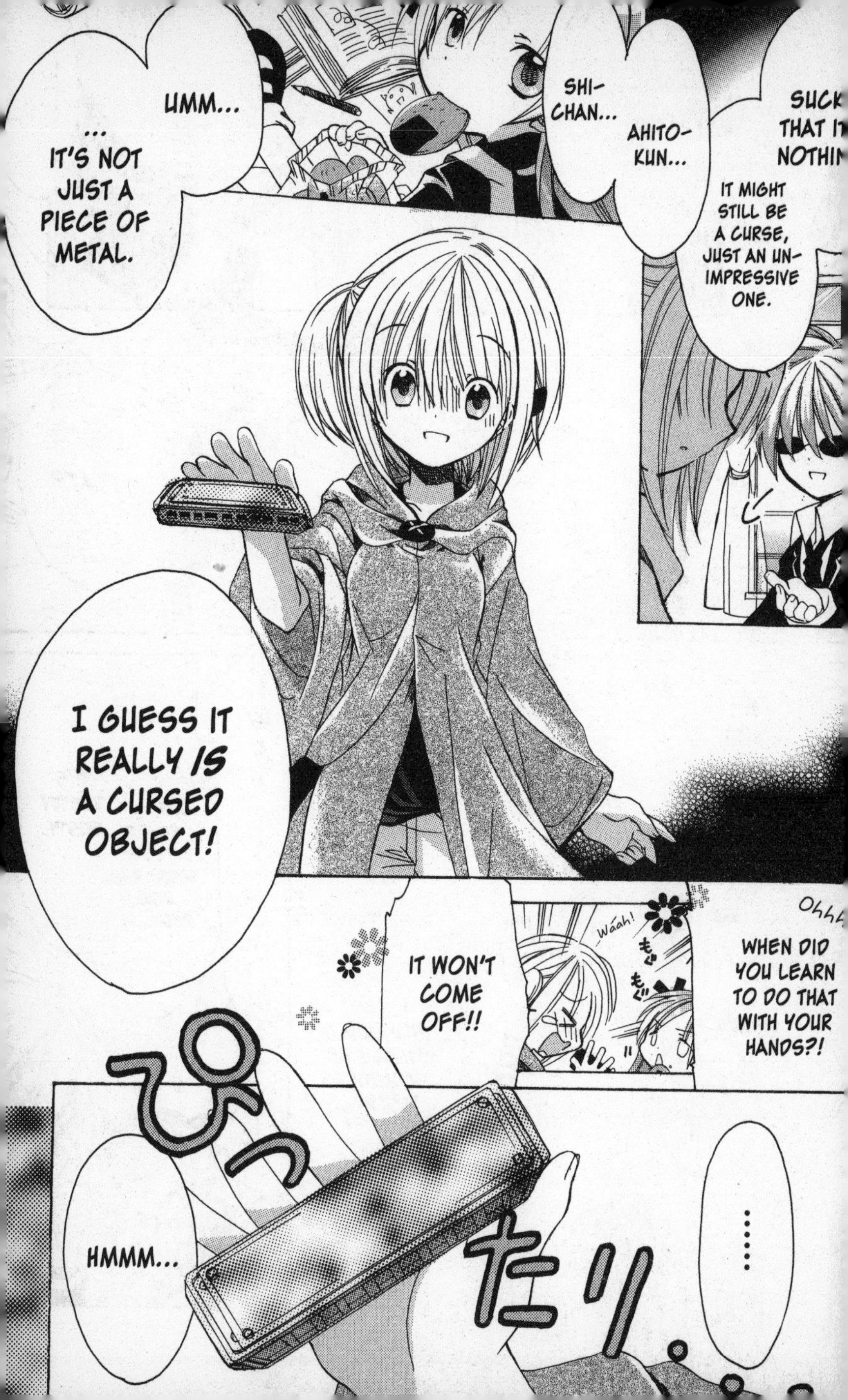
SUCK THAT IT NOTHIN
SHI-CHAN... AHITO-KUN...
UMM...
... IT'S NOT JUST A PIECE OF METAL.
IT MIGHT STILL BE A CURSE, JUST AN UN-IMPRESSIVE ONE.
I GUESS IT REALLY IS A CURSED OBJECT!
WHEN DID YOU LEARN TO DO THAT WITH YOUR HANDS?!
Wáah!
もぐもぐ
IT WON'T COME OFF!!
......
たり
ぴっ
HMMM...

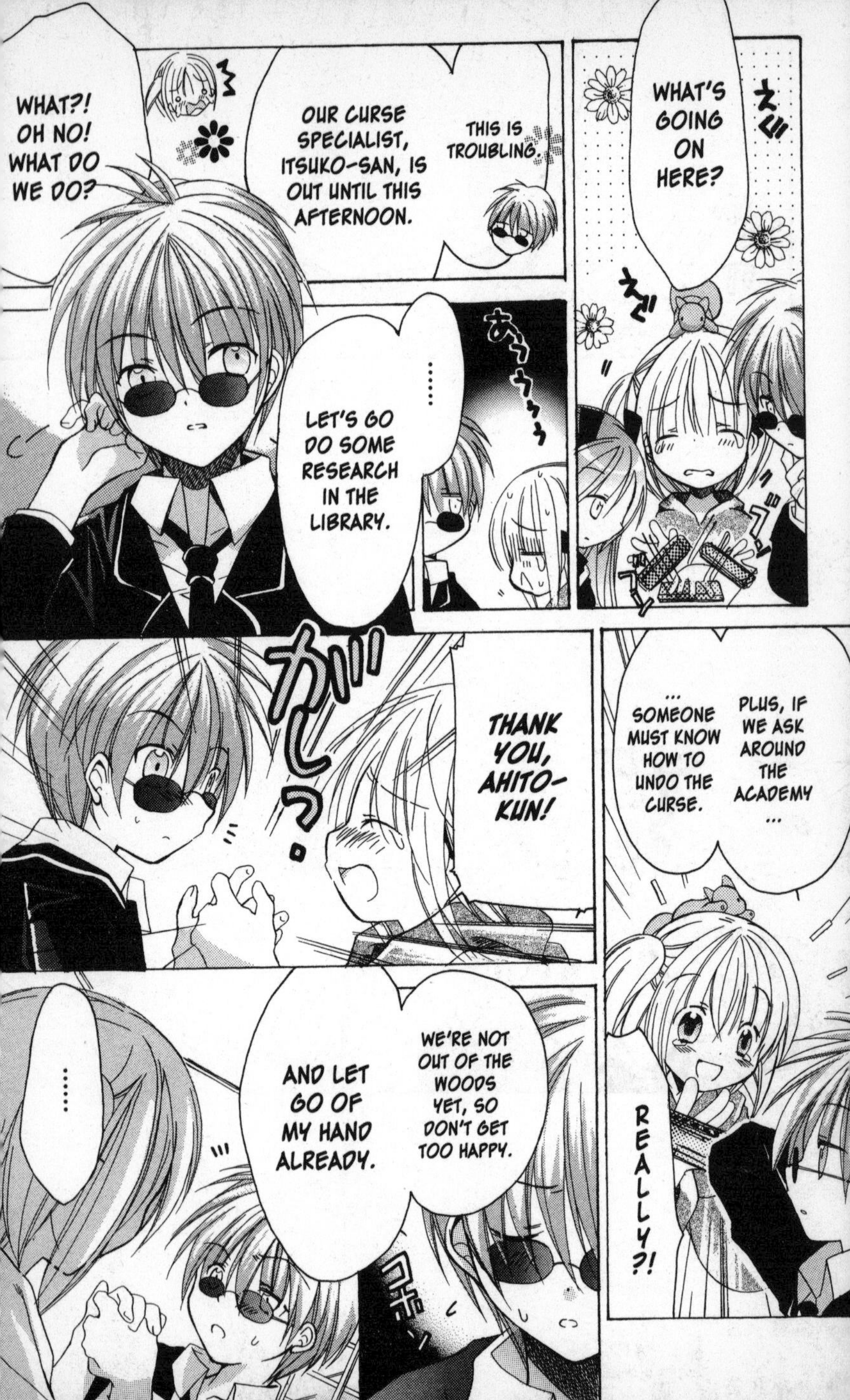

WHAT'S GOING ON HERE?
THIS IS TROUBLING.
OUR CURSE SPECIALIST, ITSUKO-SAN, IS OUT UNTIL THIS AFTERNOON.
WHAT?! OH NO! WHAT DO WE DO?
あうぅぅぅ
......
LET'S GO DO SOME RESEARCH IN THE LIBRARY.
PLUS, IF WE ASK AROUND THE ACADEMY...
...SOMEONE MUST KNOW HOW TO UNDO THE CURSE.
REALLY?!
がしっ。
THANK YOU, AHITO-KUN!
WE'RE NOT OUT OF THE WOODS YET, SO DON'T GET TOO HAPPY.
AND LET GO OF MY HAND ALREADY.
......

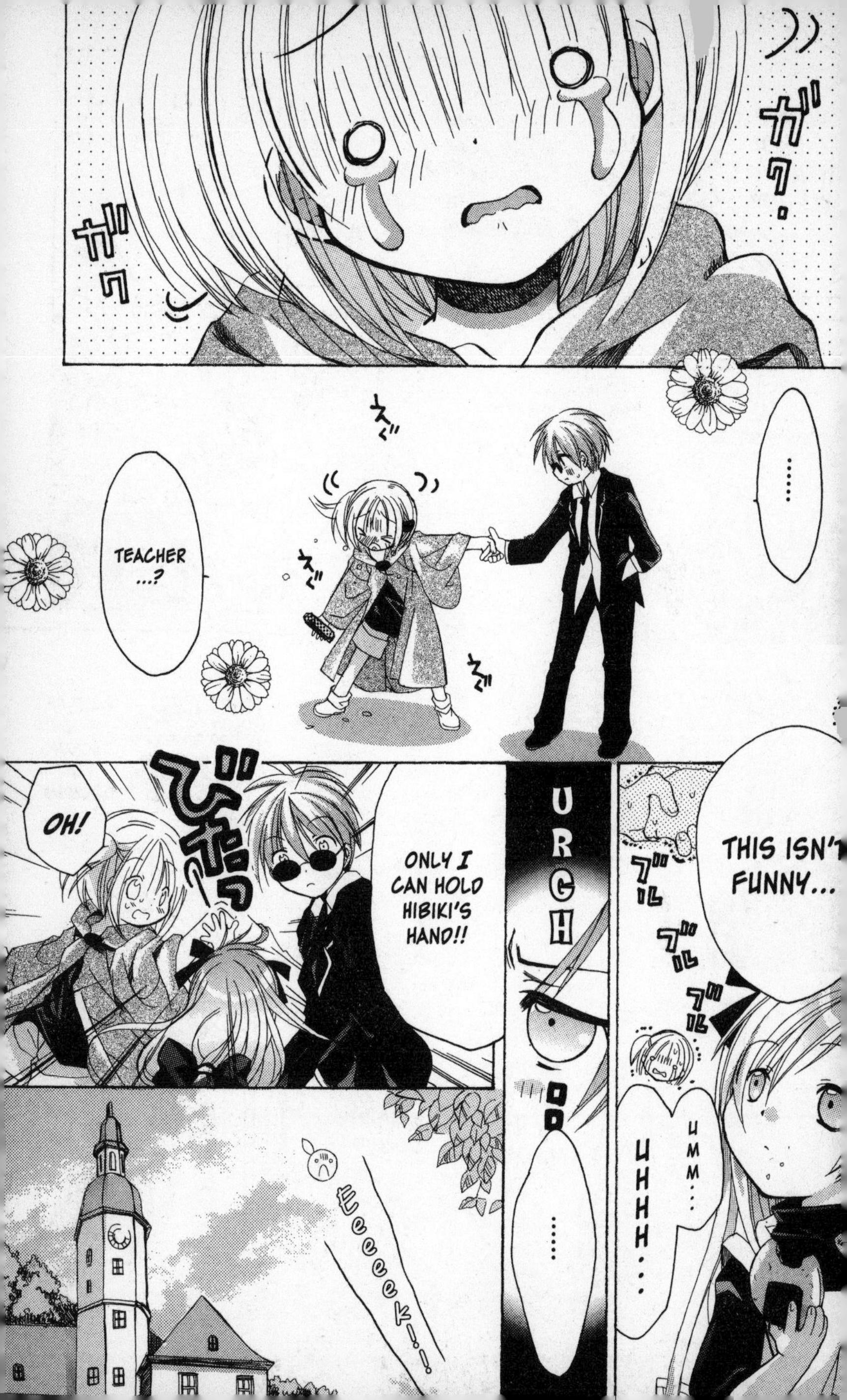
ガク。
ガク
......
えぐ
えぐ
えぐ
TEACHER ...?
THIS ISN'T FUNNY...
ブル
ブル
ブル
UMM...
UHHH...
URGH
......
ONLY I CAN HOLD HIBIKI'S HAND!!
ぴたっ
OH!
もeeeek!!

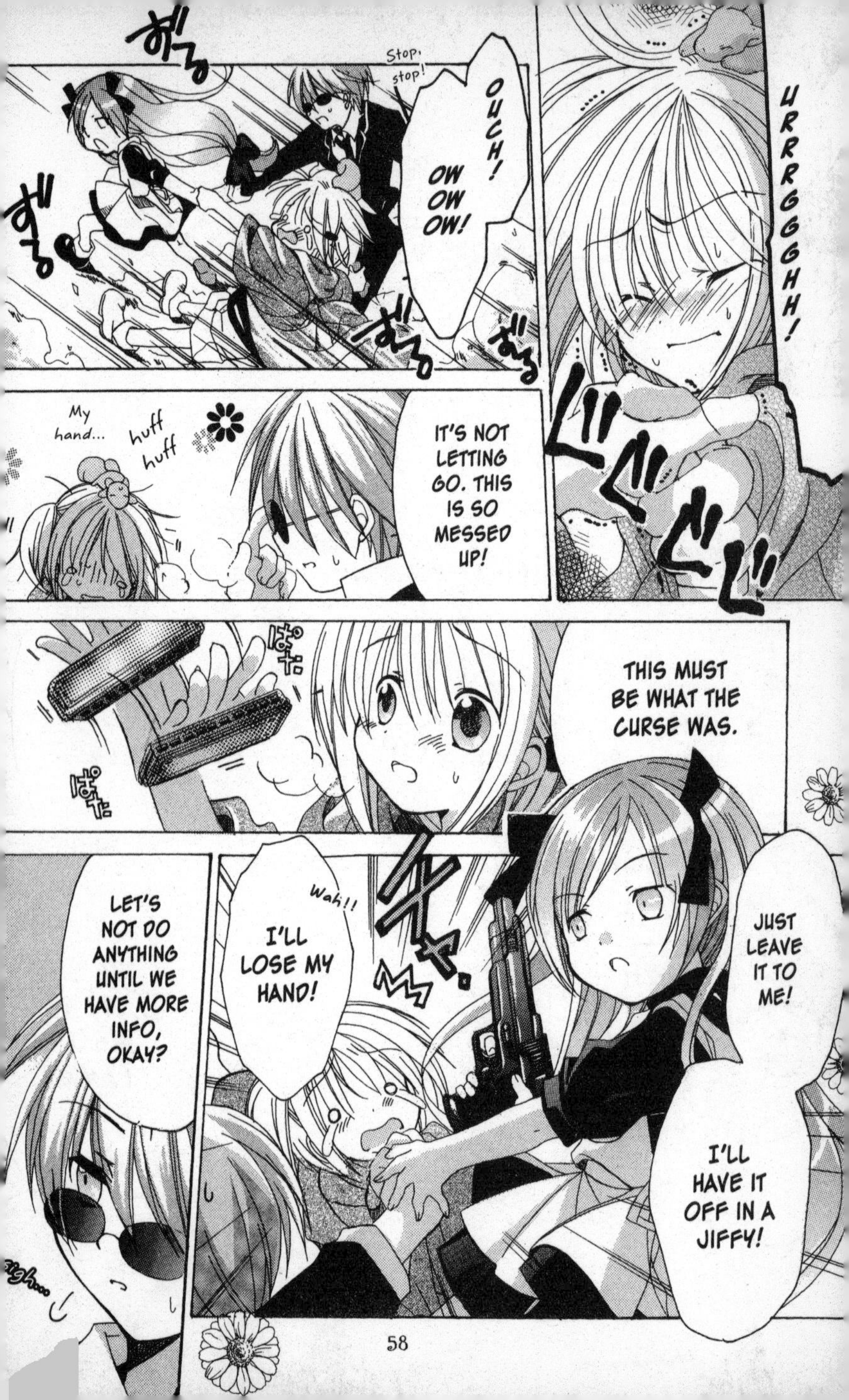
....
URRRGGGHH!
OUCH! OW OW OW!
Stop, stop!
IT'S NOT LETTING GO. THIS IS SO MESSED UP!
My hand... huff huff
THIS MUST BE WHAT THE CURSE WAS.
JUST LEAVE IT TO ME!
I'LL HAVE IT OFF IN A JIFFY!
I'LL LOSE MY HAND!
Wah!!
LET'S NOT DO ANYTHING UNTIL WE HAVE MORE INFO, OKAY?
Sigh...

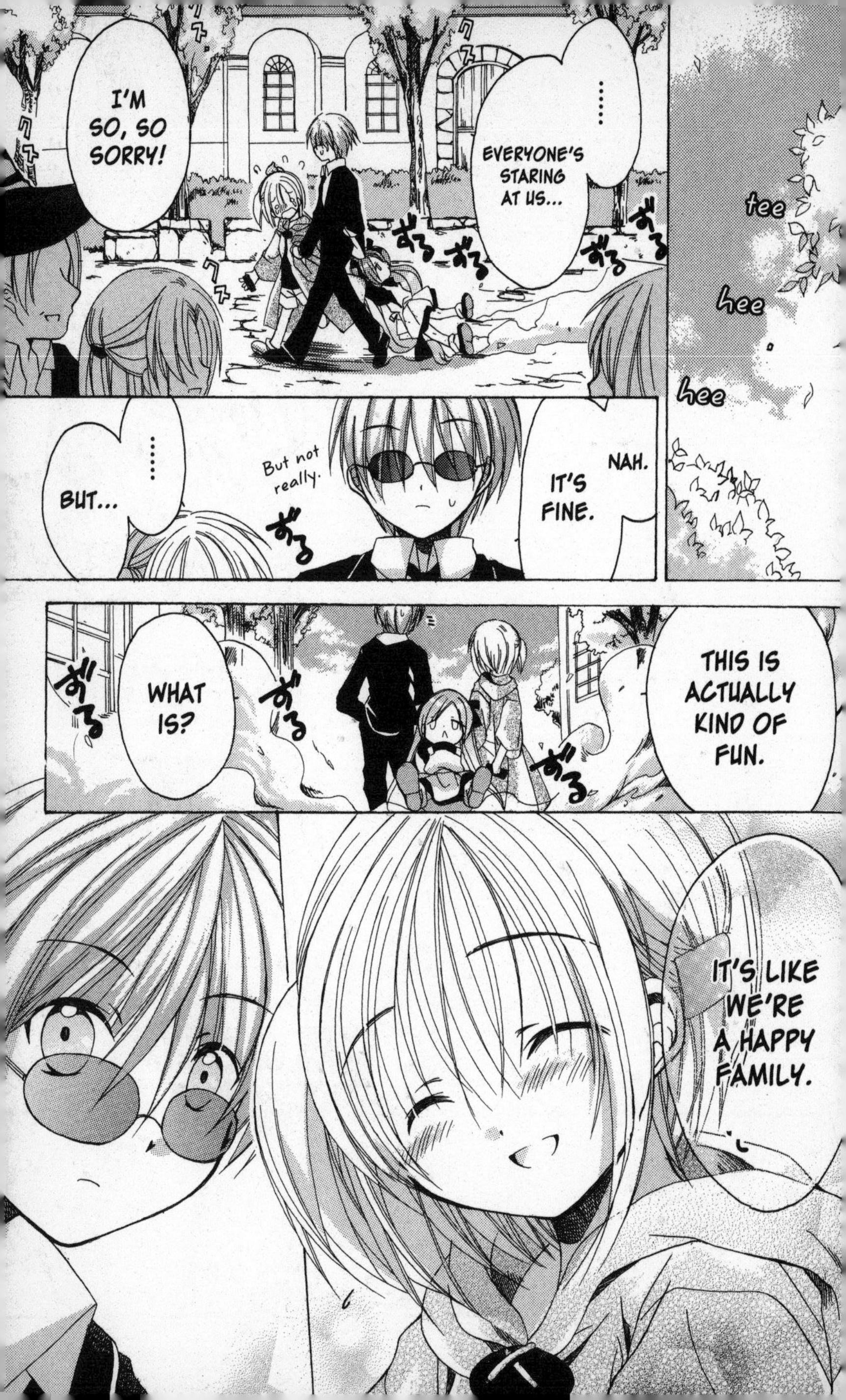
tee hee hee
......
EVERYONE'S STARING AT US...
I'M SO, SO SORRY!
ずる ずる
ずる ずる
NAH. IT'S FINE.
But not really.
ずる
......
BUT...
THIS IS ACTUALLY KIND OF FUN.
ずる
ずる
WHAT IS?
ずる
IT'S LIKE WE'RE A HAPPY FAMILY.

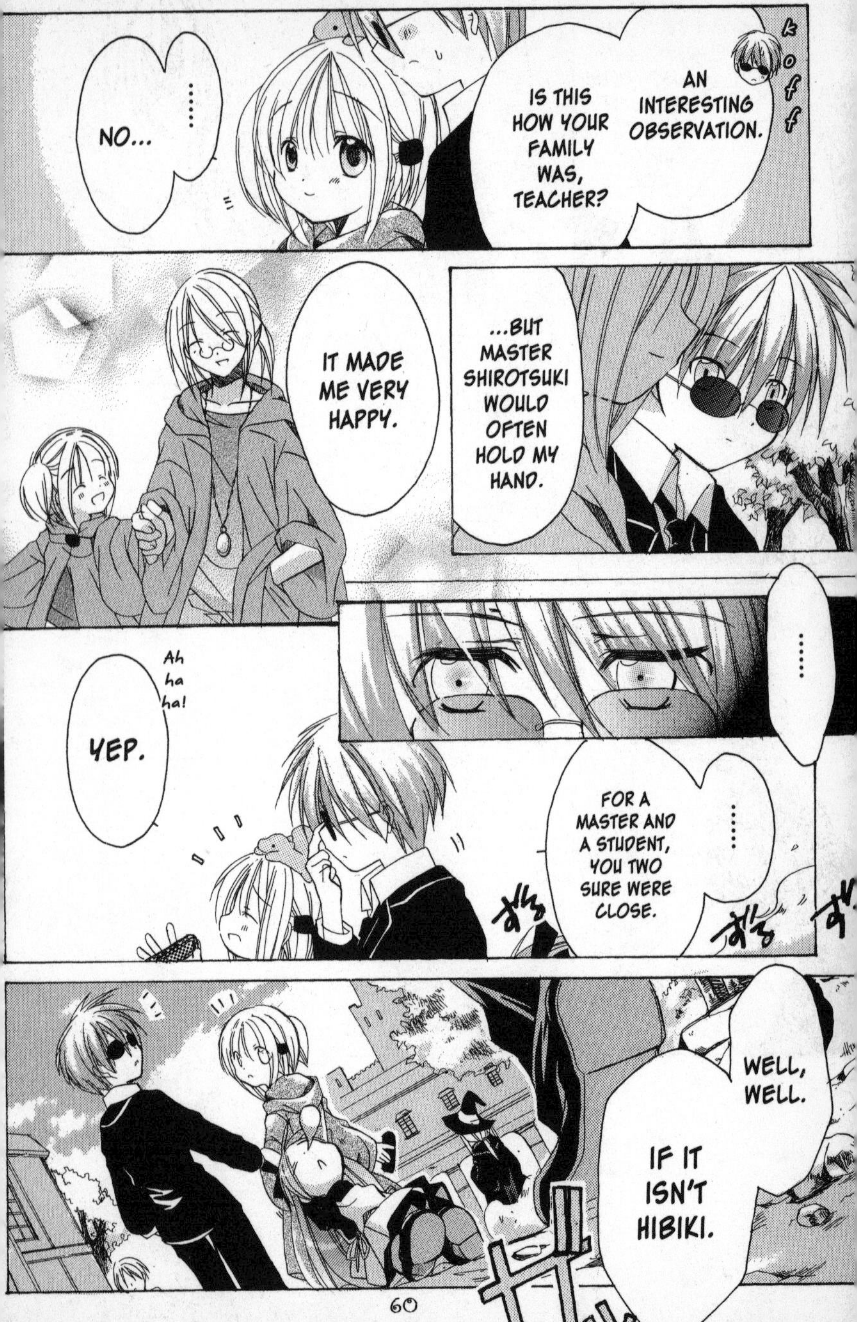
koff
AN INTERESTING OBSERVATION.
IS THIS HOW YOUR FAMILY WAS, TEACHER?
...... NO...
...BUT MASTER SHIROTSUKI WOULD OFTEN HOLD MY HAND.
IT MADE ME VERY HAPPY.
......
......
FOR A MASTER AND A STUDENT, YOU TWO SURE WERE CLOSE.
Ah ha ha!
YEP.
WELL, WELL.
IF IT ISN'T HIBIKI.

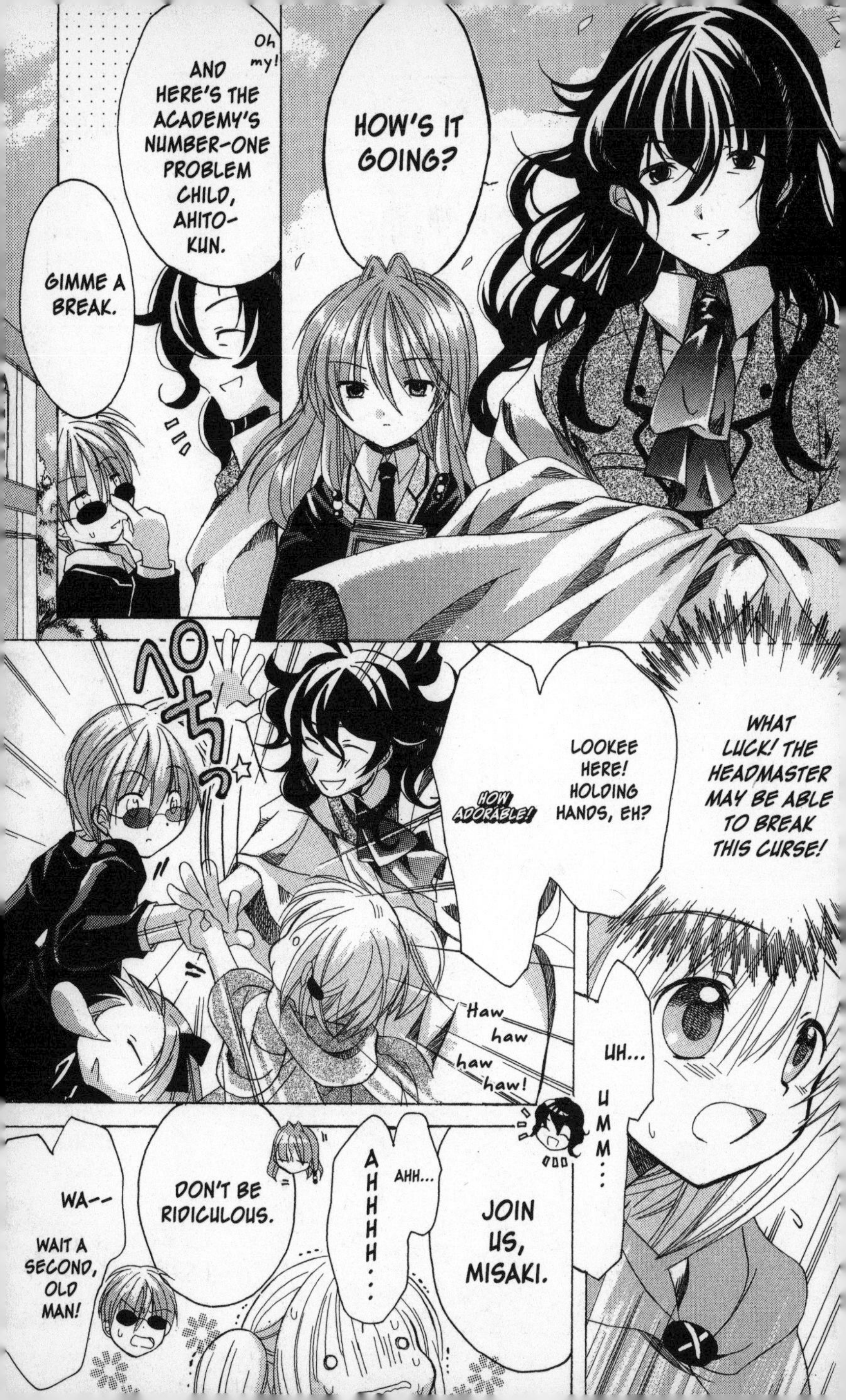
HOW'S IT GOING?
Oh my!
AND HERE'S THE ACADEMY'S NUMBER-ONE PROBLEM CHILD, AHITO-KUN.
GIMME A BREAK.
WHAT LUCK! THE HEADMASTER MAY BE ABLE TO BREAK THIS CURSE!
UH...
UMM...
LOOKEE HERE! HOLDING HANDS, EH?
HOW ADORABLE!
ペちっ
Haw haw haw haw!
JOIN US, MISAKI.
AHHHHH...
AHH...
DON'T BE RIDICULOUS.
WA--
WAIT A SECOND, OLD MAN!

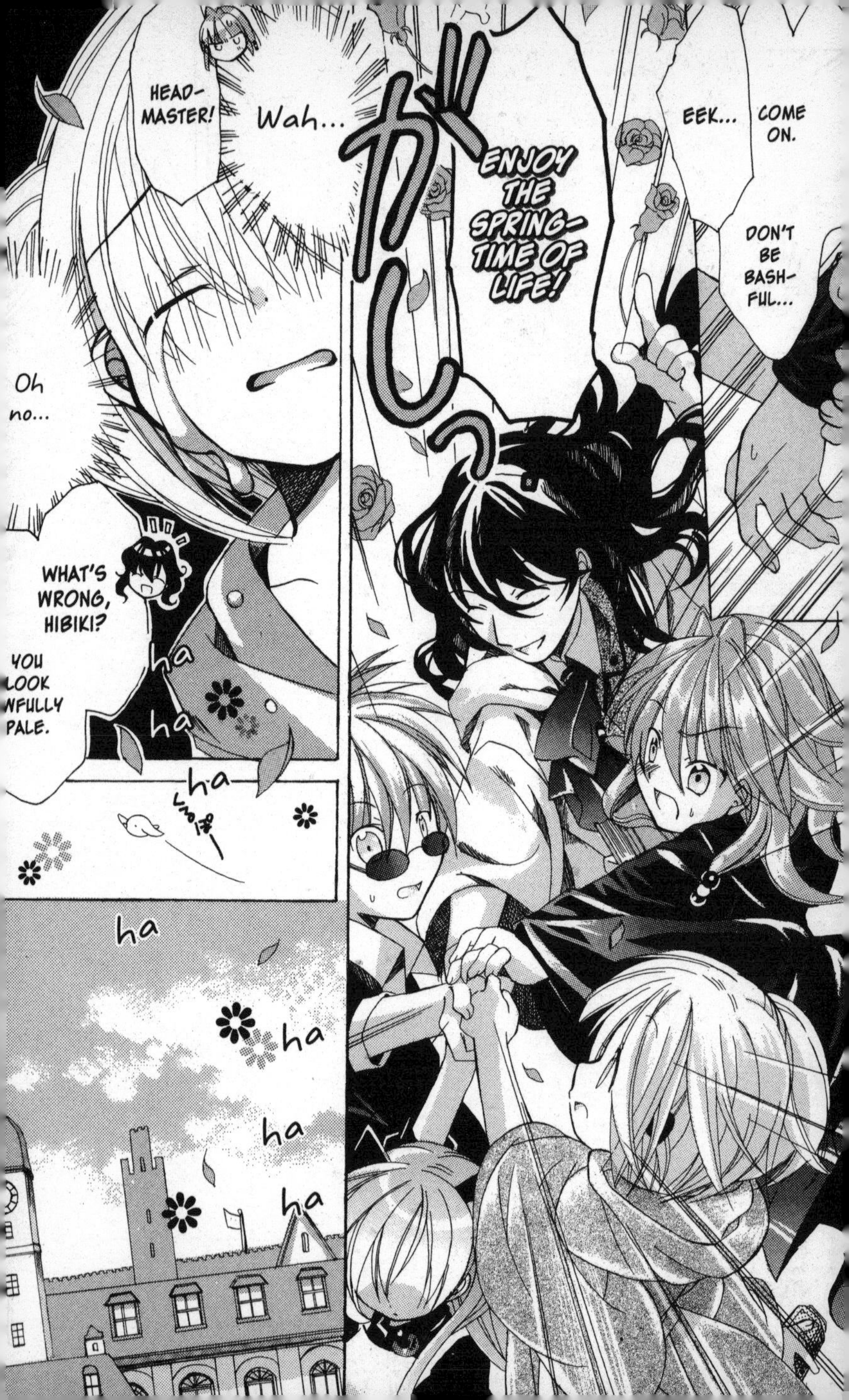
COME ON.
EEK...
DON'T BE BASHFUL...
ENJOY THE SPRING-TIME OF LIFE!
がしっ
Wah...
HEAD-MASTER!
Oh no...
WHAT'S WRONG, HIBIKI?
YOU LOOK NFULLY PALE.
ha
ha
ha
ha
ha
ha
ha

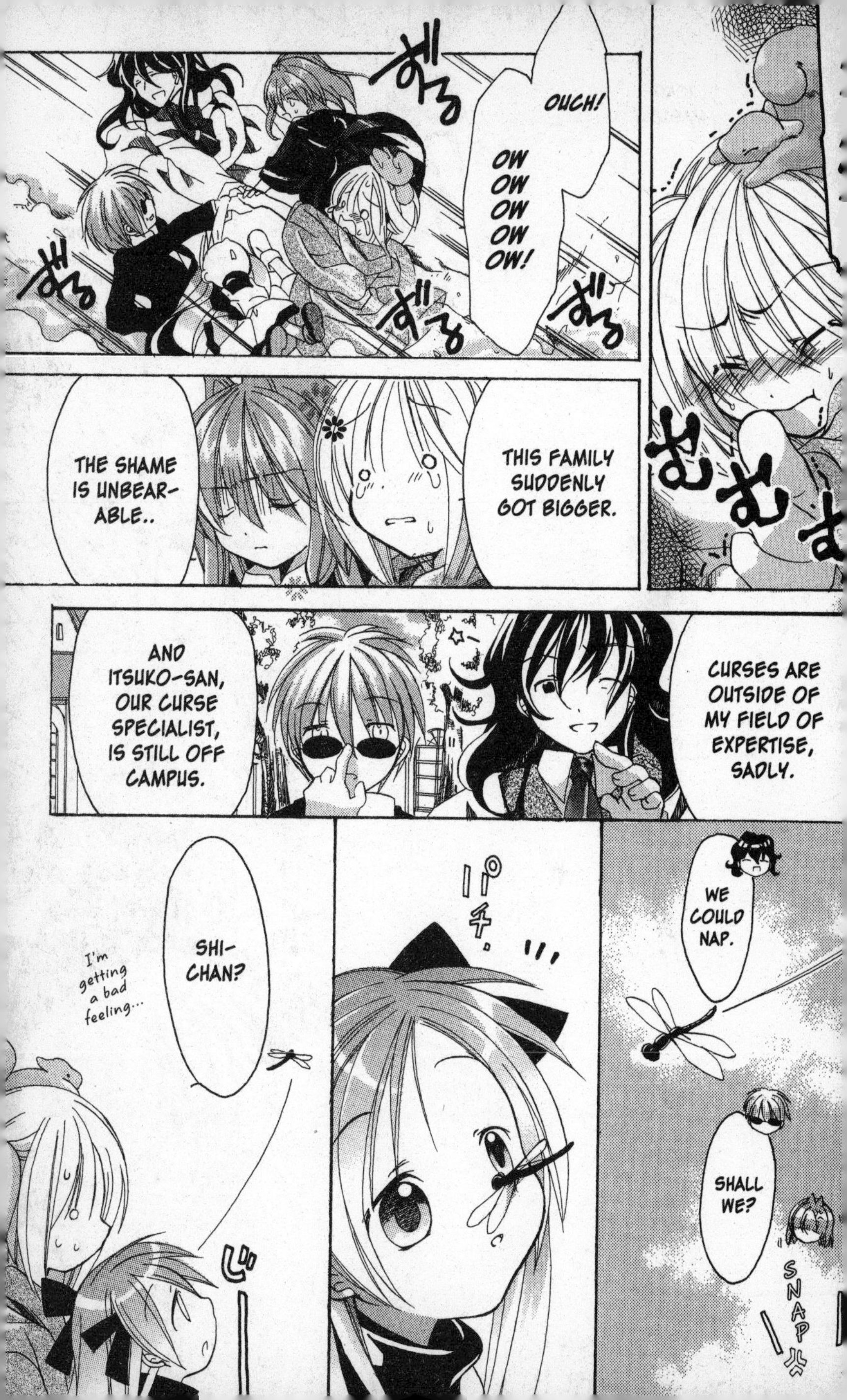

OUCH!
OW OW OW OW OW!
THIS FAMILY SUDDENLY GOT BIGGER.
THE SHAME IS UNBEARABLE..
CURSES ARE OUTSIDE OF MY FIELD OF EXPERTISE, SADLY.
AND ITSUKO-SAN, OUR CURSE SPECIALIST, IS STILL OFF CAMPUS.
WE COULD NAP.
SHALL WE?
SNAP
SHI-CHAN?
I'm getting a bad feeling...

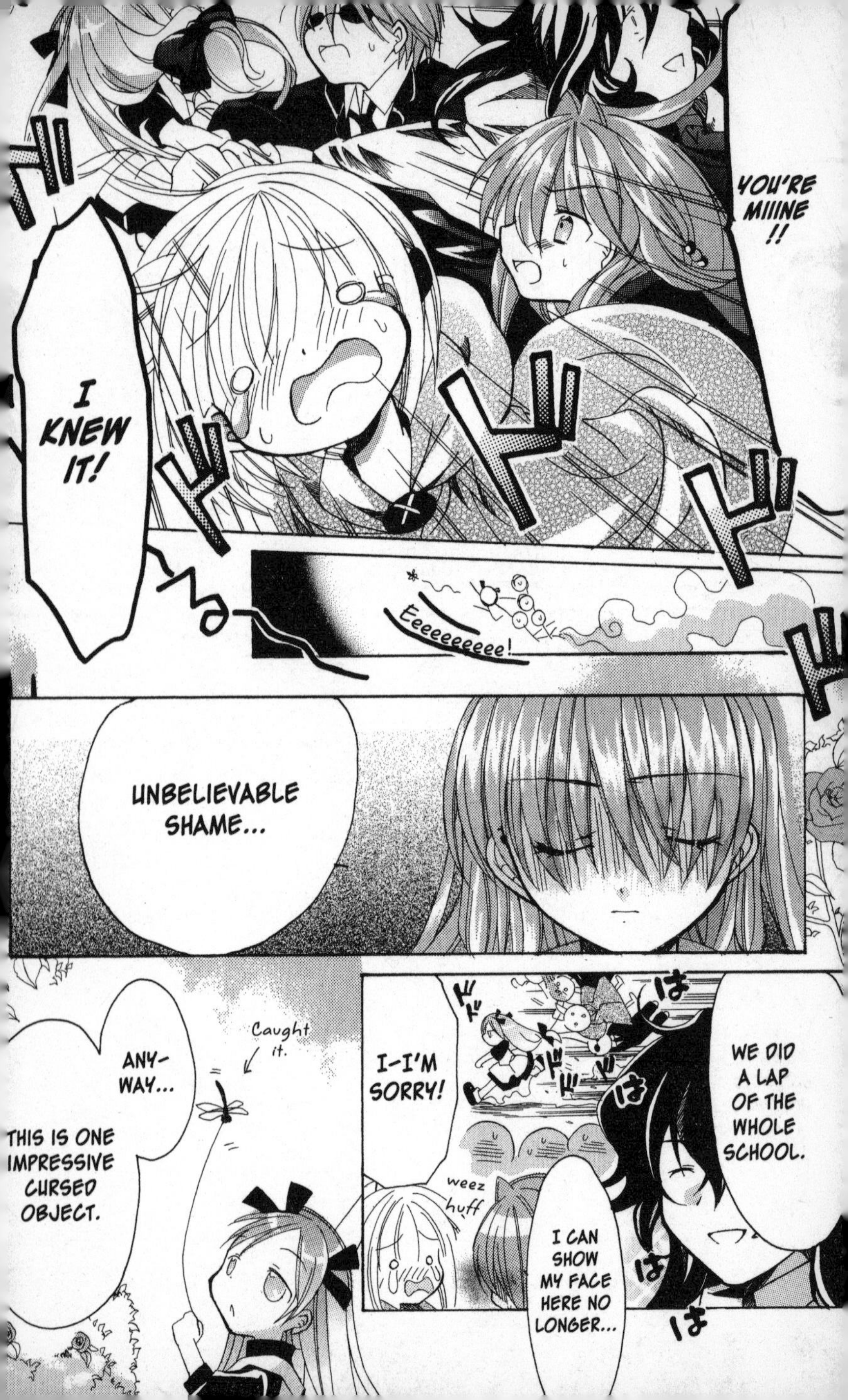
YOU'RE MIIINE !!
I KNEW IT!
ド
ド
ド
ド
Eeeeeeeeee!
UNBELIEVABLE SHAME...
WE DID A LAP OF THE WHOLE SCHOOL.
は
は
I-I'M SORRY!
weez
huff
I CAN SHOW MY FACE HERE NO LONGER...
は
は
Caught it.
ANY-WAY...
THIS IS ONE IMPRESSIVE CURSED OBJECT.

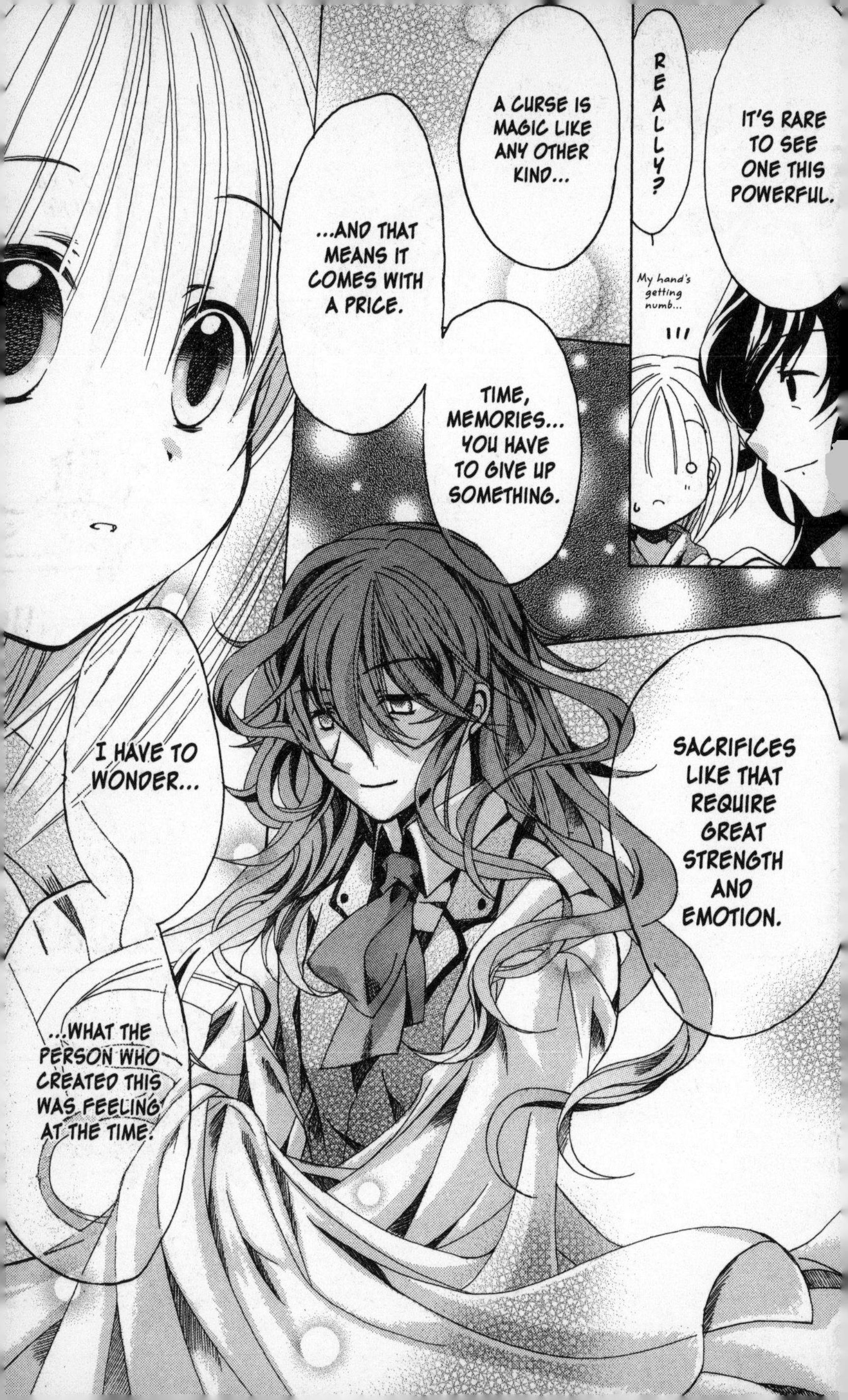
IT'S RARE TO SEE ONE THIS POWERFUL.
REALLY?
My hand's getting numb...
!!!
A CURSE IS MAGIC LIKE ANY OTHER KIND...
...AND THAT MEANS IT COMES WITH A PRICE.
TIME, MEMORIES... YOU HAVE TO GIVE UP SOMETHING.
SACRIFICES LIKE THAT REQUIRE GREAT STRENGTH AND EMOTION.
I HAVE TO WONDER...
...WHAT THE PERSON WHO CREATED THIS WAS FEELING AT THE TIME.

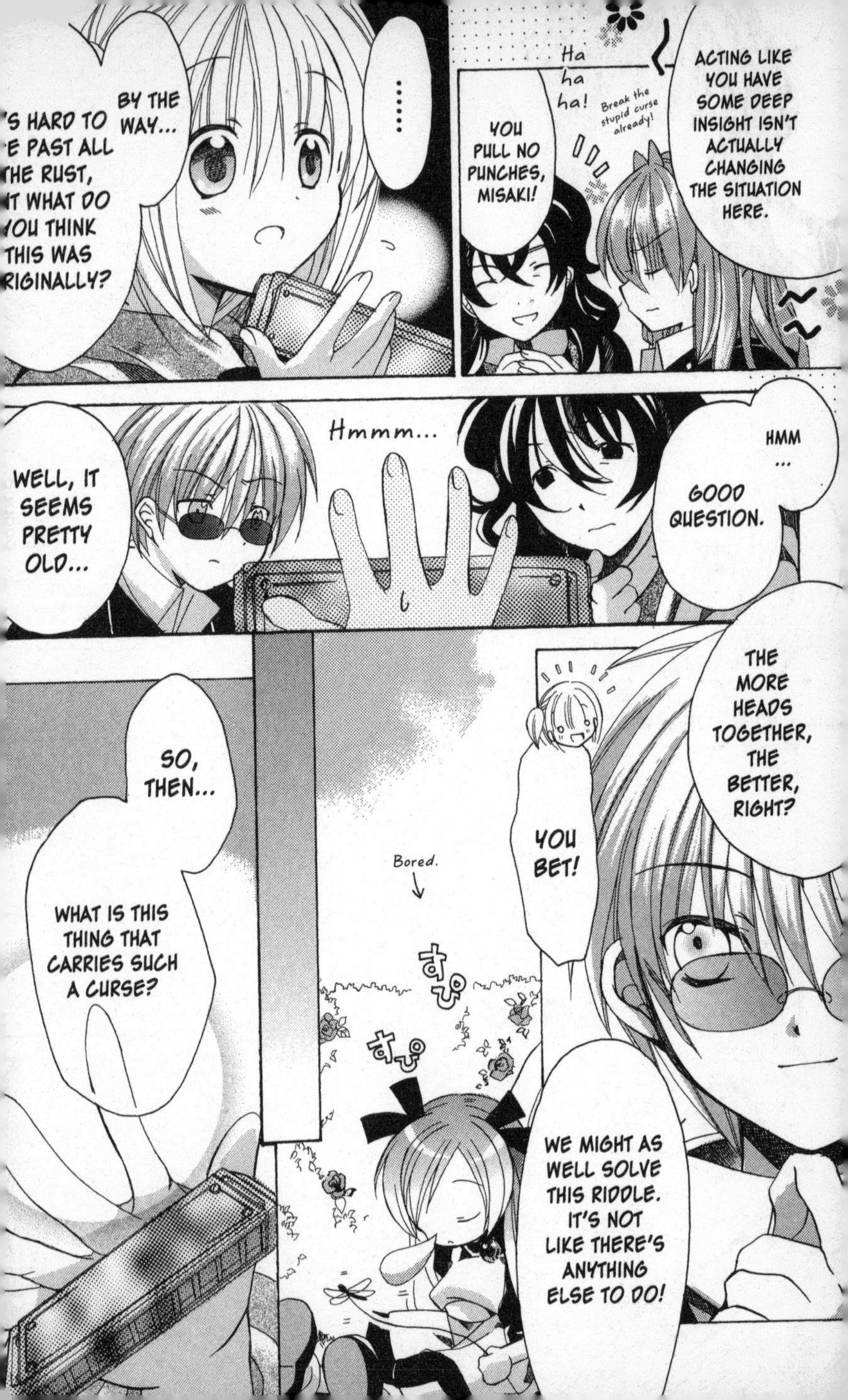

ACTING LIKE YOU HAVE SOME DEEP INSIGHT ISN'T ACTUALLY CHANGING THE SITUATION HERE.
Ha ha ha!
Break the stupid curse already!
YOU PULL NO PUNCHES, MISAKI!
......
BY THE WAY...
'S HARD TO 'E PAST ALL THE RUST, IT WHAT DO YOU THINK THIS WAS RIGINALLY?
HMM... GOOD QUESTION.
Hmmm...
WELL, IT SEEMS PRETTY OLD...
THE MORE HEADS TOGETHER, THE BETTER, RIGHT?
YOU BET!
WE MIGHT AS WELL SOLVE THIS RIDDLE. IT'S NOT LIKE THERE'S ANYTHING ELSE TO DO!
Bored.
すぴ
すぴ
SO, THEN...
WHAT IS THIS THING THAT CARRIES SUCH A CURSE?

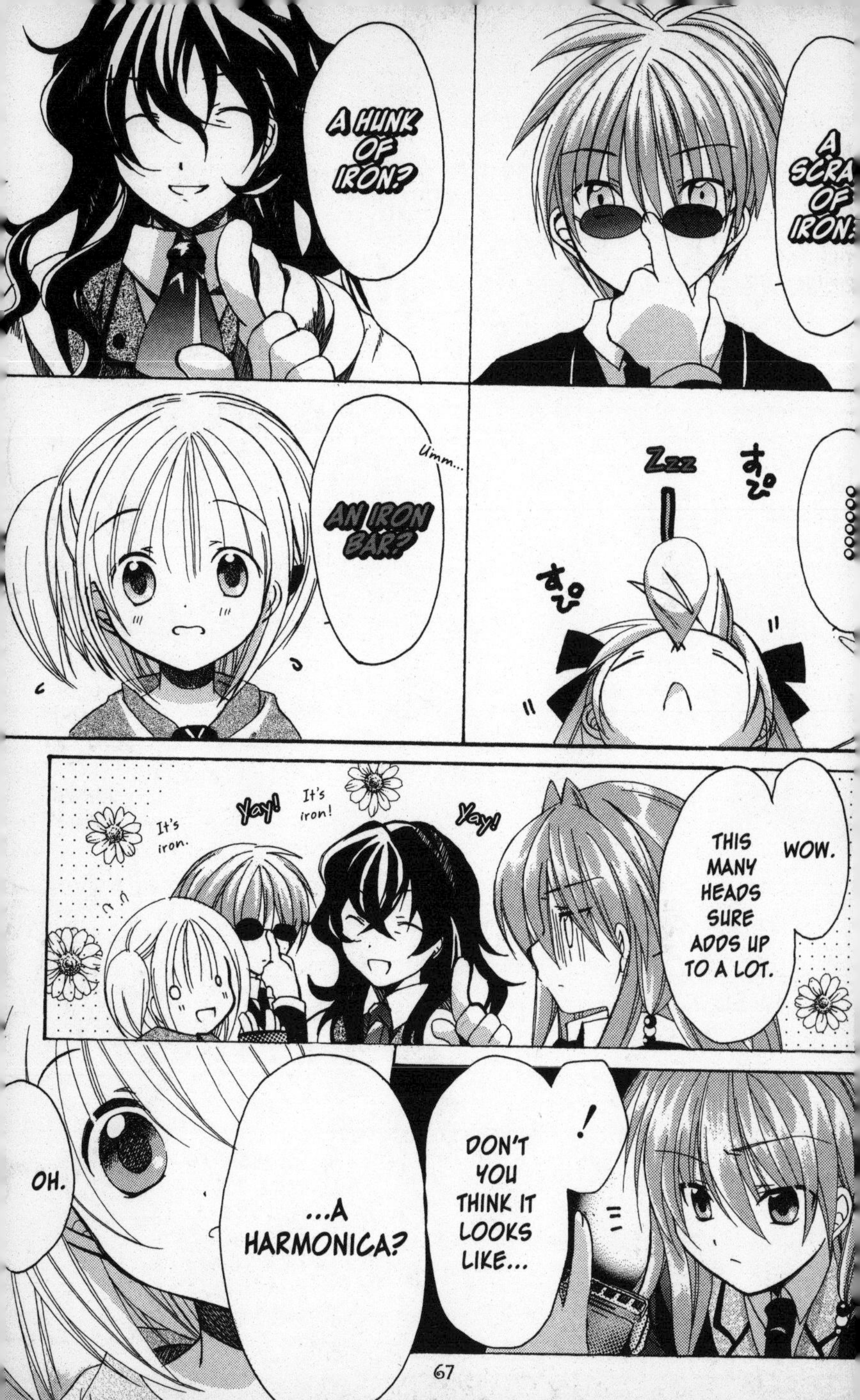
A SCRA OF IRON
A HUNK OF IRON?
Zzz
すぴ
すぴ
Umm...
AN IRON BAR?
WOW.
THIS MANY HEADS SURE ADDS UP TO A LOT.
Yay!
It's iron!
Yay!
It's iron.
!
DON'T YOU THINK IT LOOKS LIKE...
...A HARMONICA?
OH.

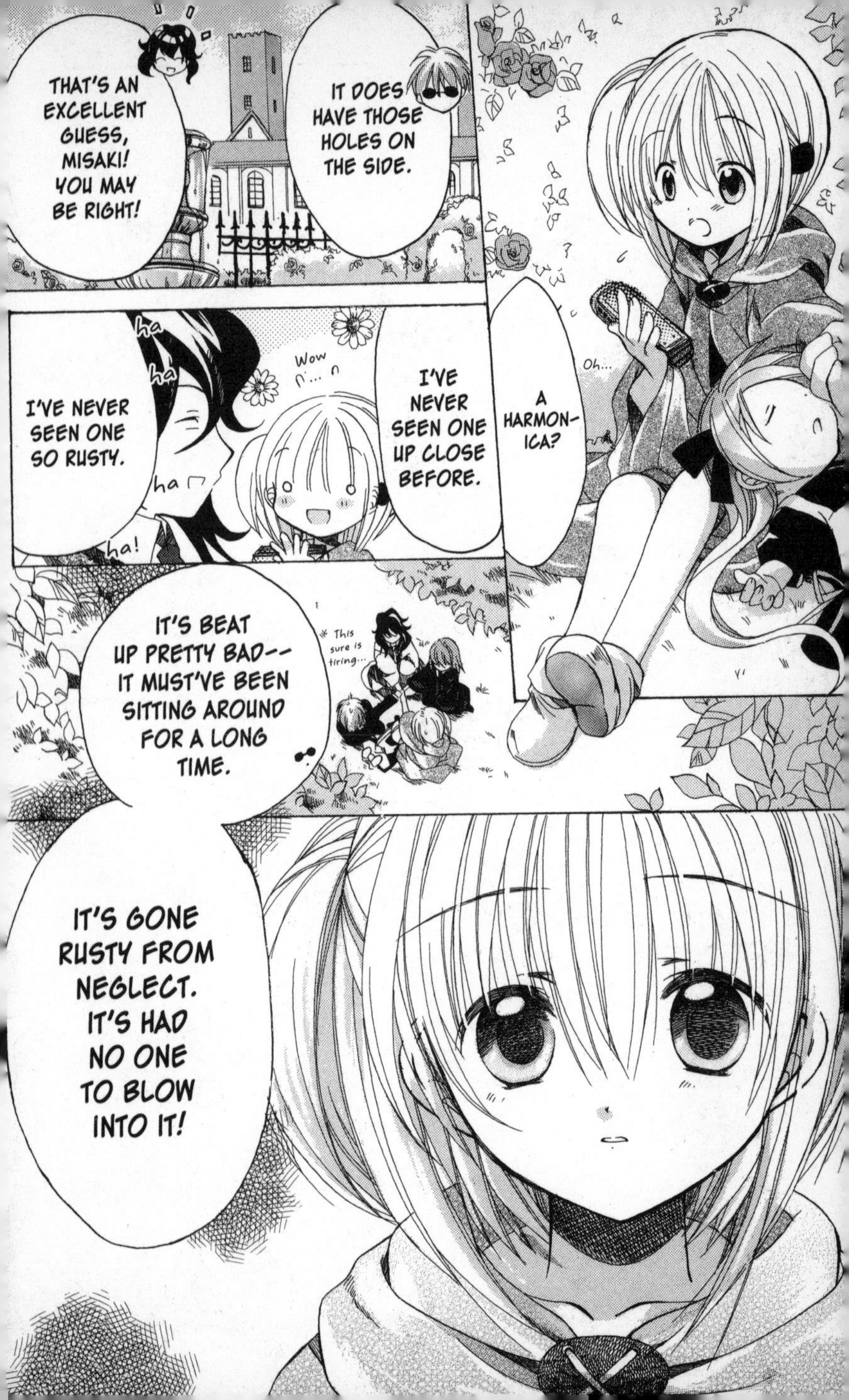

Oh...
A HARMONICA?
IT DOES HAVE THOSE HOLES ON THE SIDE.
THAT'S AN EXCELLENT GUESS, MISAKI! YOU MAY BE RIGHT!
I'VE NEVER SEEN ONE UP CLOSE BEFORE.
Wow
I'VE NEVER SEEN ONE SO RUSTY.
ha ha ha ha!
This sure is tiring...
IT'S BEAT UP PRETTY BAD-- IT MUST'VE BEEN SITTING AROUND FOR A LONG TIME.
IT'S GONE RUSTY FROM NEGLECT. IT'S HAD NO ONE TO BLOW INTO IT!

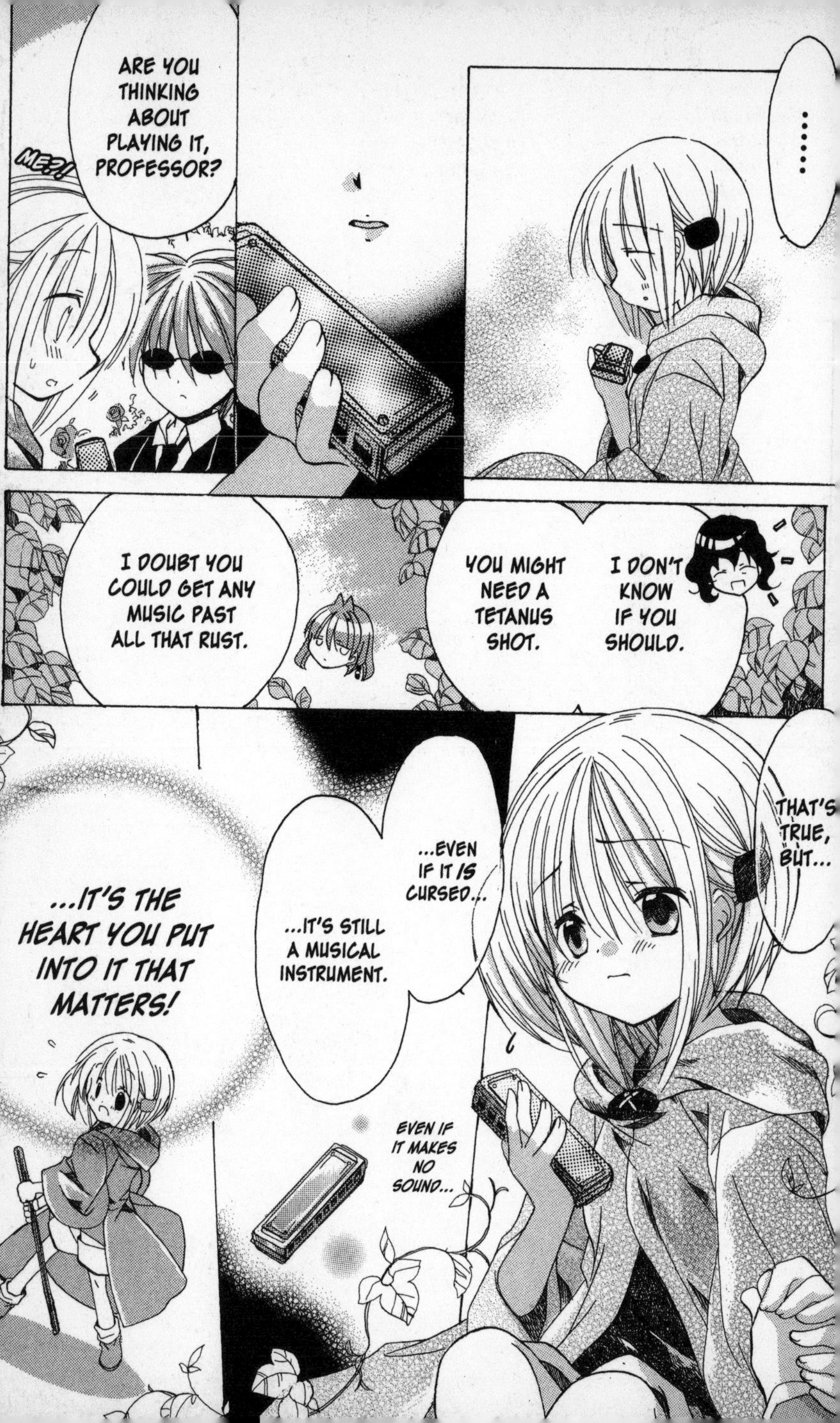
......
ARE YOU THINKING ABOUT PLAYING IT, PROFESSOR?
ME?!
I DON'T KNOW IF YOU SHOULD.
YOU MIGHT NEED A TETANUS SHOT.
I DOUBT YOU COULD GET ANY MUSIC PAST ALL THAT RUST.
THAT'S TRUE, BUT...
...EVEN IF IT *IS* CURSED...
...IT'S STILL A MUSICAL INSTRUMENT.
EVEN IF IT MAKES NO SOUND...
...IT'S THE HEART YOU PUT INTO IT THAT MATTERS!

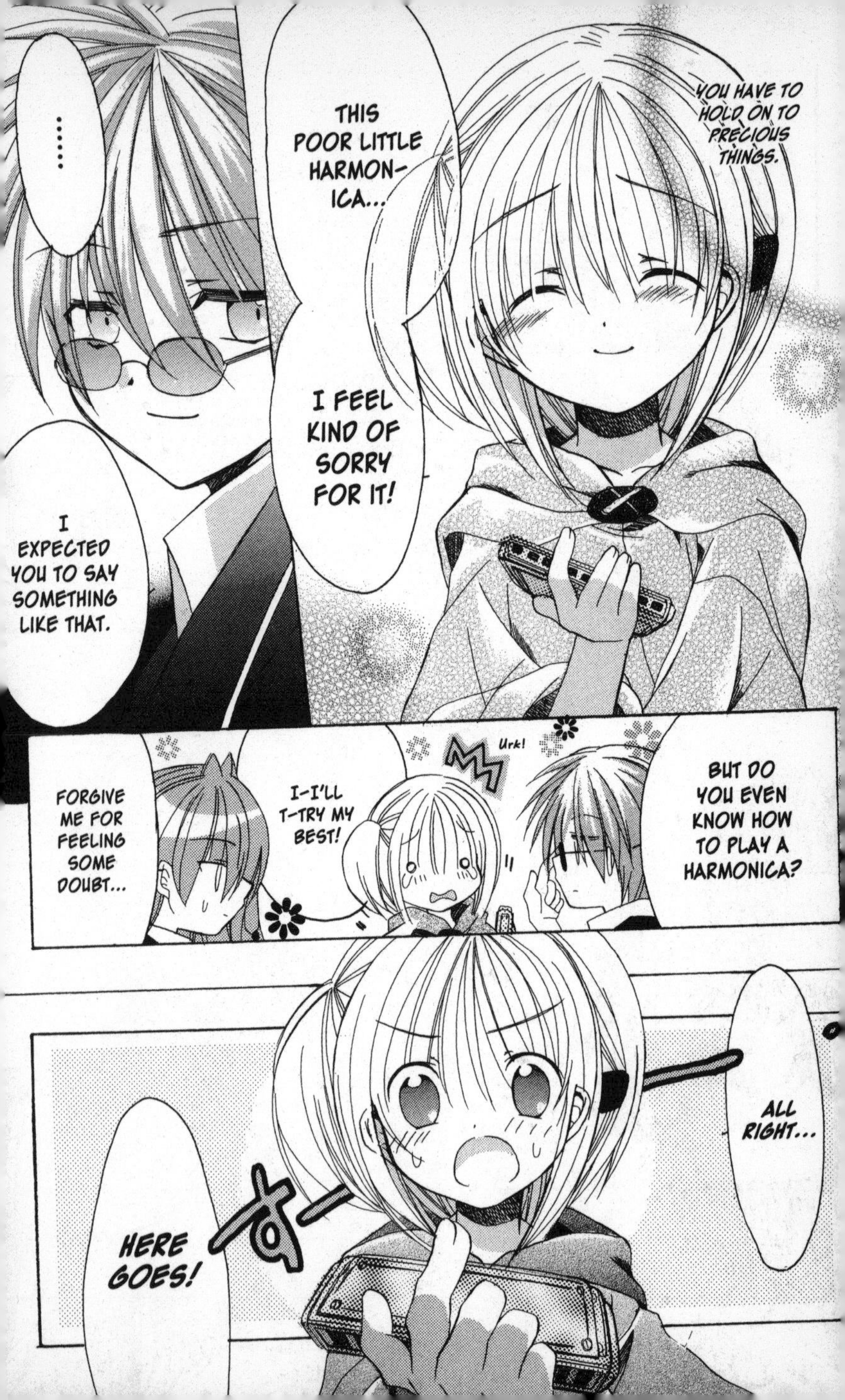
YOU HAVE TO HOLD ON TO PRECIOUS THINGS.
THIS POOR LITTLE HARMONICA...
I FEEL KIND OF SORRY FOR IT!
......
I EXPECTED YOU TO SAY SOMETHING LIKE THAT.
BUT DO YOU EVEN KNOW HOW TO PLAY A HARMONICA?
Urk!
I-I'LL T-TRY MY BEST!
FORGIVE ME FOR FEELING SOME DOUBT...
ALL RIGHT...
すー
HERE GOES!

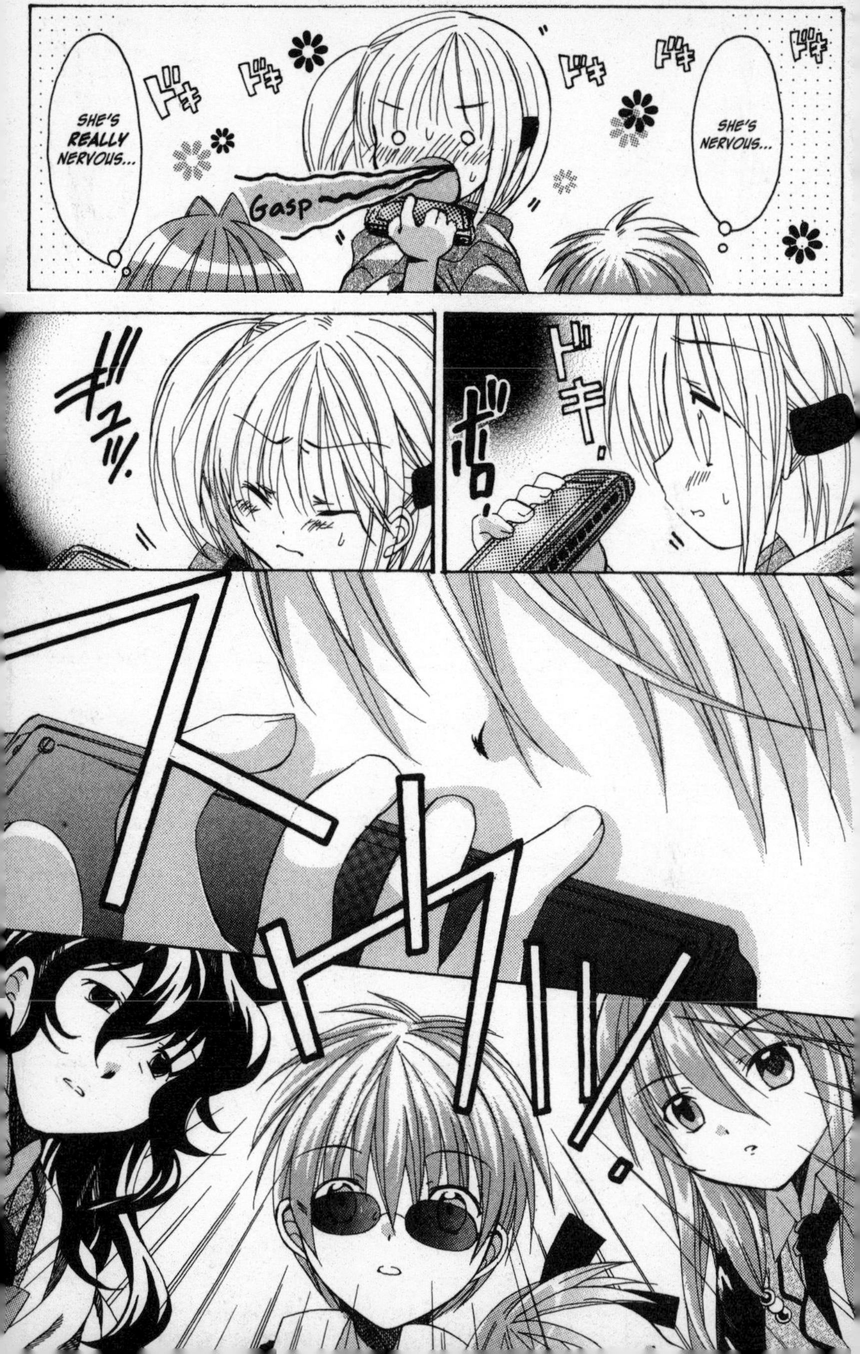

SHE'S NERVOUS...
Gasp
SHE'S REALLY NERVOUS...

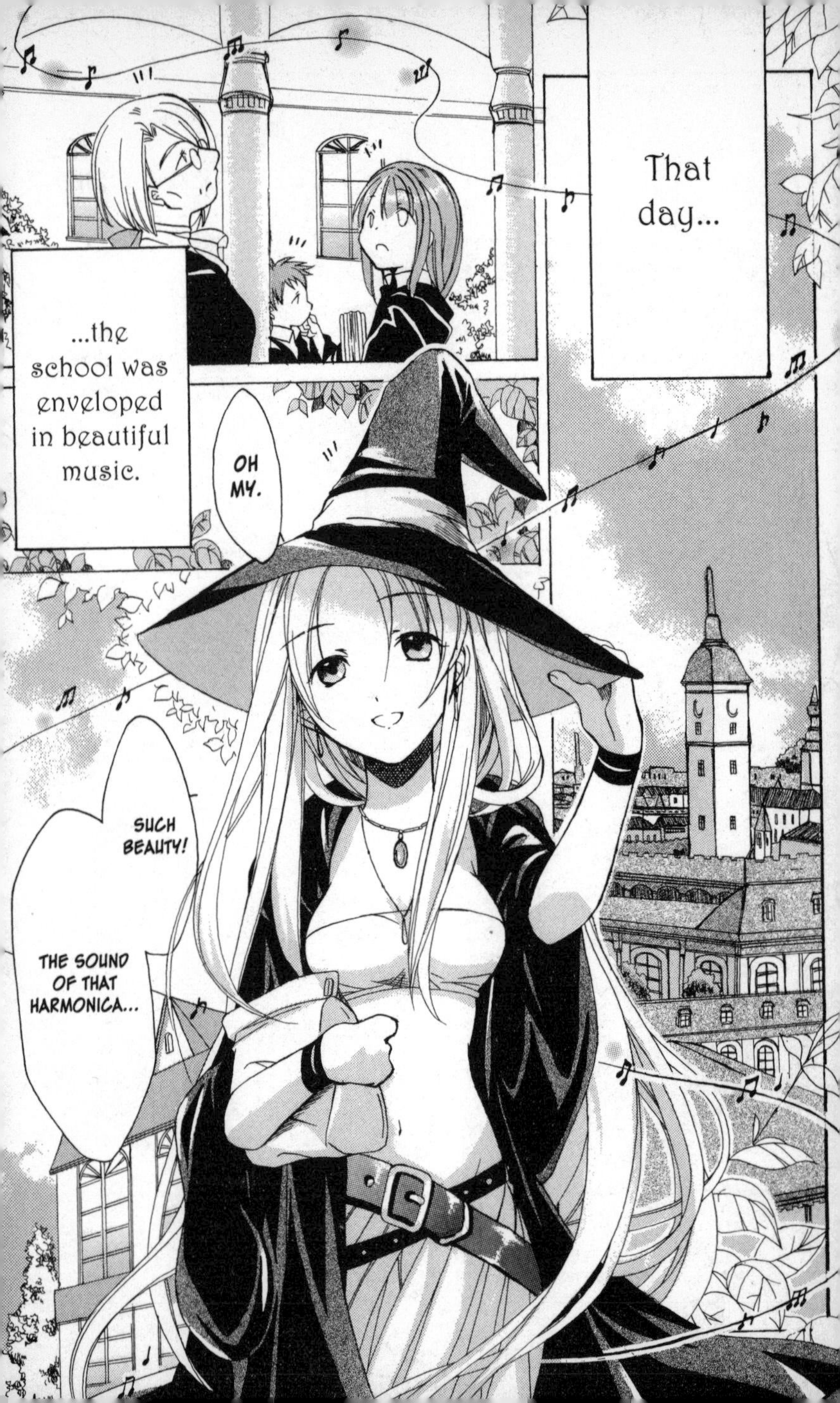
That day...
...the school was enveloped in beautiful music.
OH MY.
SUCH BEAUTY!
THE SOUND OF THAT HARMONICA...

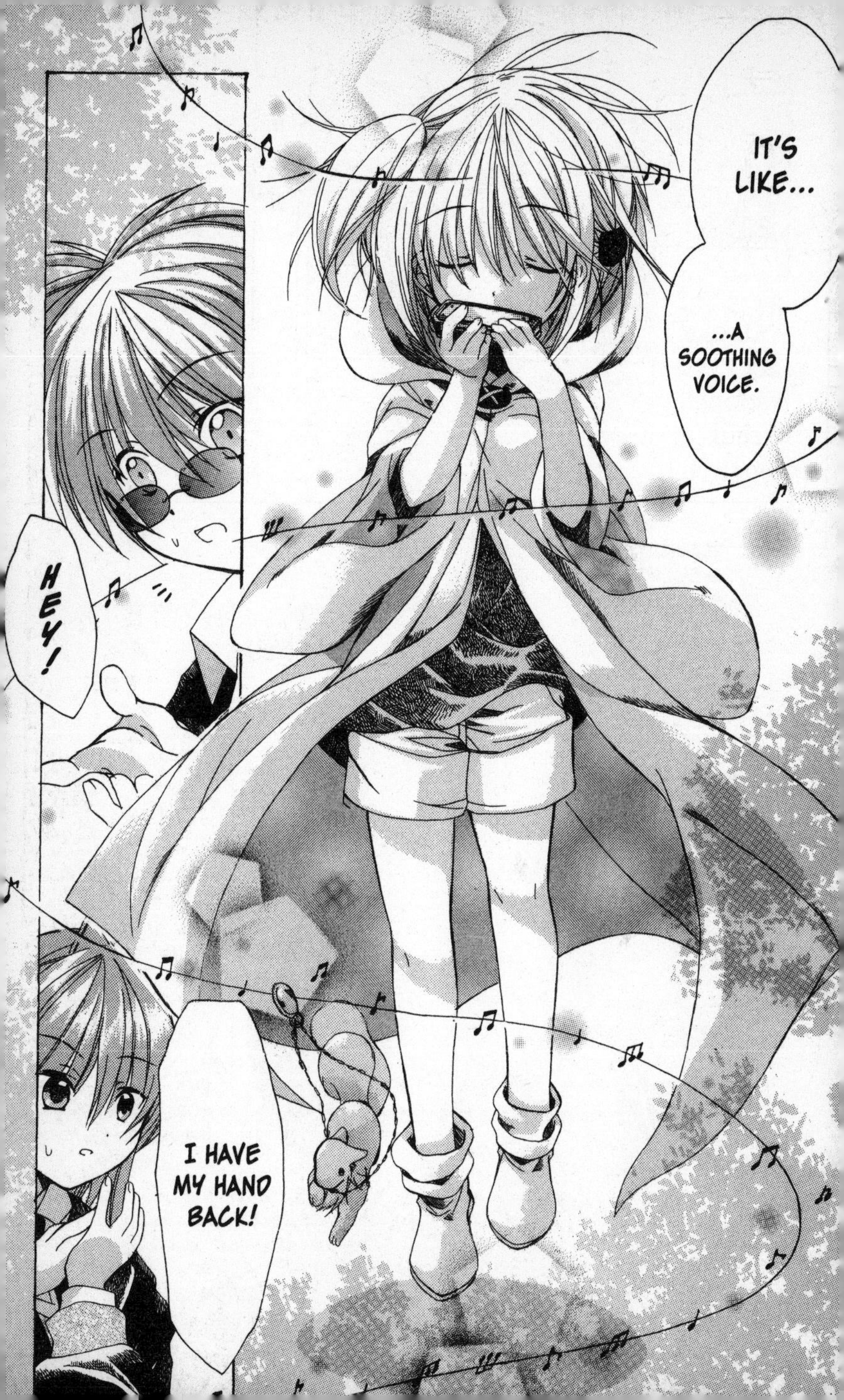
IT'S LIKE...
...A SOOTHING VOICE.
HEY!
I HAVE MY HAND BACK!

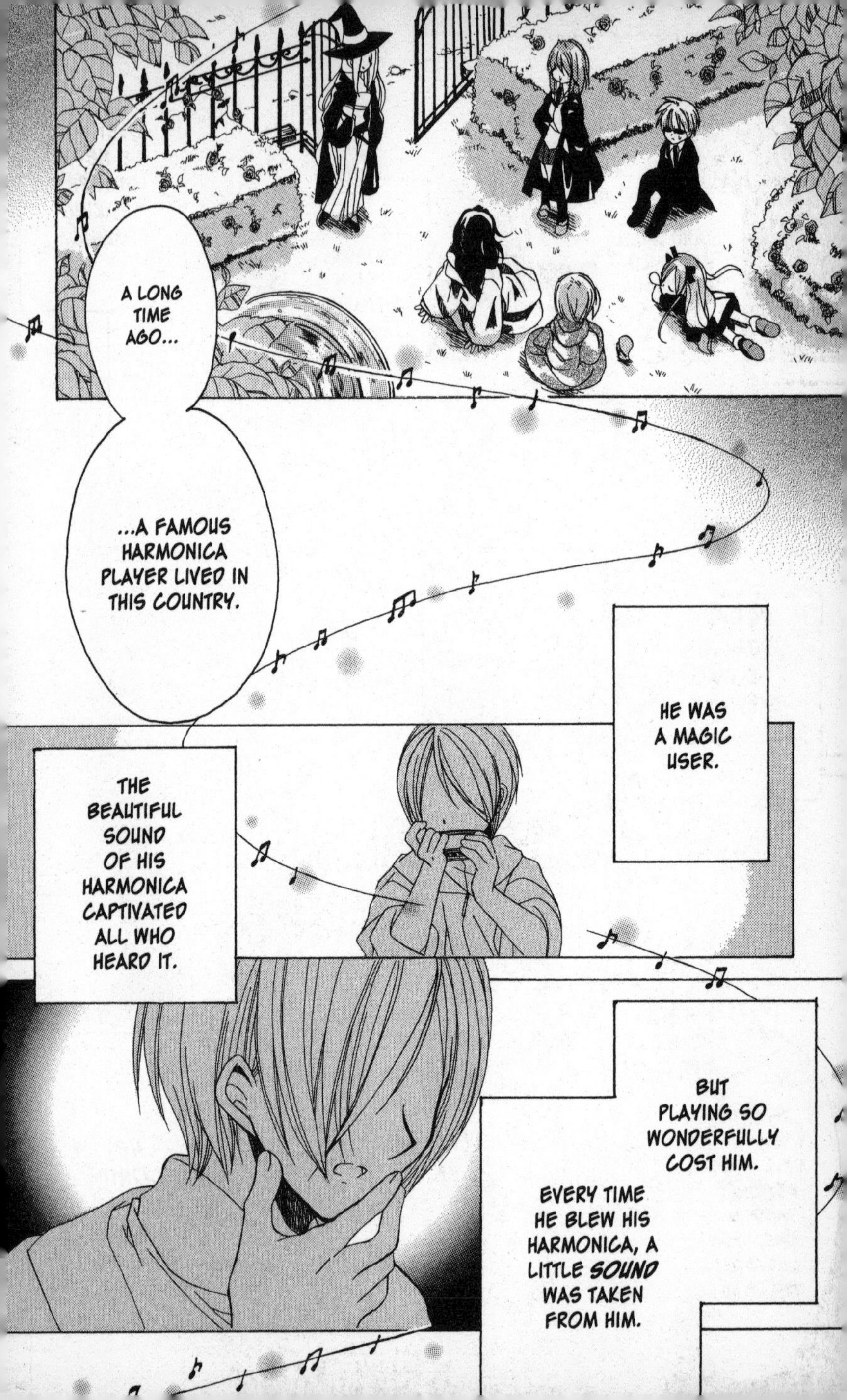
A LONG TIME AGO...
...A FAMOUS HARMONICA PLAYER LIVED IN THIS COUNTRY.
HE WAS A MAGIC USER.
THE BEAUTIFUL SOUND OF HIS HARMONICA CAPTIVATED ALL WHO HEARD IT.
BUT PLAYING SO WONDERFULLY COST HIM.
EVERY TIME HE BLEW HIS HARMONICA, A LITTLE *SOUND* WAS TAKEN FROM HIM.

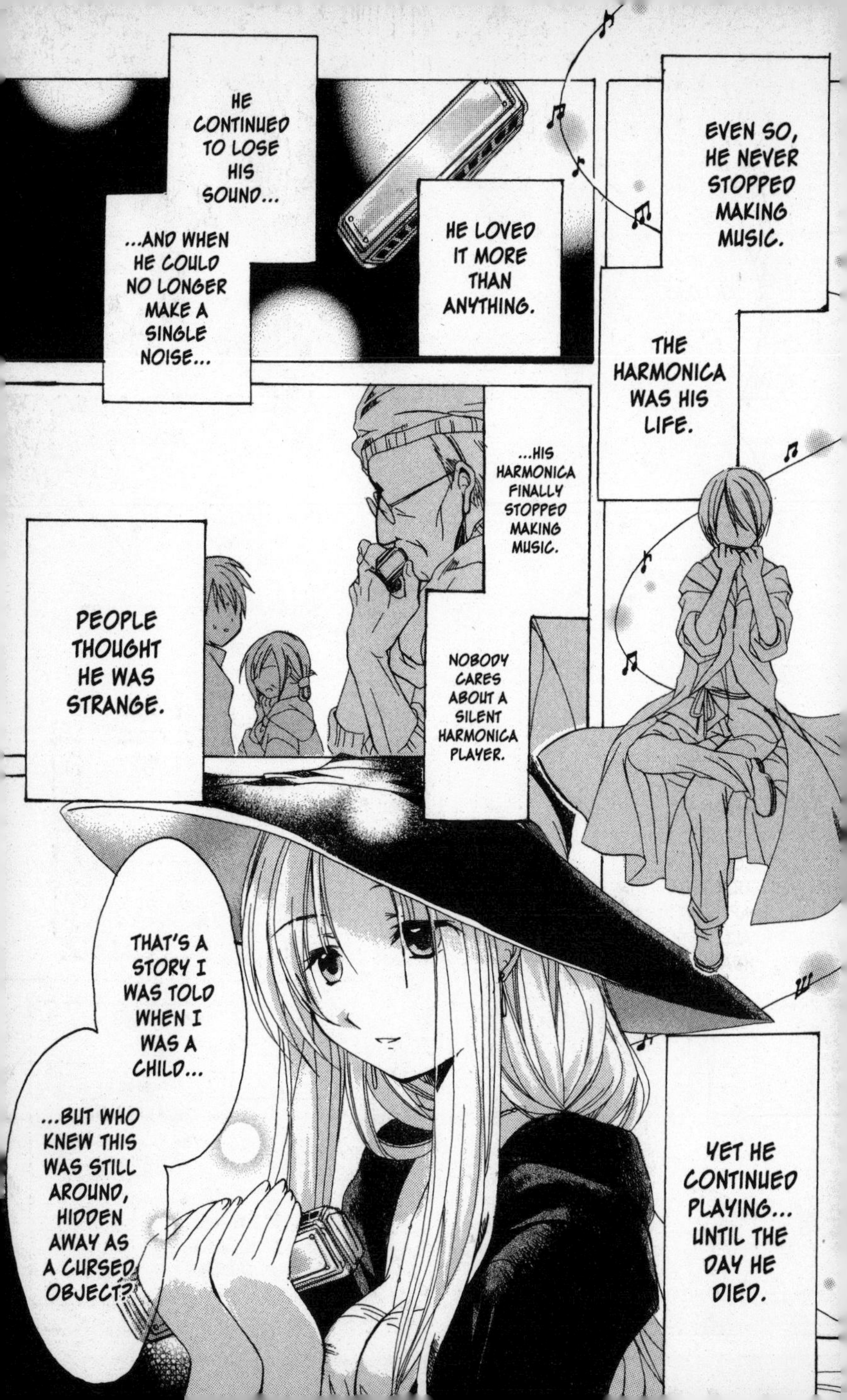
EVEN SO, HE NEVER STOPPED MAKING MUSIC.
HE LOVED IT MORE THAN ANYTHING.
HE CONTINUED TO LOSE HIS SOUND...
...AND WHEN HE COULD NO LONGER MAKE A SINGLE NOISE...
...HIS HARMONICA FINALLY STOPPED MAKING MUSIC.
THE HARMONICA WAS HIS LIFE.
NOBODY CARES ABOUT A SILENT HARMONICA PLAYER.
PEOPLE THOUGHT HE WAS STRANGE.
YET HE CONTINUED PLAYING... UNTIL THE DAY HE DIED.
THAT'S A STORY I WAS TOLD WHEN I WAS A CHILD...
...BUT WHO KNEW THIS WAS STILL AROUND, HIDDEN AWAY AS A CURSED OBJECT?

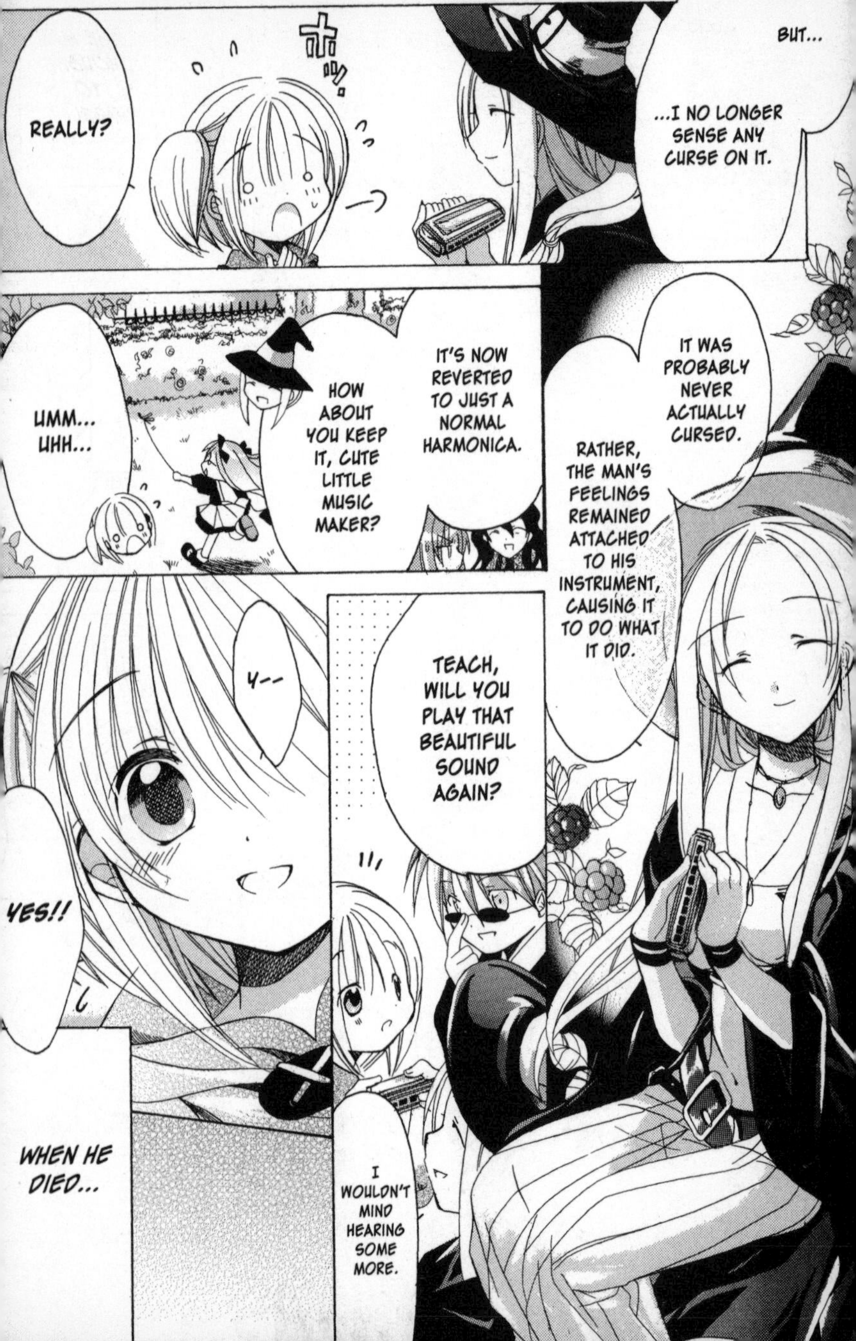
BUT...
...I NO LONGER SENSE ANY CURSE ON IT.
ホッ
REALLY?
IT WAS PROBABLY NEVER ACTUALLY CURSED.
RATHER, THE MAN'S FEELINGS REMAINED ATTACHED TO HIS INSTRUMENT, CAUSING IT TO DO WHAT IT DID.
IT'S NOW REVERTED TO JUST A NORMAL HARMONICA.
HOW ABOUT YOU KEEP IT, CUTE LITTLE MUSIC MAKER?
UMM... UHH...
TEACH, WILL YOU PLAY THAT BEAUTIFUL SOUND AGAIN?
I WOULDN'T MIND HEARING SOME MORE.
Y--
YES!!
WHEN HE DIED...

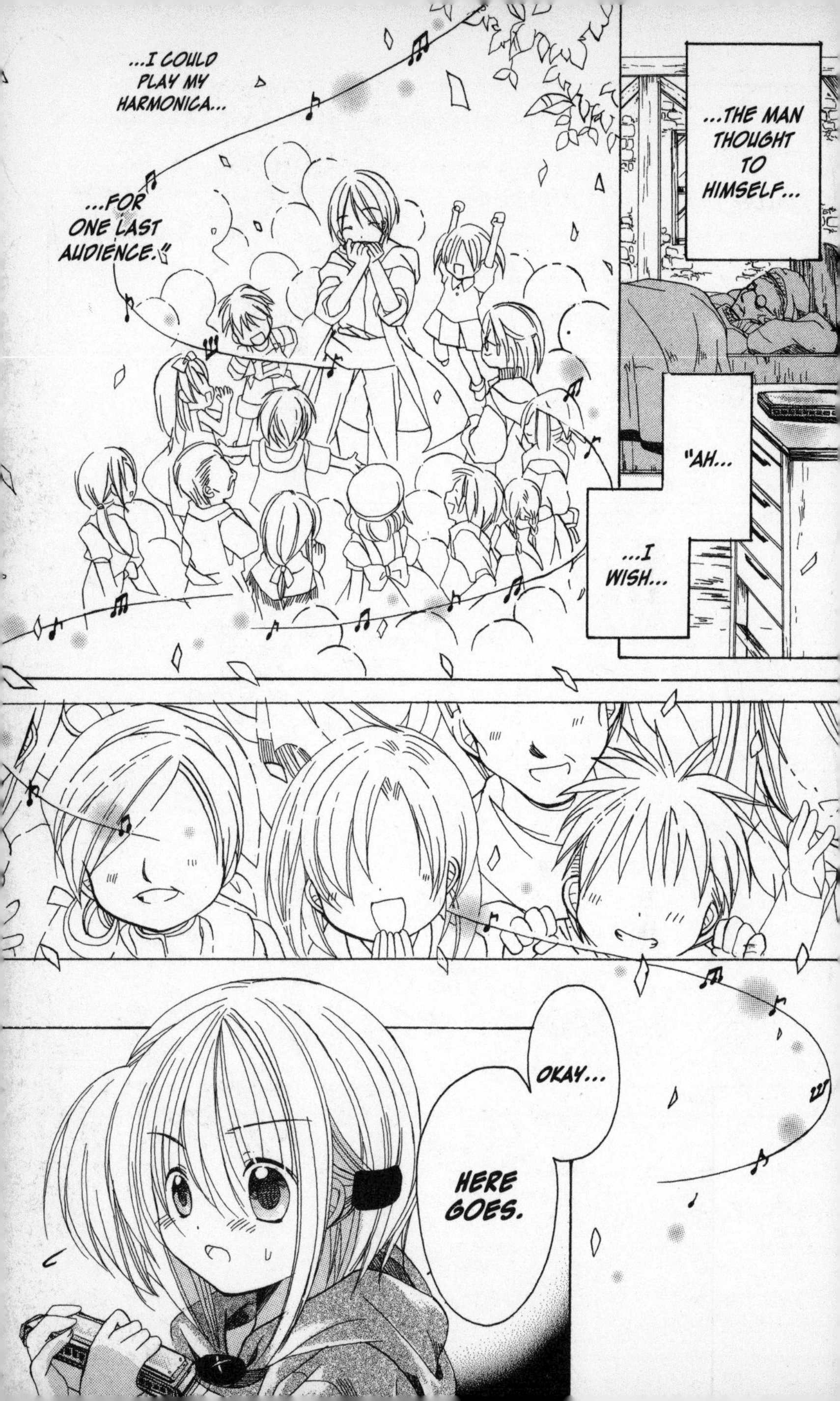
...THE MAN THOUGHT TO HIMSELF...
"AH...
...I WISH...
...I COULD PLAY MY HARMONICA...
...FOR ONE LAST AUDIENCE."
OKAY...
HERE GOES.

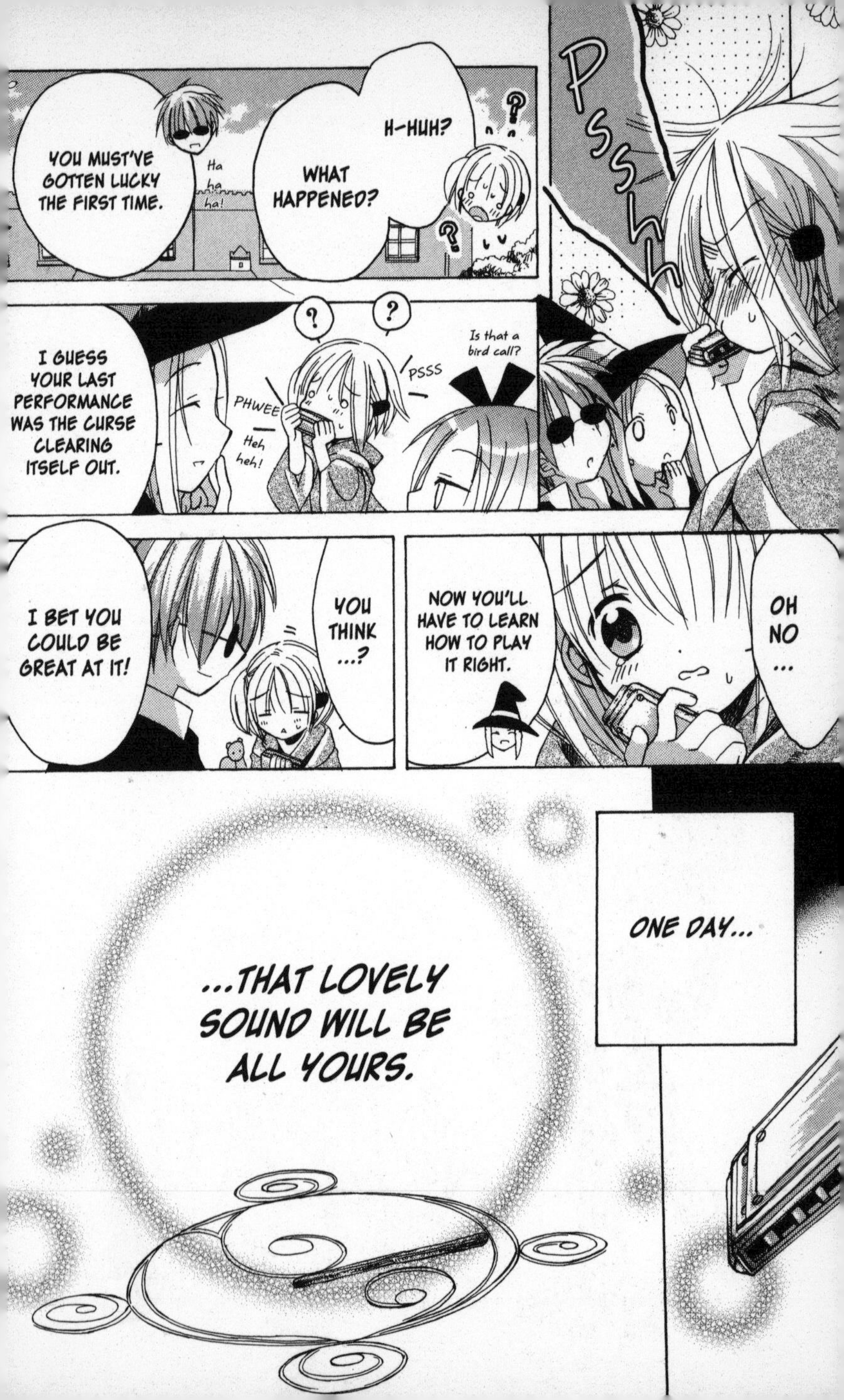
PSSHH
H-HUH?
WHAT HAPPENED?
YOU MUST'VE GOTTEN LUCKY THE FIRST TIME.
Ha ha ha!
Is that a bird call?
PSSS
PHWEE
Heh heh!
I GUESS YOUR LAST PERFORMANCE WAS THE CURSE CLEARING ITSELF OUT.
OH NO...
NOW YOU'LL HAVE TO LEARN HOW TO PLAY IT RIGHT.
YOU THINK...?
I BET YOU COULD BE GREAT AT IT!
ONE DAY...
...THAT LOVELY SOUND WILL BE ALL YOURS.

HIBIKI'S MAGIC™

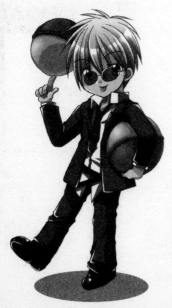

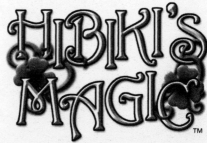

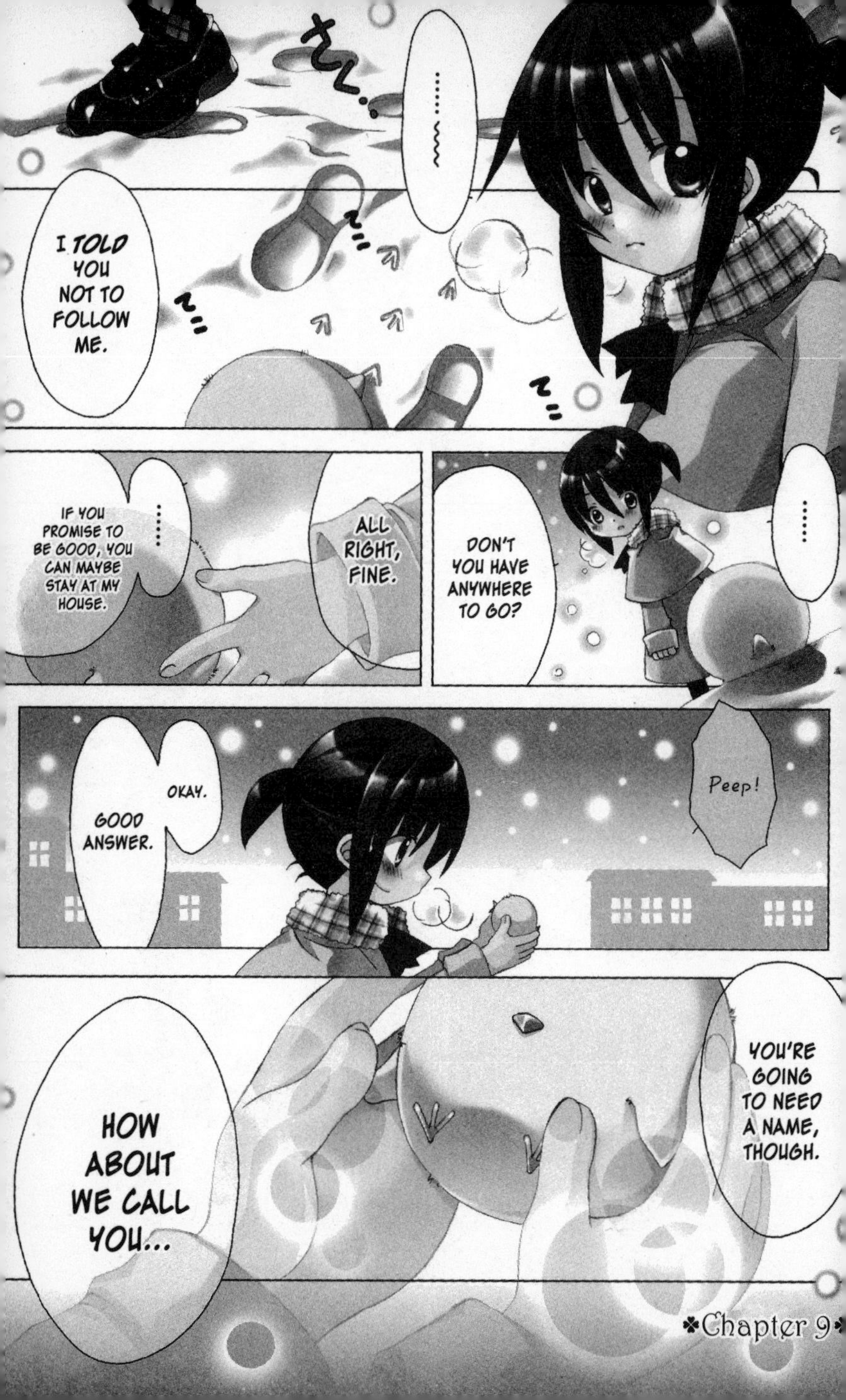
......~
I TOLD YOU NOT TO FOLLOW ME.
......
DON'T YOU HAVE ANYWHERE TO GO?
ALL RIGHT, FINE.
......
IF YOU PROMISE TO BE GOOD, YOU CAN MAYBE STAY AT MY HOUSE.
Peep!
OKAY.
GOOD ANSWER.
YOU'RE GOING TO NEED A NAME, THOUGH.
HOW ABOUT WE CALL YOU...
Chapter 9

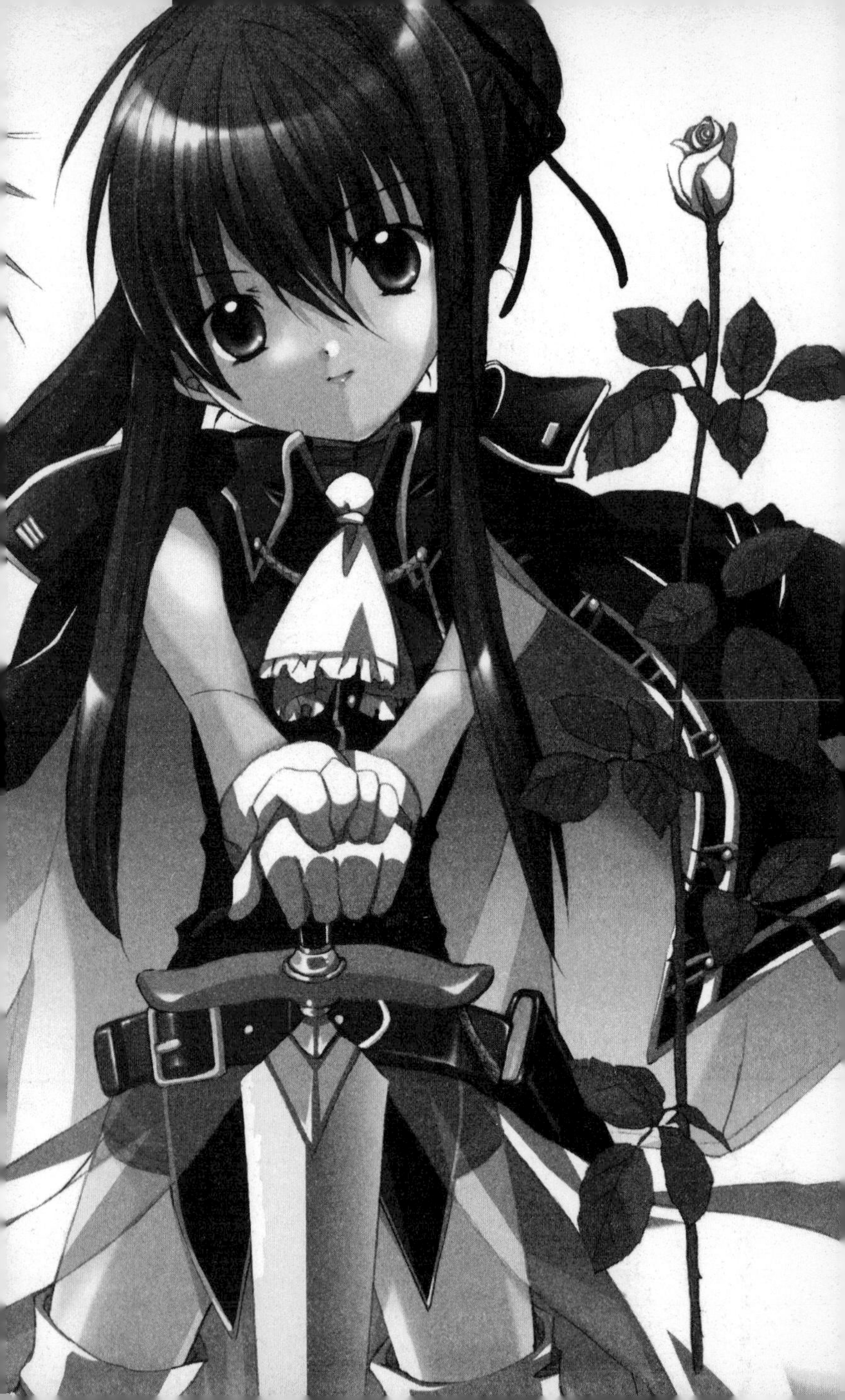

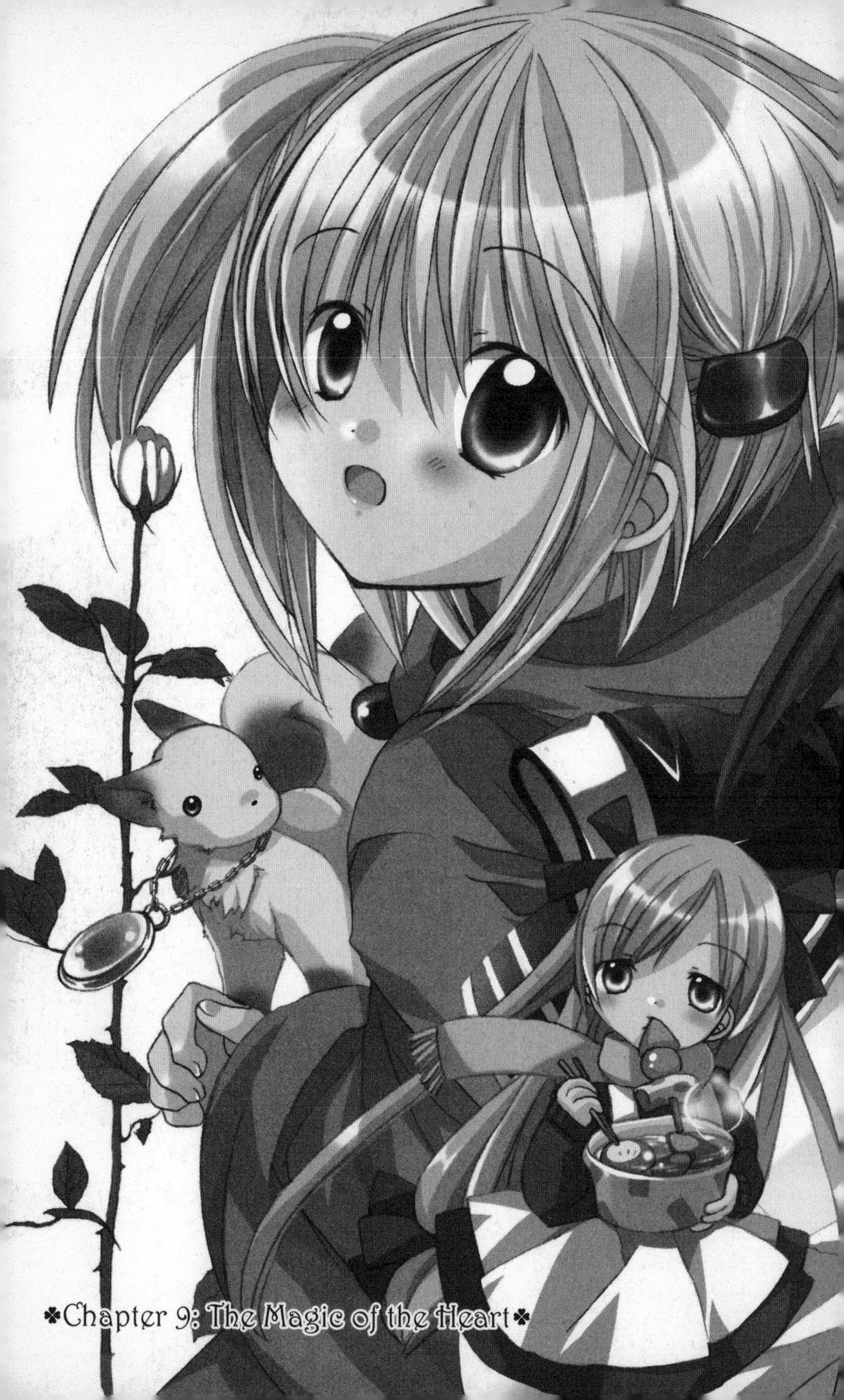

Chapter 9: The Magic of the Heart

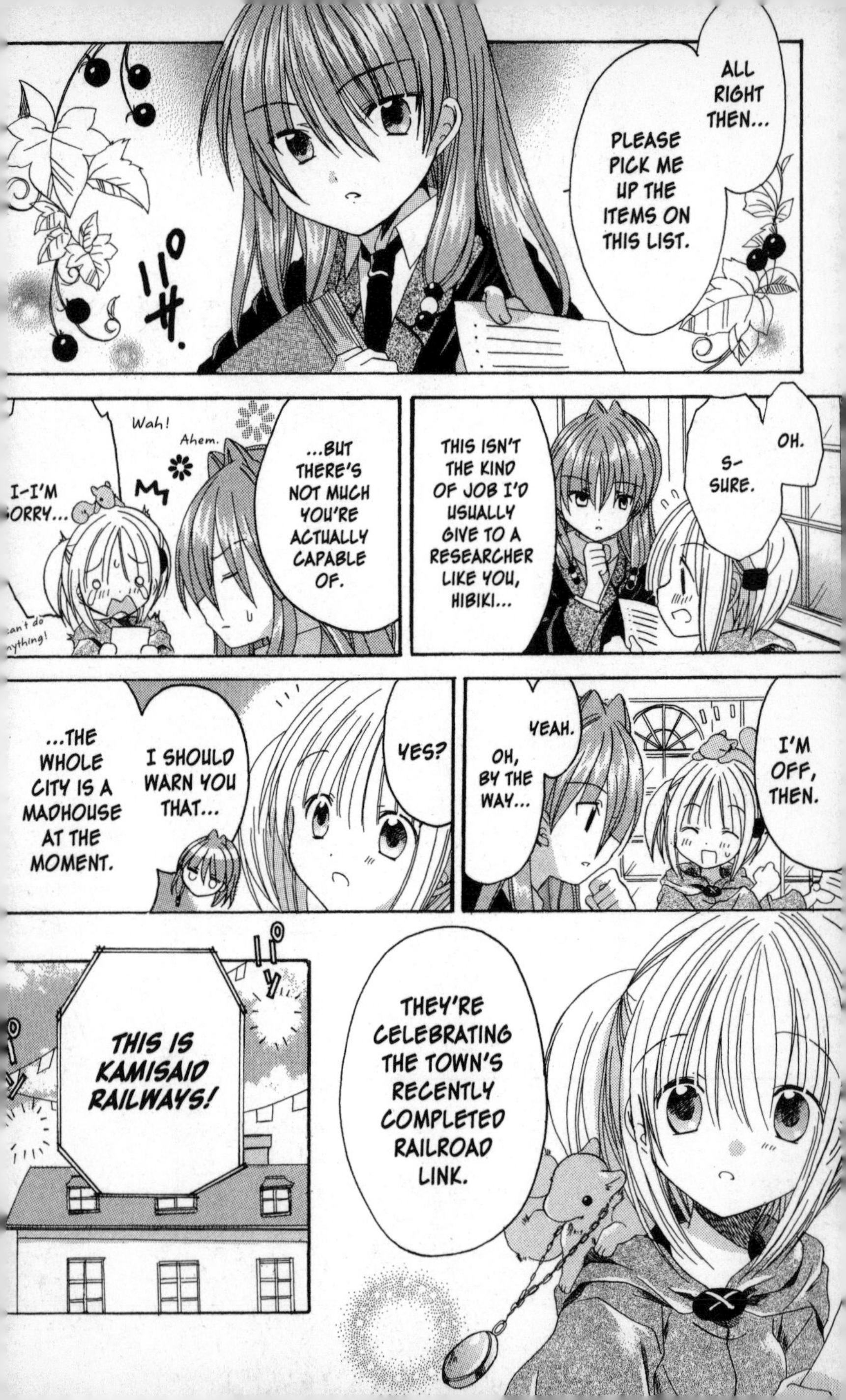
ALL RIGHT THEN...
PLEASE PICK ME UP THE ITEMS ON THIS LIST.
OH.
S-SURE.
THIS ISN'T THE KIND OF JOB I'D USUALLY GIVE TO A RESEARCHER LIKE YOU, HIBIKI...
...BUT THERE'S NOT MUCH YOU'RE ACTUALLY CAPABLE OF.
Ahem.
Wah!
I-I'M ORRY...
can't do nything!
I'M OFF, THEN.
YEAH.
OH, BY THE WAY...
YES?
I SHOULD WARN YOU THAT...
...THE WHOLE CITY IS A MADHOUSE AT THE MOMENT.
THEY'RE CELEBRATING THE TOWN'S RECENTLY COMPLETED RAILROAD LINK.
THIS IS KAMISAID RAILWAYS!

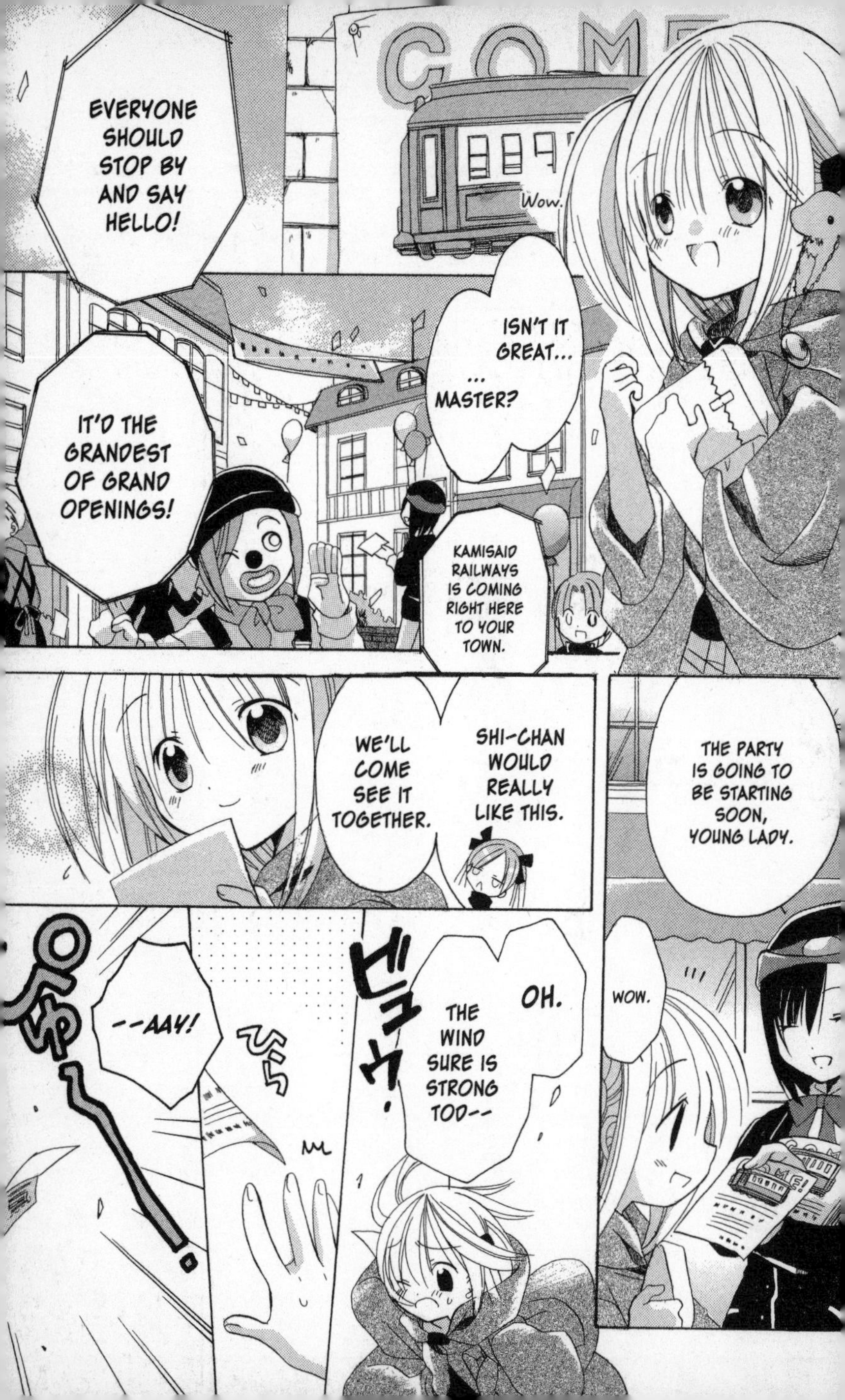
Wow.
ISN'T IT GREAT... ...MASTER?
KAMISAID RAILWAYS IS COMING RIGHT HERE TO YOUR TOWN.
EVERYONE SHOULD STOP BY AND SAY HELLO!
IT'D THE GRANDEST OF GRAND OPENINGS!
THE PARTY IS GOING TO BE STARTING SOON, YOUNG LADY.
SHI-CHAN WOULD REALLY LIKE THIS.
WE'LL COME SEE IT TOGETHER.
WOW.
OH.
THE WIND SURE IS STRONG TOO--
--AAY!

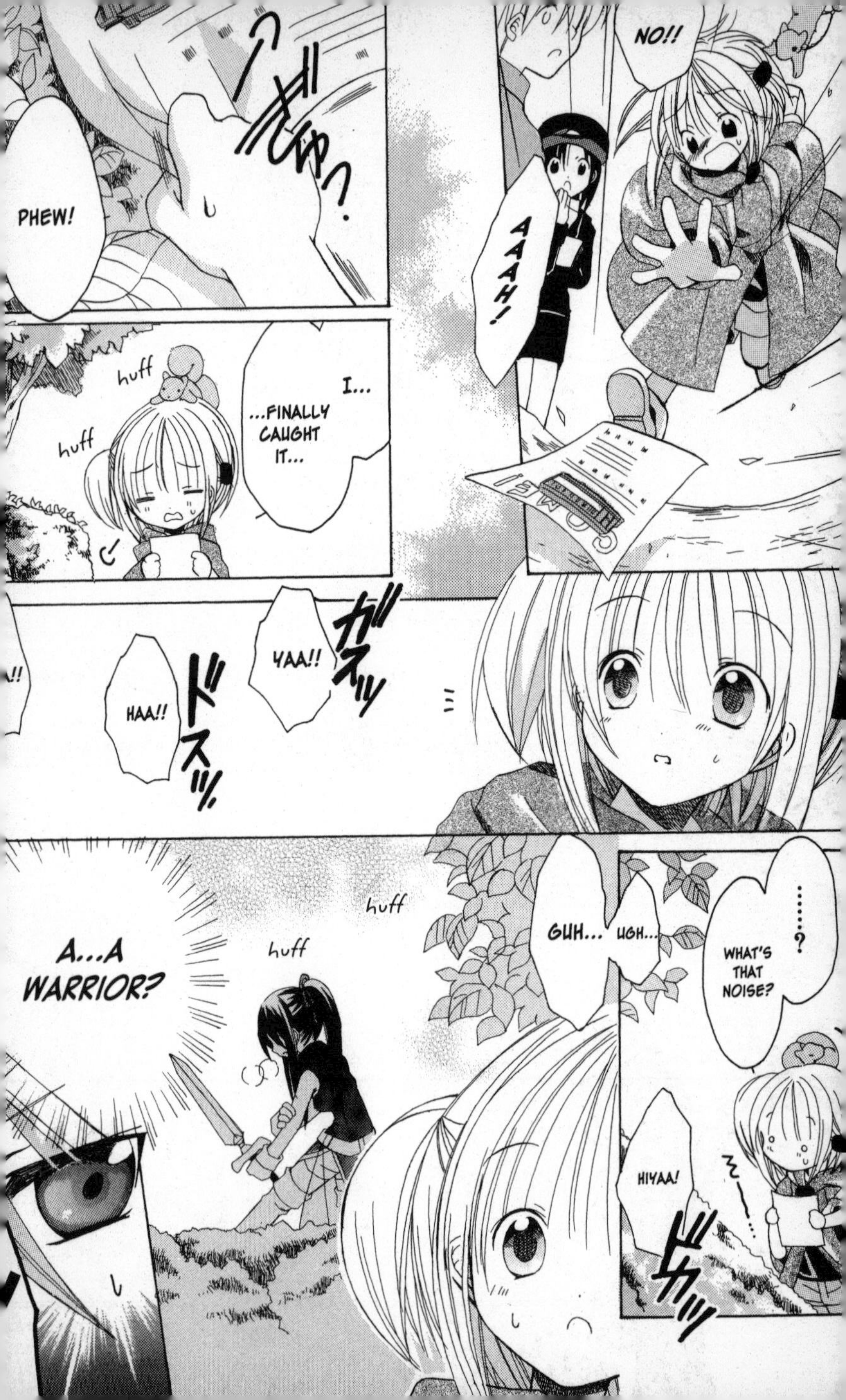
NO!!
AAAAH!
PHEW!
huff
huff
I...
...FINALLY CAUGHT IT...
YAA!!
HAA!!
!!
......?
WHAT'S THAT NOISE?
HIYAA!
GUH...
UGH...
huff
huff
A...A WARRIOR?

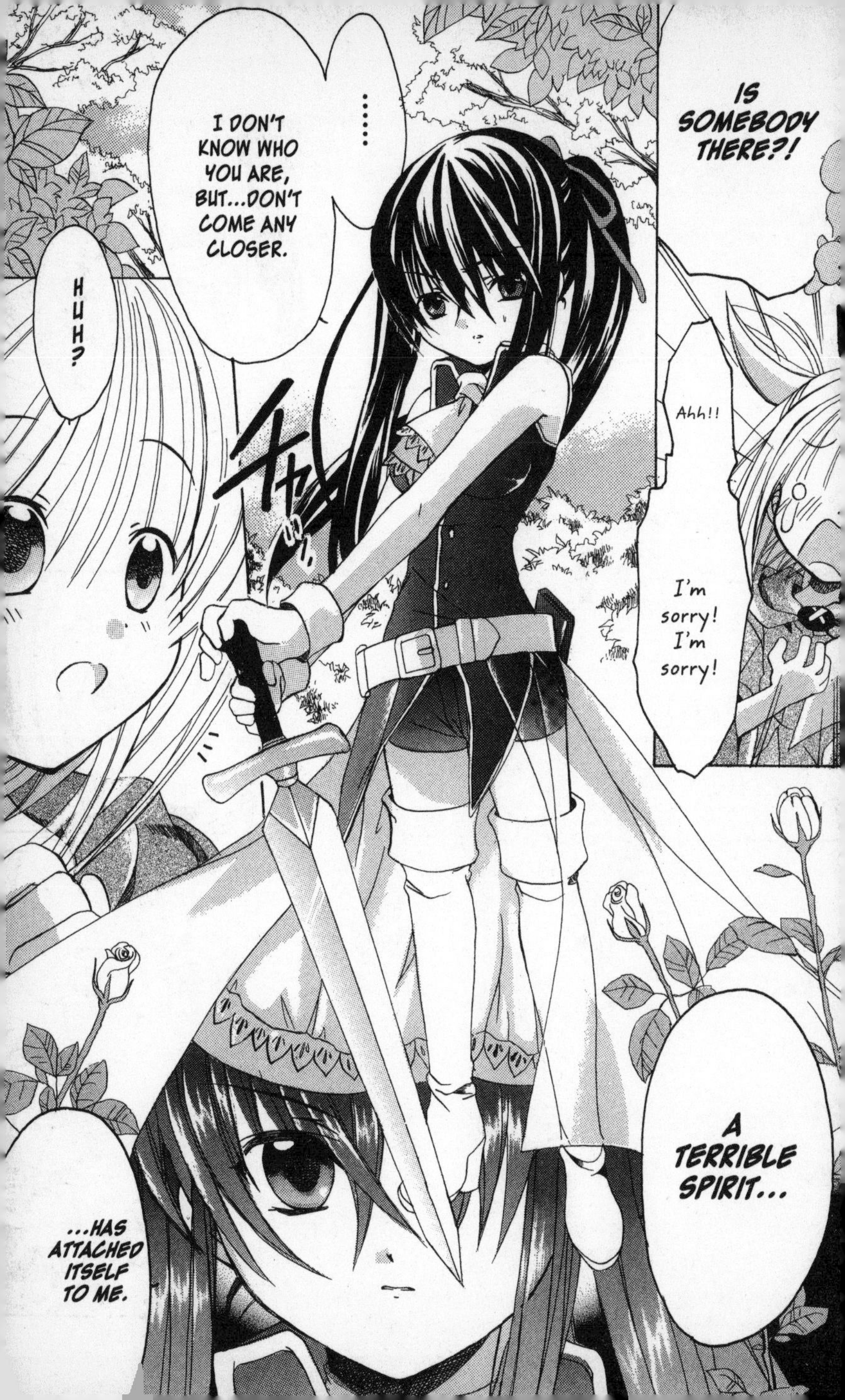
IS SOMEBODY THERE?!
......
I DON'T KNOW WHO YOU ARE, BUT...DON'T COME ANY CLOSER.
HUH?
Ahh!!
I'm sorry! I'm sorry!
A TERRIBLE SPIRIT...
...HAS ATTACHED ITSELF TO ME.

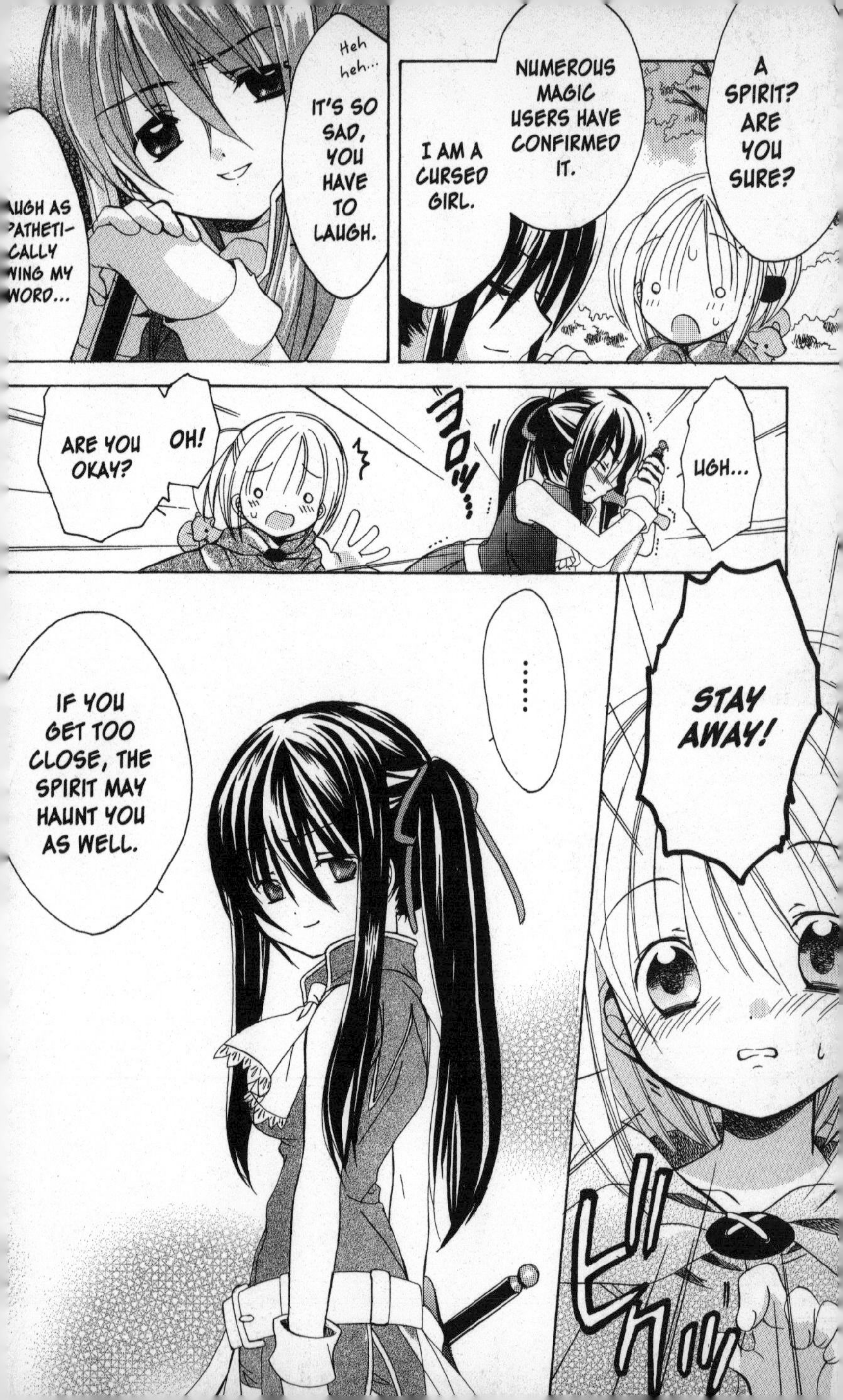
A SPIRIT? ARE YOU SURE?
NUMEROUS MAGIC USERS HAVE CONFIRMED IT.
I AM A CURSED GIRL.
Heh heh...
IT'S SO SAD, YOU HAVE TO LAUGH.
AUGH AS PATHETI-CALLY WING MY WORD...
UGH...
ヨロッ...
OH!
ARE YOU OKAY?
STAY AWAY!
......
IF YOU GET TOO CLOSE, THE SPIRIT MAY HAUNT YOU AS WELL.

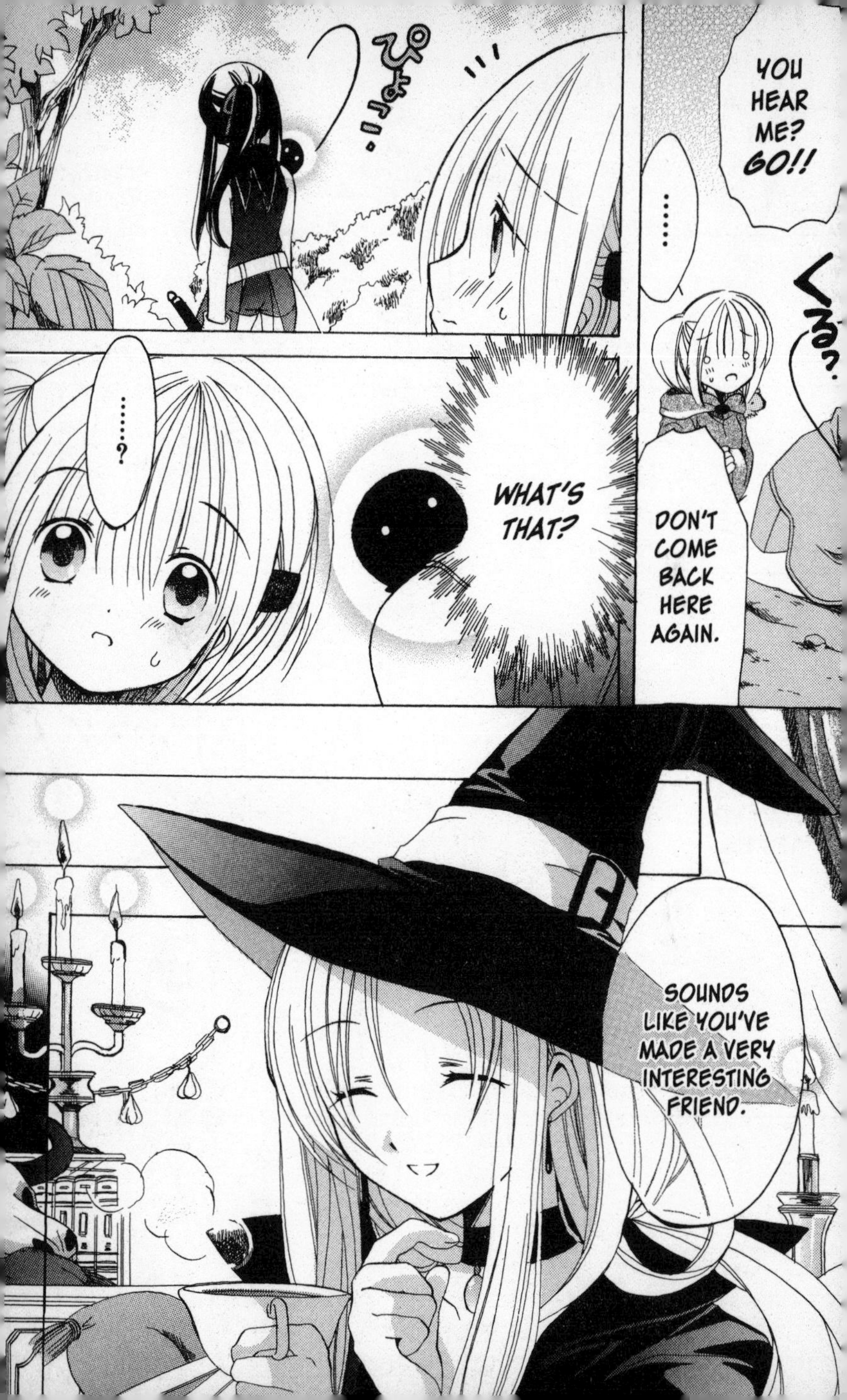
YOU HEAR ME? GO!!
……
くるっ?
DON'T COME BACK HERE AGAIN.
ぴょこ!?
……?
WHAT'S THAT?
SOUNDS LIKE YOU'VE MADE A VERY INTERESTING FRIEND.

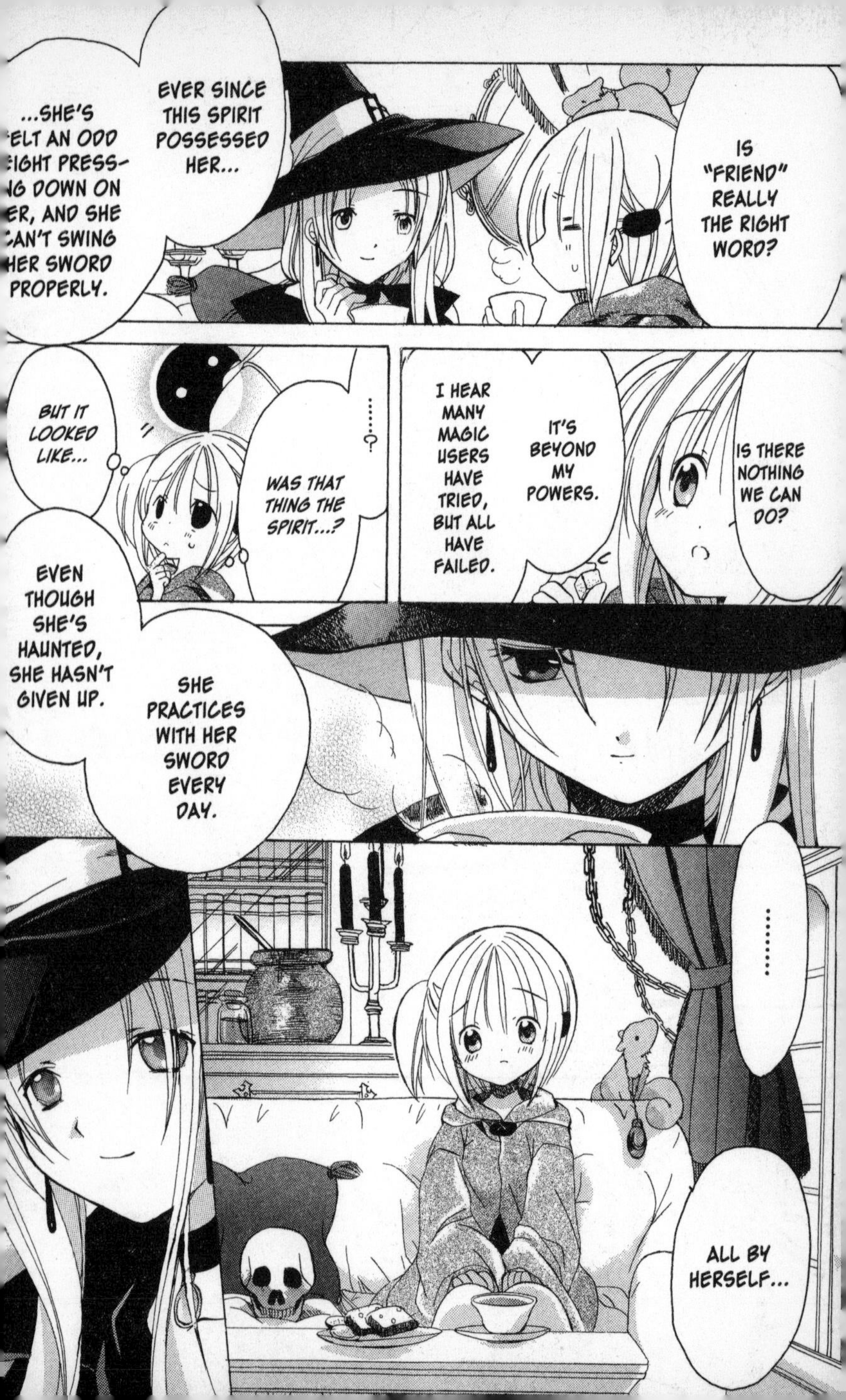

IS "FRIEND" REALLY THE RIGHT WORD?
EVER SINCE THIS SPIRIT POSSESSED HER...
...SHE'S FELT AN ODD WEIGHT PRESSING DOWN ON HER, AND SHE CAN'T SWING HER SWORD PROPERLY.
IS THERE NOTHING WE CAN DO?
IT'S BEYOND MY POWERS.
I HEAR MANY MAGIC USERS HAVE TRIED, BUT ALL HAVE FAILED.
......?
WAS THAT THING THE SPIRIT...?
BUT IT LOOKED LIKE...
EVEN THOUGH SHE'S HAUNTED, SHE HASN'T GIVEN UP.
SHE PRACTICES WITH HER SWORD EVERY DAY.
......
ALL BY HERSELF...

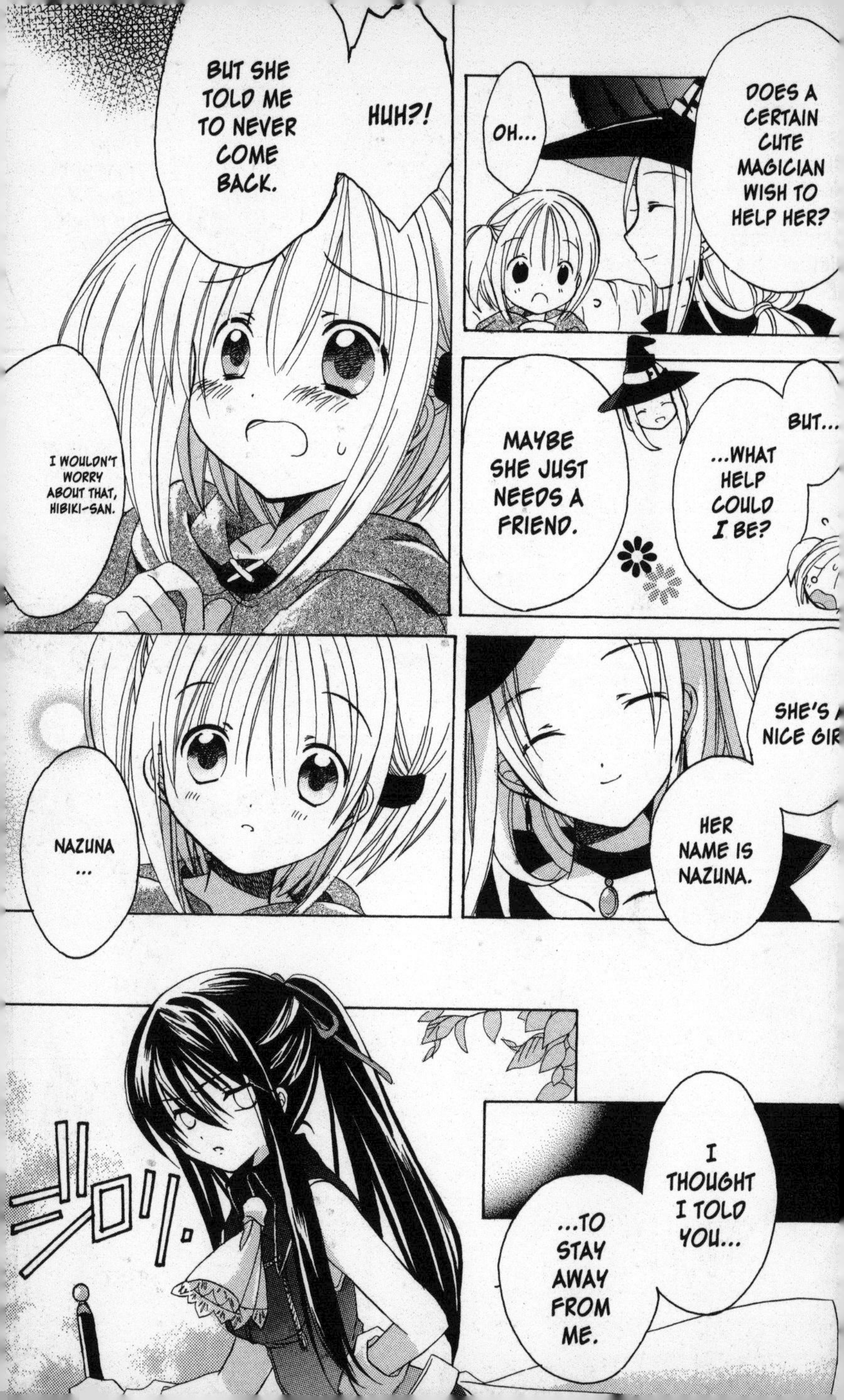
DOES A CERTAIN CUTE MAGICIAN WISH TO HELP HER?
OH...
BUT...
...WHAT HELP COULD I BE?
MAYBE SHE JUST NEEDS A FRIEND.
HUH?!
BUT SHE TOLD ME TO NEVER COME BACK.
I WOULDN'T WORRY ABOUT THAT, HIBIKI-SAN.
SHE'S A NICE GIR
HER NAME IS NAZUNA.
NAZUNA ...
I THOUGHT I TOLD YOU...
...TO STAY AWAY FROM ME.

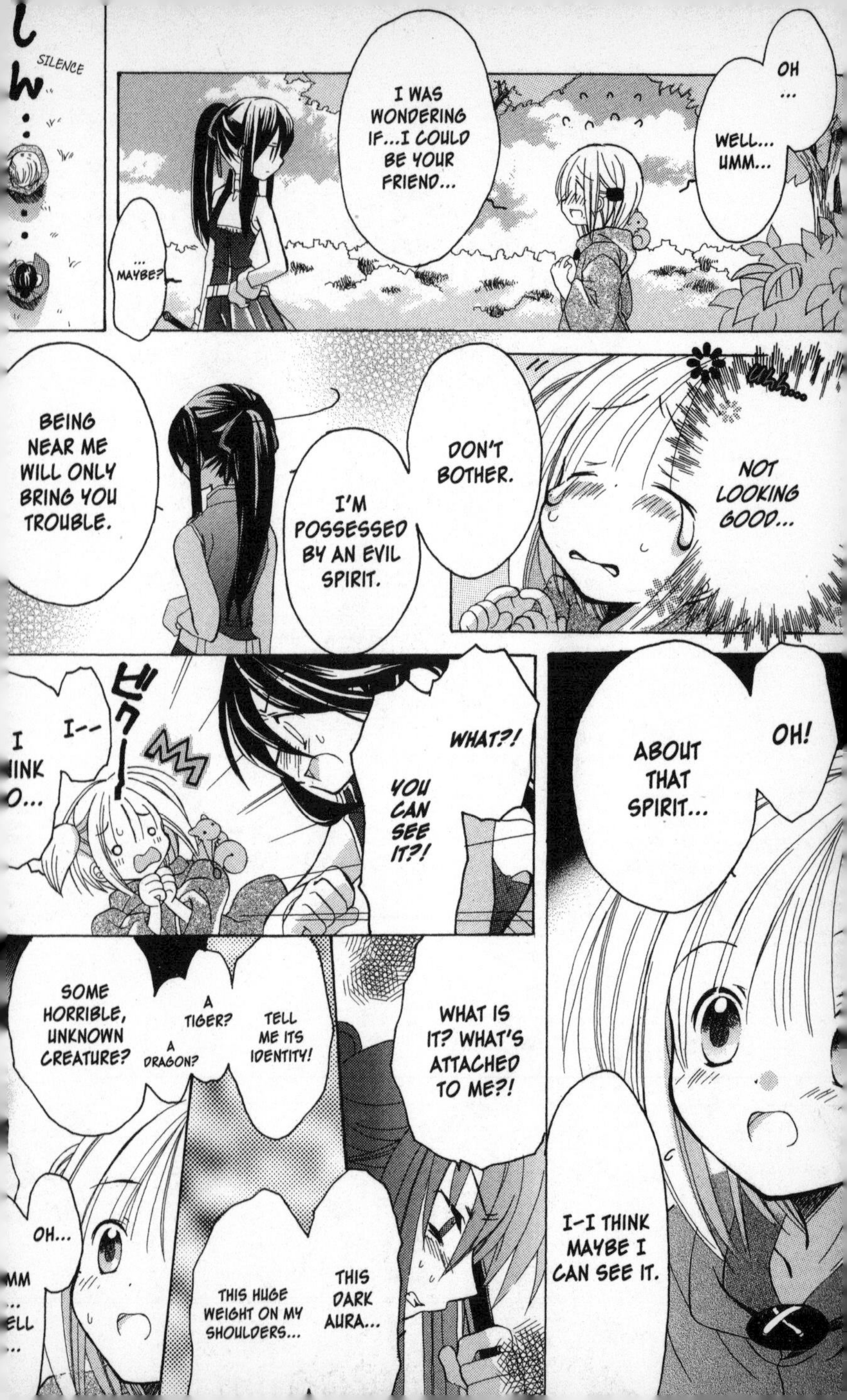
OH ... WELL... UMM...
I WAS WONDERING IF...I COULD BE YOUR FRIEND...
... MAYBE?
SILENCE
Uhh...
NOT LOOKING GOOD...
DON'T BOTHER.
I'M POSSESSED BY AN EVIL SPIRIT.
BEING NEAR ME WILL ONLY BRING YOU TROUBLE.
OH!
ABOUT THAT SPIRIT...
I-I THINK MAYBE I CAN SEE IT.
WHAT?!
YOU CAN SEE IT?!
ビクー
I--
I INK O...
WHAT IS IT? WHAT'S ATTACHED TO ME?!
TELL ME ITS IDENTITY!
A TIGER?
A DRAGON?
SOME HORRIBLE, UNKNOWN CREATURE?
THIS DARK AURA...
THIS HUGE WEIGHT ON MY SHOULDERS...
OH...
MM ... ELL ...

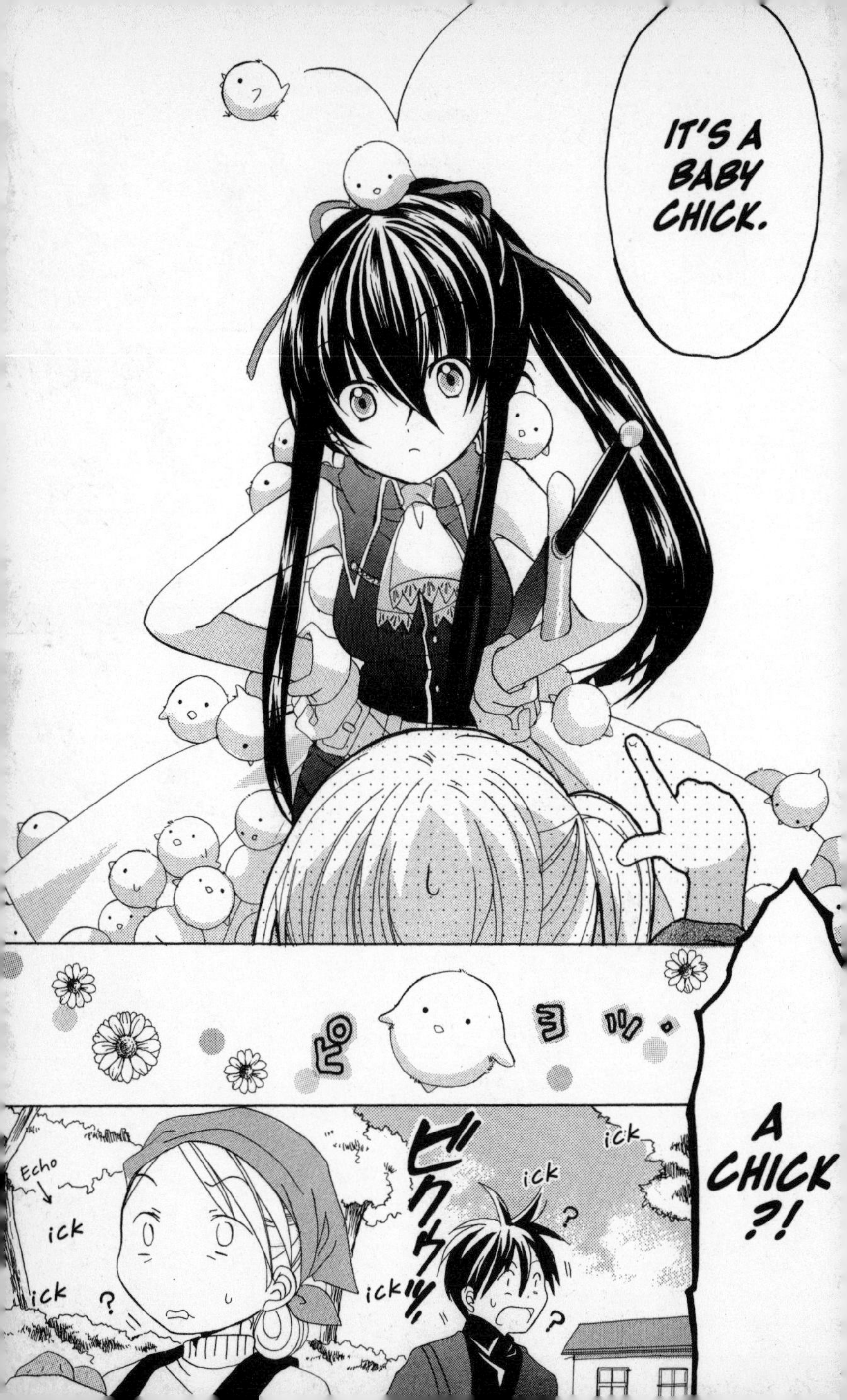
IT'S A BABY CHICK.
ピヨッ。
A CHICK ?!
ビクゥッ
ick
ick
ick
ick
Echo
ick
ick
?
?
?

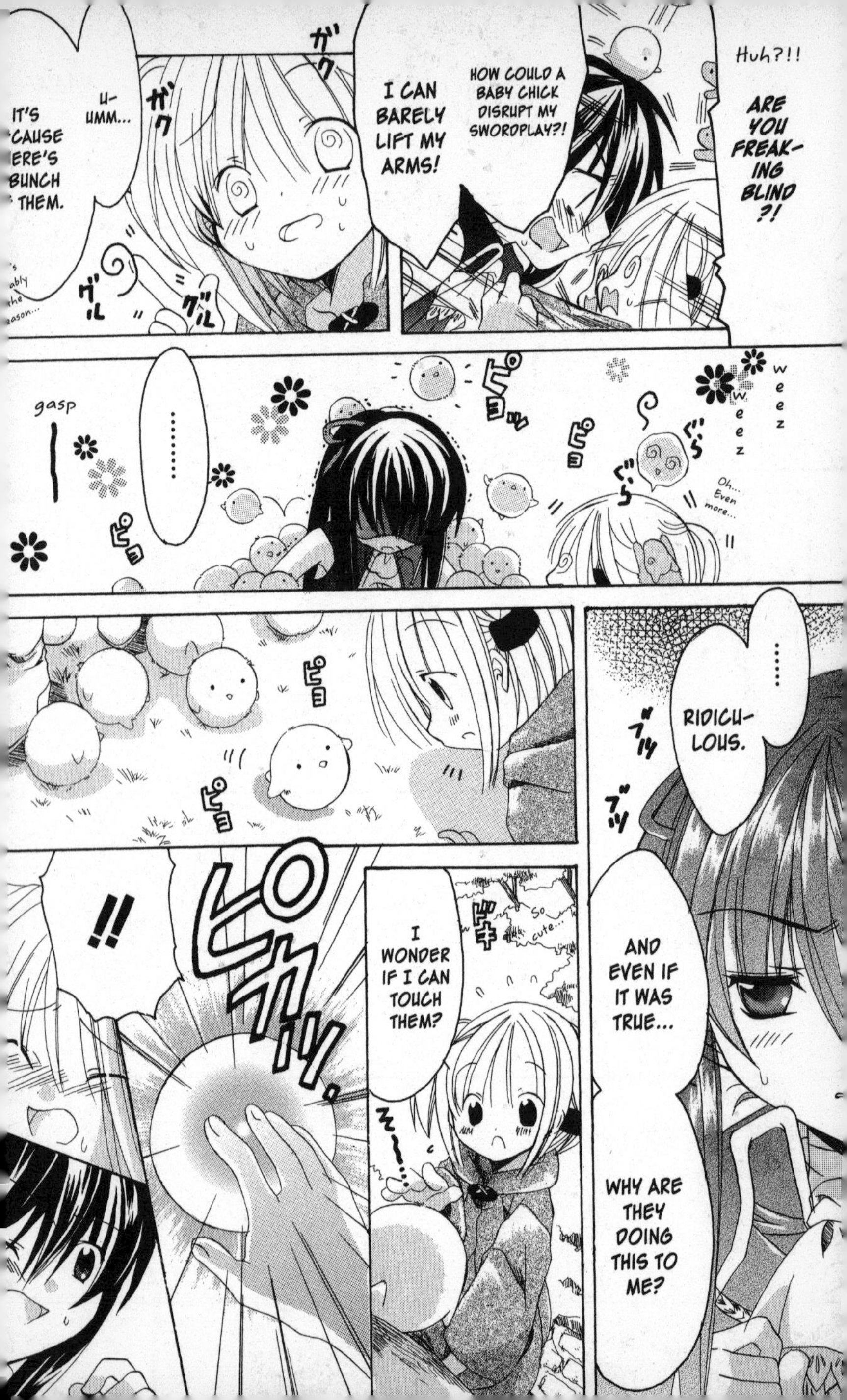
Huh?!!
ARE YOU FREAK-ING BLIND?!
HOW COULD A BABY CHICK DISRUPT MY SWORDPLAY?!
ガク
ガク
I CAN BARELY LIFT MY ARMS!
U-UMM...
IT'S 'CAUSE ERE'S BUNCH THEM.
グル
グル
weez
weez
ぐら
ぐら
Oh... Even more...
ピョッ
ピヨ
ピヨ
......
gasp
......
RIDICULOUS.
ブツ
ブツ
ピヨ
ピヨ
AND EVEN IF IT WAS TRUE...
WHY ARE THEY DOING THIS TO ME?
ドキ
So cute...
I WONDER IF I CAN TOUCH THEM?
ス~...
ピカッ。
!!

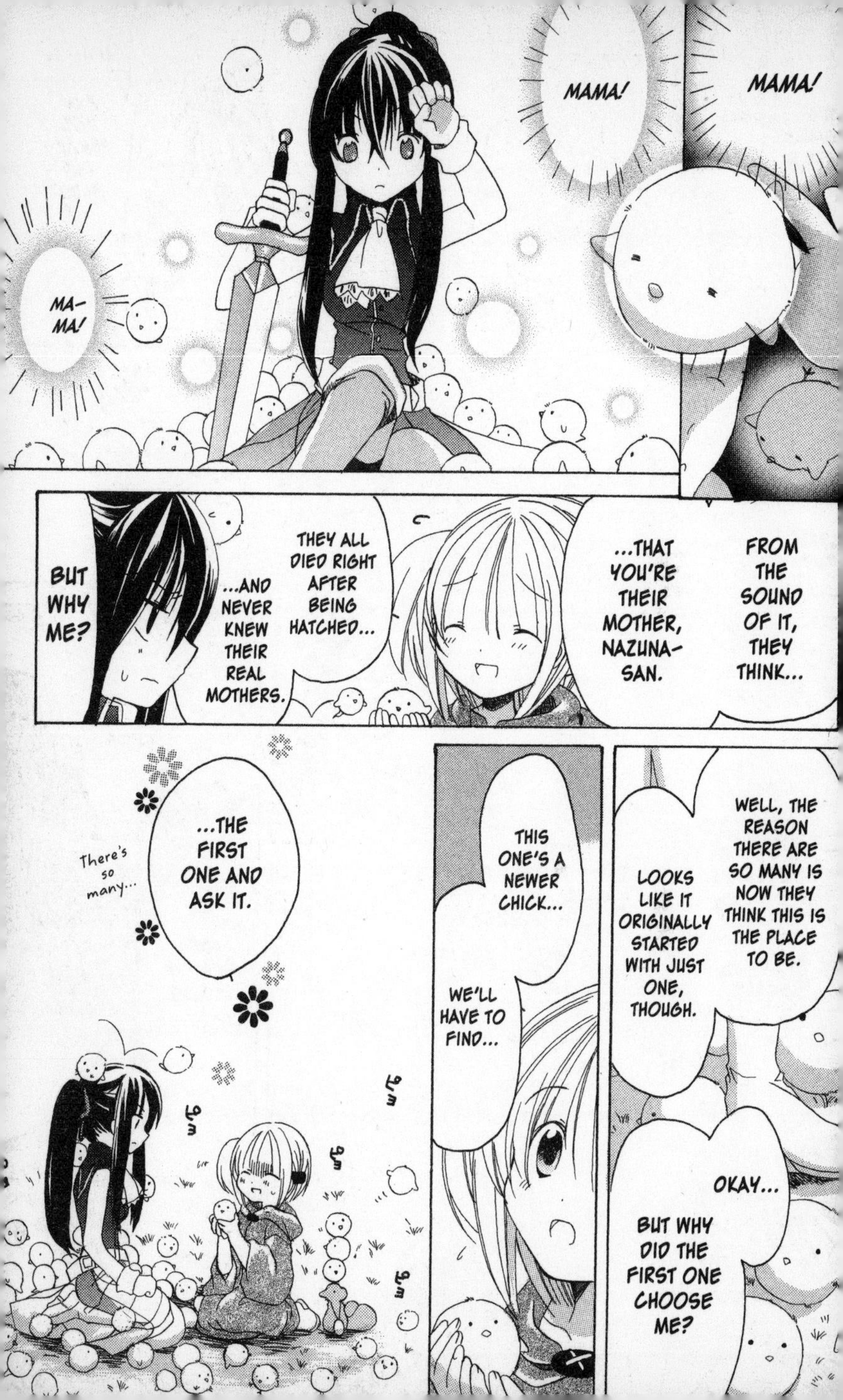
MAMA!
MAMA!
MA-MA!
FROM THE SOUND OF IT, THEY THINK...
...THAT YOU'RE THEIR MOTHER, NAZUNA-SAN.
THEY ALL DIED RIGHT AFTER BEING HATCHED...
...AND NEVER KNEW THEIR REAL MOTHERS.
BUT WHY ME?
WELL, THE REASON THERE ARE SO MANY IS NOW THEY THINK THIS IS THE PLACE TO BE.
LOOKS LIKE IT ORIGINALLY STARTED WITH JUST ONE, THOUGH.
OKAY...
BUT WHY DID THE FIRST ONE CHOOSE ME?
THIS ONE'S A NEWER CHICK...
WE'LL HAVE TO FIND...
...THE FIRST ONE AND ASK IT.
There's so many...

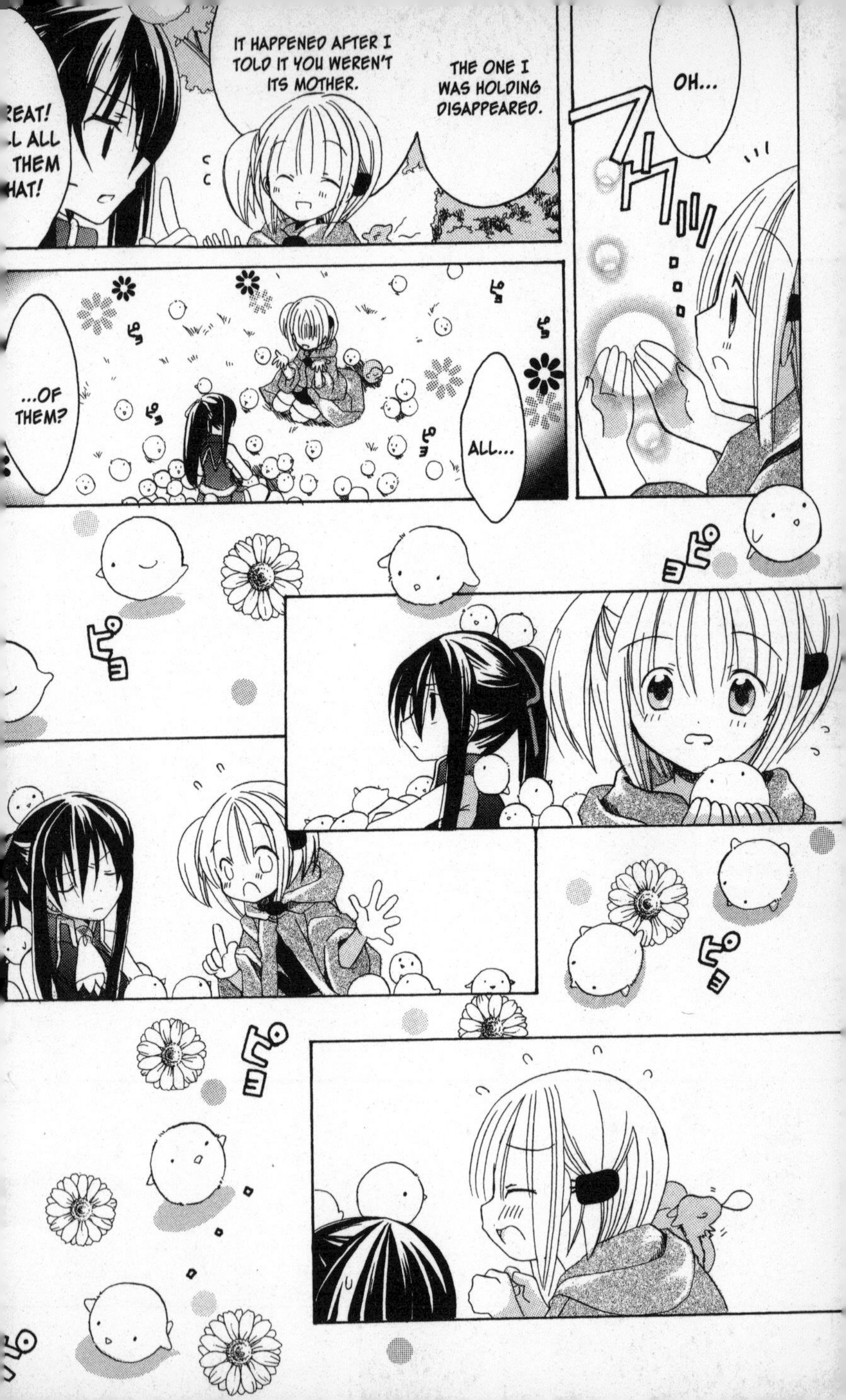
OH...
THE ONE I WAS HOLDING DISAPPEARED.
IT HAPPENED AFTER I TOLD IT YOU WEREN'T ITS MOTHER.
ALL...
...OF THEM?

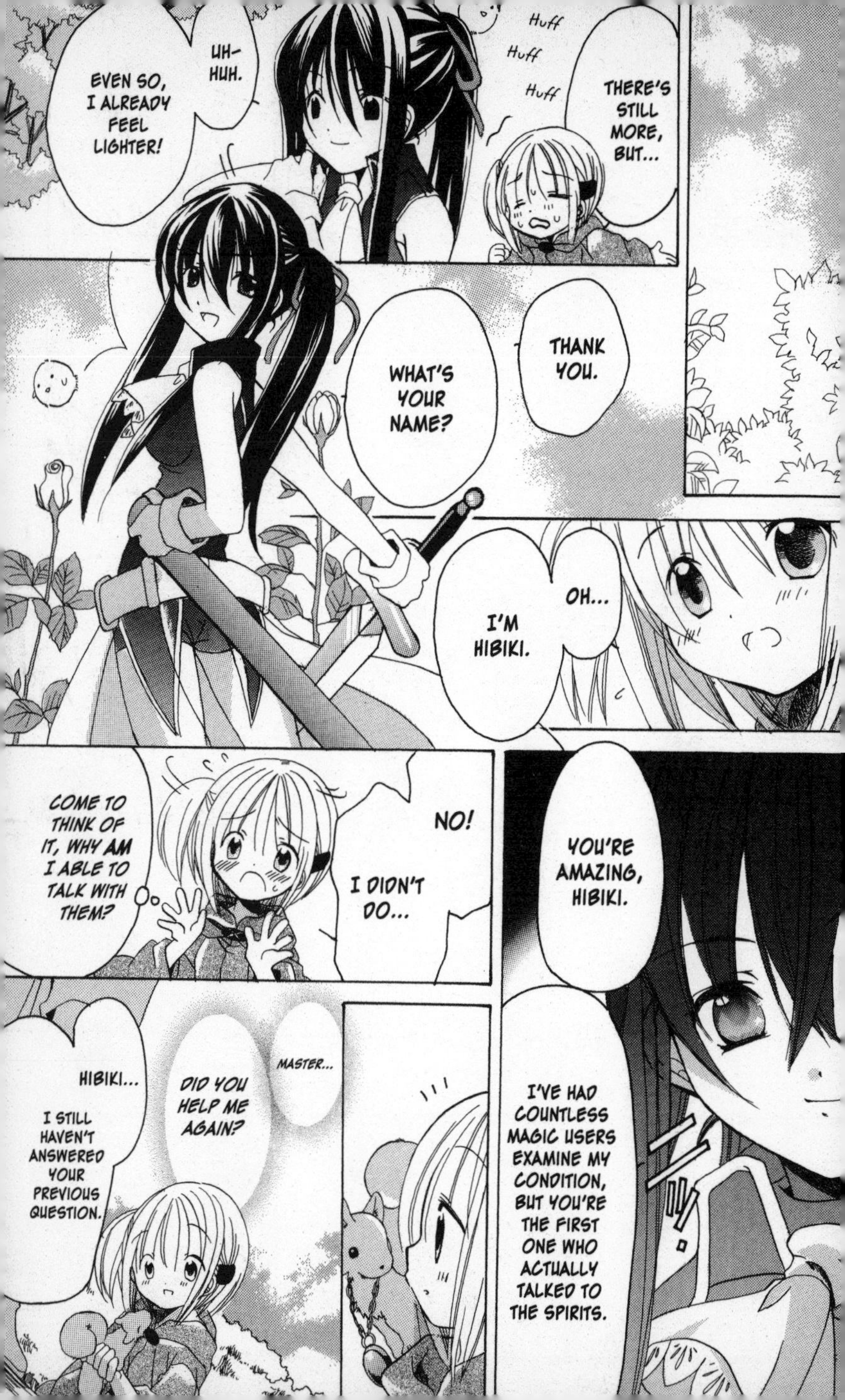

Huff
Huff
Huff
THERE'S STILL MORE, BUT...
UH-HUH.
EVEN SO, I ALREADY FEEL LIGHTER!
THANK YOU.
WHAT'S YOUR NAME?
OH...
I'M HIBIKI.
YOU'RE AMAZING, HIBIKI.
I'VE HAD COUNTLESS MAGIC USERS EXAMINE MY CONDITION, BUT YOU'RE THE FIRST ONE WHO ACTUALLY TALKED TO THE SPIRITS.
NO!
I DIDN'T DO...
COME TO THINK OF IT, WHY AM I ABLE TO TALK WITH THEM?
MASTER...
DID YOU HELP ME AGAIN?
HIBIKI...
I STILL HAVEN'T ANSWERED YOUR PREVIOUS QUESTION.

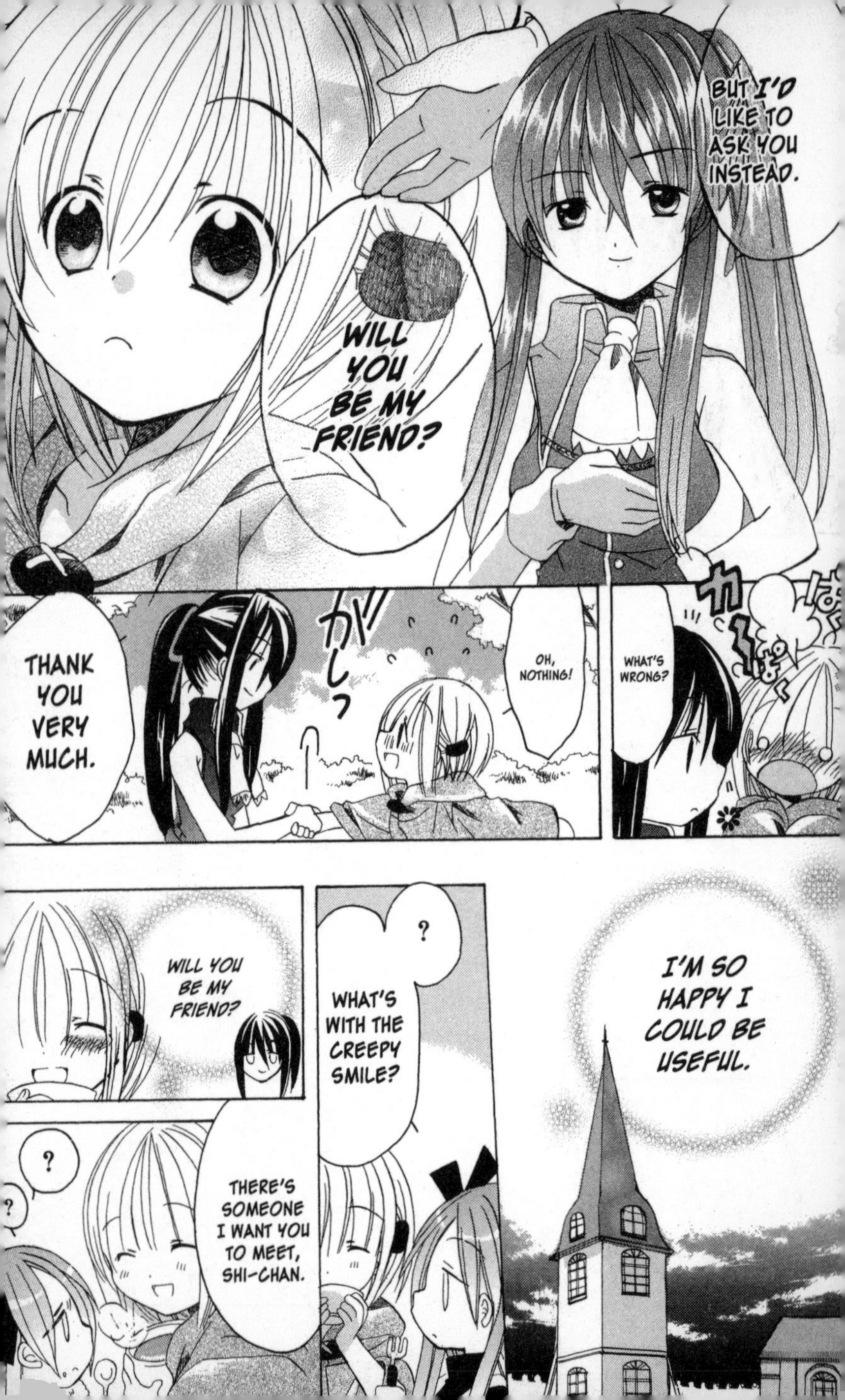
BUT I'D LIKE TO ASK YOU INSTEAD.
WILL YOU BE MY FRIEND?
WHAT'S WRONG?
OH, NOTHING!
THANK YOU VERY MUCH.
I'M SO HAPPY I COULD BE USEFUL.
?
WHAT'S WITH THE CREEPY SMILE?
WILL YOU BE MY FRIEND?
THERE'S SOMEONE I WANT YOU TO MEET, SHI-CHAN.
?
?

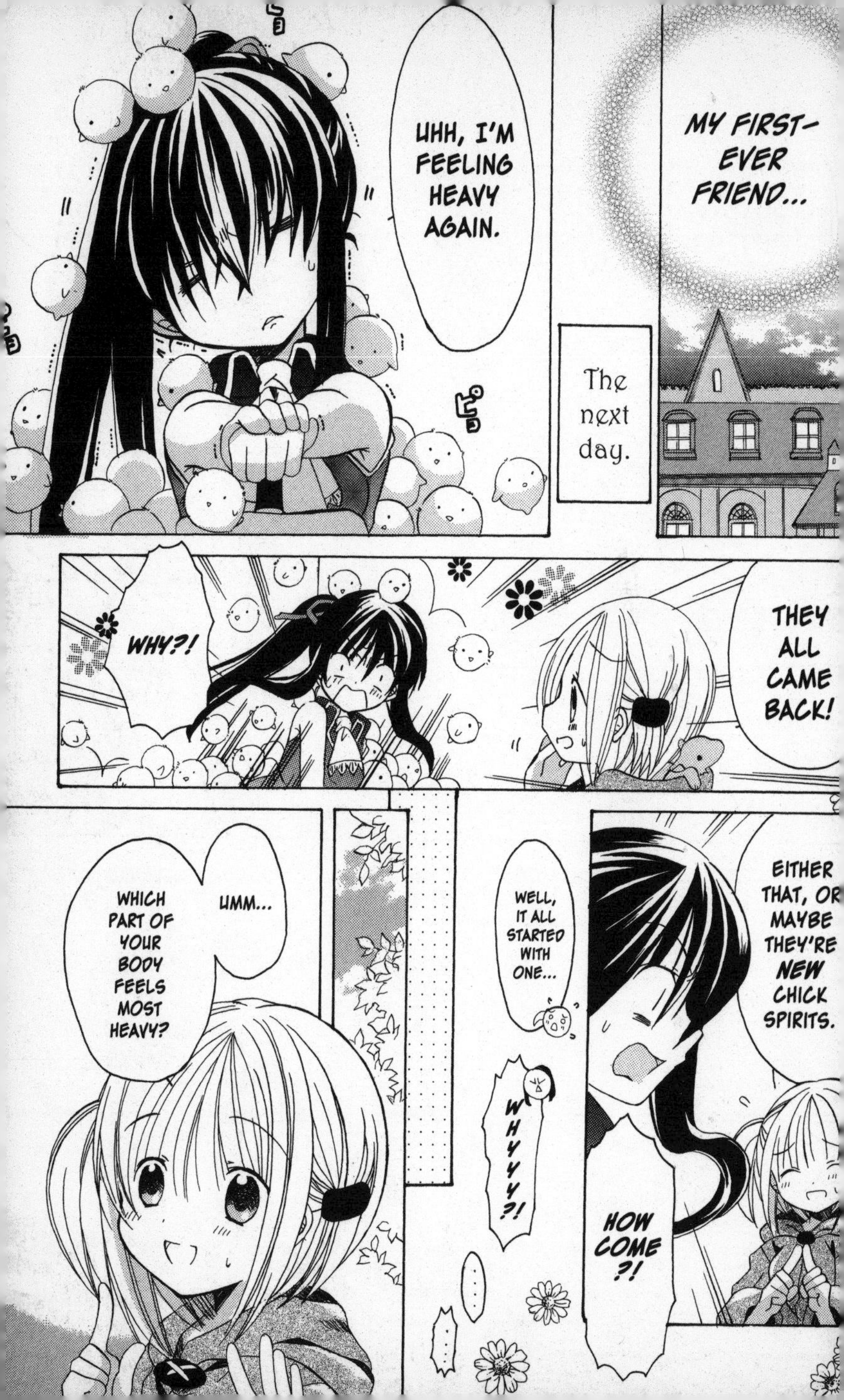
MY FIRST-EVER FRIEND...
The next day.
UHH, I'M FEELING HEAVY AGAIN.
THEY ALL CAME BACK!
WHY?!
EITHER THAT, OR MAYBE THEY'RE NEW CHICK SPIRITS.
HOW COME?!
WELL, IT ALL STARTED WITH ONE...
WHYYYY?!
...
...
UMM...
WHICH PART OF YOUR BODY FEELS MOST HEAVY?

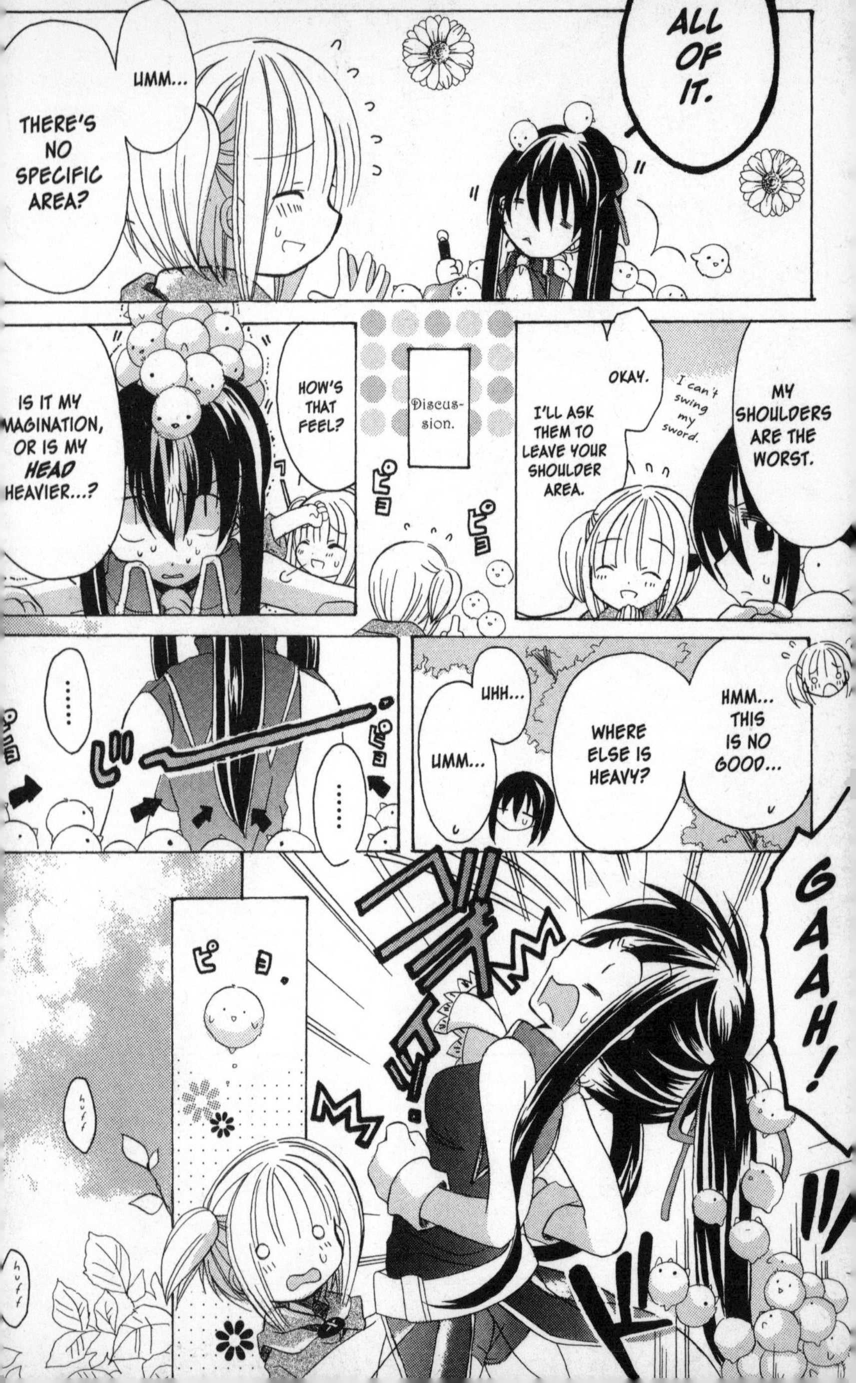

ALL OF IT.
UMM...
THERE'S NO SPECIFIC AREA?
MY SHOULDERS ARE THE WORST.
I can't swing my sword.
OKAY.
I'LL ASK THEM TO LEAVE YOUR SHOULDER AREA.
Discus-sion.
HOW'S THAT FEEL?
IS IT MY MAGINATION, OR IS MY *HEAD* HEAVIER...?
HMM... THIS IS NO GOOD...
WHERE ELSE IS HEAVY?
UHH...
UMM...
......
......
GAAH!
ピヨ。
huff
huff

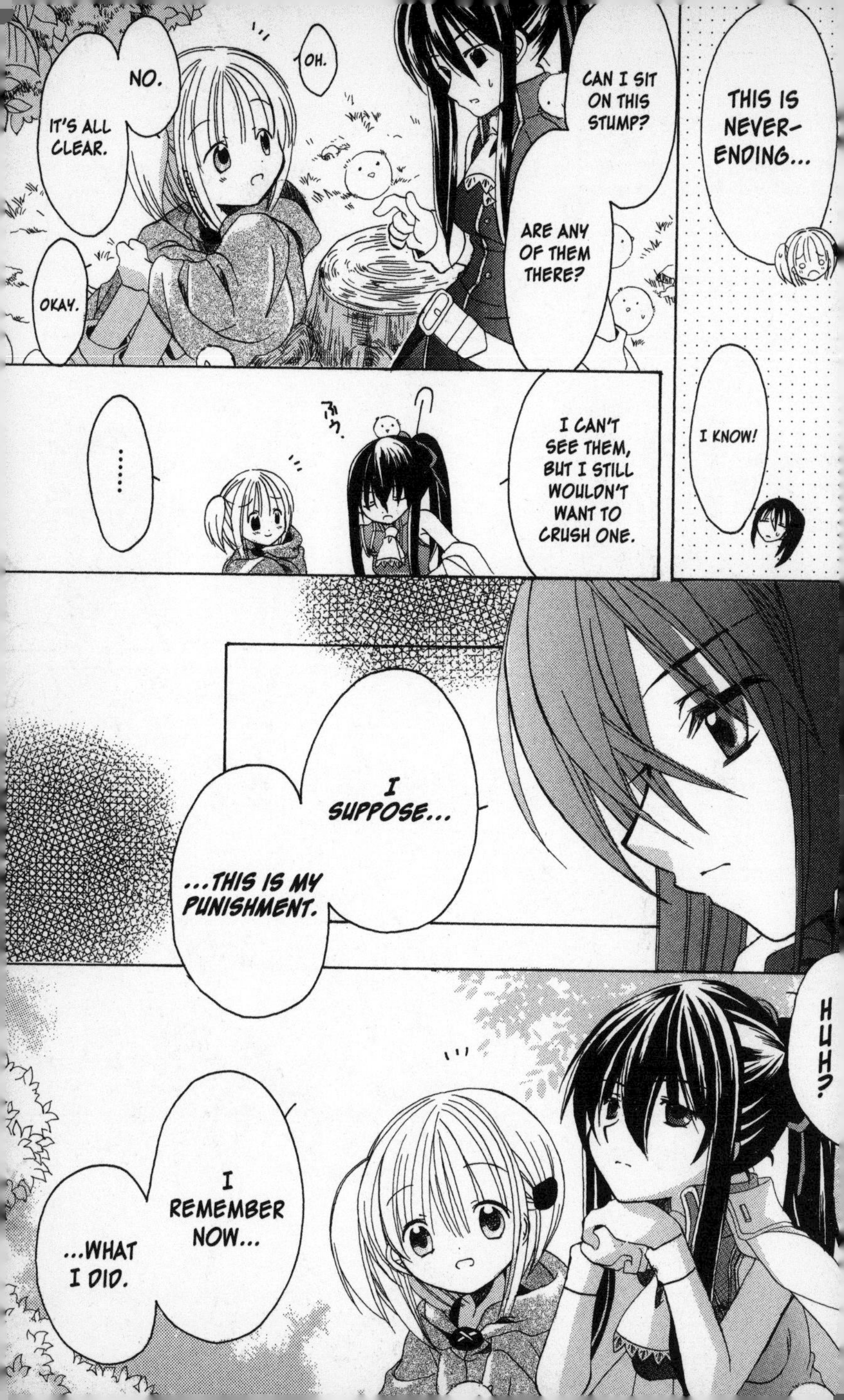
THIS IS NEVER-ENDING...
I KNOW!
CAN I SIT ON THIS STUMP?
ARE ANY OF THEM THERE?
OH.
NO.
IT'S ALL CLEAR.
OKAY.
I CAN'T SEE THEM, BUT I STILL WOULDN'T WANT TO CRUSH ONE.
......
I SUPPOSE...
...THIS IS MY PUNISHMENT.
HUH?
I REMEMBER NOW...
...WHAT I DID.

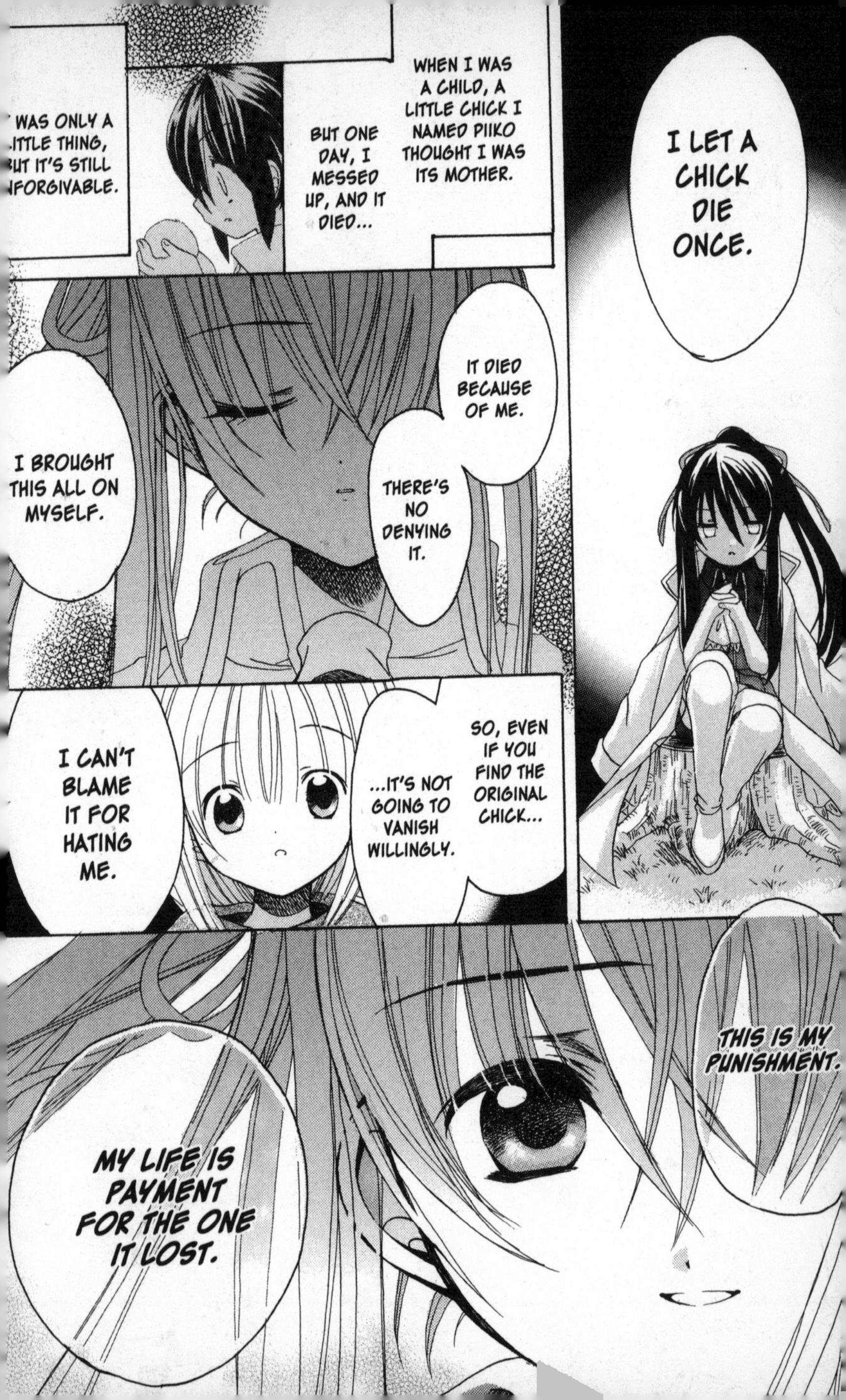
I LET A CHICK DIE ONCE.
WHEN I WAS A CHILD, A LITTLE CHICK I NAMED PIIKO THOUGHT I WAS ITS MOTHER.
BUT ONE DAY, I MESSED UP, AND IT DIED...
WAS ONLY A ITTLE THING, UT IT'S STILL NFORGIVABLE.
IT DIED BECAUSE OF ME.
THERE'S NO DENYING IT.
I BROUGHT THIS ALL ON MYSELF.
SO, EVEN IF YOU FIND THE ORIGINAL CHICK...
...IT'S NOT GOING TO VANISH WILLINGLY.
I CAN'T BLAME IT FOR HATING ME.
THIS IS MY PUNISHMENT.
MY LIFE IS PAYMENT FOR THE ONE IT LOST.

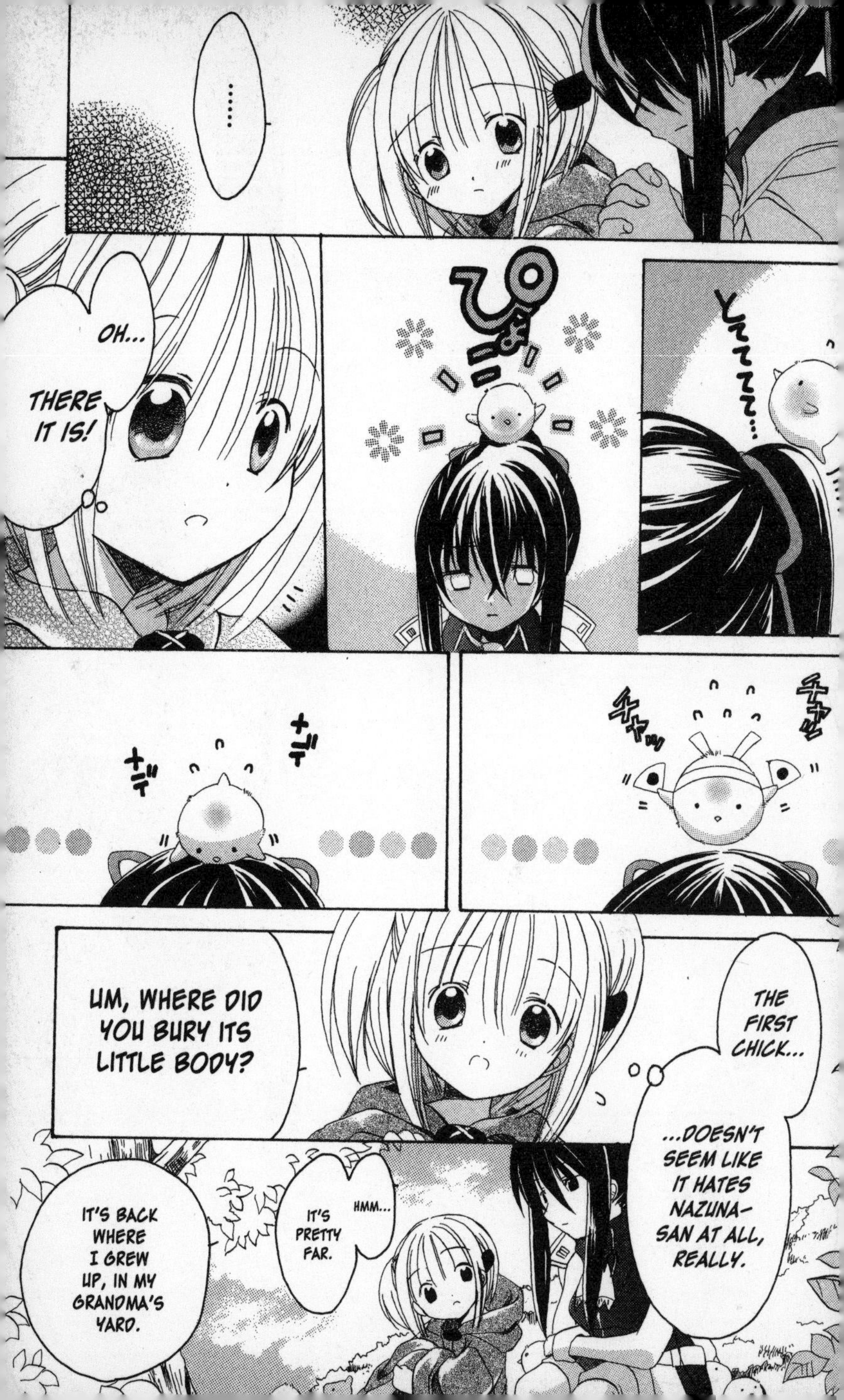
......
YZZZZ...
OH... THERE IT IS!
THE FIRST CHICK...
...DOESN'T SEEM LIKE IT HATES NAZUNA-SAN AT ALL, REALLY.
UM, WHERE DID YOU BURY ITS LITTLE BODY?
HMM...
IT'S PRETTY FAR.
IT'S BACK WHERE I GREW UP, IN MY GRANDMA'S YARD.

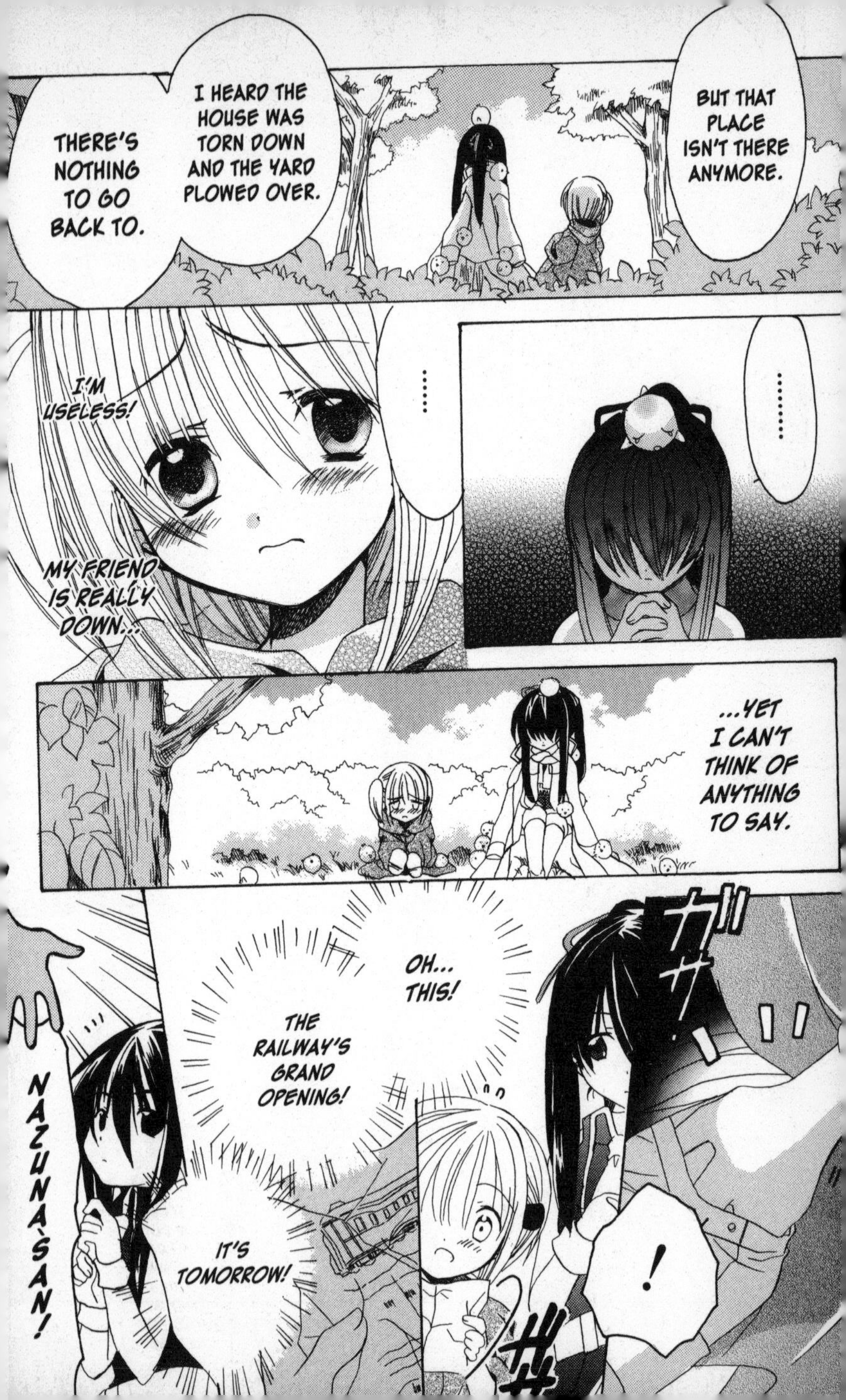
BUT THAT PLACE ISN'T THERE ANYMORE.
I HEARD THE HOUSE WAS TORN DOWN AND THE YARD PLOWED OVER.
THERE'S NOTHING TO GO BACK TO.
......
......
I'M USELESS!
MY FRIEND IS REALLY DOWN...
...YET I CAN'T THINK OF ANYTHING TO SAY.
!!
!
OH... THIS!
THE RAILWAY'S GRAND OPENING!
IT'S TOMORROW!
...!
NAZUNA-SAN!

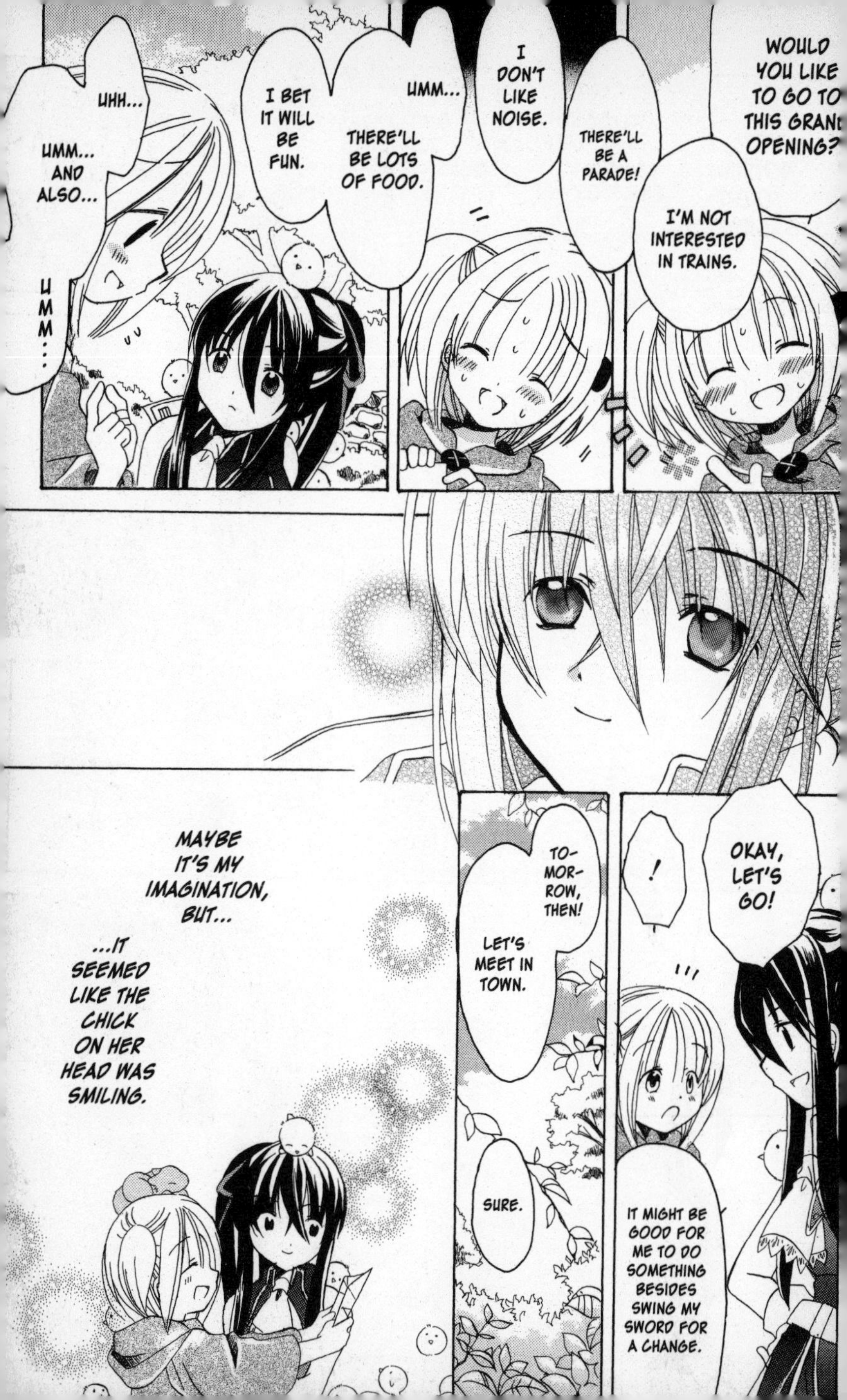
WOULD YOU LIKE TO GO TO THIS GRAN OPENING?
I'M NOT INTERESTED IN TRAINS.
THERE'LL BE A PARADE!
I DON'T LIKE NOISE.
UMM...
THERE'LL BE LOTS OF FOOD.
I BET IT WILL BE FUN.
UHH...
UMM... AND ALSO...
UMM...
OKAY, LET'S GO!
!
IT MIGHT BE GOOD FOR ME TO DO SOMETHING BESIDES SWING MY SWORD FOR A CHANGE.
TO-MOR-ROW, THEN!
LET'S MEET IN TOWN.
SURE.
MAYBE IT'S MY IMAGINATION, BUT...
...IT SEEMED LIKE THE CHICK ON HER HEAD WAS SMILING.

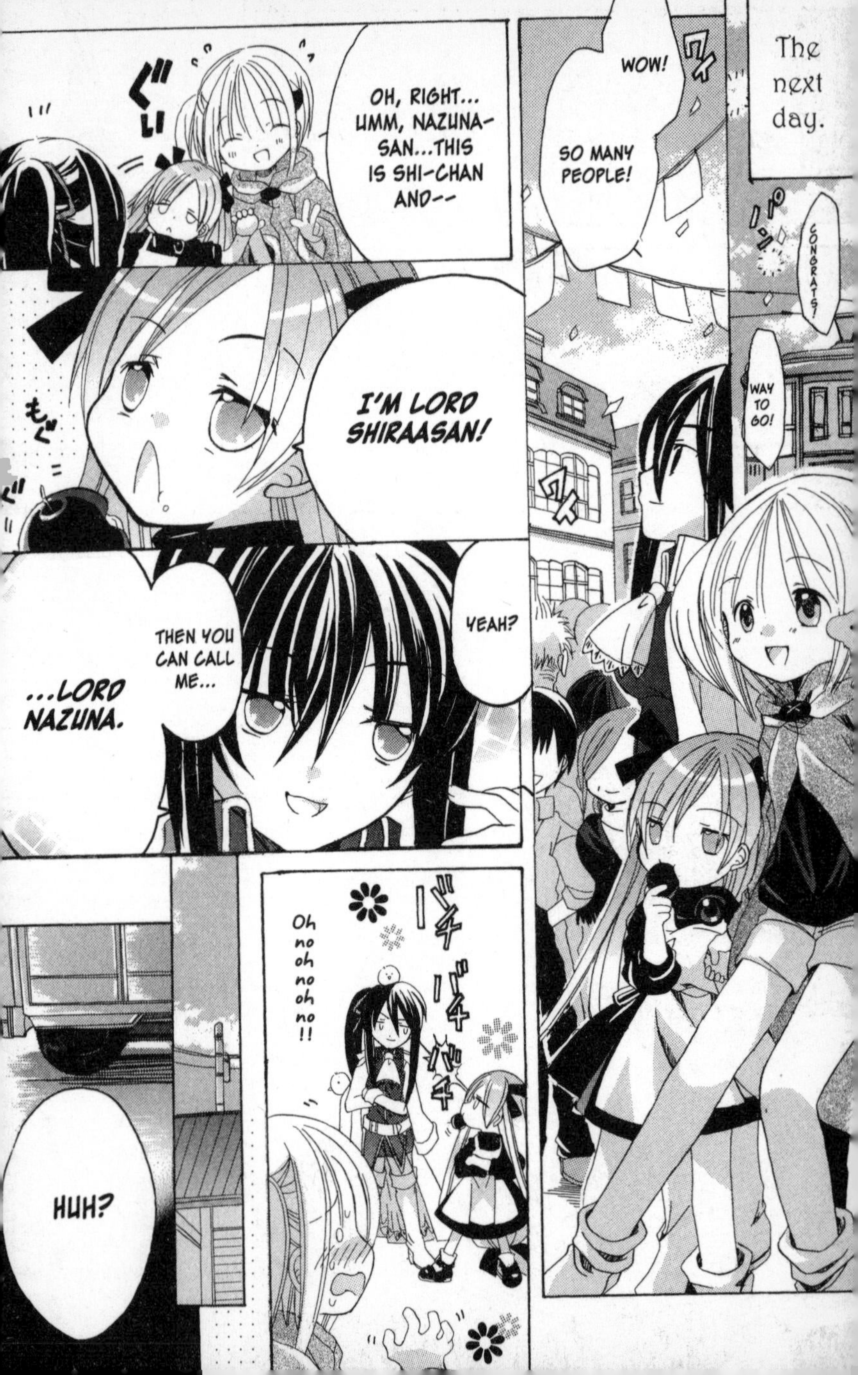
The next day.
WOW!
SO MANY PEOPLE!
CONGRATS!
WAY TO GO!
OH, RIGHT... UMM, NAZUNA-SAN...THIS IS SHI-CHAN AND--
I'M LORD SHIRAASAN!
YEAH?
THEN YOU CAN CALL ME...
...LORD NAZUNA.
Oh no oh no oh no!!
HUH?

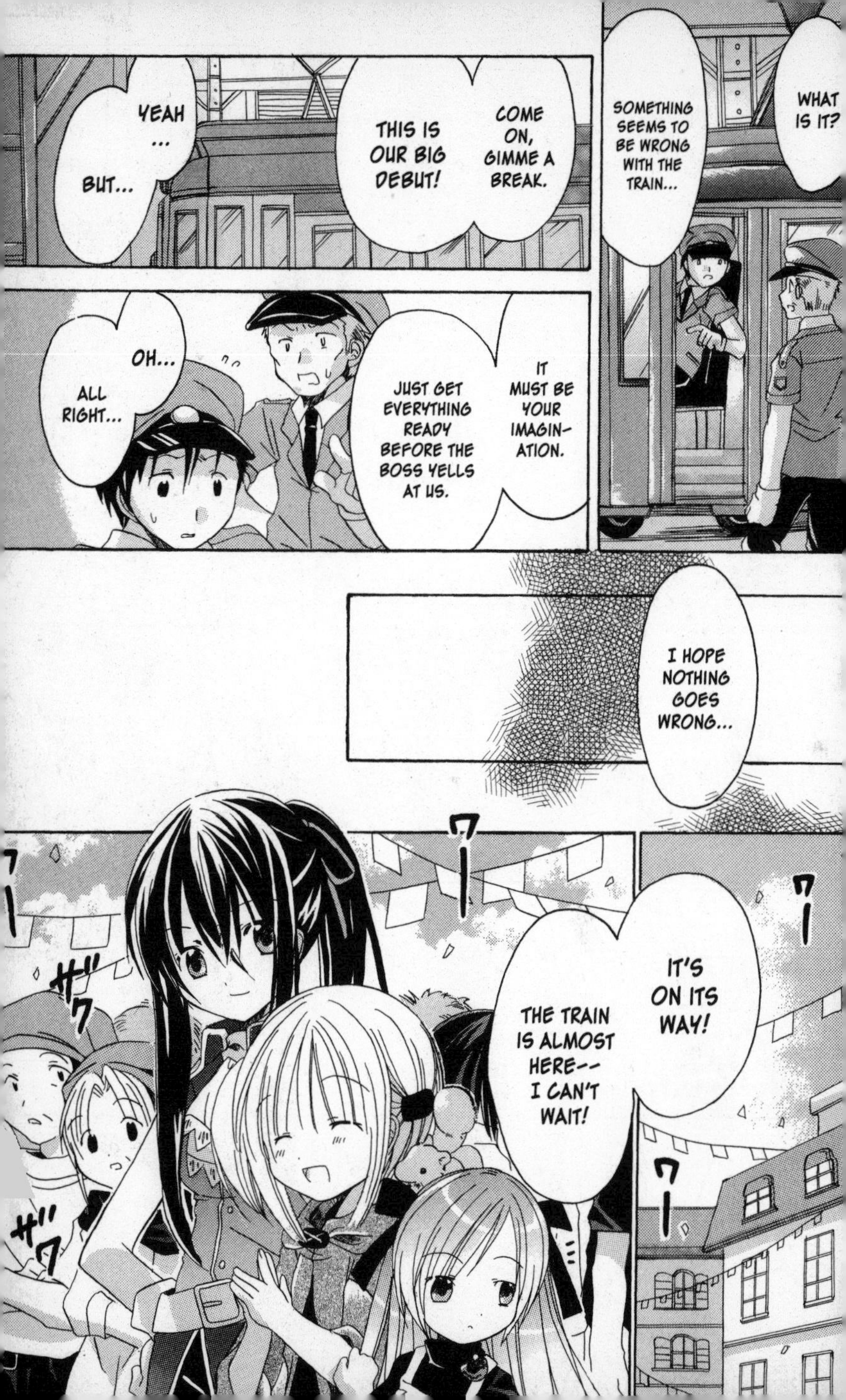
WHAT IS IT?
SOMETHING SEEMS TO BE WRONG WITH THE TRAIN...
COME ON, GIMME A BREAK.
THIS IS OUR BIG DEBUT!
YEAH ... BUT...
IT MUST BE YOUR IMAGINATION.
JUST GET EVERYTHING READY BEFORE THE BOSS YELLS AT US.
OH... ALL RIGHT...
I HOPE NOTHING GOES WRONG...
ワー
IT'S ON ITS WAY!
THE TRAIN IS ALMOST HERE-- I CAN'T WAIT!
ザワ ザワ

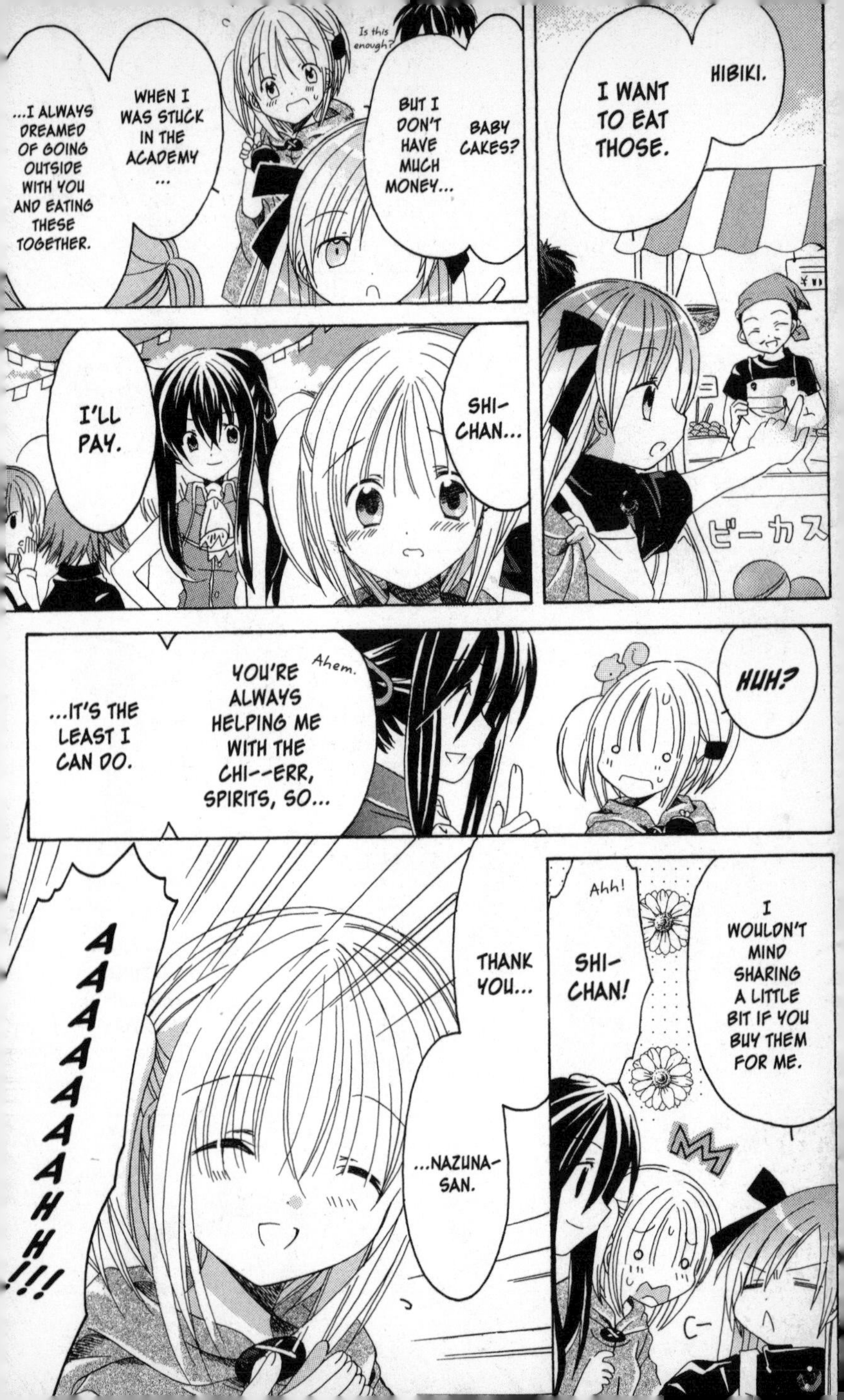
HIBIKI.
I WANT TO EAT THOSE.
ビーカス
Is this enough?
BABY CAKES?
BUT I DON'T HAVE MUCH MONEY...
WHEN I WAS STUCK IN THE ACADEMY...
...I ALWAYS DREAMED OF GOING OUTSIDE WITH YOU AND EATING THESE TOGETHER.
SHI-CHAN...
I'LL PAY.
HUH?
Ahem.
YOU'RE ALWAYS HELPING ME WITH THE CHI--ERR, SPIRITS, SO...
...IT'S THE LEAST I CAN DO.
I WOULDN'T MIND SHARING A LITTLE BIT IF YOU BUY THEM FOR ME.
Ahh!
SHI-CHAN!
THANK YOU...
...NAZUNA-SAN.
AAAAAAAAAAHHH!!!

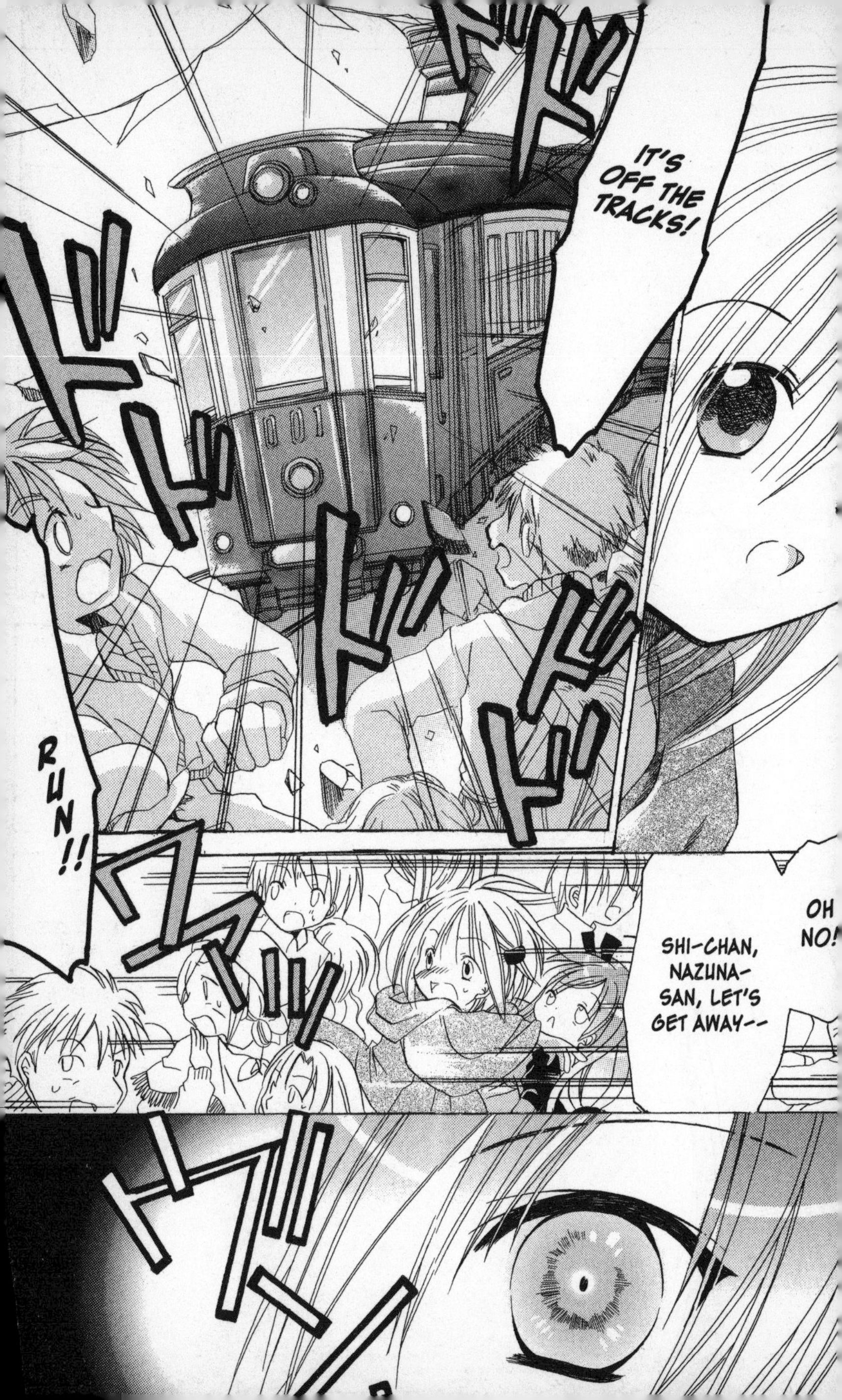
IT'S OFF THE TRACKS!
RUN!!
OH NO!
SHI-CHAN, NAZUNA-SAN, LET'S GET AWAY--

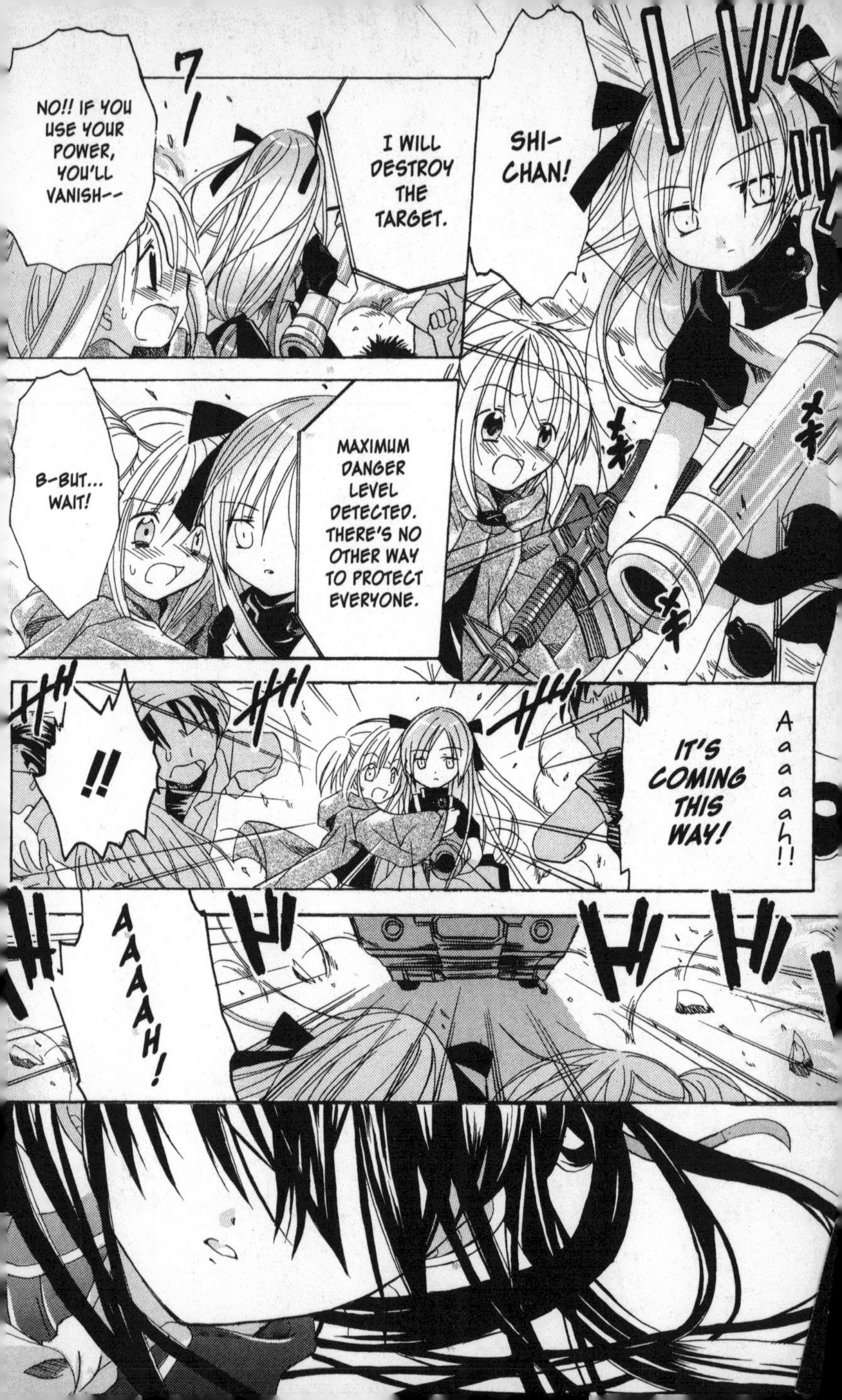
SHI-CHAN!
I WILL DESTROY THE TARGET.
NO!! IF YOU USE YOUR POWER, YOU'LL VANISH--
MAXIMUM DANGER LEVEL DETECTED. THERE'S NO OTHER WAY TO PROTECT EVERYONE.
B-BUT... WAIT!
Aaaaaah!!
IT'S COMING THIS WAY!
!!
AAAAAH!

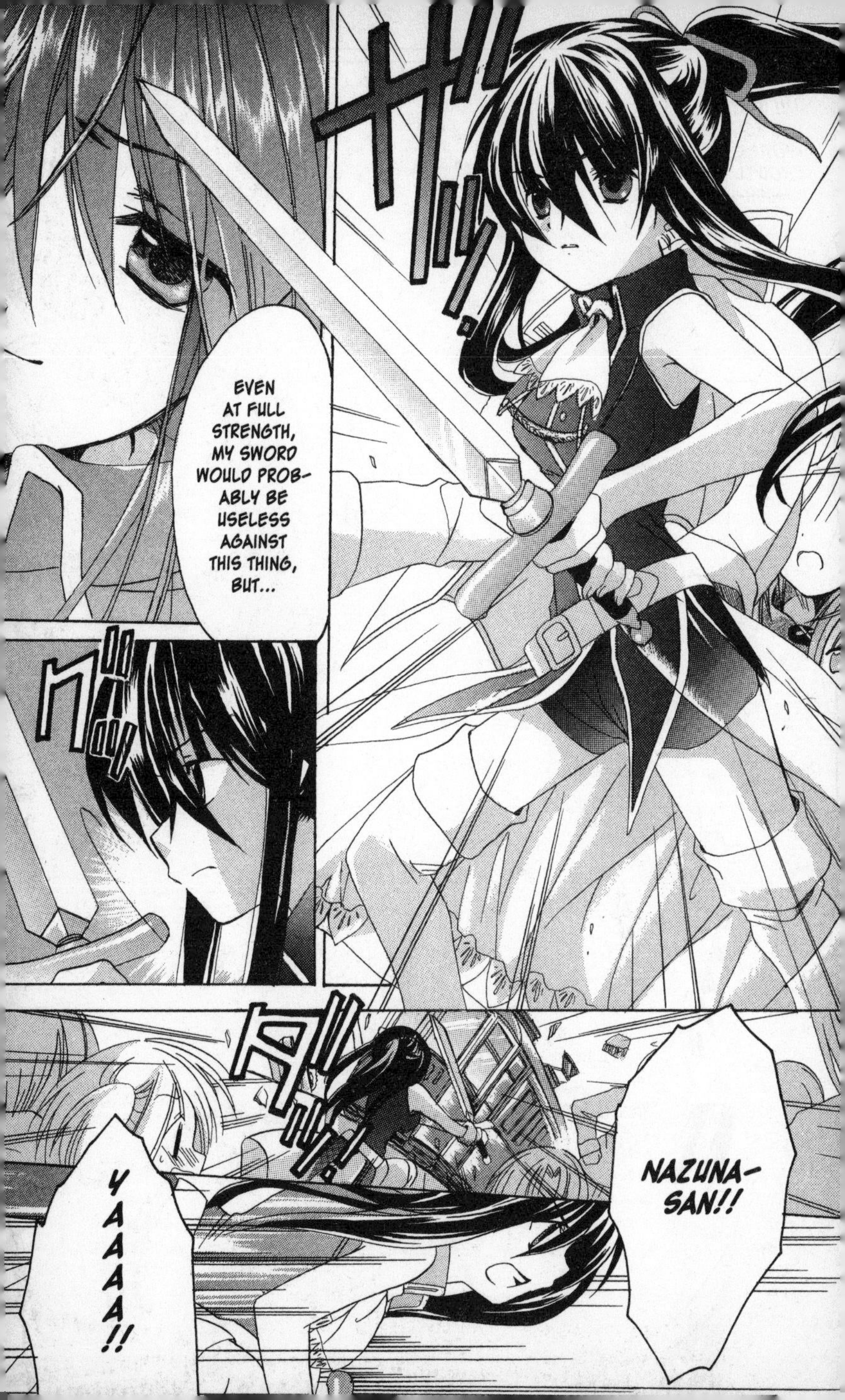
EVEN AT FULL STRENGTH, MY SWORD WOULD PROBABLY BE USELESS AGAINST THIS THING, BUT...
NAZUNA-SAN!!
YAAAAA!!

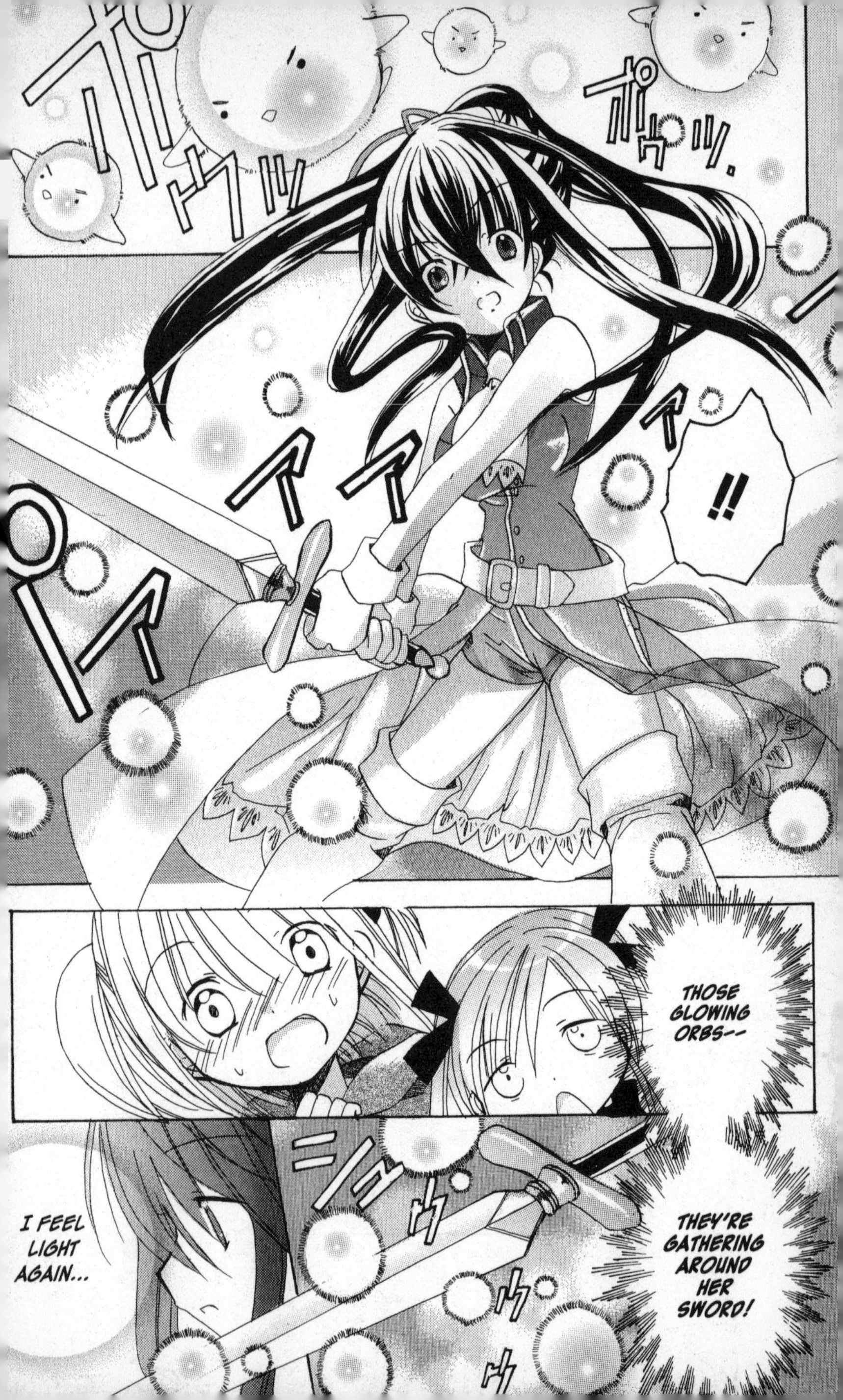
!!
THOSE GLOWING ORBS--
THEY'RE GATHERING AROUND HER SWORD!
I FEEL LIGHT AGAIN...

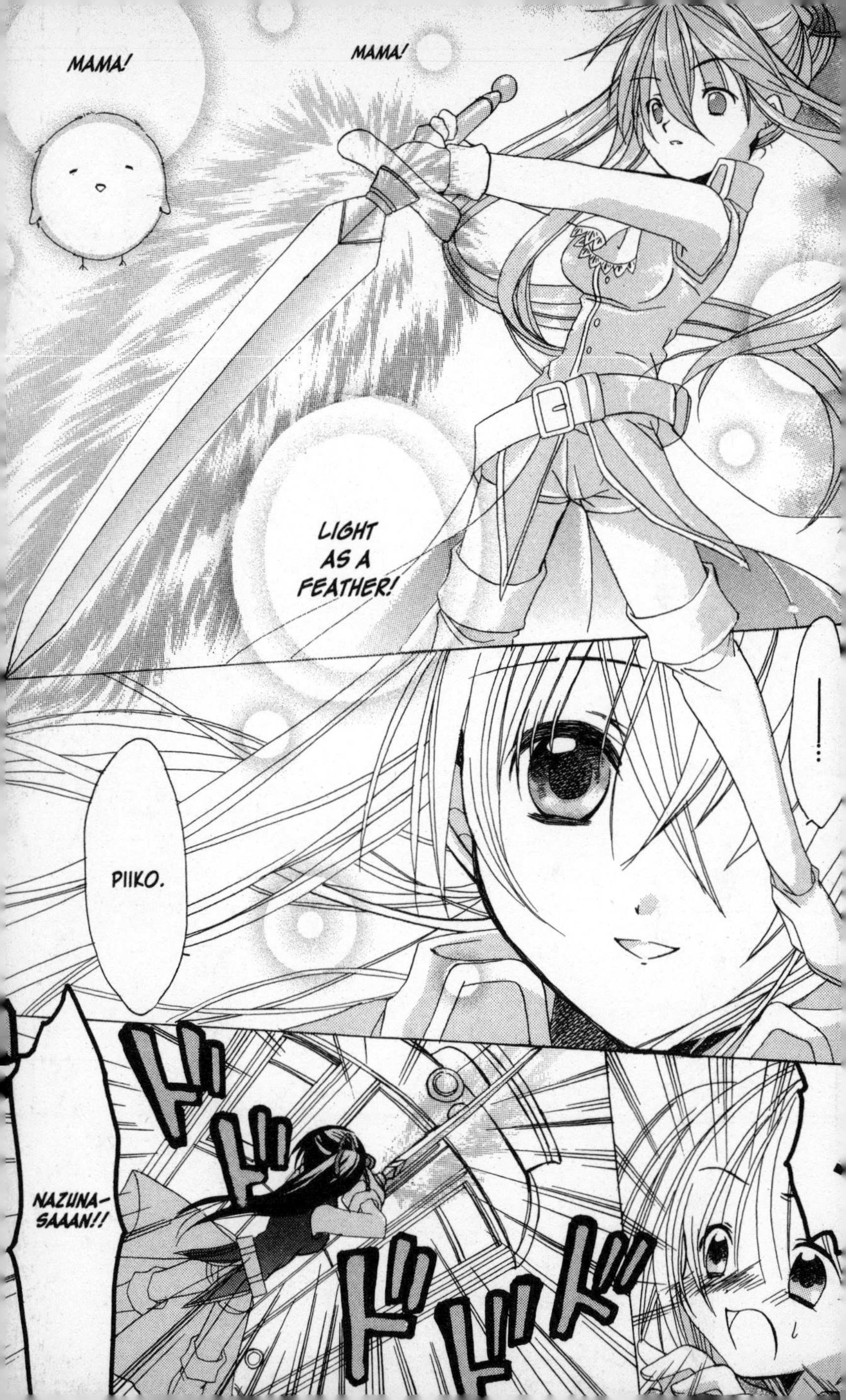
MAMA!
MAMA!
LIGHT AS A FEATHER!
...!
PIIKO.
ドド
ドドドド
NAZUNA-SAAAN!!

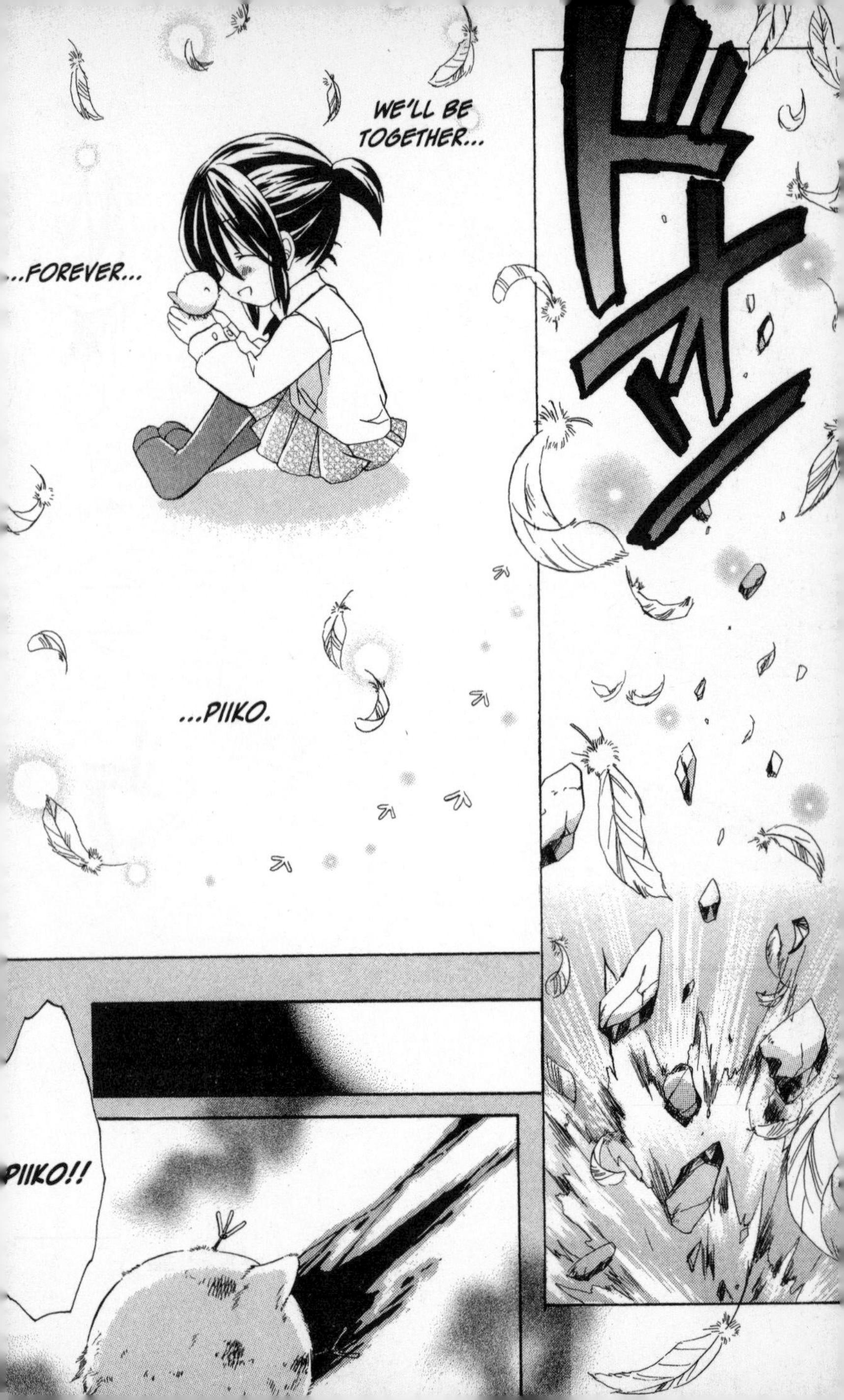
ドォン
WE'LL BE TOGETHER...
...FOREVER...
...PIIKO.
PIIKO!!

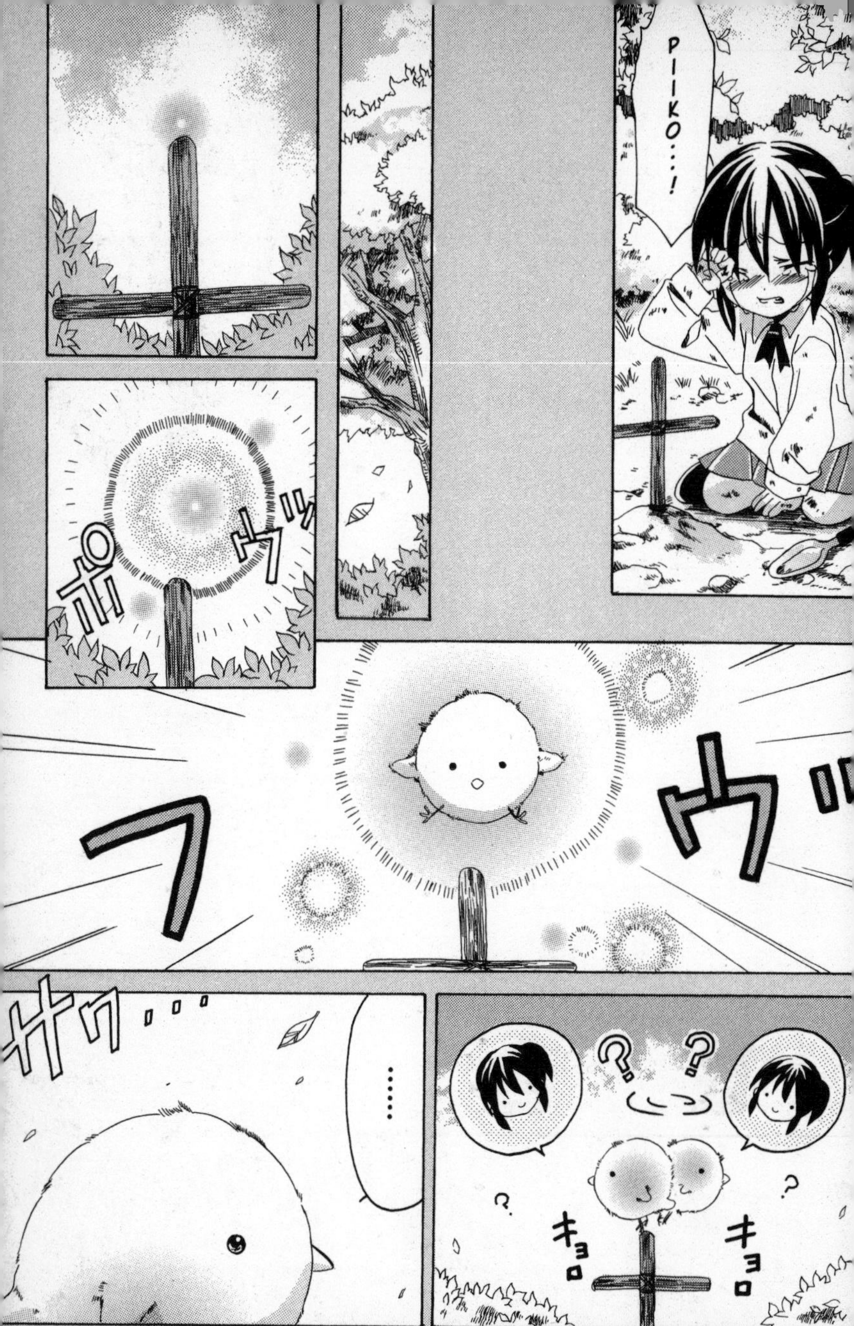

PIIKO...!
ポウッ
フ
ウッ
? ?
?
?
キョロ
キョロ
サワ...
......

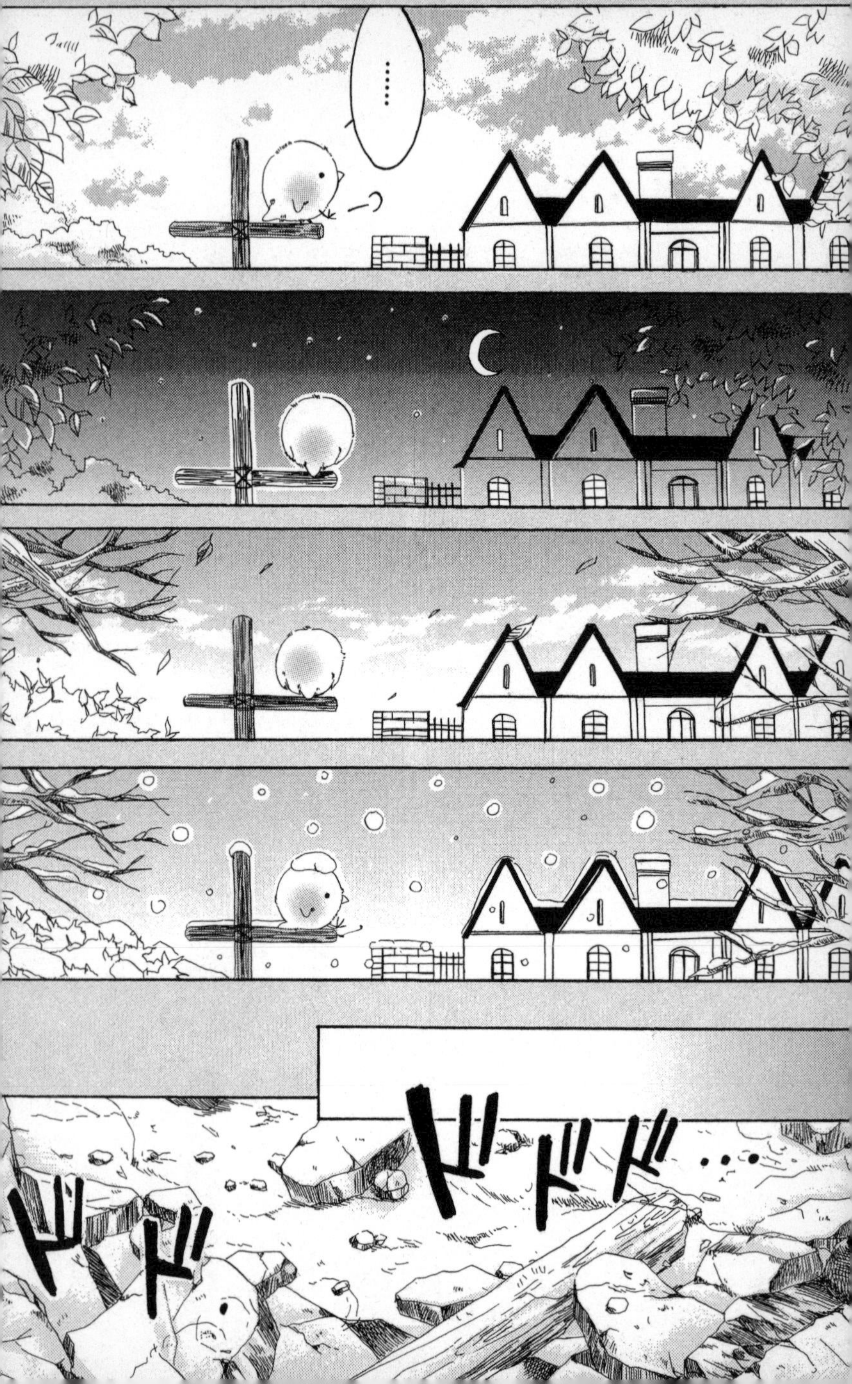
……
ドドド…
ドド

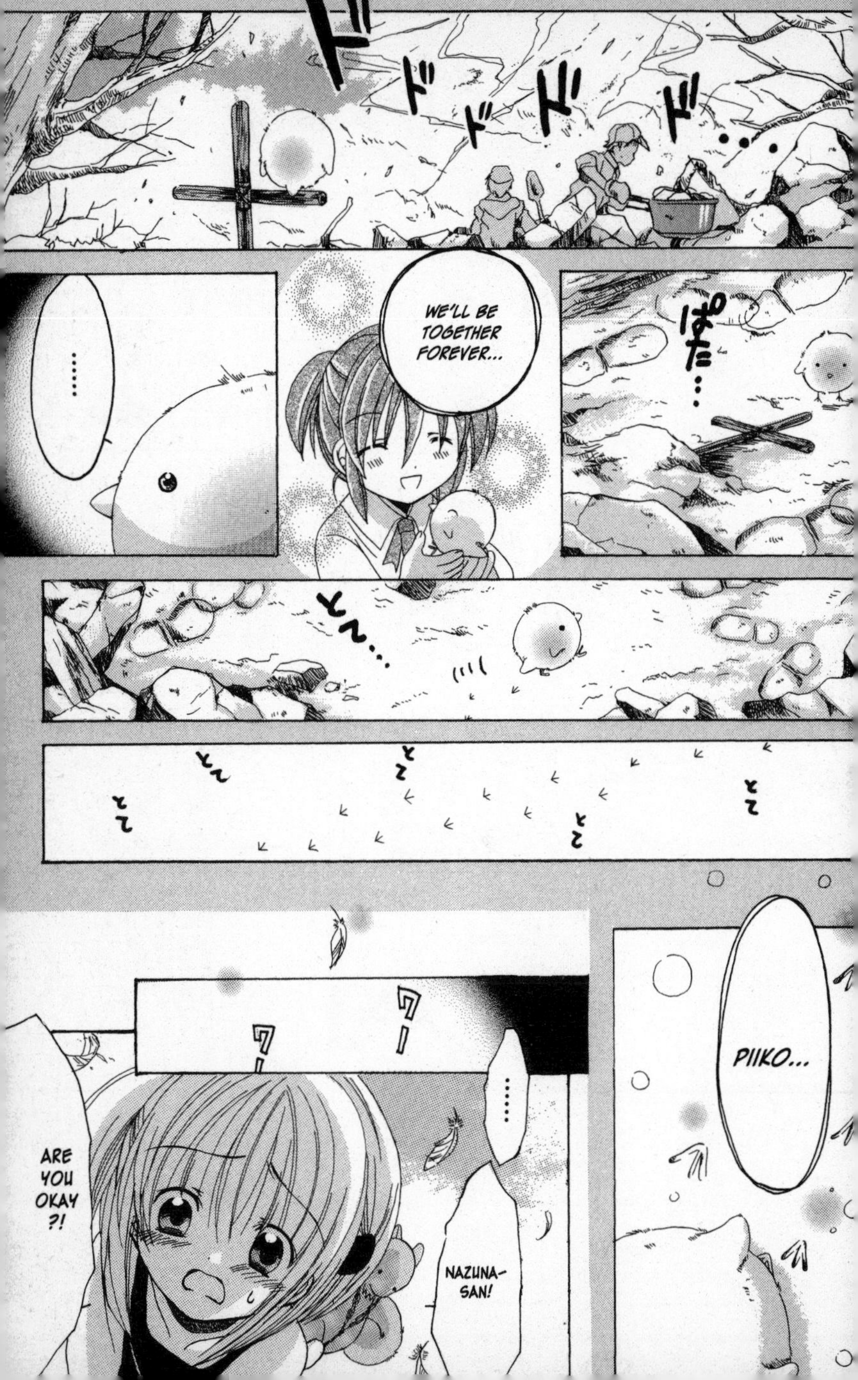
ドドドドド…
ぽた…
WE'LL BE TOGETHER FOREVER...
......
とん…
PIIKO...
ワー
ワー
......
NAZUNA-SAN!
ARE YOU OKAY?!

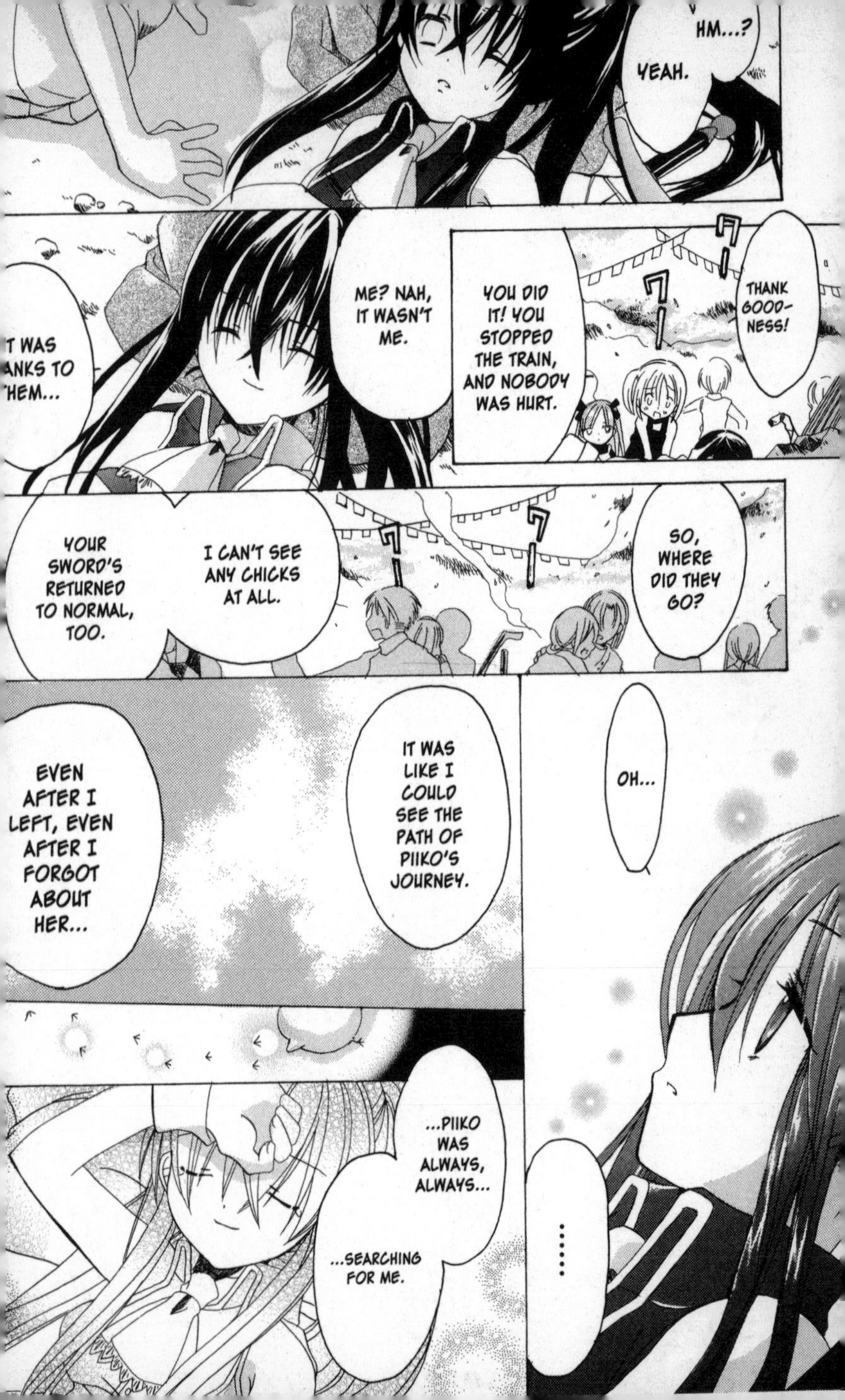
HM...?
YEAH.
THANK GOODNESS!
YOU DID IT! YOU STOPPED THE TRAIN, AND NOBODY WAS HURT.
ME? NAH, IT WASN'T ME.
T WAS ANKS TO HEM...
SO, WHERE DID THEY GO?
I CAN'T SEE ANY CHICKS AT ALL.
YOUR SWORD'S RETURNED TO NORMAL, TOO.
OH...
......
IT WAS LIKE I COULD SEE THE PATH OF PIIKO'S JOURNEY.
EVEN AFTER I LEFT, EVEN AFTER I FORGOT ABOUT HER...
...PIIKO WAS ALWAYS, ALWAYS...
...SEARCHING FOR ME.

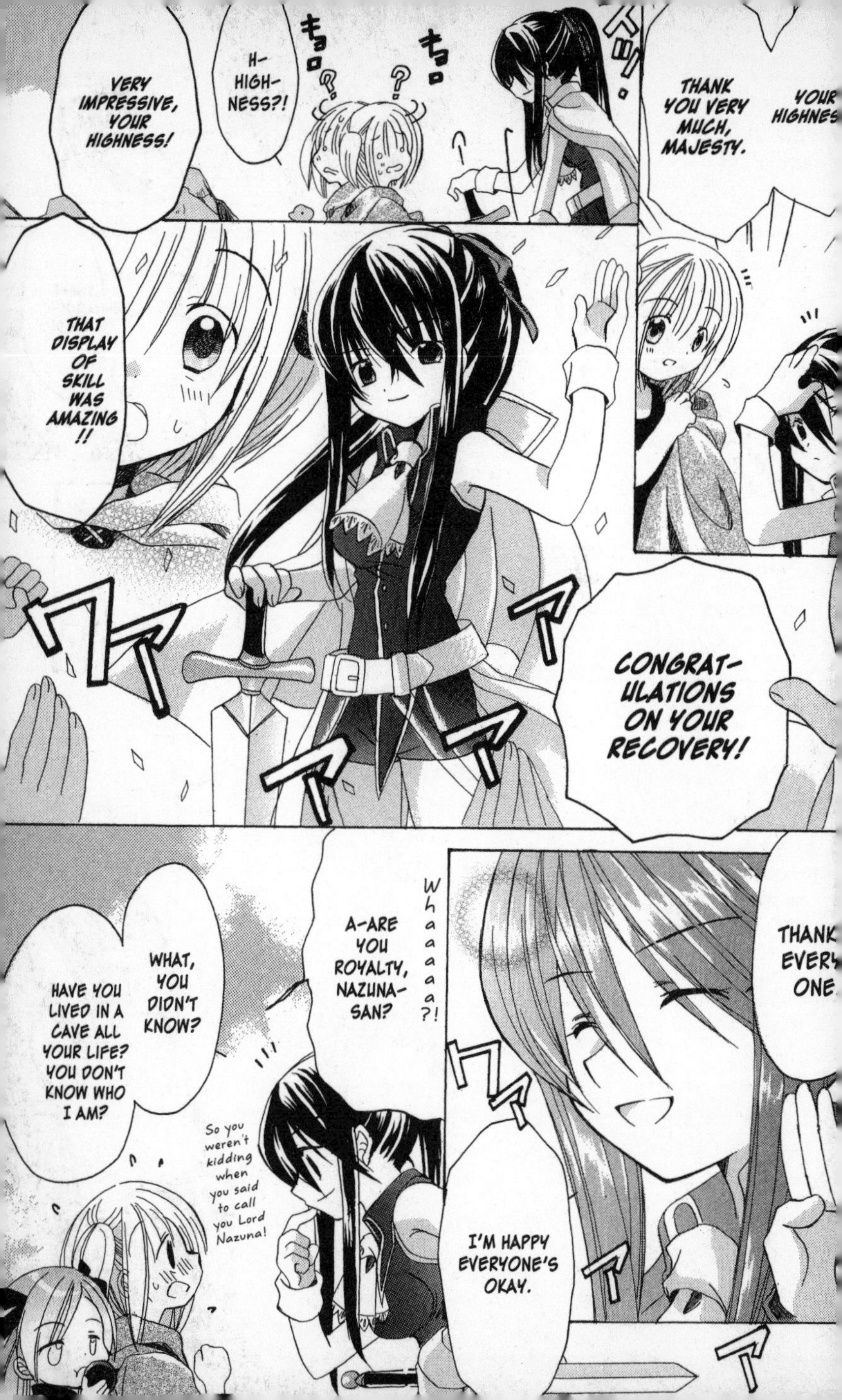

YOUR HIGHNES
THANK YOU VERY MUCH, MAJESTY.
H-HIGH-NESS?!
VERY IMPRESSIVE, YOUR HIGHNESS!
CONGRAT-ULATIONS ON YOUR RECOVERY!
THAT DISPLAY OF SKILL WAS AMAZING!!
THANK EVERY ONE
I'M HAPPY EVERYONE'S OKAY.
Whaaaaaaa?!
A-ARE YOU ROYALTY, NAZUNA-SAN?
WHAT, YOU DIDN'T KNOW?
HAVE YOU LIVED IN A CAVE ALL YOUR LIFE? YOU DON'T KNOW WHO I AM?
So you weren't kidding when you said to call you Lord Nazuna!

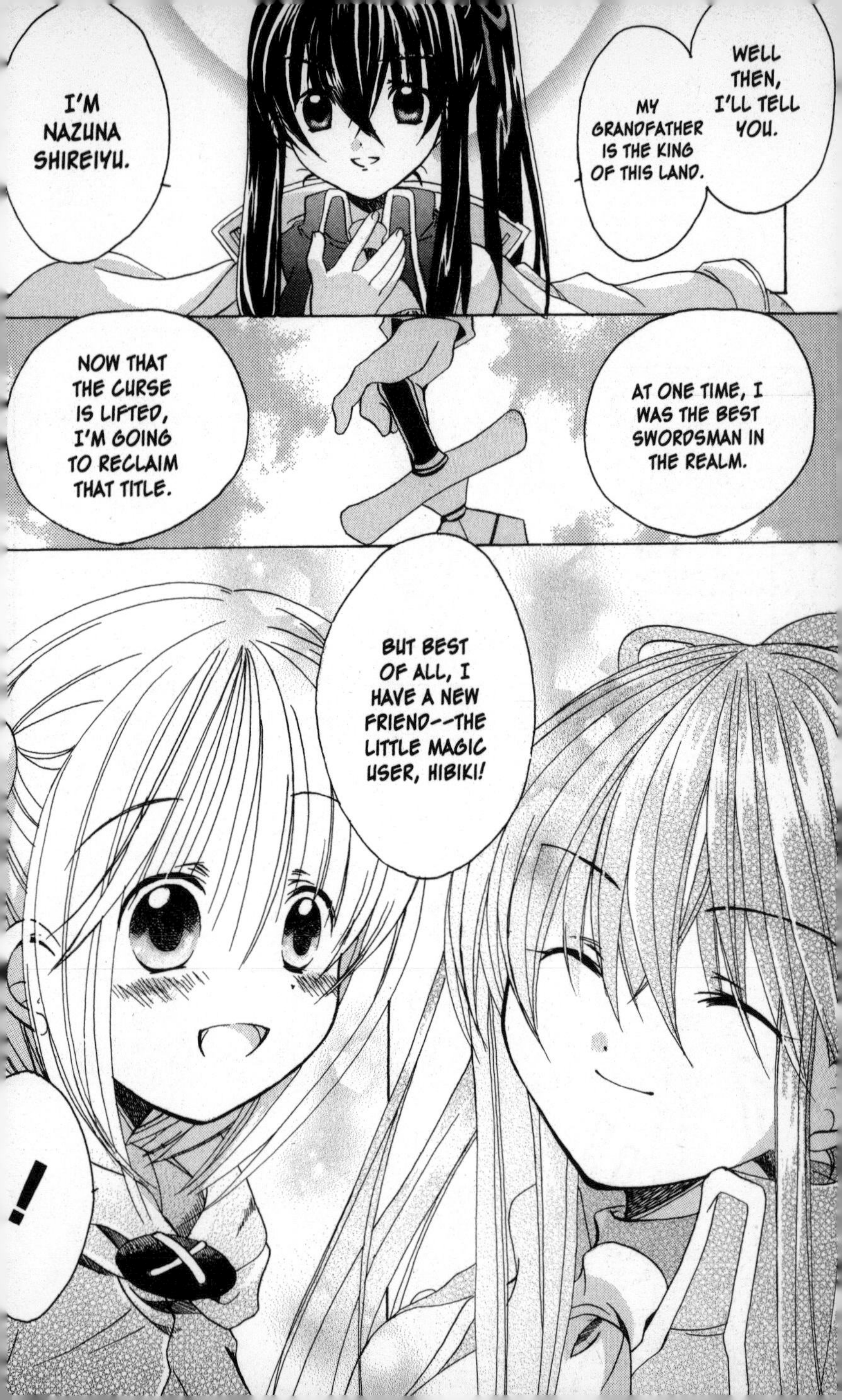
WELL THEN, I'LL TELL YOU.
MY GRANDFATHER IS THE KING OF THIS LAND.
I'M NAZUNA SHIREIYU.
AT ONE TIME, I WAS THE BEST SWORDSMAN IN THE REALM.
NOW THAT THE CURSE IS LIFTED, I'M GOING TO RECLAIM THAT TITLE.
BUT BEST OF ALL, I HAVE A NEW FRIEND--THE LITTLE MAGIC USER, HIBIKI!
!

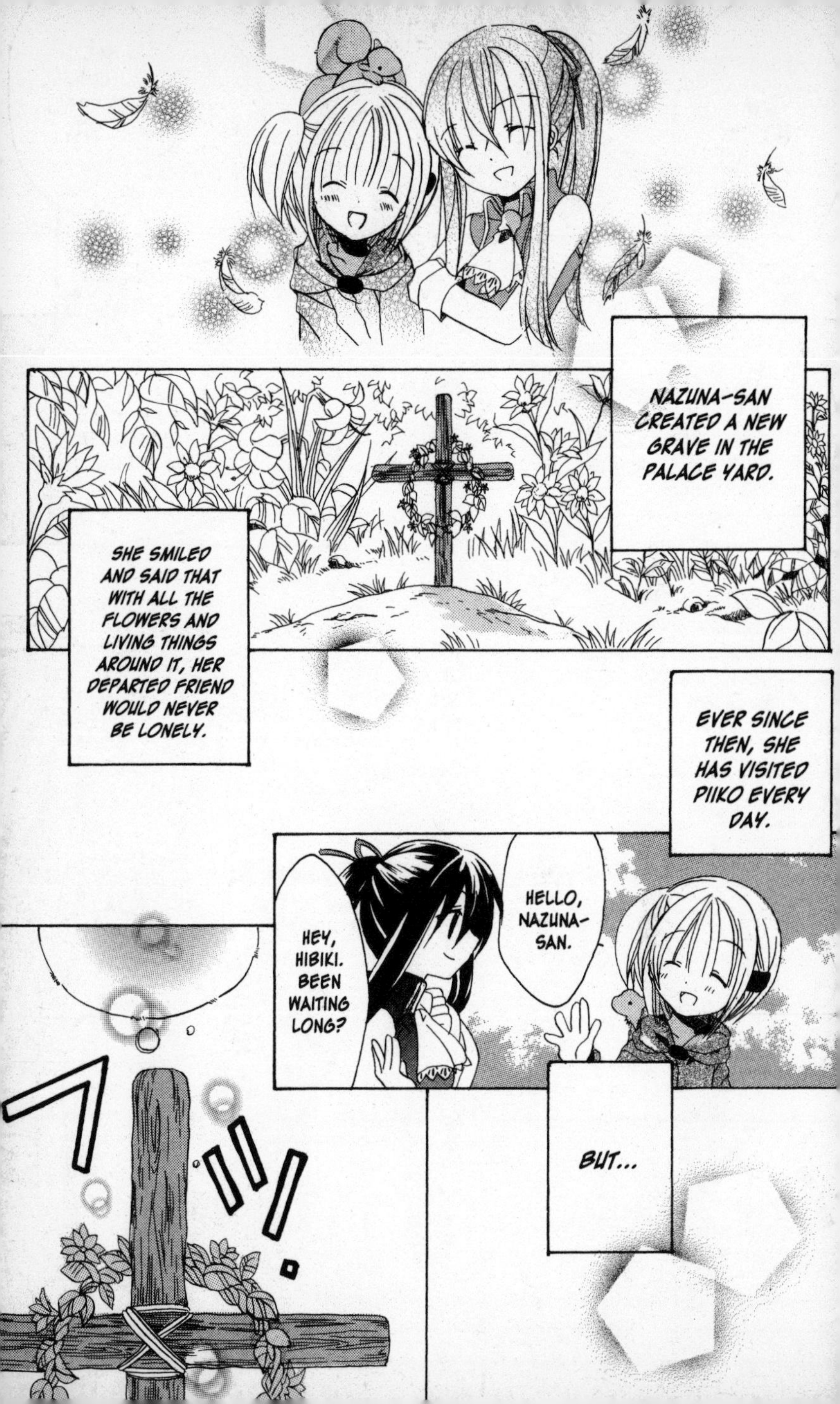
NAZUNA-SAN CREATED A NEW GRAVE IN THE PALACE YARD.
SHE SMILED AND SAID THAT WITH ALL THE FLOWERS AND LIVING THINGS AROUND IT, HER DEPARTED FRIEND WOULD NEVER BE LONELY.
EVER SINCE THEN, SHE HAS VISITED PIIKO EVERY DAY.
HELLO, NAZUNA-SAN.
HEY, HIBIKI. BEEN WAITING LONG?
BUT...

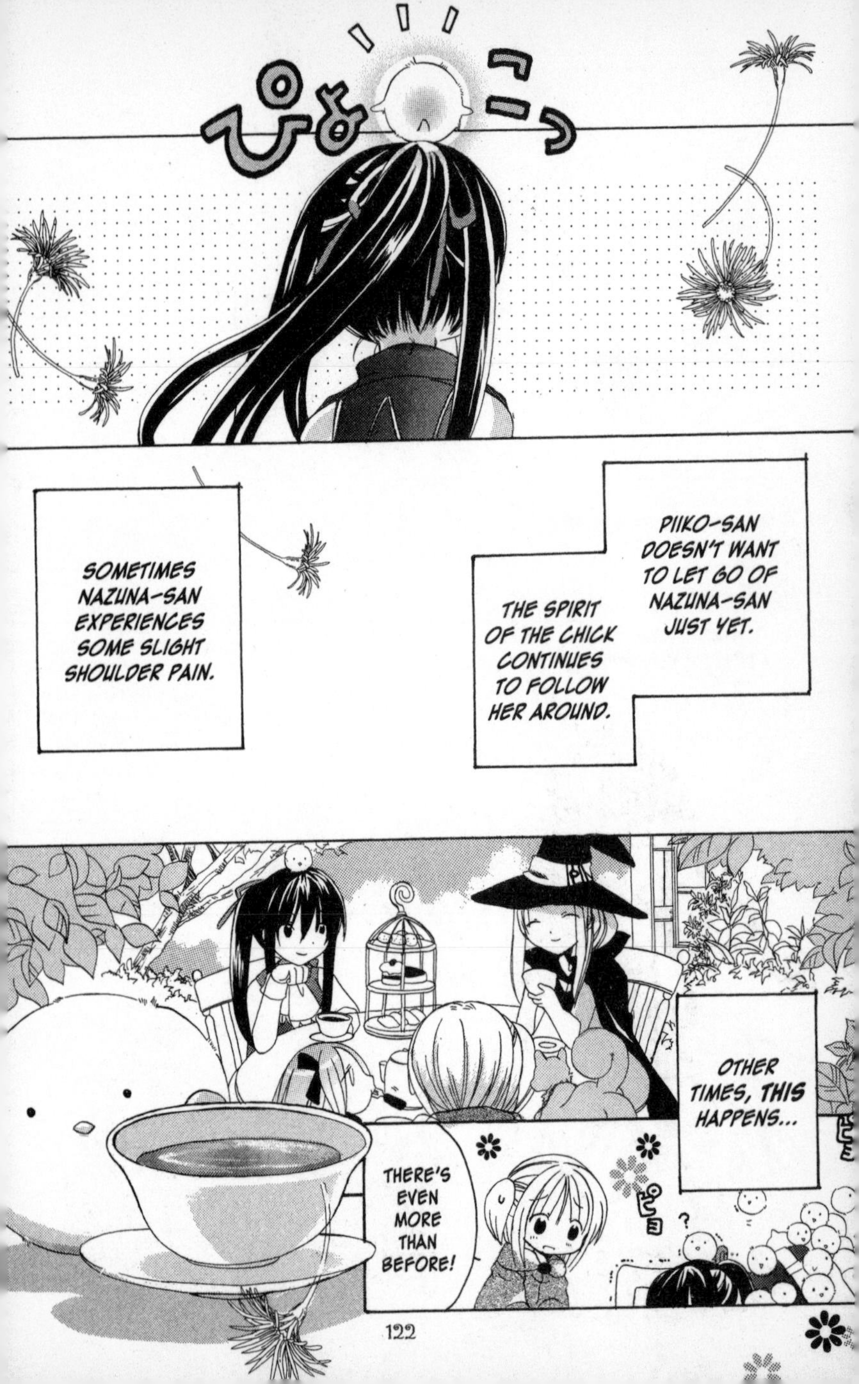
ぴよーっ
PIIKO-SAN DOESN'T WANT TO LET GO OF NAZUNA-SAN JUST YET.
THE SPIRIT OF THE CHICK CONTINUES TO FOLLOW HER AROUND.
SOMETIMES NAZUNA-SAN EXPERIENCES SOME SLIGHT SHOULDER PAIN.
OTHER TIMES, THIS HAPPENS...
THERE'S EVEN MORE THAN BEFORE!

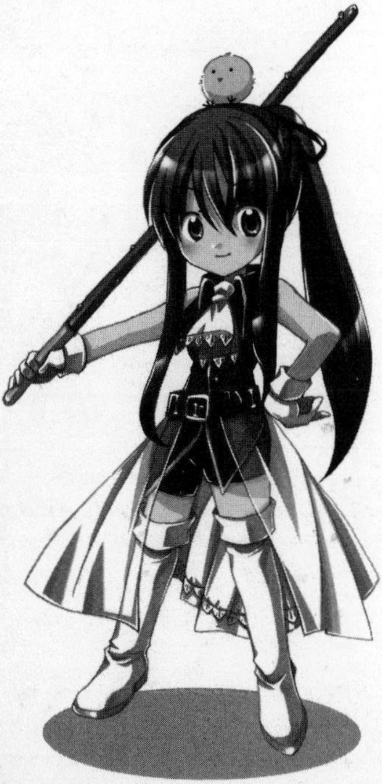

HIBIKI'S MAGIC™

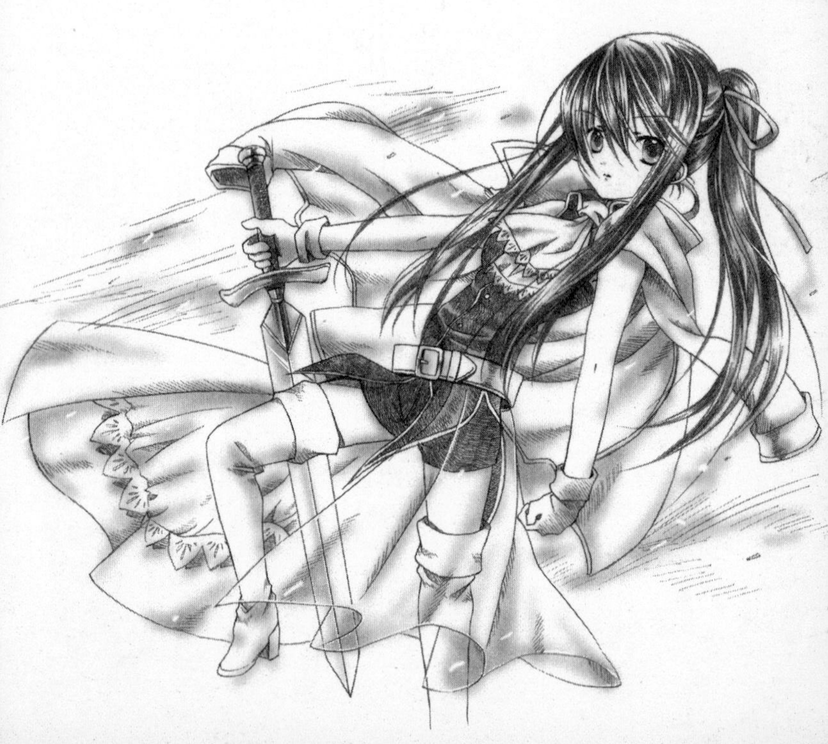

There's a legend about a demon who appears at this intersection.

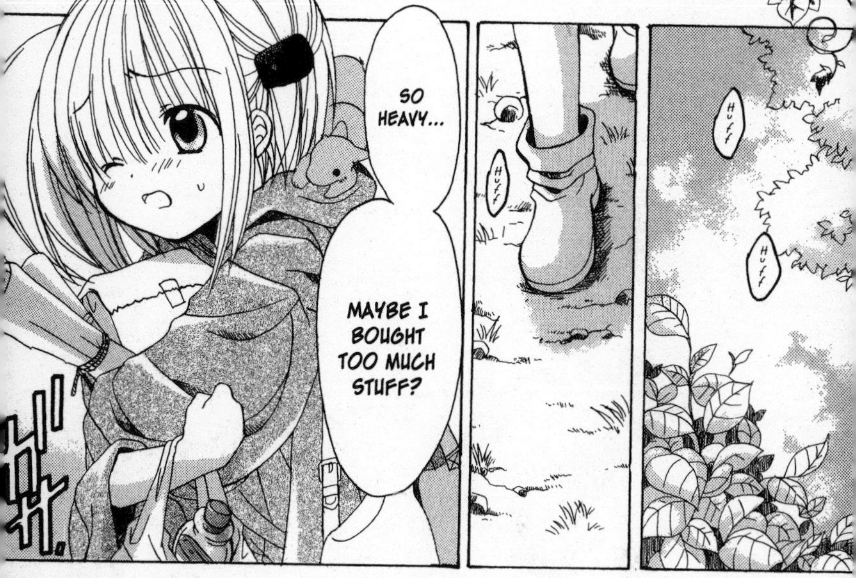
Huff
Huff
Huff
SO HEAVY...
MAYBE I BOUGHT TOO MUCH STUFF?

A demon who will grant you any wish in exchange for your soul.

✤Chapter 10✤

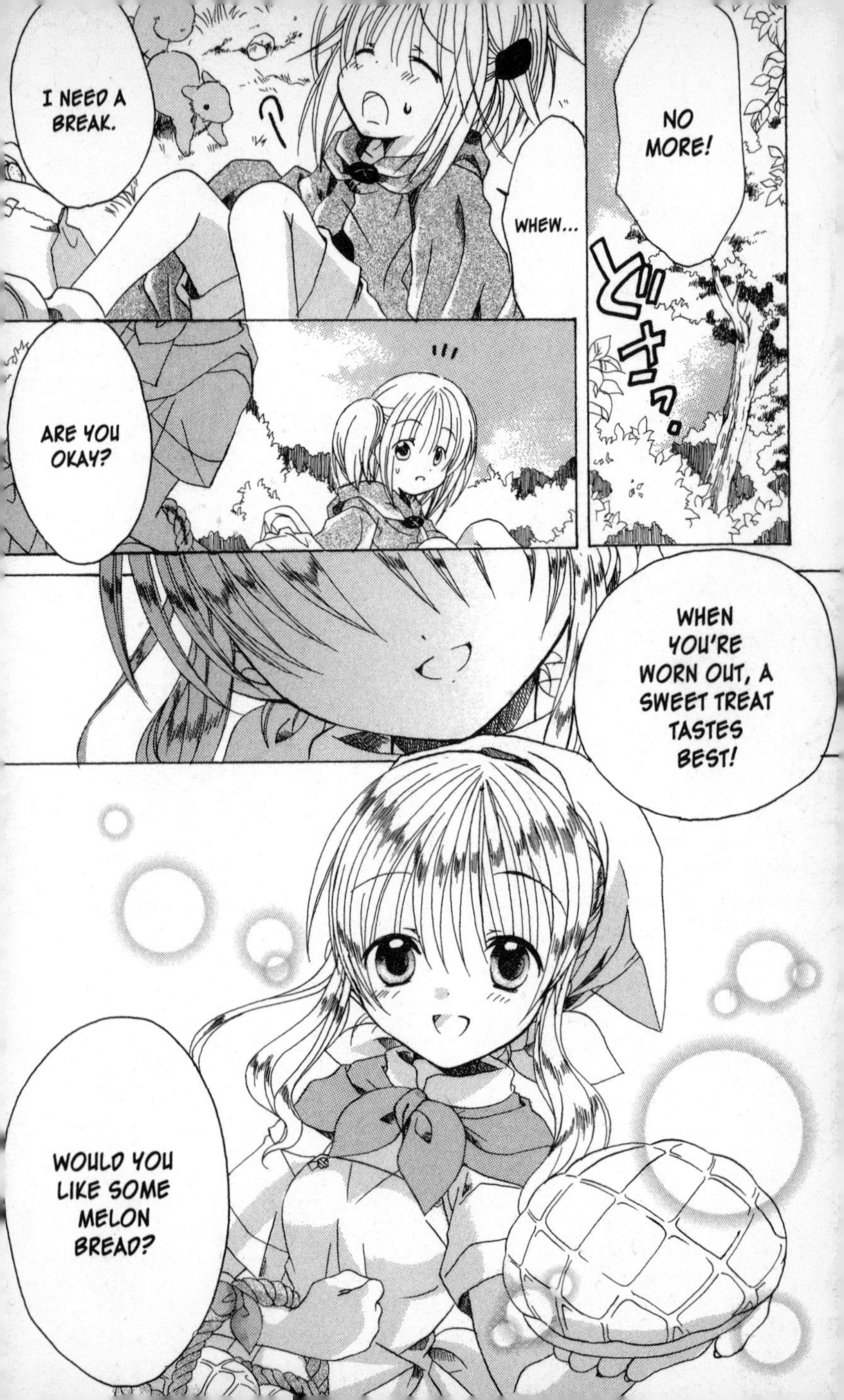
NO MORE!
どさっ
WHEW...
I NEED A BREAK.
ARE YOU OKAY?
WHEN YOU'RE WORN OUT, A SWEET TREAT TASTES BEST!
WOULD YOU LIKE SOME MELON BREAD?

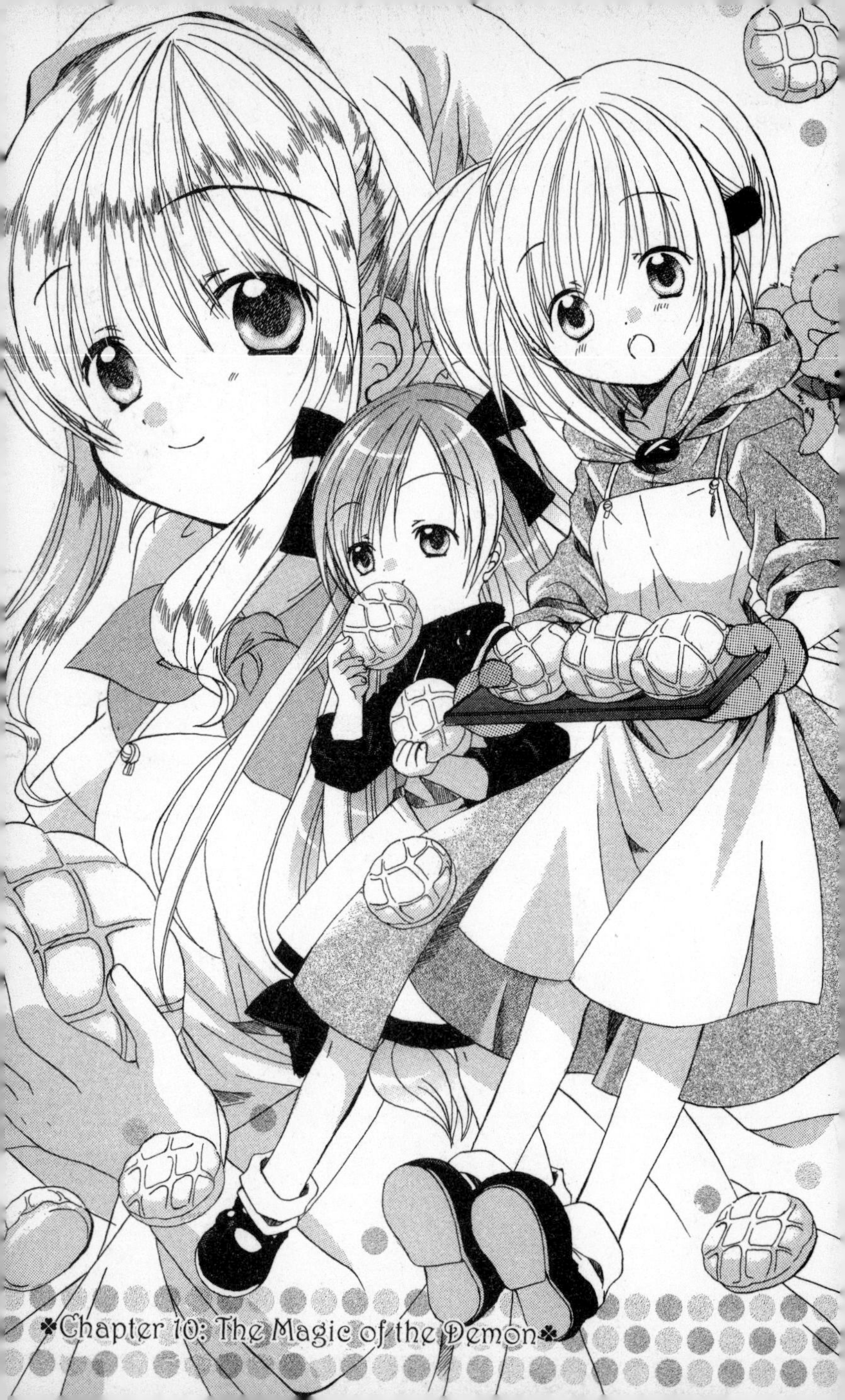
Chapter 10: The Magic of the Demon

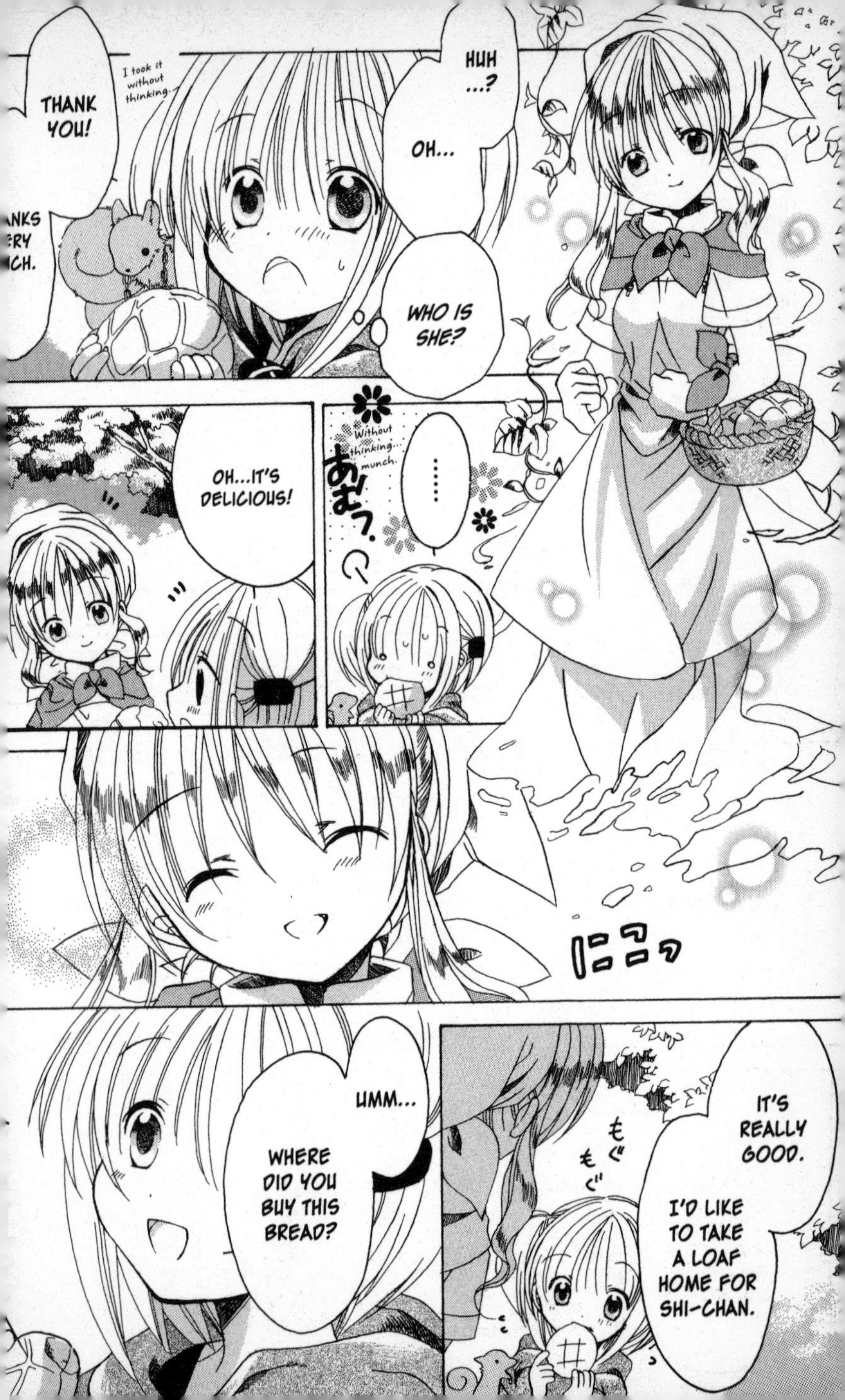
HUH ...?
OH...
WHO IS SHE?
I took it without thinking...
THANK YOU!
......
Without thinking... munch.
あむっ
OH...IT'S DELICIOUS!
にコっ
IT'S REALLY GOOD.
I'D LIKE TO TAKE A LOAF HOME FOR SHI-CHAN.
もぐ もぐ
UMM...
WHERE DID YOU BUY THIS BREAD?

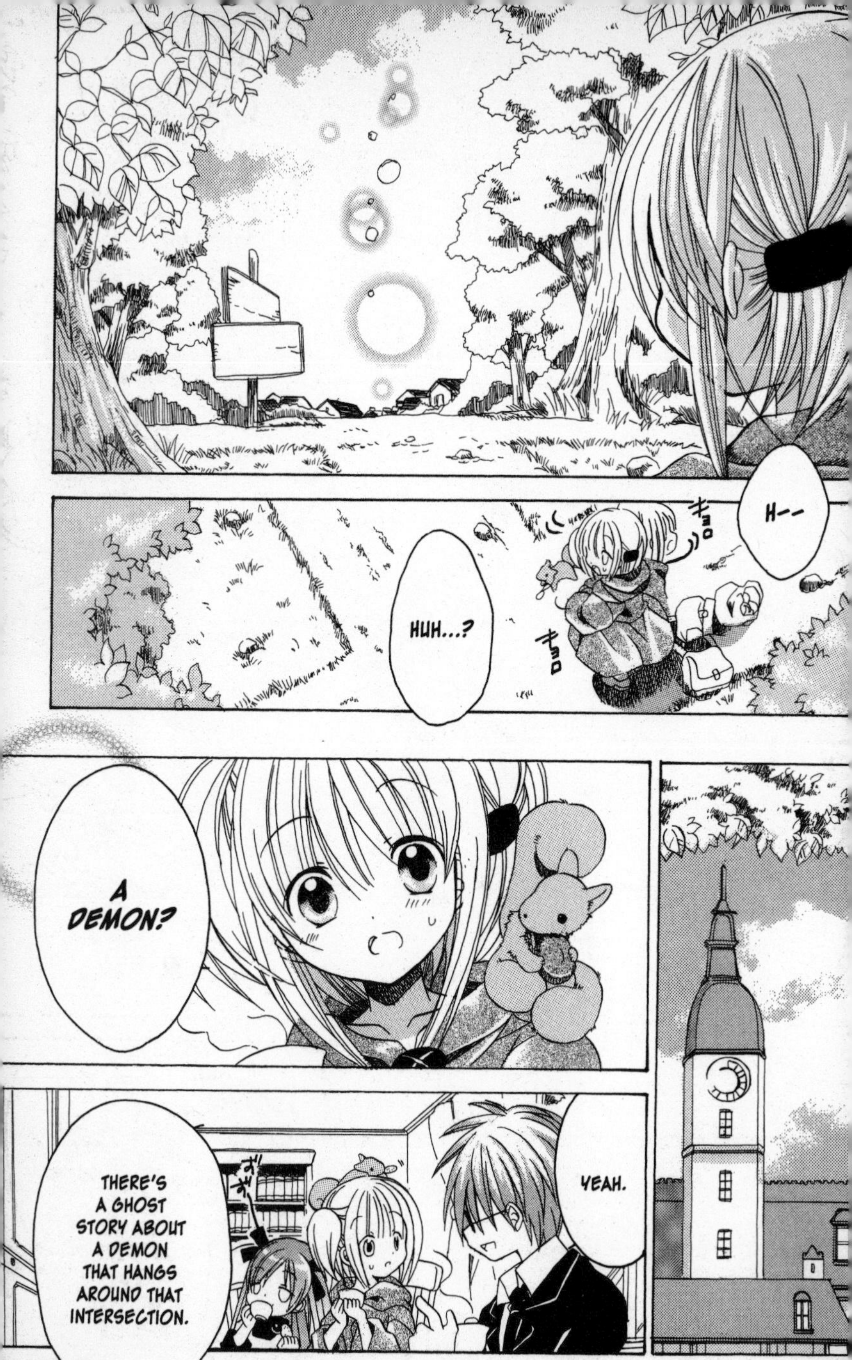
H--
キョロ
HUH...?
キョロ
A DEMON?
YEAH.
THERE'S A GHOST STORY ABOUT A DEMON THAT HANGS AROUND THAT INTERSECTION.

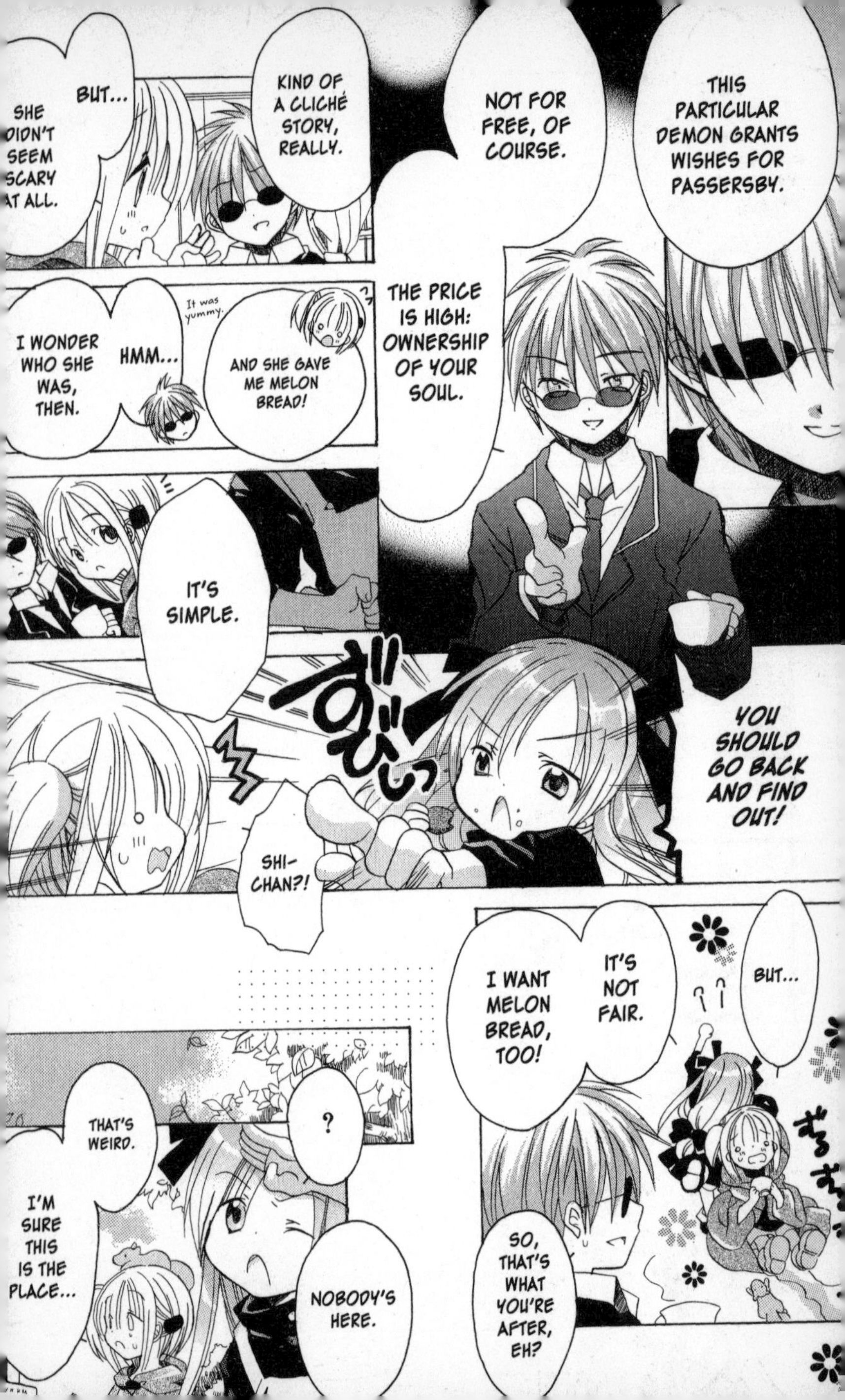
THIS PARTICULAR DEMON GRANTS WISHES FOR PASSERSBY.
NOT FOR FREE, OF COURSE.
THE PRICE IS HIGH: OWNERSHIP OF YOUR SOUL.
KIND OF A CLICHÉ STORY, REALLY.
BUT...
SHE DIDN'T SEEM SCARY AT ALL.
AND SHE GAVE ME MELON BREAD!
It was yummy.
HMM...
I WONDER WHO SHE WAS, THEN.
IT'S SIMPLE.
YOU SHOULD GO BACK AND FIND OUT!
ずびしっ
SHI-CHAN?!
BUT...
IT'S NOT FAIR.
I WANT MELON BREAD, TOO!
ずるずる
SO, THAT'S WHAT YOU'RE AFTER, EH?
?
THAT'S WEIRD.
I'M SURE THIS IS THE PLACE...
NOBODY'S HERE.

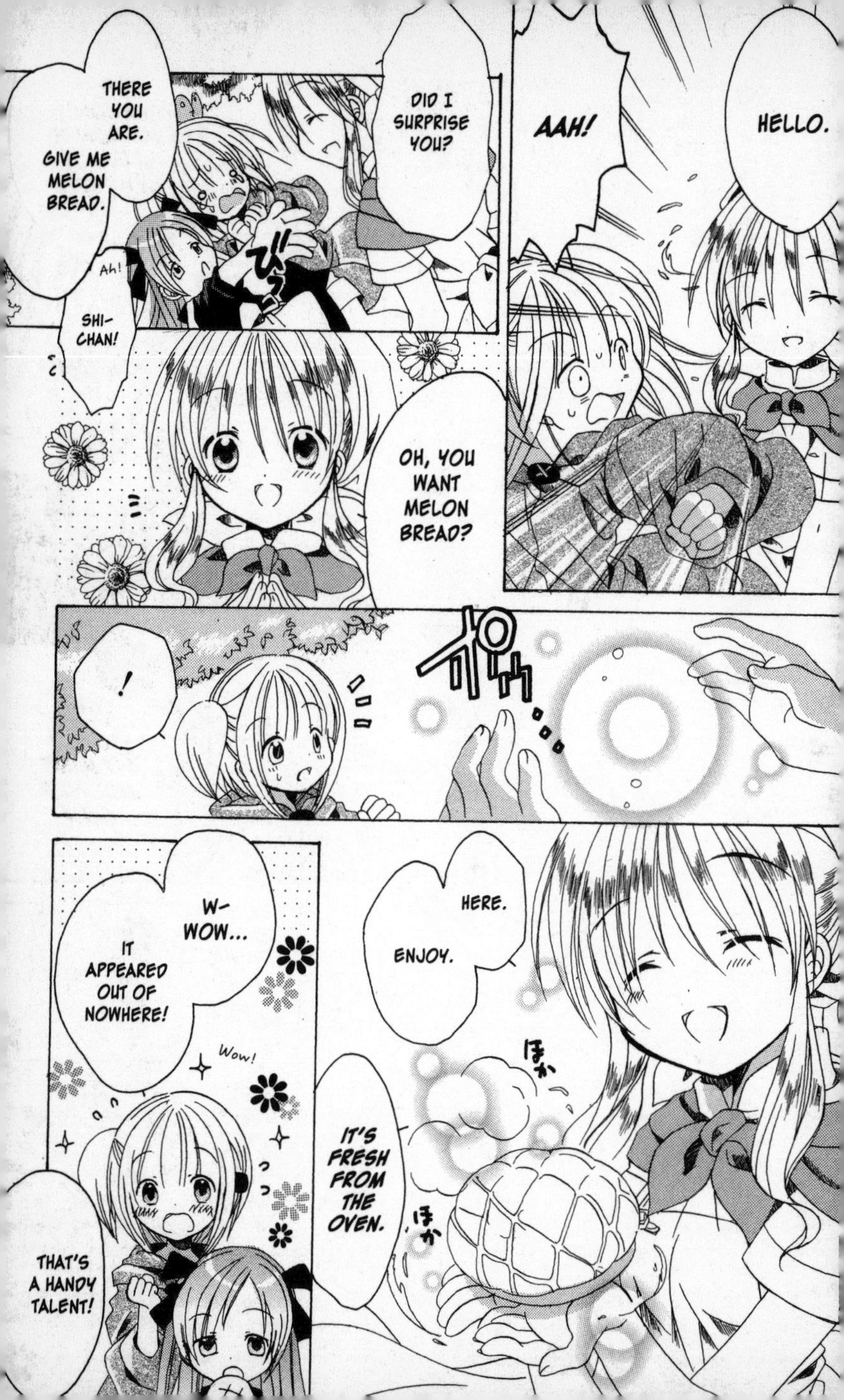
HELLO.
AAH!
DID I SURPRISE YOU?
THERE YOU ARE.
GIVE ME MELON BREAD.
Ah!
SHI-CHAN!
OH, YOU WANT MELON BREAD?
!
ポッ
HERE.
ENJOY.
IT'S FRESH FROM THE OVEN.
ほか
ほか
W-WOW...
IT APPEARED OUT OF NOWHERE!
Wow!
THAT'S A HANDY TALENT!

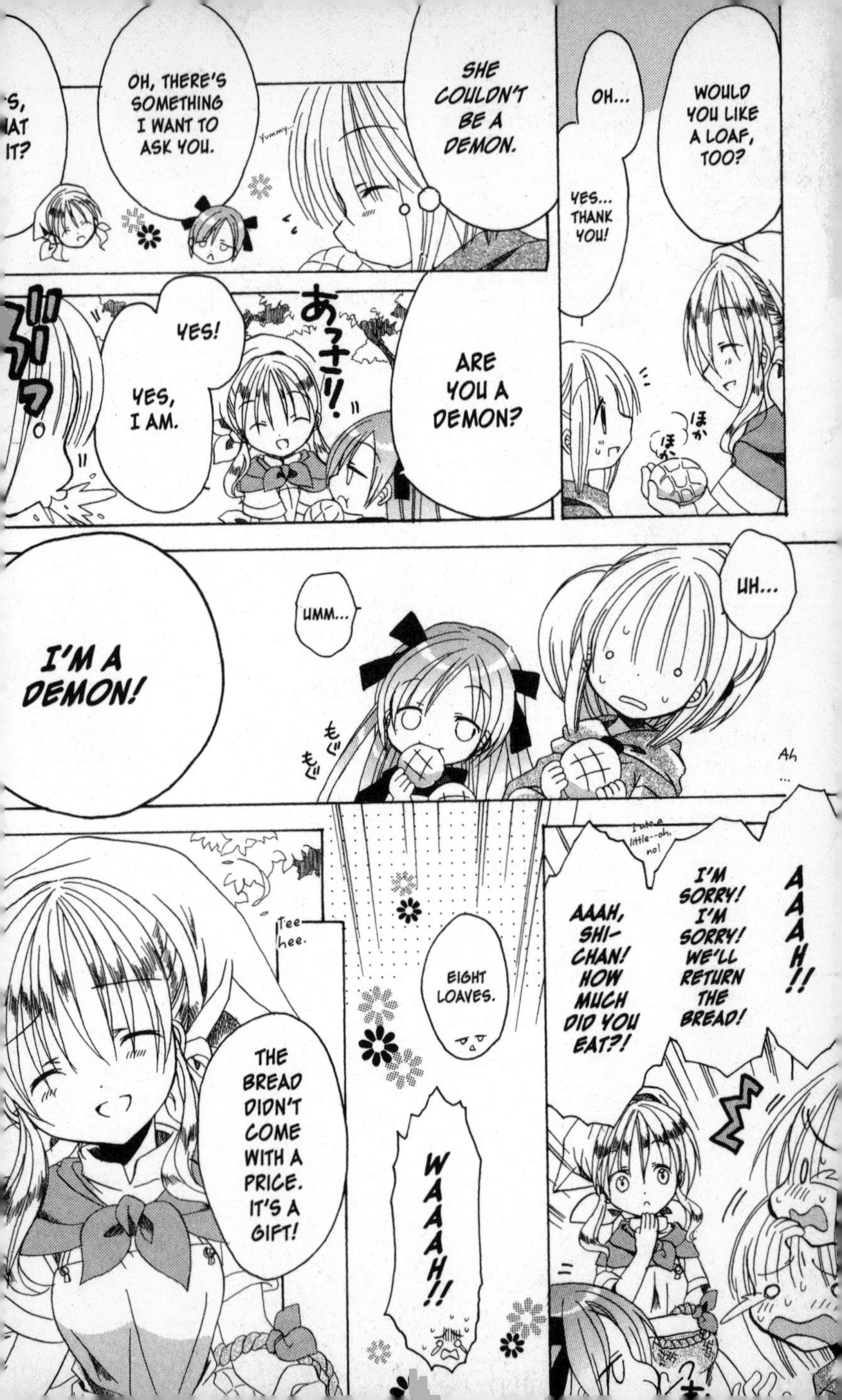

WOULD YOU LIKE A LOAF, TOO?
OH...
YES... THANK YOU!
ほかほか
SHE COULDN'T BE A DEMON.
Yummy...
OH, THERE'S SOMETHING I WANT TO ASK YOU.
ARE YOU A DEMON?
あっさり!
YES!
YES, I AM.
UH...
Ah...
UMM...
もぐもぐ
I'M A DEMON!
AAAAH!!
I'M SORRY! I'M SORRY! WE'LL RETURN THE BREAD!
AAAH, SHI-CHAN! HOW MUCH DID YOU EAT?!
I ate a little--oh, no!
EIGHT LOAVES.
WAAAAH!!
Tee hee.
THE BREAD DIDN'T COME WITH A PRICE. IT'S A GIFT!

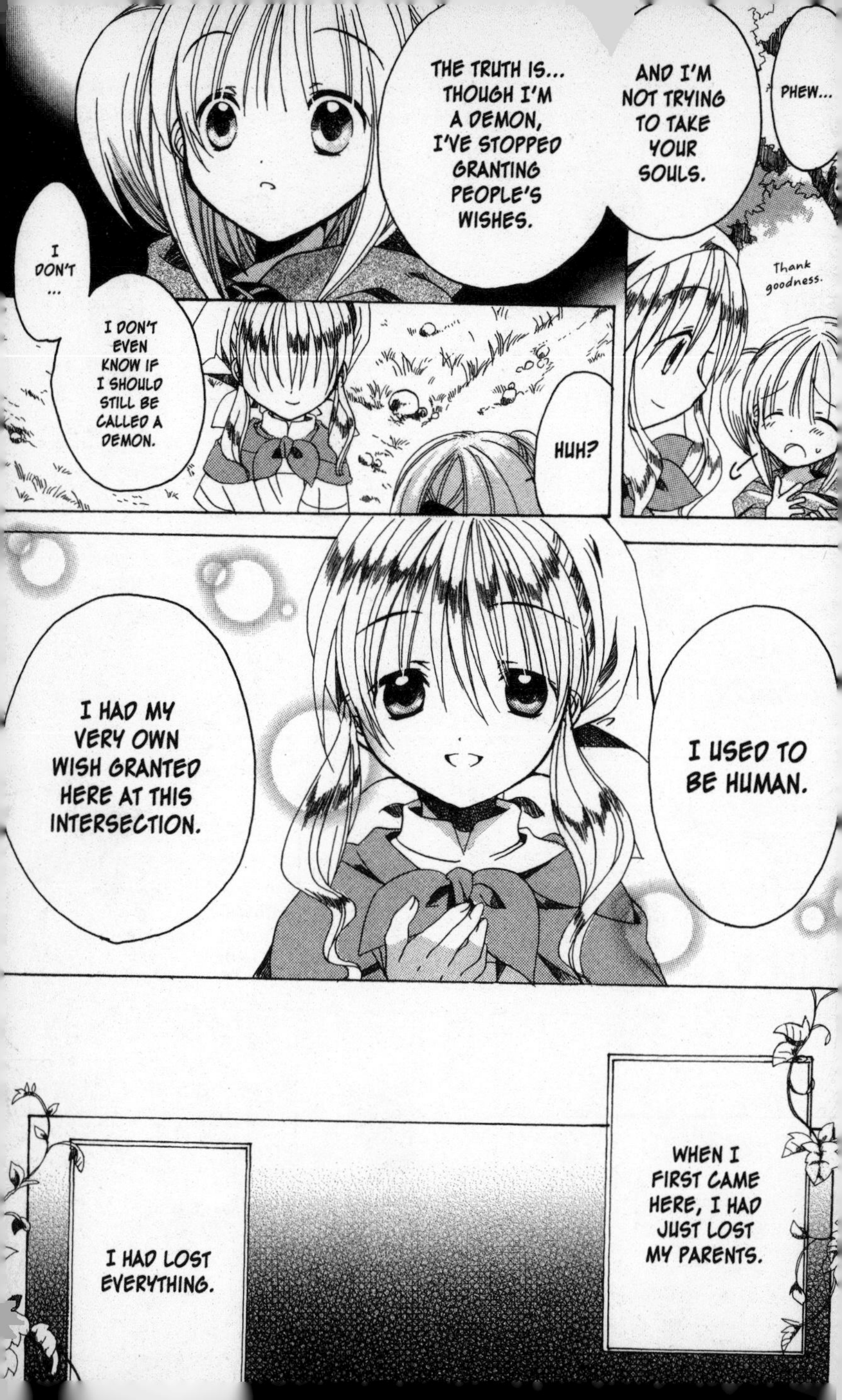
THE TRUTH IS... THOUGH I'M A DEMON, I'VE STOPPED GRANTING PEOPLE'S WISHES.
AND I'M NOT TRYING TO TAKE YOUR SOULS.
PHEW...
Thank goodness.
HUH?
I DON'T ...
I DON'T EVEN KNOW IF I SHOULD STILL BE CALLED A DEMON.
I USED TO BE HUMAN.
I HAD MY VERY OWN WISH GRANTED HERE AT THIS INTERSECTION.
WHEN I FIRST CAME HERE, I HAD JUST LOST MY PARENTS.
I HAD LOST EVERYTHING.

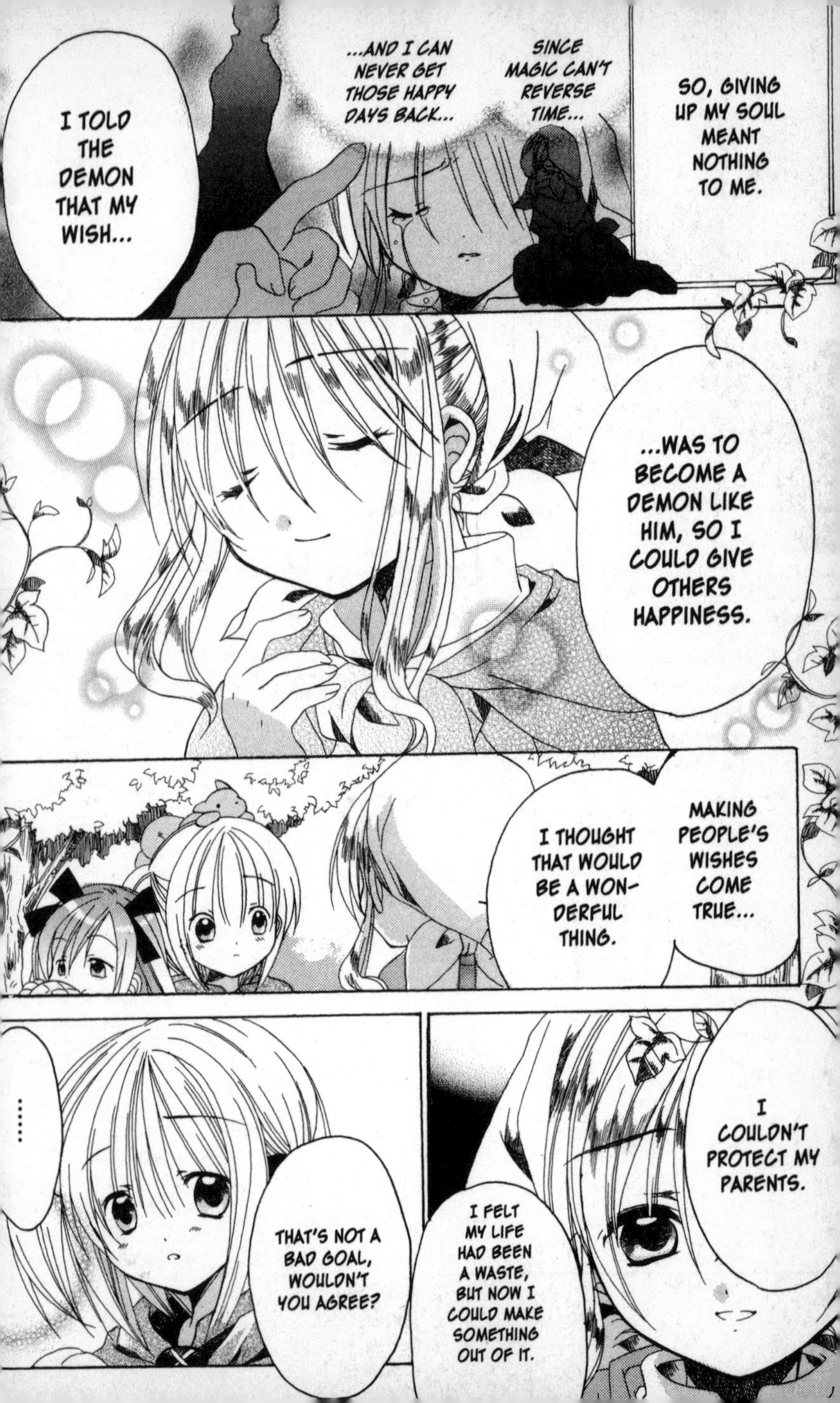
SO, GIVING UP MY SOUL MEANT NOTHING TO ME.
SINCE MAGIC CAN'T REVERSE TIME...
...AND I CAN NEVER GET THOSE HAPPY DAYS BACK...
I TOLD THE DEMON THAT MY WISH...
...WAS TO BECOME A DEMON LIKE HIM, SO I COULD GIVE OTHERS HAPPINESS.
MAKING PEOPLE'S WISHES COME TRUE...
I THOUGHT THAT WOULD BE A WON-DERFUL THING.
I COULDN'T PROTECT MY PARENTS.
I FELT MY LIFE HAD BEEN A WASTE, BUT NOW I COULD MAKE SOMETHING OUT OF IT.
THAT'S NOT A BAD GOAL, WOULDN'T YOU AGREE?
......

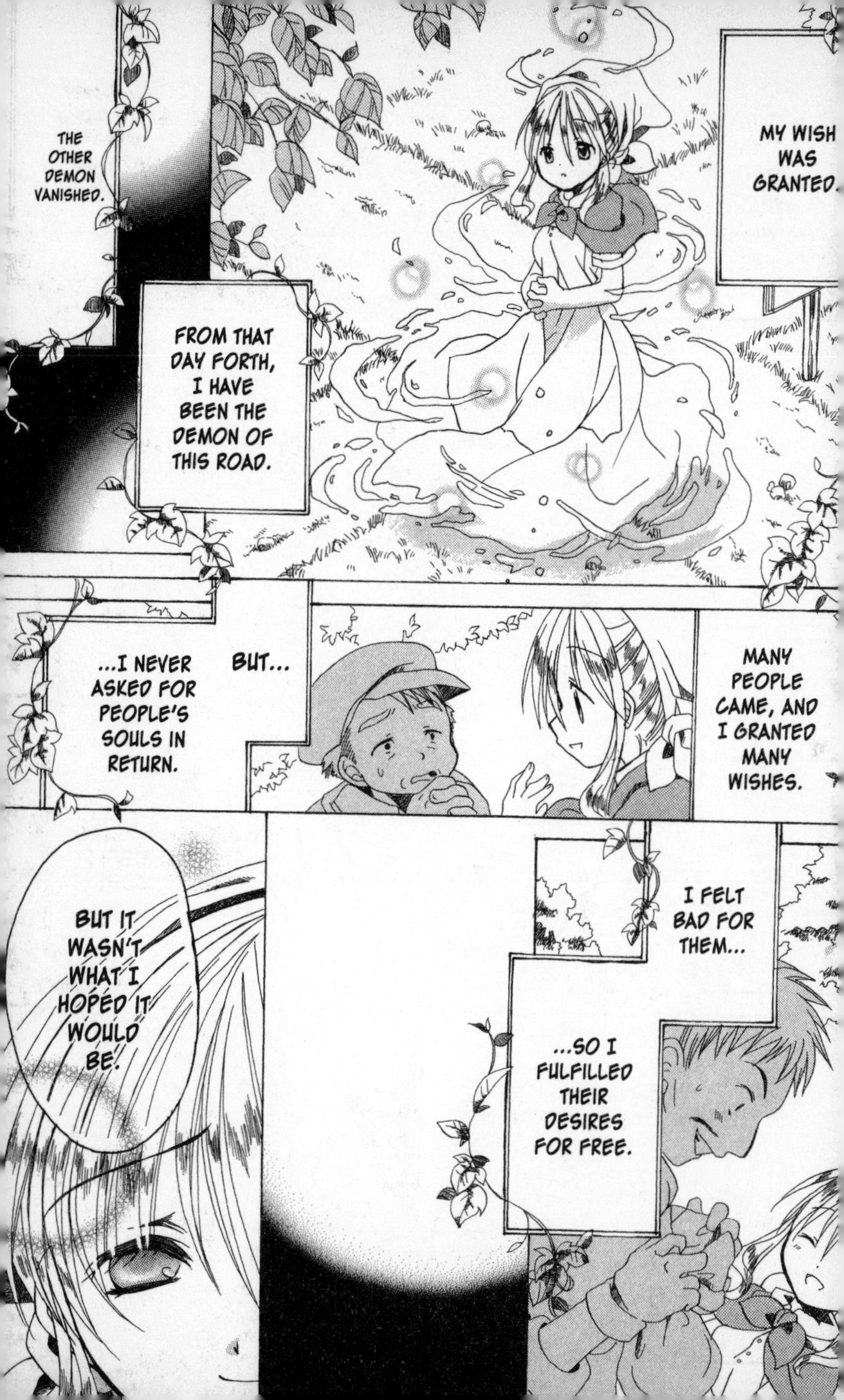

MY WISH WAS GRANTED.
FROM THAT DAY FORTH, I HAVE BEEN THE DEMON OF THIS ROAD.
THE OTHER DEMON VANISHED.
MANY PEOPLE CAME, AND I GRANTED MANY WISHES.
BUT...
...I NEVER ASKED FOR PEOPLE'S SOULS IN RETURN.
I FELT BAD FOR THEM...
...SO I FULFILLED THEIR DESIRES FOR FREE.
BUT IT WASN'T WHAT I HOPED IT WOULD BE.

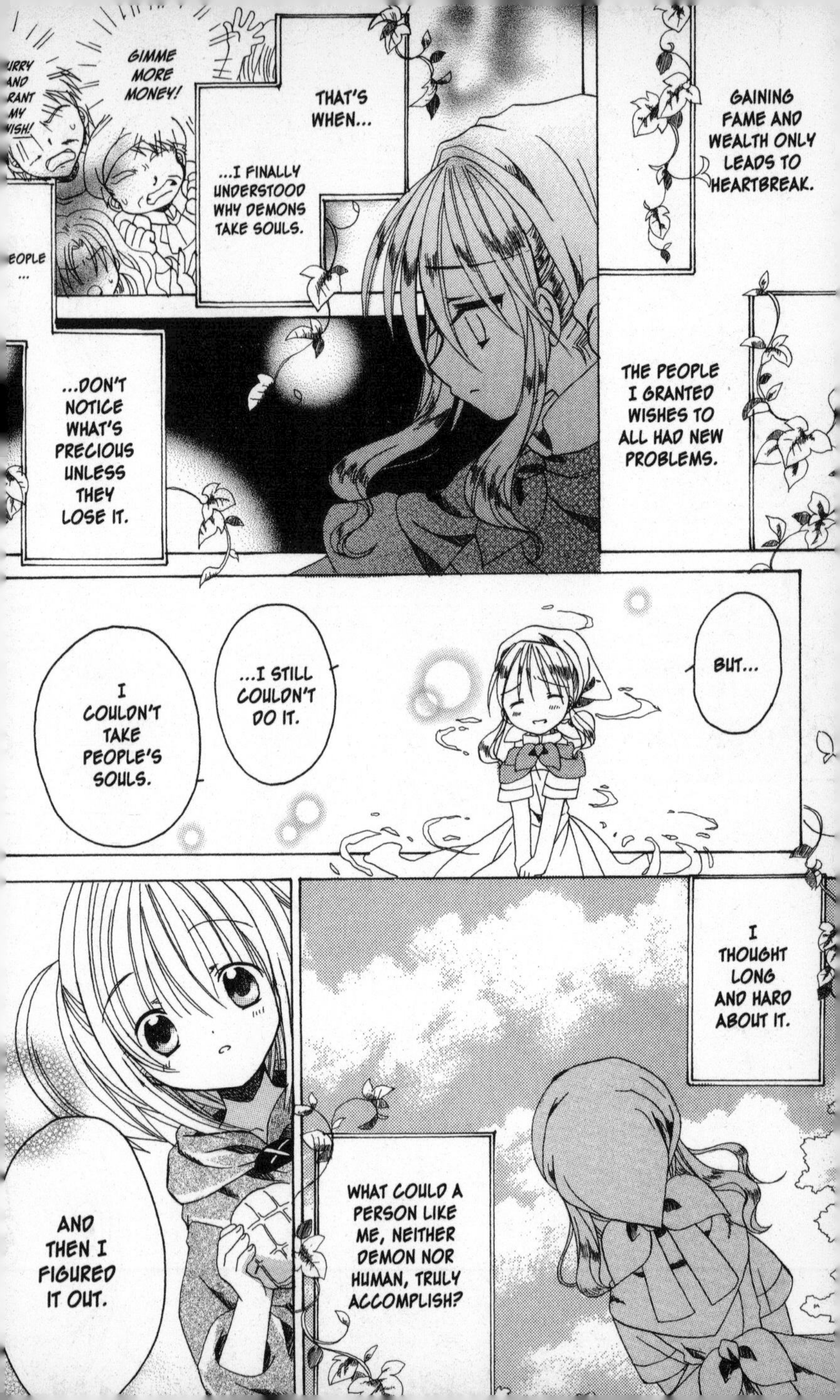
GAINING FAME AND WEALTH ONLY LEADS TO HEARTBREAK.
THE PEOPLE I GRANTED WISHES TO ALL HAD NEW PROBLEMS.
GIMME MORE MONEY!
URRY AND RANT MY WISH!
EOPLE ...
...DON'T NOTICE WHAT'S PRECIOUS UNLESS THEY LOSE IT.
THAT'S WHEN...
...I FINALLY UNDERSTOOD WHY DEMONS TAKE SOULS.
BUT...
...I STILL COULDN'T DO IT.
I COULDN'T TAKE PEOPLE'S SOULS.
I THOUGHT LONG AND HARD ABOUT IT.
WHAT COULD A PERSON LIKE ME, NEITHER DEMON NOR HUMAN, TRULY ACCOMPLISH?
AND THEN I FIGURED IT OUT.

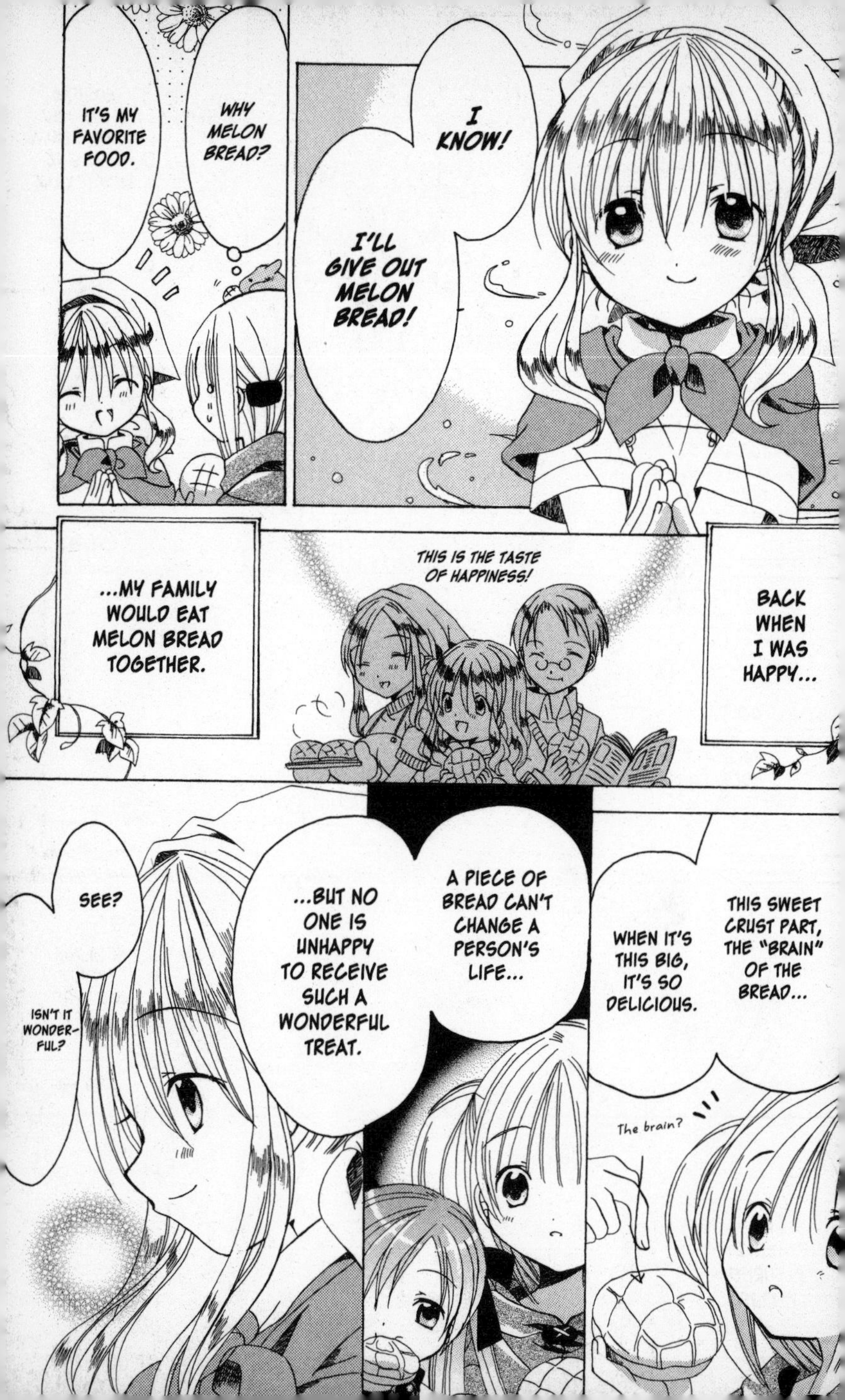

I KNOW!
I'LL GIVE OUT MELON BREAD!
WHY MELON BREAD?
IT'S MY FAVORITE FOOD.
BACK WHEN I WAS HAPPY...
THIS IS THE TASTE OF HAPPINESS!
...MY FAMILY WOULD EAT MELON BREAD TOGETHER.
THIS SWEET CRUST PART, THE "BRAIN" OF THE BREAD...
WHEN IT'S THIS BIG, IT'S SO DELICIOUS.
The brain?
A PIECE OF BREAD CAN'T CHANGE A PERSON'S LIFE...
...BUT NO ONE IS UNHAPPY TO RECEIVE SUCH A WONDERFUL TREAT.
SEE?
ISN'T IT WONDER-FUL?

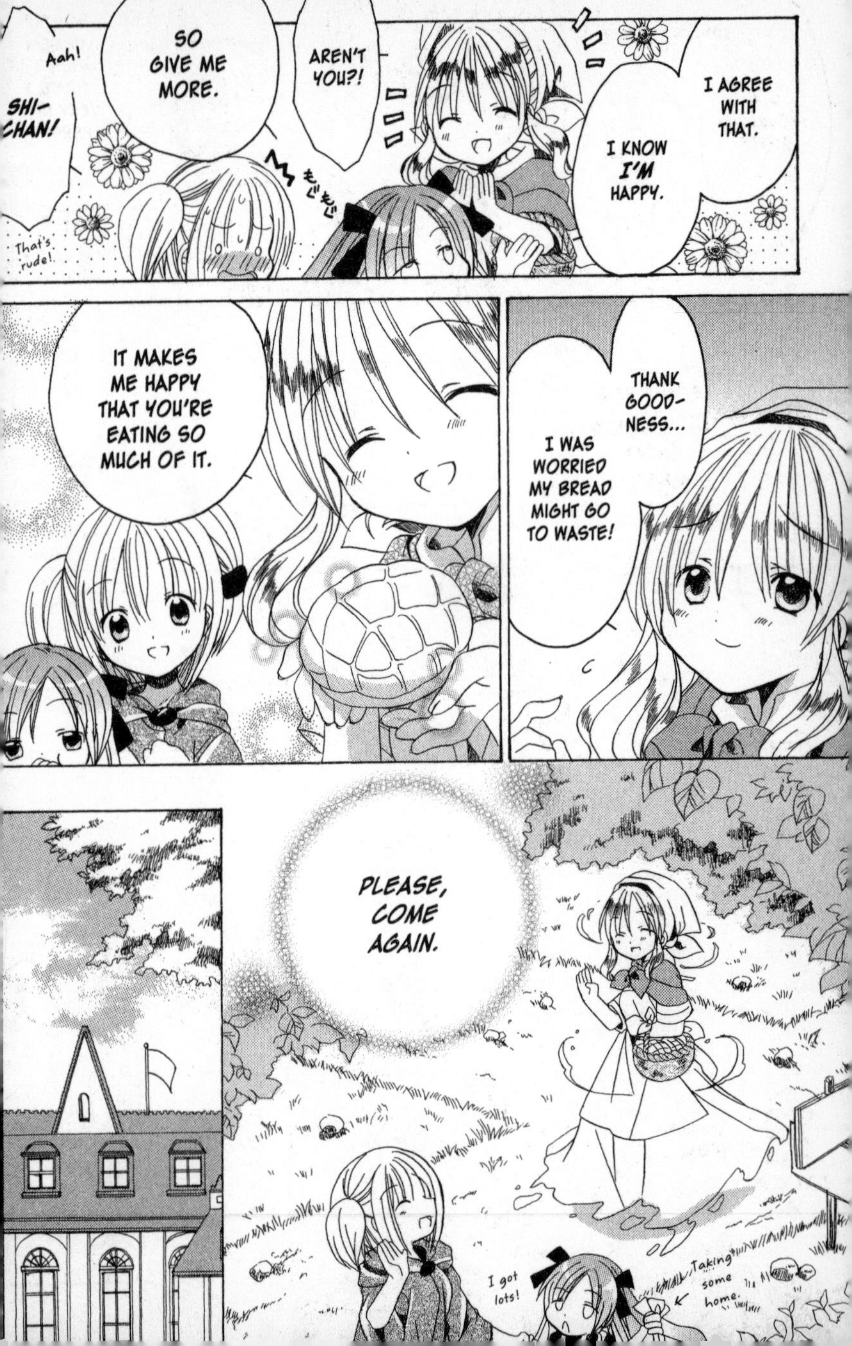
I AGREE WITH THAT.
I KNOW I'M HAPPY.
AREN'T YOU?!
SO GIVE ME MORE.
もぐもぐ
Aah!
SHI-CHAN!
That's rude!
THANK GOODNESS...
I WAS WORRIED MY BREAD MIGHT GO TO WASTE!
IT MAKES ME HAPPY THAT YOU'RE EATING SO MUCH OF IT.
PLEASE, COME AGAIN.
Taking some home.
I got lots!

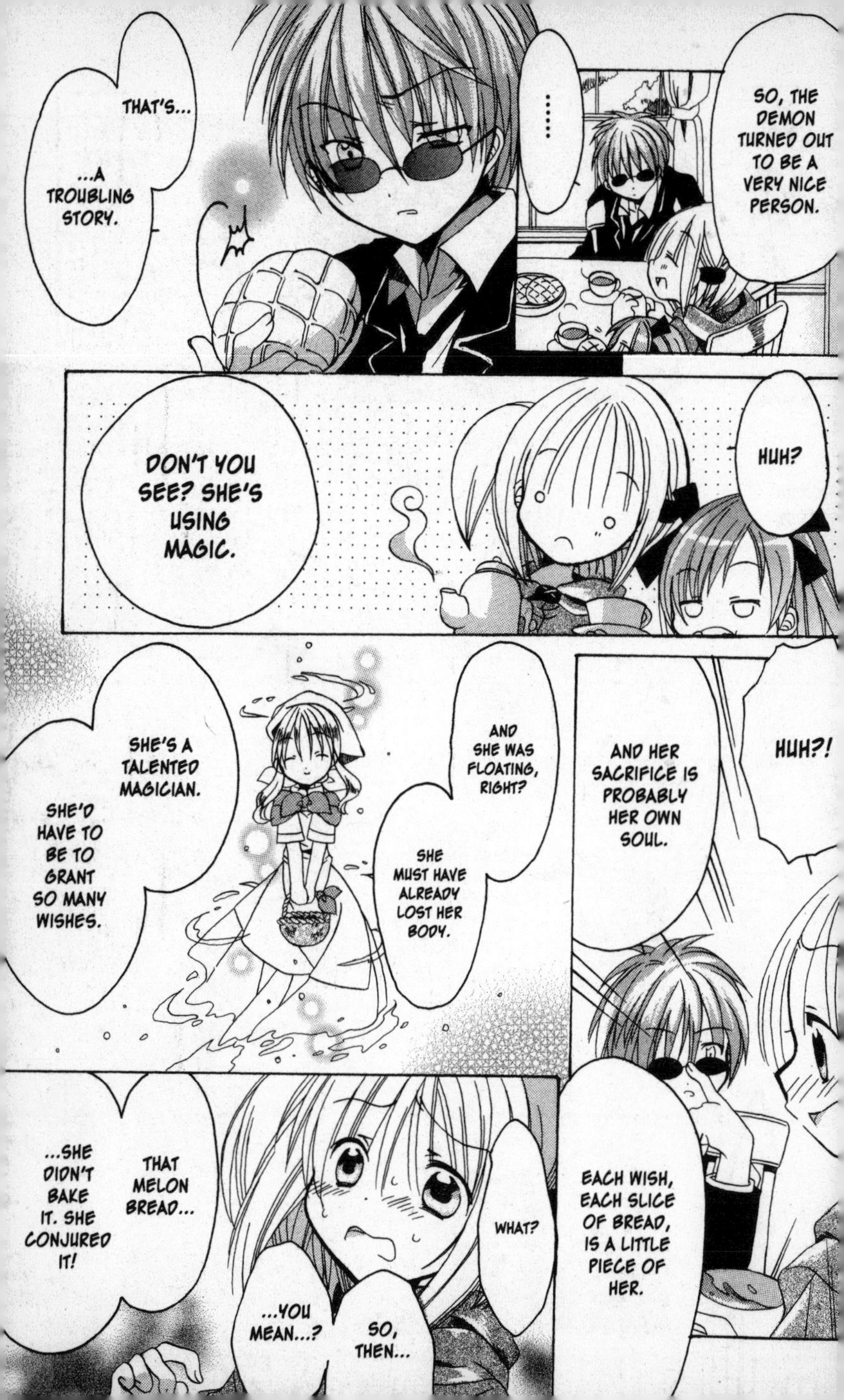
SO, THE DEMON TURNED OUT TO BE A VERY NICE PERSON.
......
THAT'S...
...A TROUBLING STORY.
HUH?
DON'T YOU SEE? SHE'S USING MAGIC.
HUH?!
AND HER SACRIFICE IS PROBABLY HER OWN SOUL.
EACH WISH, EACH SLICE OF BREAD, IS A LITTLE PIECE OF HER.
AND SHE WAS FLOATING, RIGHT?
SHE MUST HAVE ALREADY LOST HER BODY.
SHE'S A TALENTED MAGICIAN.
SHE'D HAVE TO BE TO GRANT SO MANY WISHES.
WHAT?
SO, THEN...
...YOU MEAN...?
THAT MELON BREAD...
...SHE DIDN'T BAKE IT. SHE CONJURED IT!

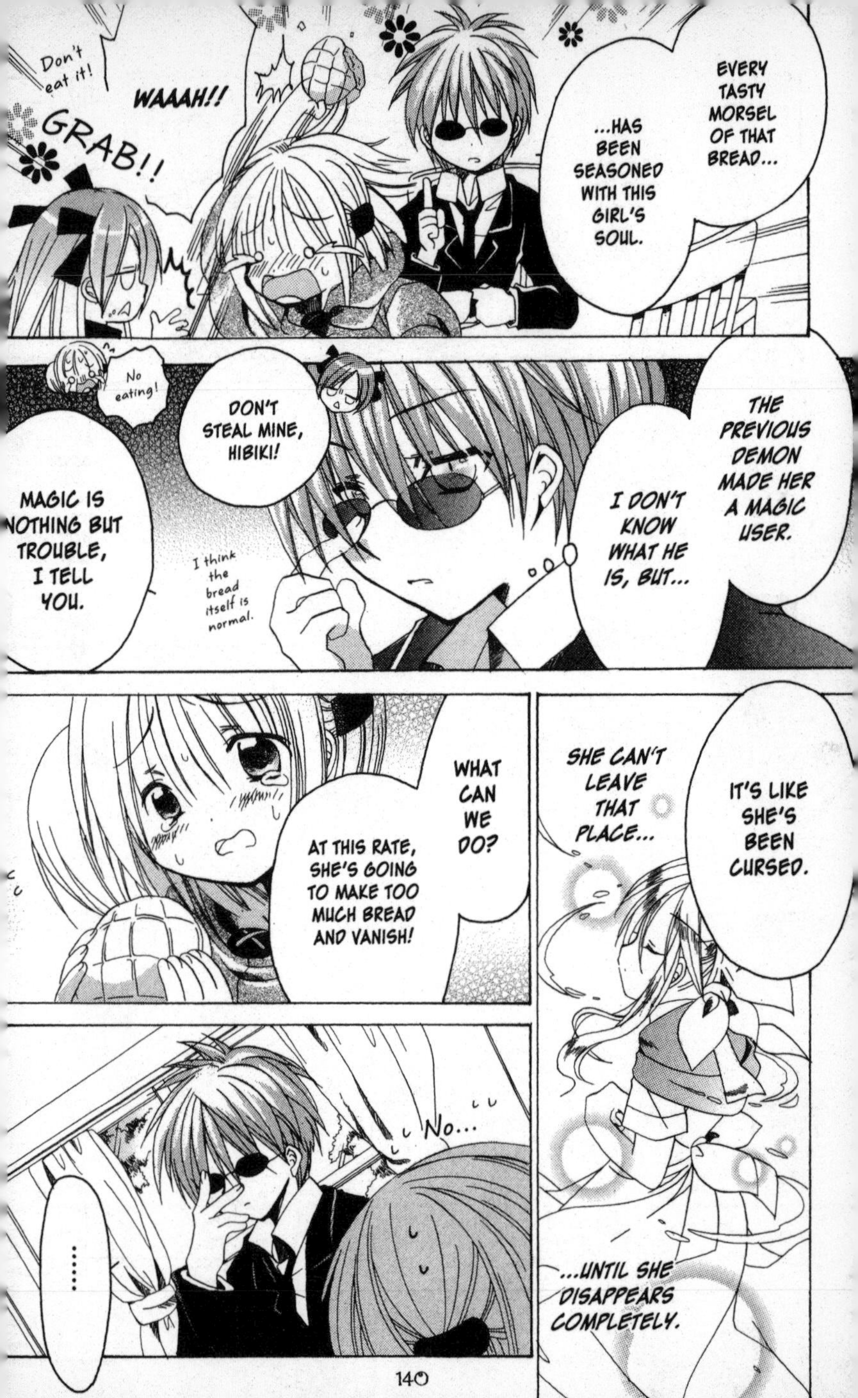
EVERY TASTY MORSEL OF THAT BREAD...
...HAS BEEN SEASONED WITH THIS GIRL'S SOUL.
WAAAH!!
Don't eat it!
GRAB!!
THE PREVIOUS DEMON MADE HER A MAGIC USER.
I DON'T KNOW WHAT HE IS, BUT...
DON'T STEAL MINE, HIBIKI!
No eating!
MAGIC IS NOTHING BUT TROUBLE, I TELL YOU.
I think the bread itself is normal.
IT'S LIKE SHE'S BEEN CURSED.
SHE CAN'T LEAVE THAT PLACE...
...UNTIL SHE DISAPPEARS COMPLETELY.
WHAT CAN WE DO?
AT THIS RATE, SHE'S GOING TO MAKE TOO MUCH BREAD AND VANISH!
No...
......

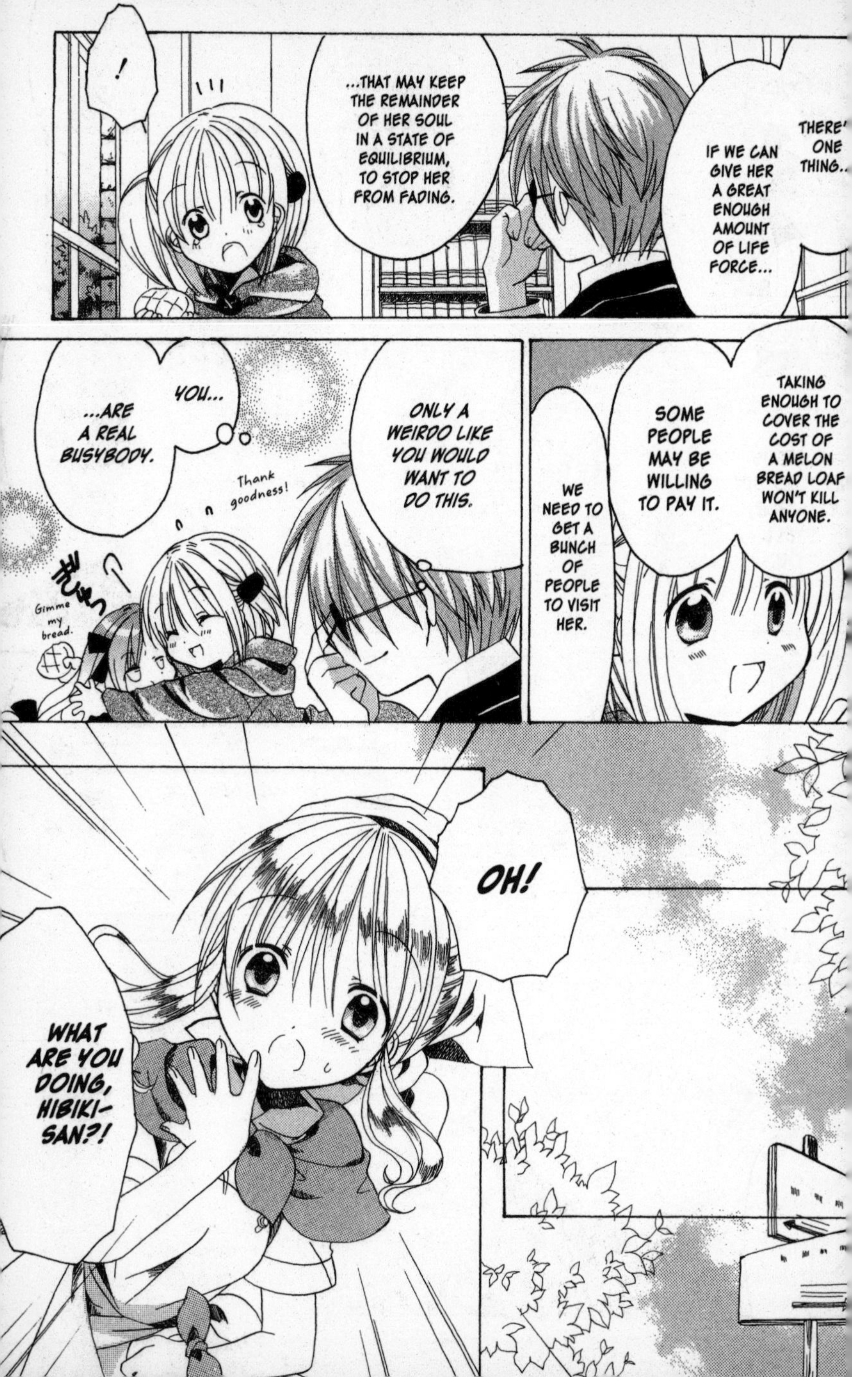
THERE' ONE THING..
IF WE CAN GIVE HER A GREAT ENOUGH AMOUNT OF LIFE FORCE...
...THAT MAY KEEP THE REMAINDER OF HER SOUL IN A STATE OF EQUILIBRIUM, TO STOP HER FROM FADING.
!
TAKING ENOUGH TO COVER THE COST OF A MELON BREAD LOAF WON'T KILL ANYONE.
SOME PEOPLE MAY BE WILLING TO PAY IT.
WE NEED TO GET A BUNCH OF PEOPLE TO VISIT HER.
ONLY A WEIRDO LIKE YOU WOULD WANT TO DO THIS.
YOU...
...ARE A REAL BUSYBODY.
Thank goodness!
Gimme my bread.
OH!
WHAT ARE YOU DOING, HIBIKI-SAN?!

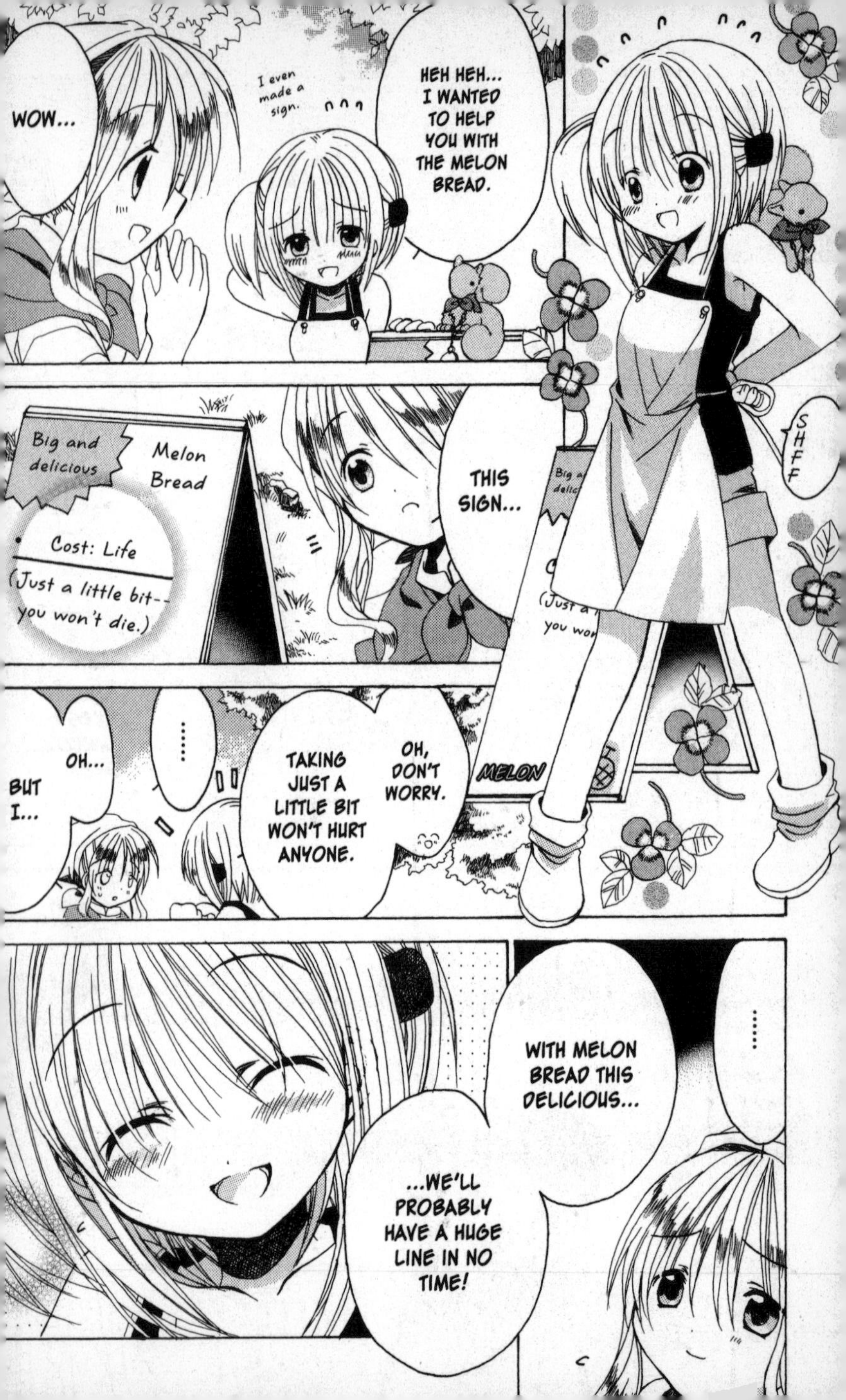
SHFF
MELON
HEH HEH... I WANTED TO HELP YOU WITH THE MELON BREAD.
I even made a sign.
WOW...
THIS SIGN...
Big and delicious
Melon Bread
Cost: Life
(Just a little bit--you won't die.)
OH, DON'T WORRY.
TAKING JUST A LITTLE BIT WON'T HURT ANYONE.
......
OH...
BUT I...
......
WITH MELON BREAD THIS DELICIOUS...
...WE'LL PROBABLY HAVE A HUGE LINE IN NO TIME!

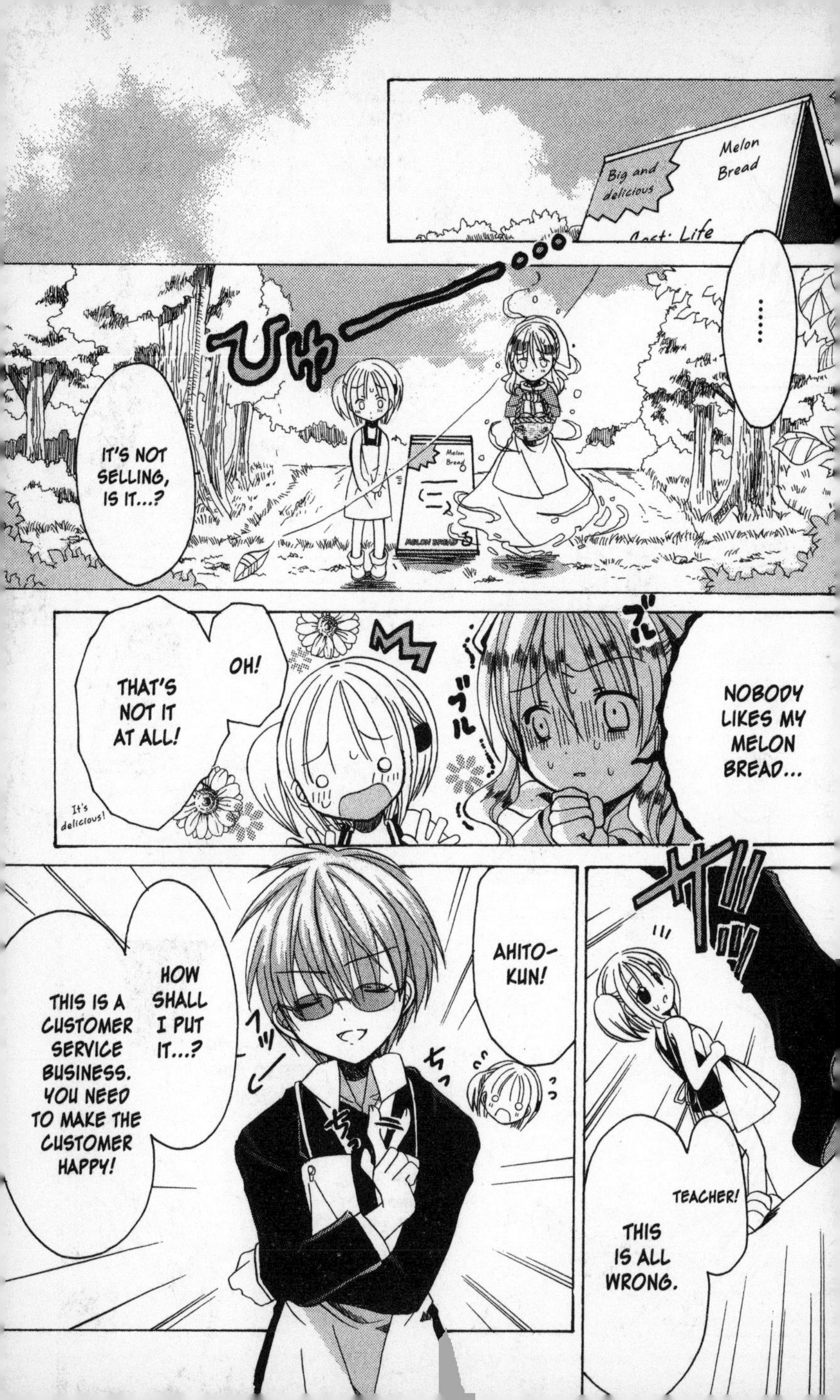
Melon Bread
Big and delicious
Cost: Life
......
ひゅー
IT'S NOT SELLING, IS IT...?
Melon Bread
MELON BREAD
NOBODY LIKES MY MELON BREAD...
ブル
ブル
OH!
THAT'S NOT IT AT ALL!
It's delicious!
TEACHER!
THIS IS ALL WRONG.
AHITO-KUN!
HOW SHALL I PUT IT...?
THIS IS A CUSTOMER SERVICE BUSINESS. YOU NEED TO MAKE THE CUSTOMER HAPPY!

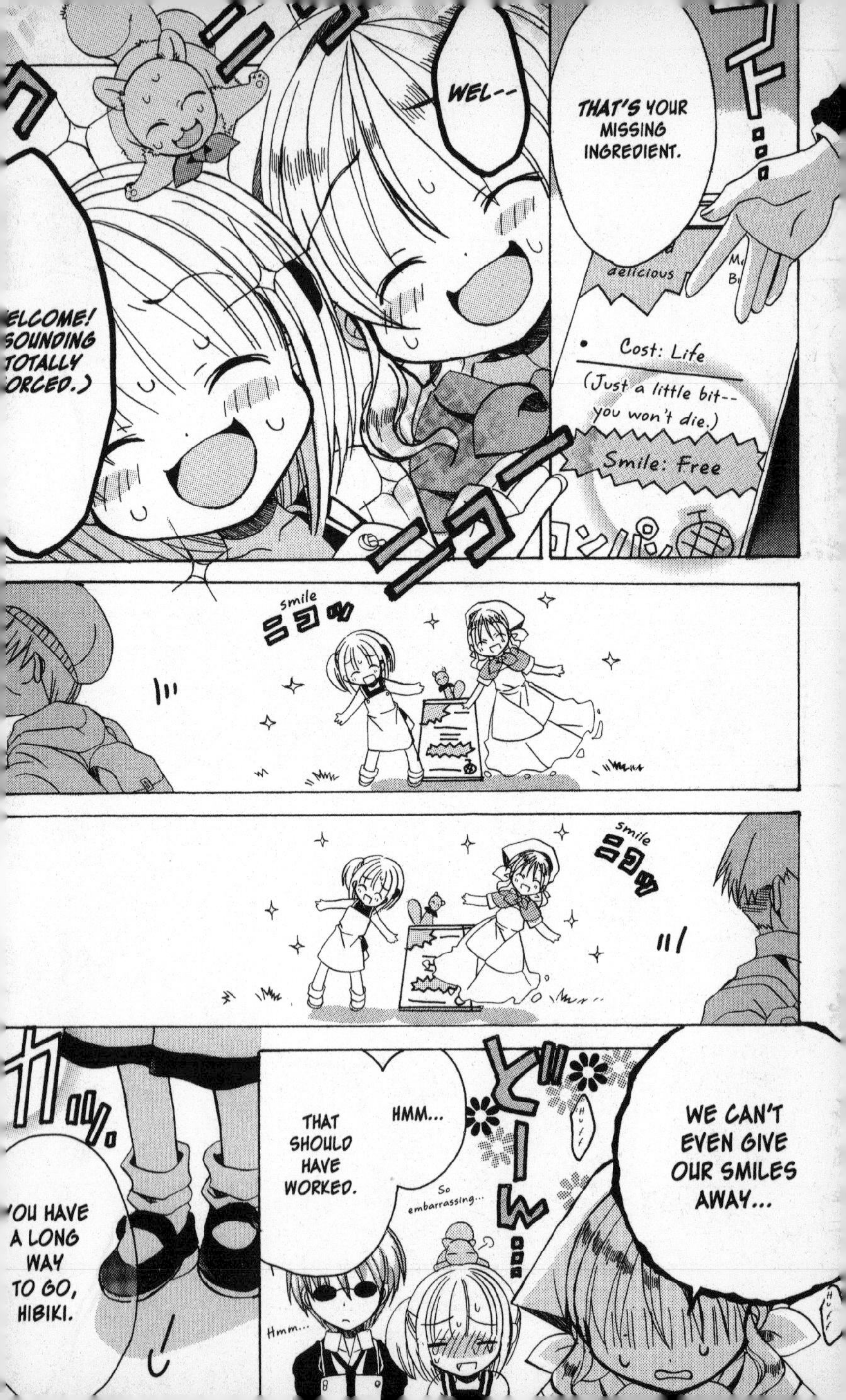
THAT'S YOUR MISSING INGREDIENT.
delicious
Cost: Life
(Just a little bit-- you won't die.)
Smile: Free
WEL--
ELCOME! SOUNDING TOTALLY ORCED.)
smile
smile
WE CAN'T EVEN GIVE OUR SMILES AWAY...
Huff
Huff
HMM...
THAT SHOULD HAVE WORKED.
So embarrassing...
Hmm...
OU HAVE A LONG WAY TO GO, HIBIKI.

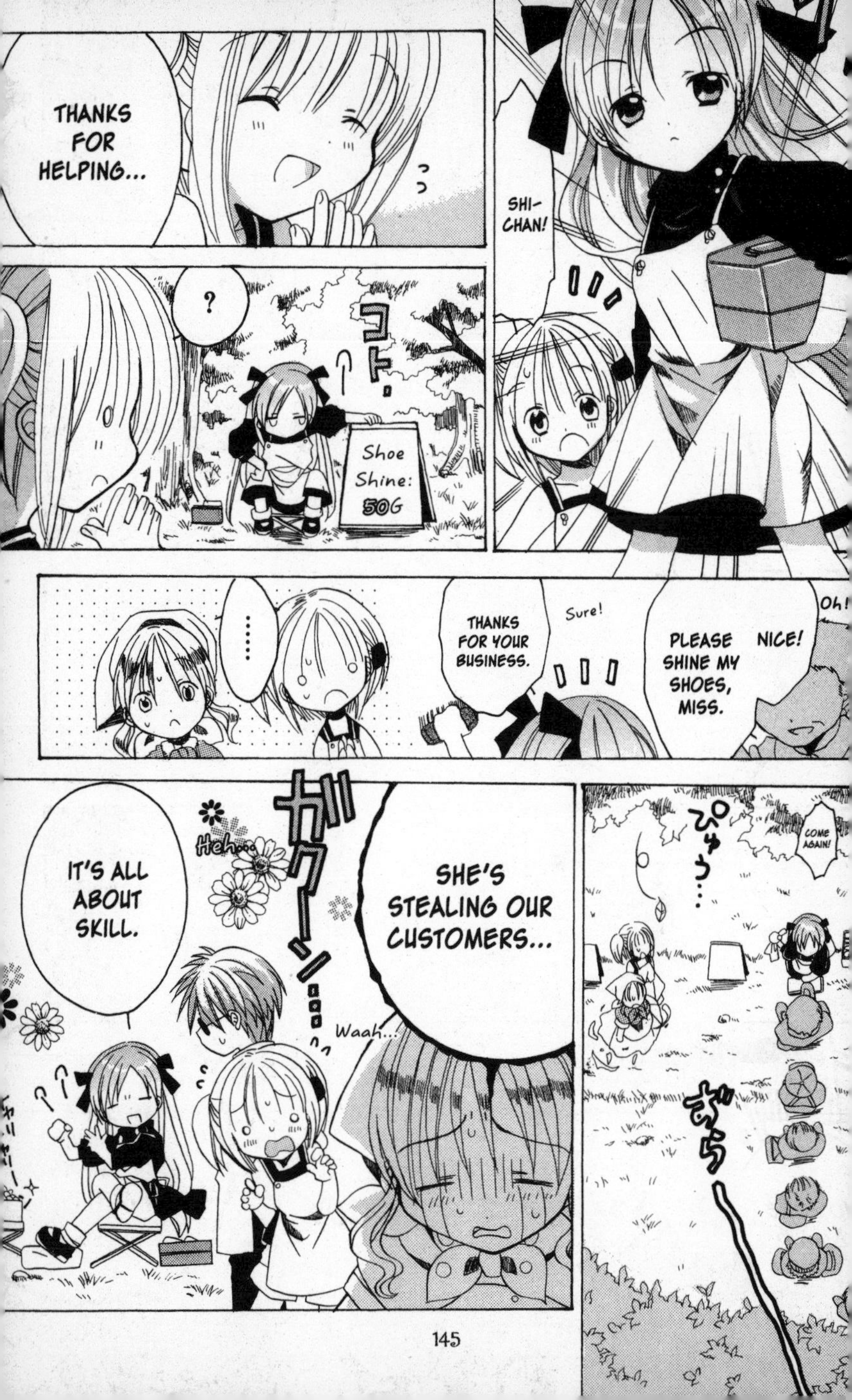
SHI-CHAN!
THANKS FOR HELPING...
?
コト。
Shoe Shine: 50G
Oh!
NICE!
PLEASE SHINE MY SHOES, MISS.
Sure!
THANKS FOR YOUR BUSINESS.
......
COME AGAIN!
ぴゅう…
SHE'S STEALING OUR CUSTOMERS...
ガクーン…
Waah...
Heh...
IT'S ALL ABOUT SKILL.

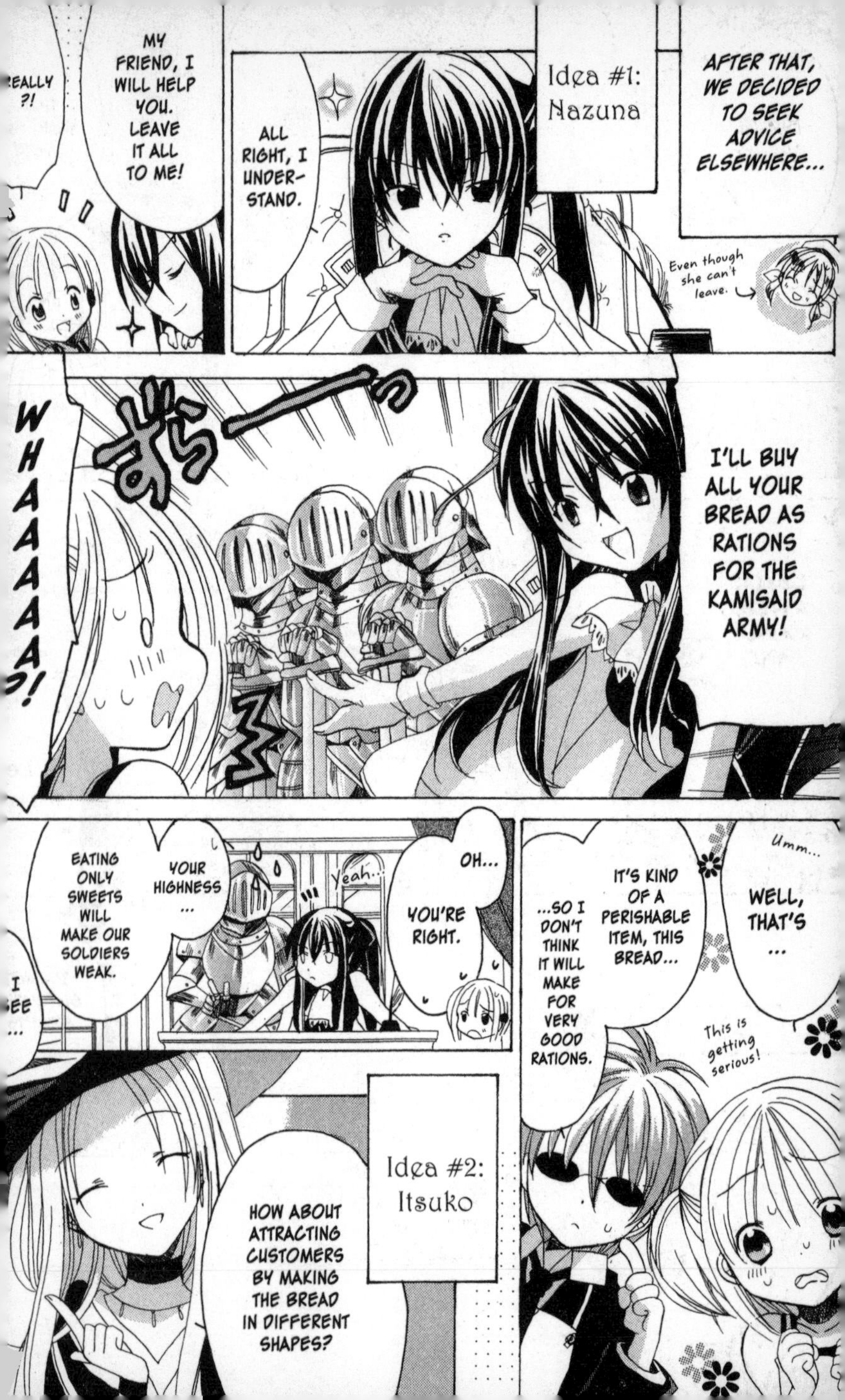
AFTER THAT, WE DECIDED TO SEEK ADVICE ELSEWHERE...
Even though she can't leave.
Idea #1: Nazuna
ALL RIGHT, I UNDER-STAND.
MY FRIEND, I WILL HELP YOU. LEAVE IT ALL TO ME!
EALLY ?!
I'LL BUY ALL YOUR BREAD AS RATIONS FOR THE KAMISAID ARMY!
ずら—っ
WHAAAAAAA?!
Umm...
WELL, THAT'S ...
IT'S KIND OF A PERISHABLE ITEM, THIS BREAD...
...SO I DON'T THINK IT WILL MAKE FOR VERY GOOD RATIONS.
This is getting serious!
OH...
YOU'RE RIGHT.
Yeah...
YOUR HIGHNESS ...
EATING ONLY SWEETS WILL MAKE OUR SOLDIERS WEAK.
I EE ...
Idea #2: Itsuko
HOW ABOUT ATTRACTING CUSTOMERS BY MAKING THE BREAD IN DIFFERENT SHAPES?

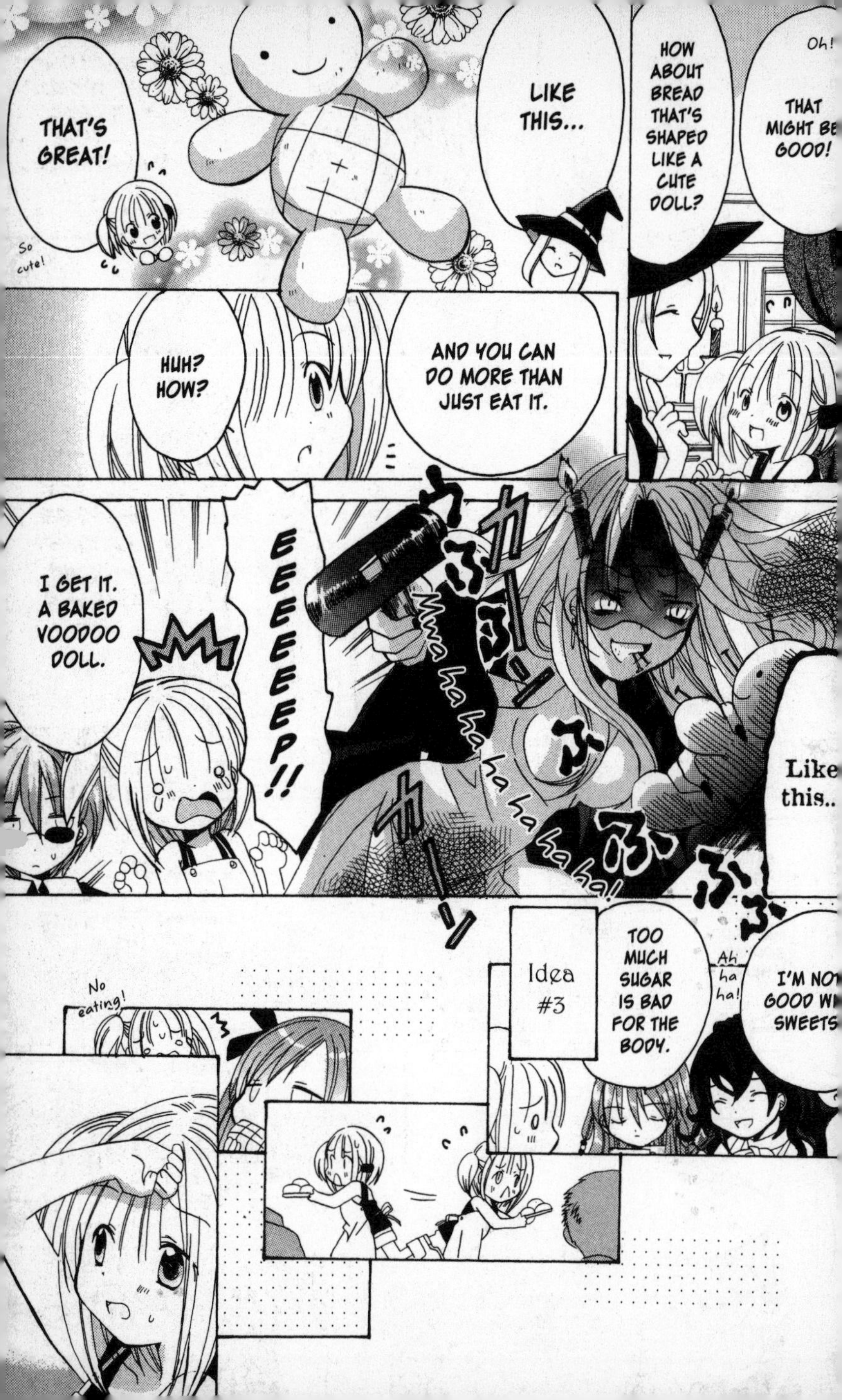
Oh!
THAT MIGHT BE GOOD!
HOW ABOUT BREAD THAT'S SHAPED LIKE A CUTE DOLL?
LIKE THIS...
THAT'S GREAT!
So cute!
AND YOU CAN DO MORE THAN JUST EAT IT.
HUH? HOW?
Like this..
Mwa ha ha ha ha ha ha!
EEEEEEEP!!
I GET IT. A BAKED VOODOO DOLL.
I'M NO GOOD WI SWEETS
Ah ha ha!
TOO MUCH SUGAR IS BAD FOR THE BODY.
Idea #3
No eating!

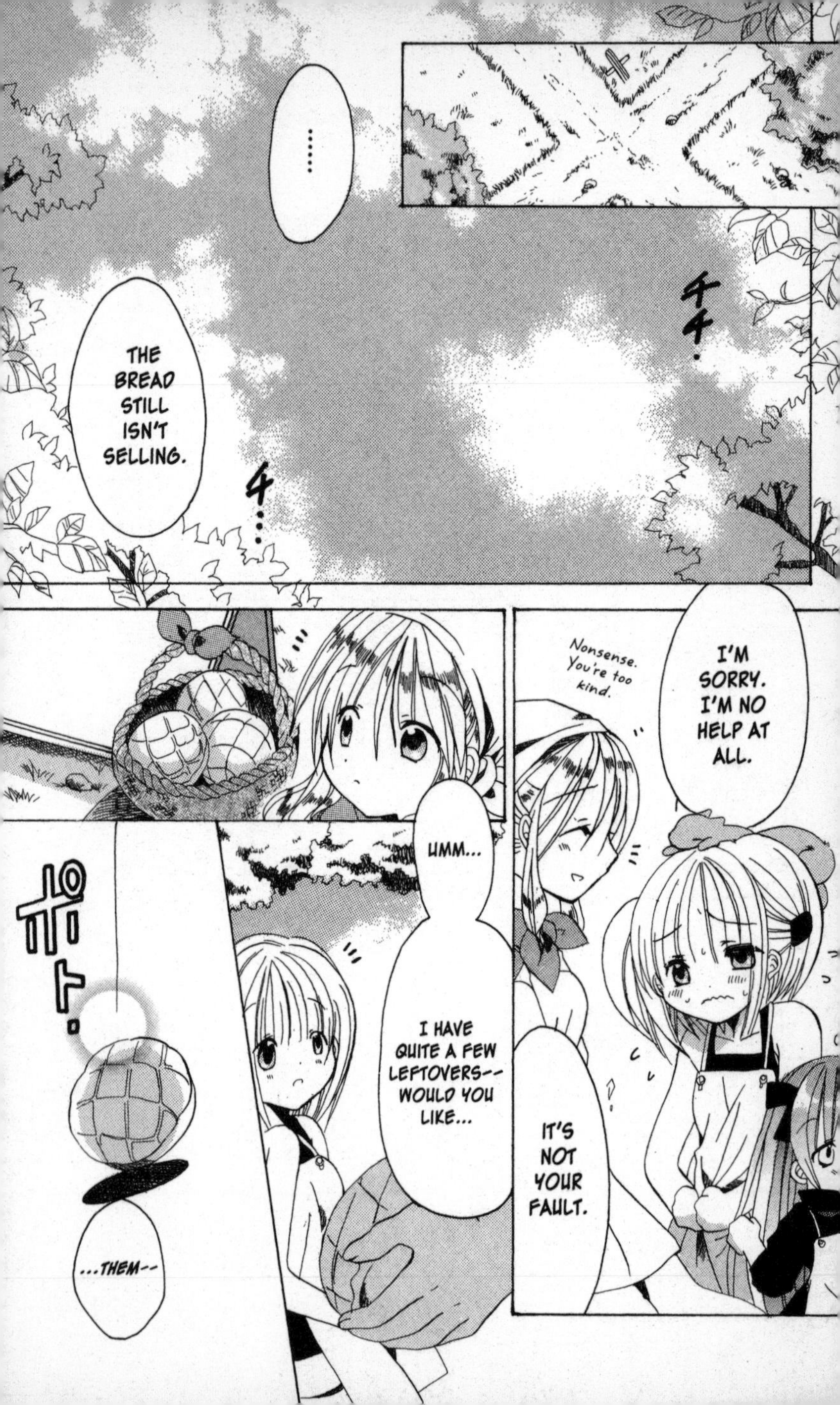

......
チチ・
THE BREAD STILL ISN'T SELLING.
チ・・・
I'M SORRY. I'M NO HELP AT ALL.
Nonsense. You're too kind.
IT'S NOT YOUR FAULT.
UMM...
I HAVE QUITE A FEW LEFTOVERS-- WOULD YOU LIKE...
...THEM--
ポト。

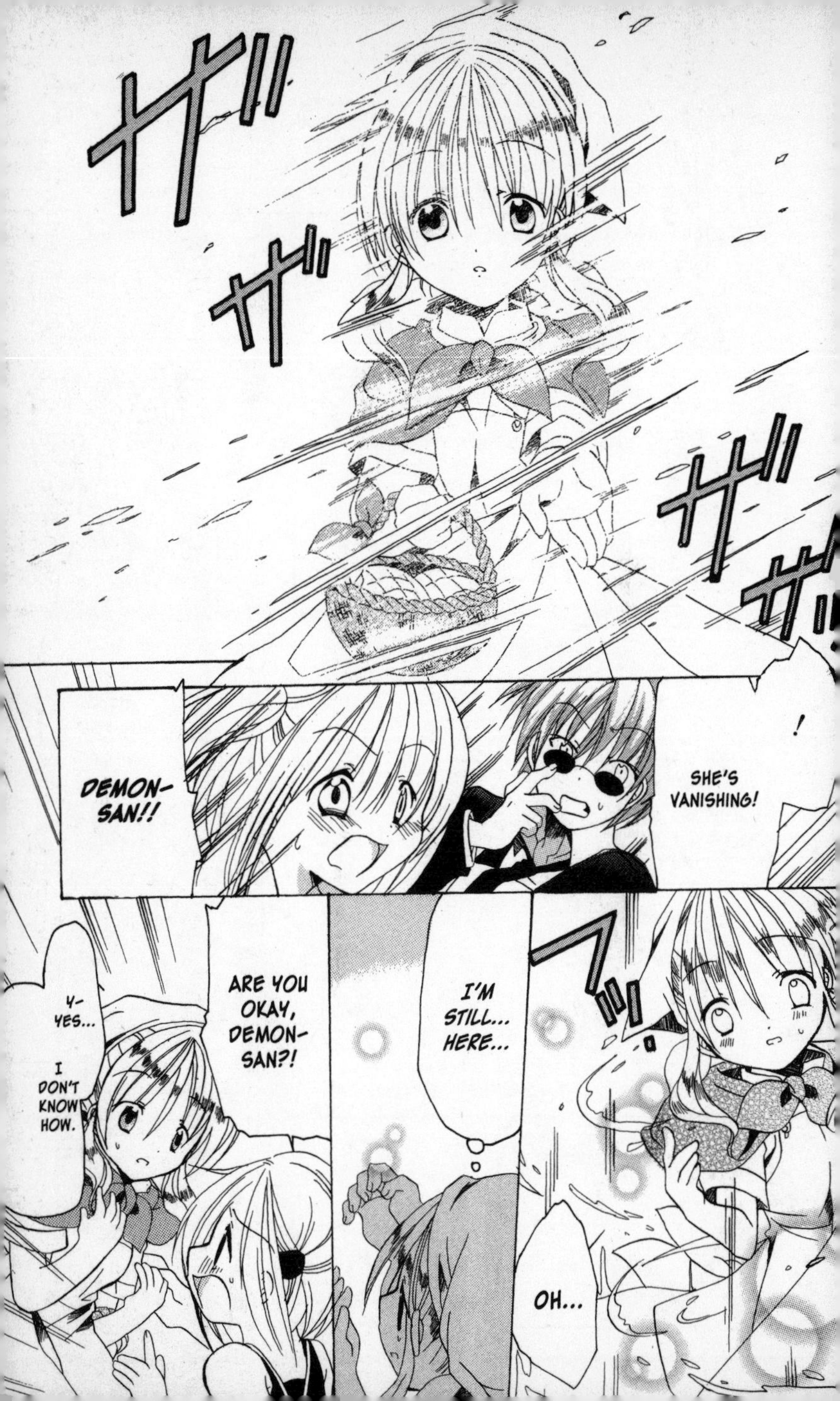
ザザ
ザザ
ザザ
ザッ
!
SHE'S VANISHING!
DEMON-SAN!!
OH...
I'M STILL... HERE...
ARE YOU OKAY, DEMON-SAN?!
Y-YES...
I DON'T KNOW HOW.

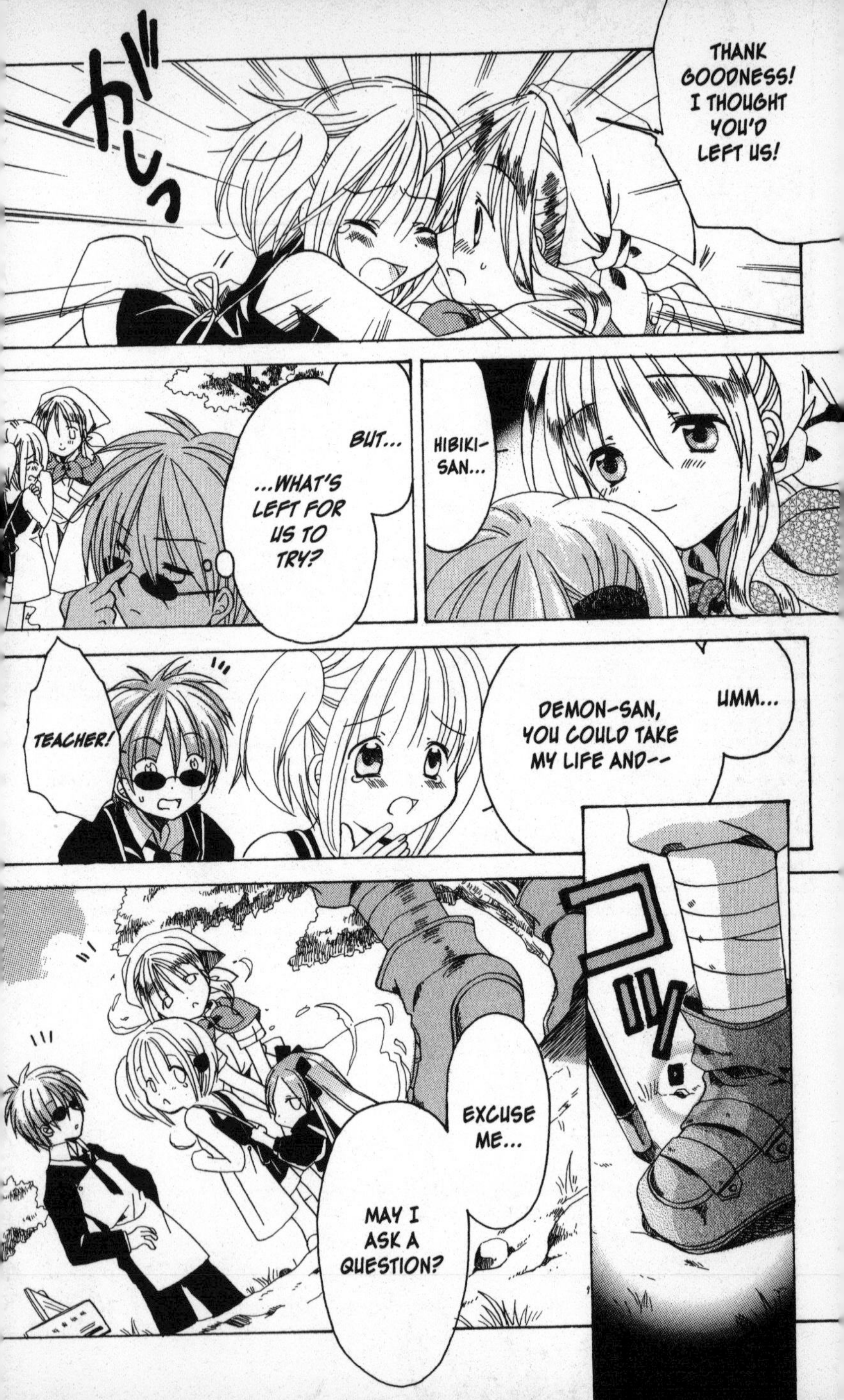

がしっ
THANK GOODNESS! I THOUGHT YOU'D LEFT US!
HIBIKI-SAN...
BUT...
...WHAT'S LEFT FOR US TO TRY?
UMM...
DEMON-SAN, YOU COULD TAKE MY LIFE AND--
TEACHER!
EXCUSE ME...
MAY I ASK A QUESTION?

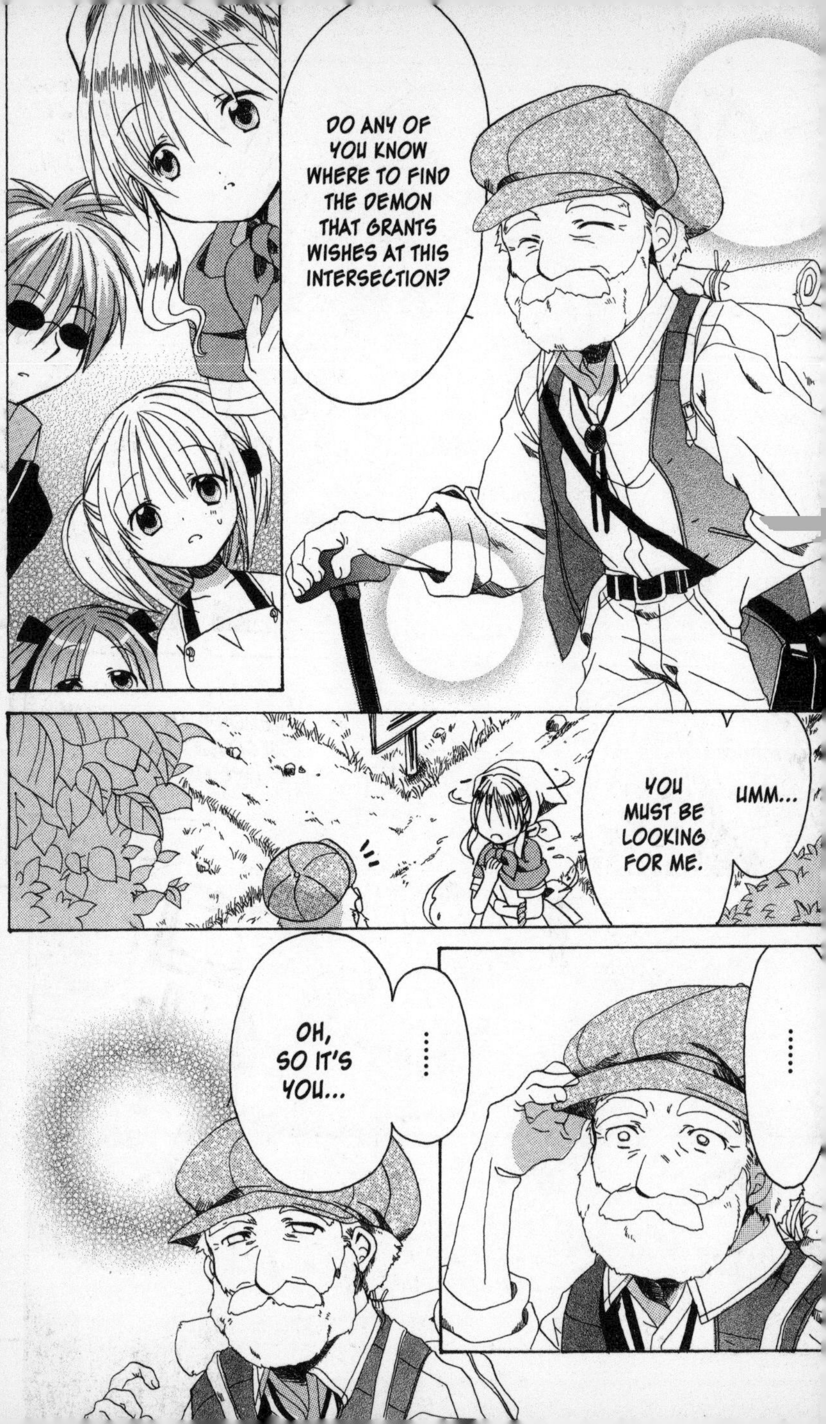
DO ANY OF YOU KNOW WHERE TO FIND THE DEMON THAT GRANTS WISHES AT THIS INTERSECTION?
UMM...
YOU MUST BE LOOKING FOR ME.
......
......
OH, SO IT'S YOU...

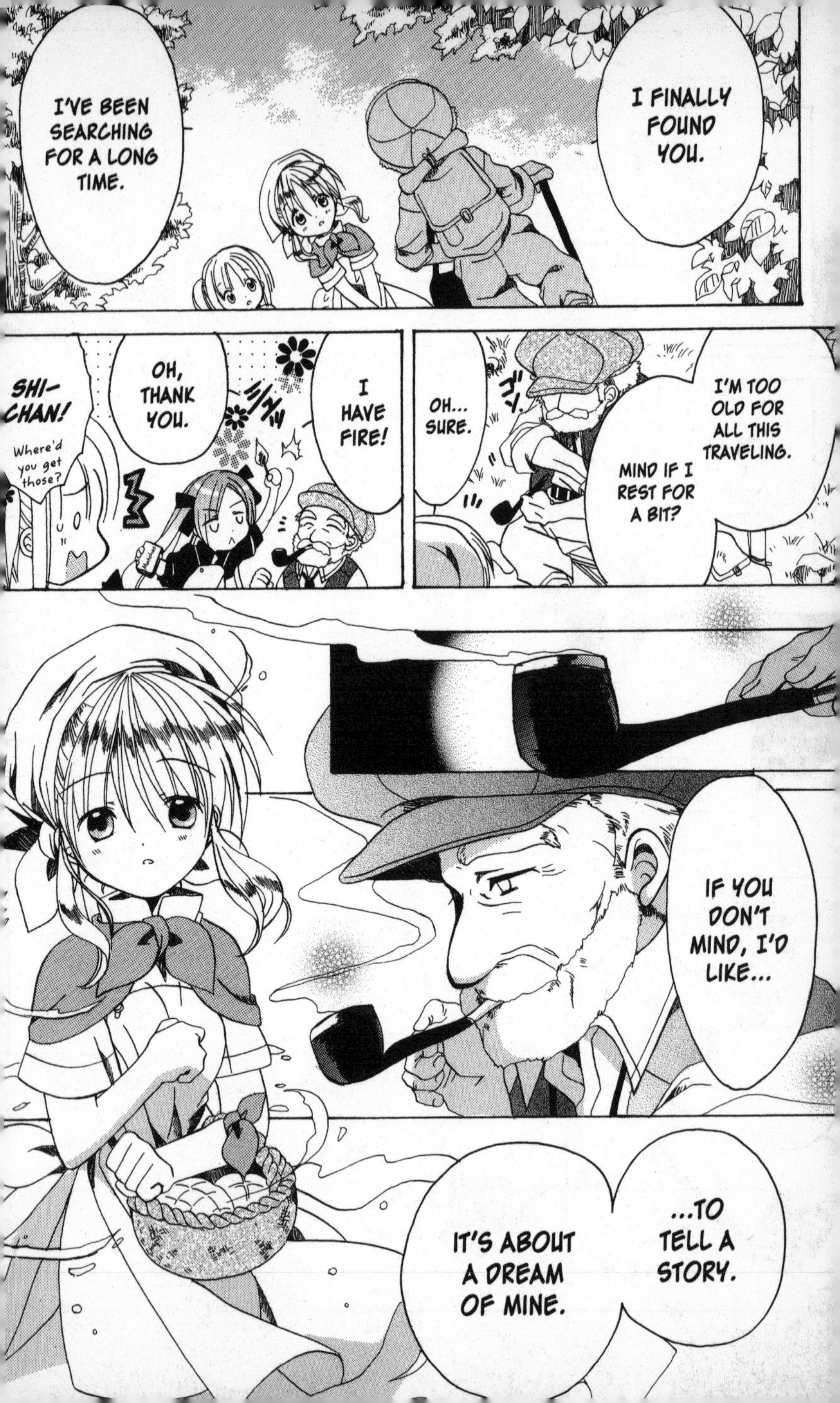
I FINALLY FOUND YOU.
I'VE BEEN SEARCHING FOR A LONG TIME.
I'M TOO OLD FOR ALL THIS TRAVELING.
MIND IF I REST FOR A BIT?
OH... SURE.
I HAVE FIRE!
OH, THANK YOU.
SHI-CHAN!
Where'd you get those?
IF YOU DON'T MIND, I'D LIKE...
...TO TELL A STORY.
IT'S ABOUT A DREAM OF MINE.

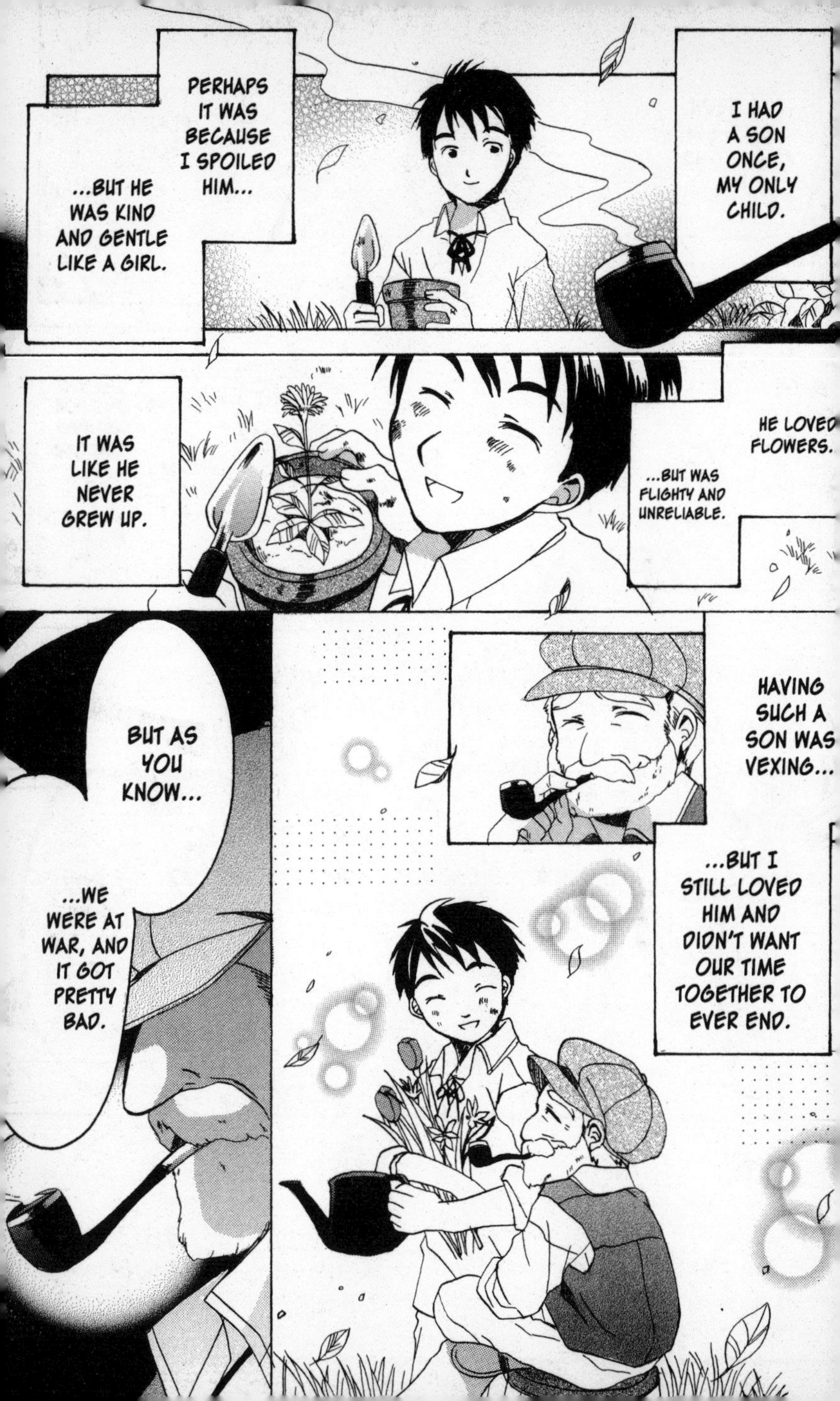
I HAD A SON ONCE, MY ONLY CHILD.
PERHAPS IT WAS BECAUSE I SPOILED HIM...
...BUT HE WAS KIND AND GENTLE LIKE A GIRL.
HE LOVED FLOWERS.
...BUT WAS FLIGHTY AND UNRELIABLE.
IT WAS LIKE HE NEVER GREW UP.
HAVING SUCH A SON WAS VEXING...
...BUT I STILL LOVED HIM AND DIDN'T WANT OUR TIME TOGETHER TO EVER END.
BUT AS YOU KNOW...
...WE WERE AT WAR, AND IT GOT PRETTY BAD.

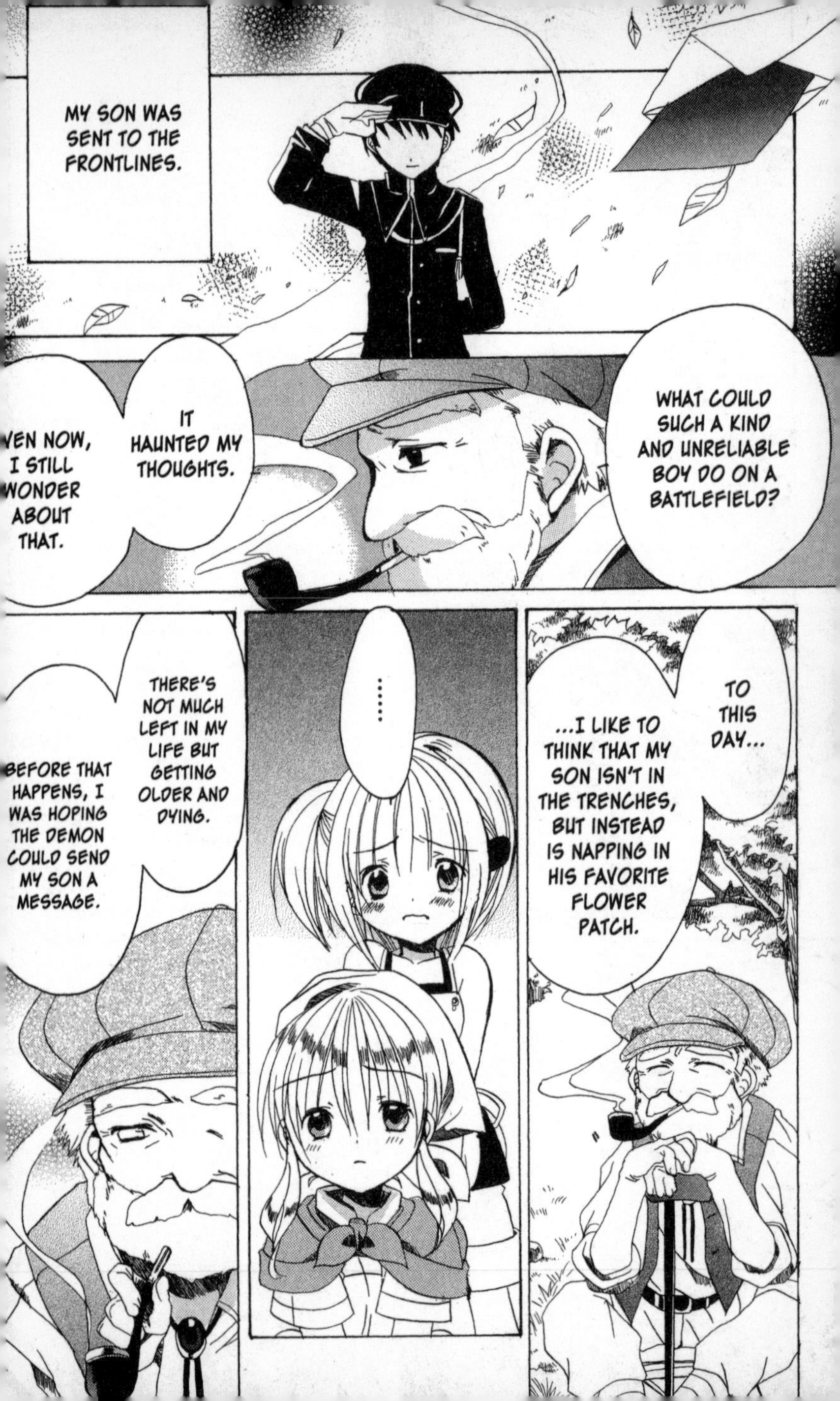
MY SON WAS SENT TO THE FRONTLINES.
WHAT COULD SUCH A KIND AND UNRELIABLE BOY DO ON A BATTLEFIELD?
IT HAUNTED MY THOUGHTS.
VEN NOW, I STILL WONDER ABOUT THAT.
TO THIS DAY...
...I LIKE TO THINK THAT MY SON ISN'T IN THE TRENCHES, BUT INSTEAD IS NAPPING IN HIS FAVORITE FLOWER PATCH.
......
THERE'S NOT MUCH LEFT IN MY LIFE BUT GETTING OLDER AND DYING.
BEFORE THAT HAPPENS, I WAS HOPING THE DEMON COULD SEND MY SON A MESSAGE.

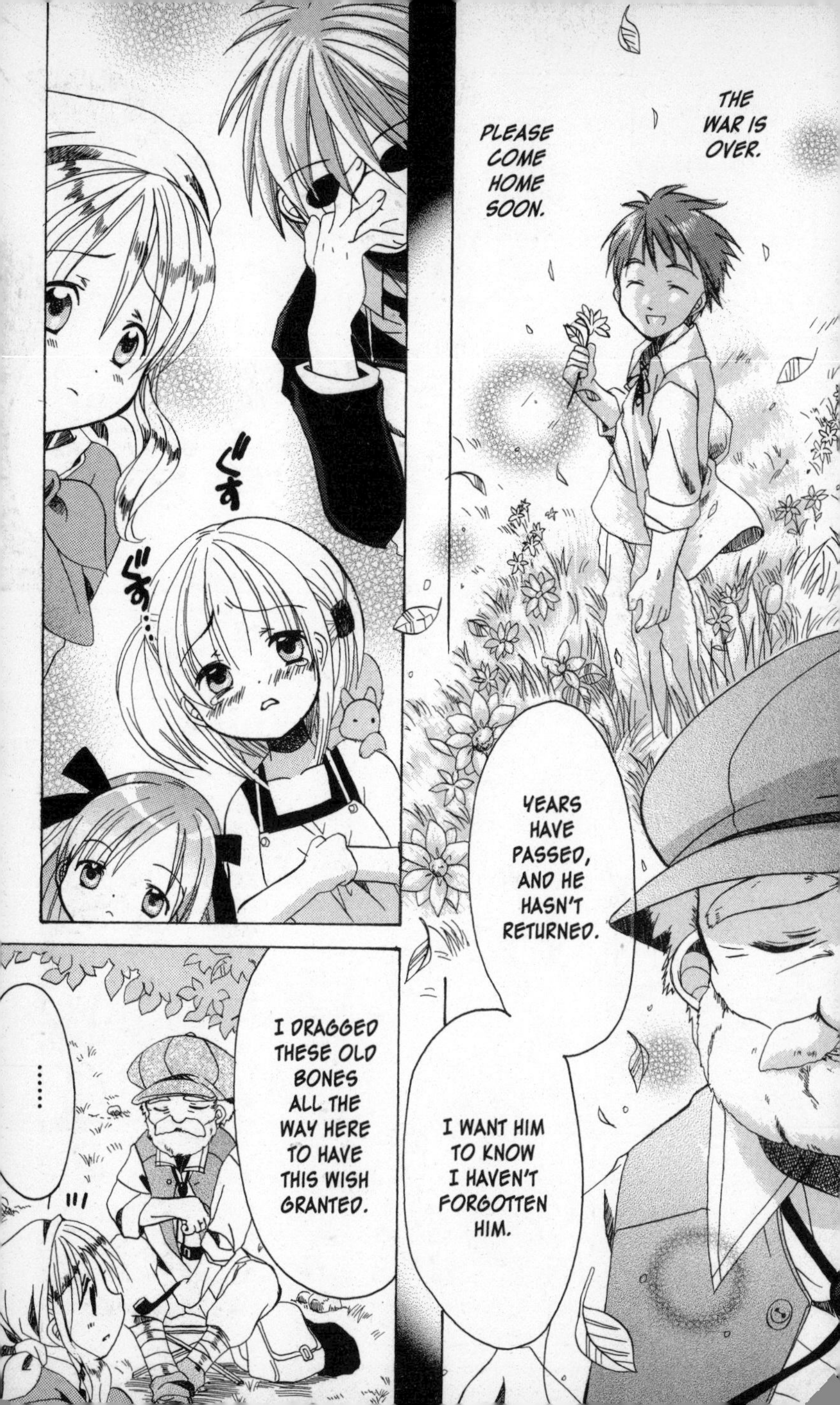
THE WAR IS OVER.
PLEASE COME HOME SOON.
ぐす
ぐす...
YEARS HAVE PASSED, AND HE HASN'T RETURNED.
I WANT HIM TO KNOW I HAVEN'T FORGOTTEN HIM.
I DRAGGED THESE OLD BONES ALL THE WAY HERE TO HAVE THIS WISH GRANTED.
......
!!!

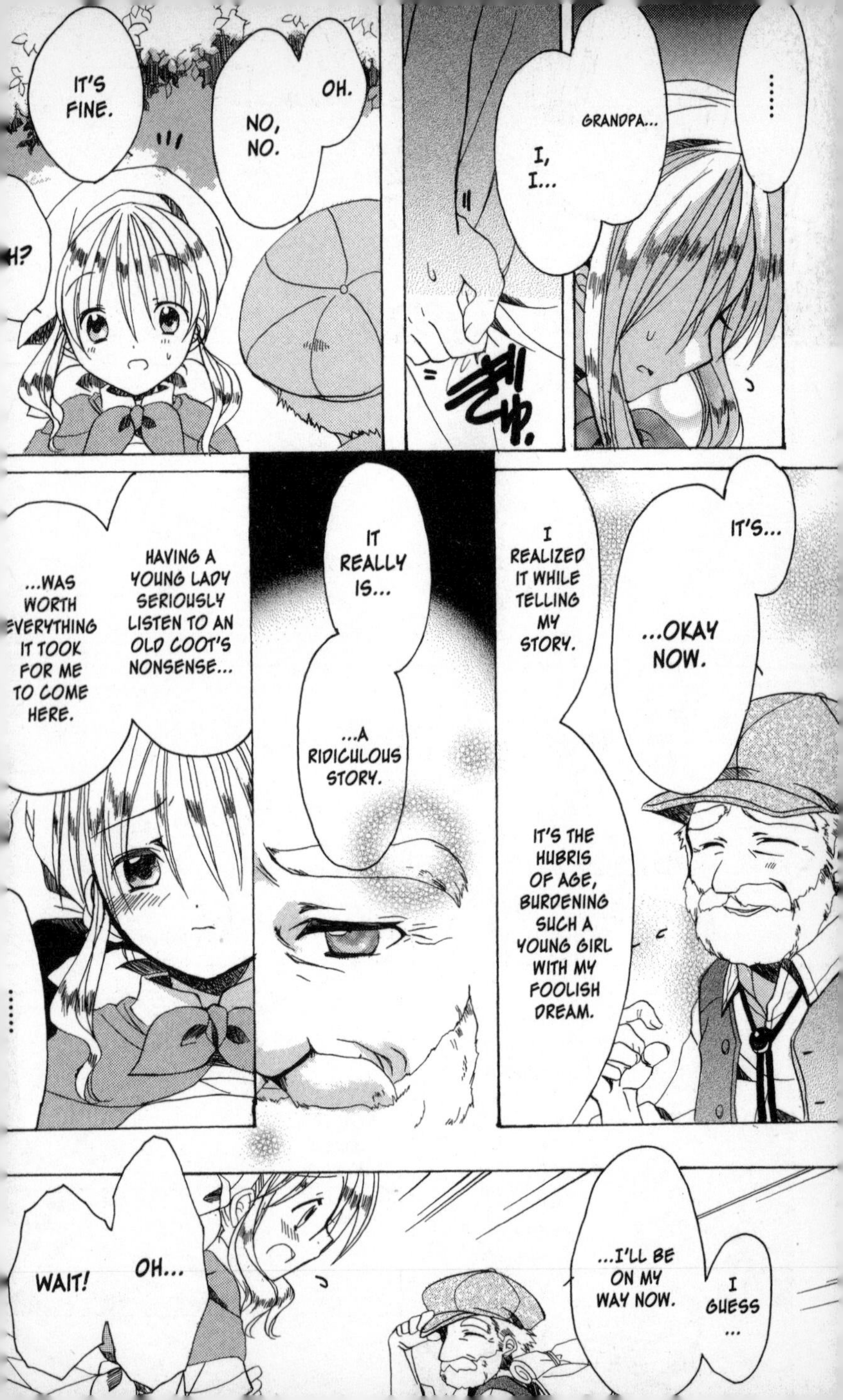

......
GRANDPA...
I, I...
OH.
NO, NO.
IT'S FINE.
IT'S...
...OKAY NOW.
I REALIZED IT WHILE TELLING MY STORY.
IT'S THE HUBRIS OF AGE, BURDENING SUCH A YOUNG GIRL WITH MY FOOLISH DREAM.
IT REALLY IS...
...A RIDICULOUS STORY.
HAVING A YOUNG LADY SERIOUSLY LISTEN TO AN OLD COOT'S NONSENSE...
...WAS WORTH EVERYTHING IT TOOK FOR ME TO COME HERE.
......
I GUESS...
...I'LL BE ON MY WAY NOW.
OH...
WAIT!

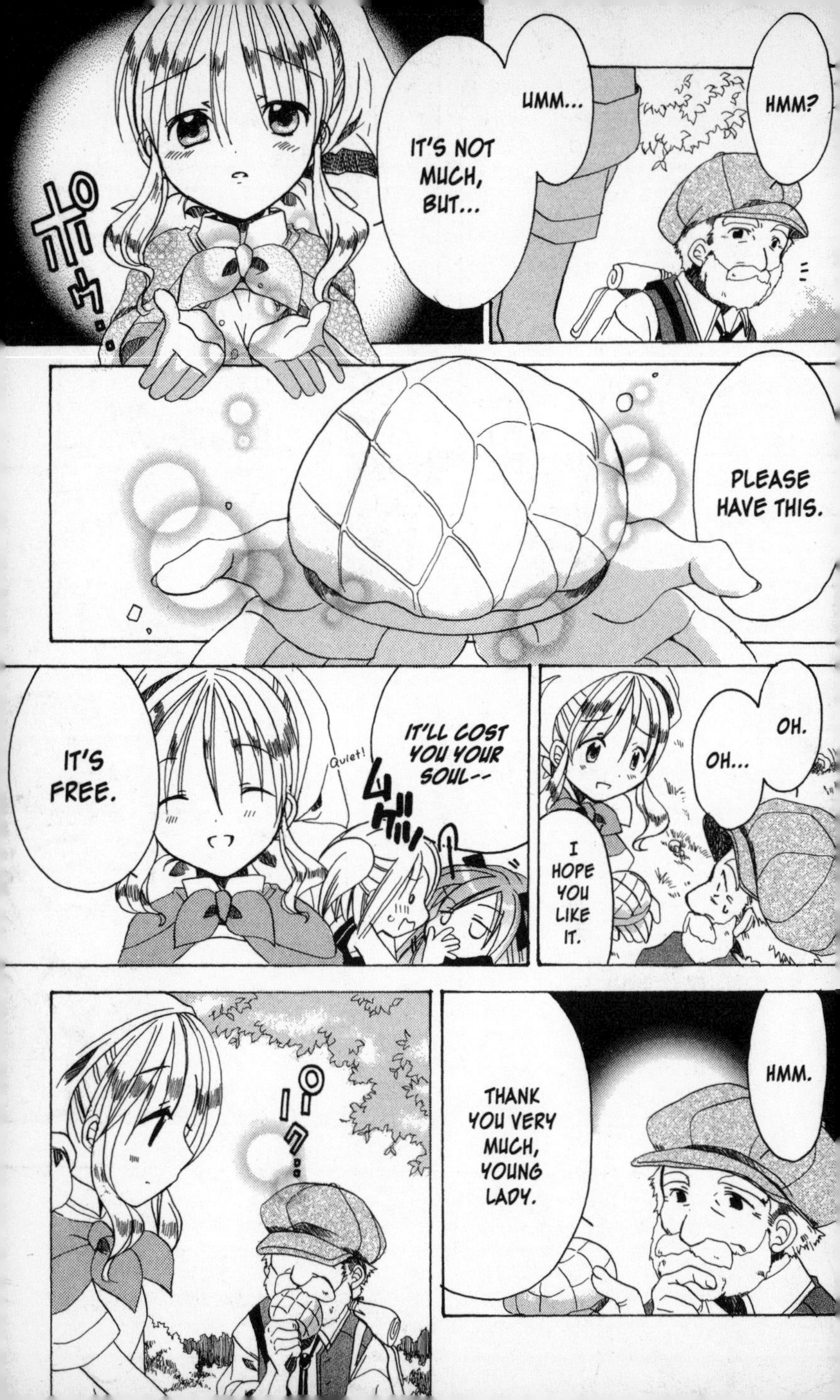
HMM?
UMM...
IT'S NOT MUCH, BUT...
PLEASE HAVE THIS.
OH.
OH...
I HOPE YOU LIKE IT.
IT'LL COST YOU YOUR SOUL--
Quiet!
IT'S FREE.
HMM.
THANK YOU VERY MUCH, YOUNG LADY.

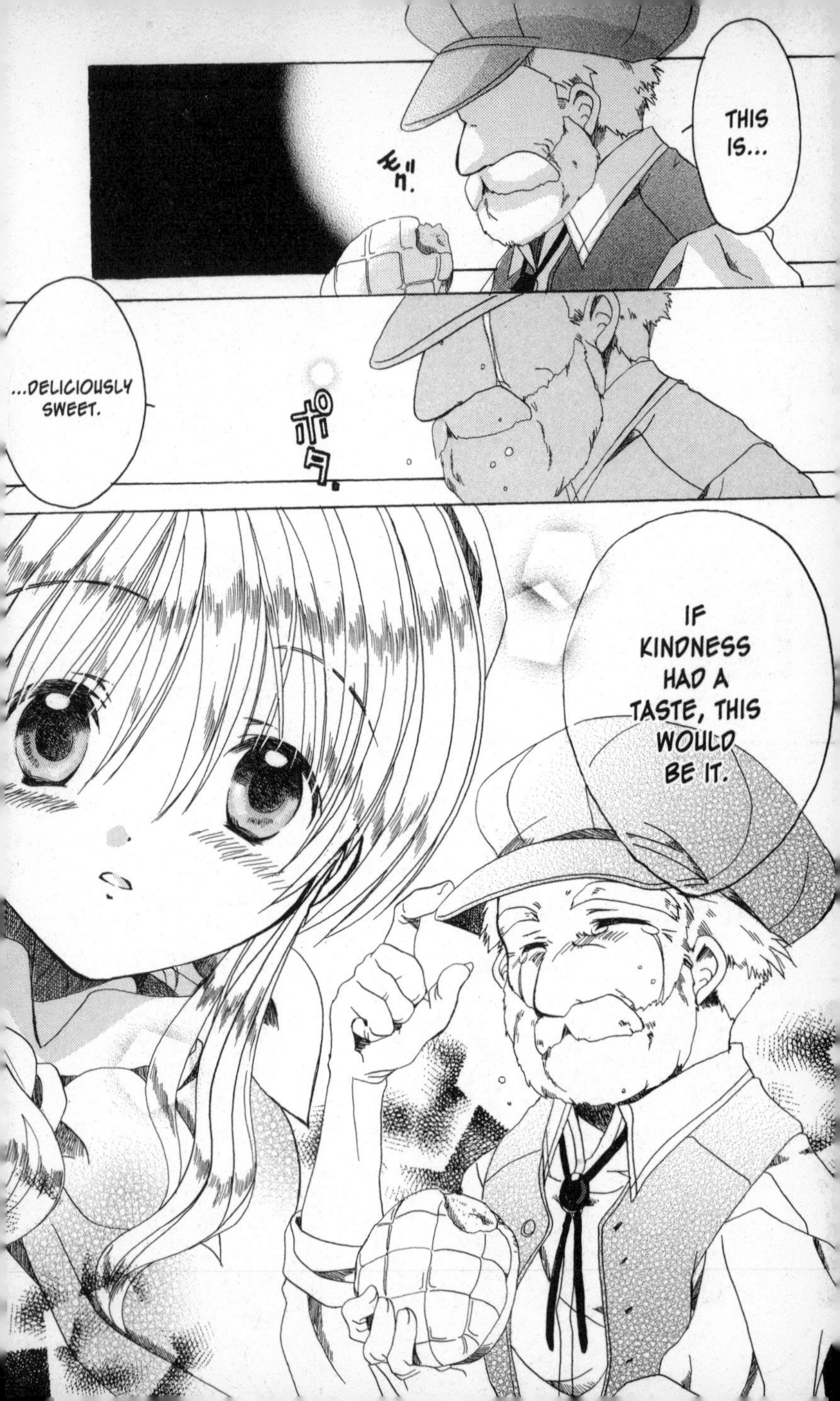
THIS IS...
モグ.
ポタ.
...DELICIOUSLY SWEET.
IF KINDNESS HAD A TASTE, THIS WOULD BE IT.

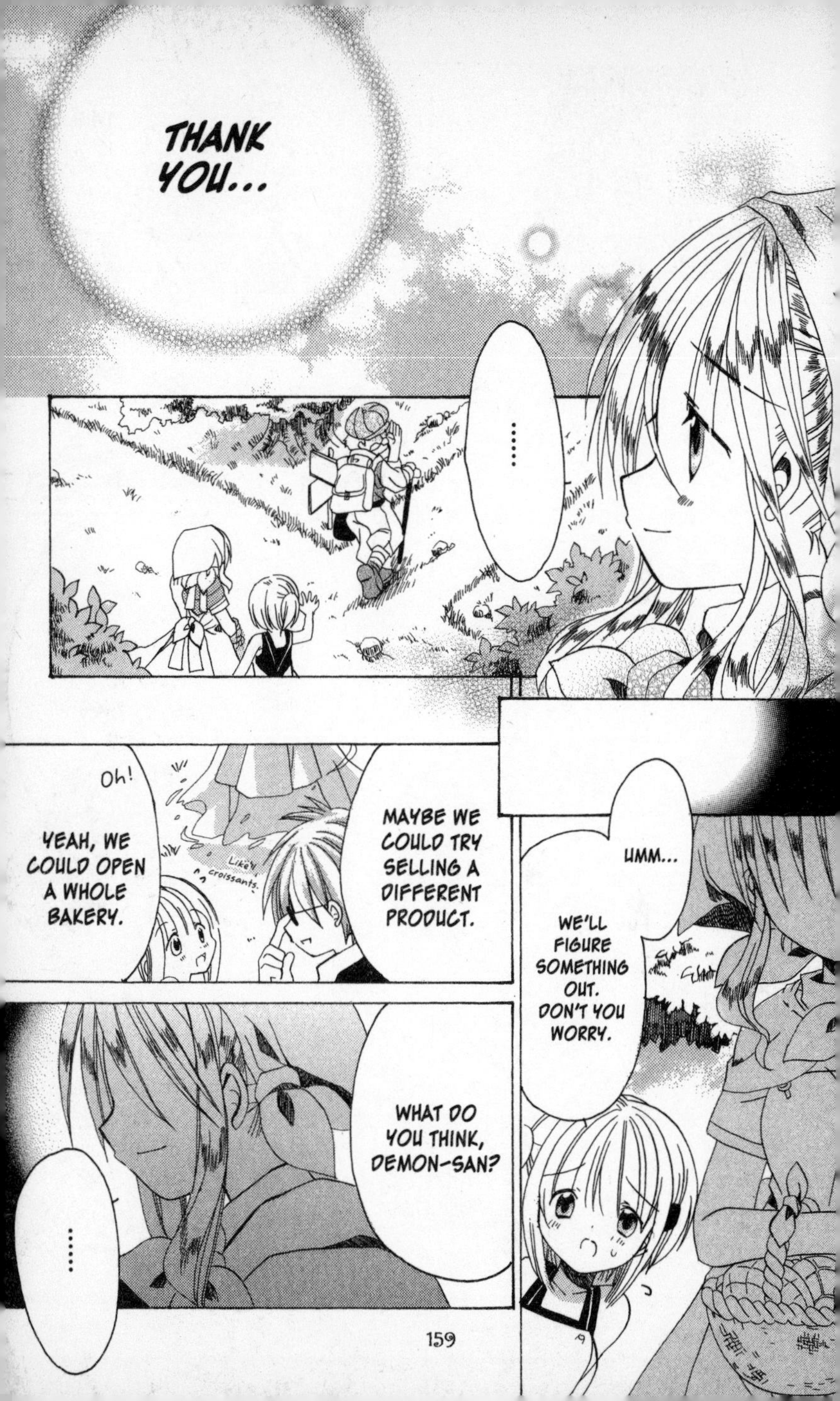
THANK YOU...
......
UMM...
WE'LL FIGURE SOMETHING OUT. DON'T YOU WORRY.
MAYBE WE COULD TRY SELLING A DIFFERENT PRODUCT.
Oh!
YEAH, WE COULD OPEN A WHOLE BAKERY.
Like croissants.
WHAT DO YOU THINK, DEMON-SAN?
......

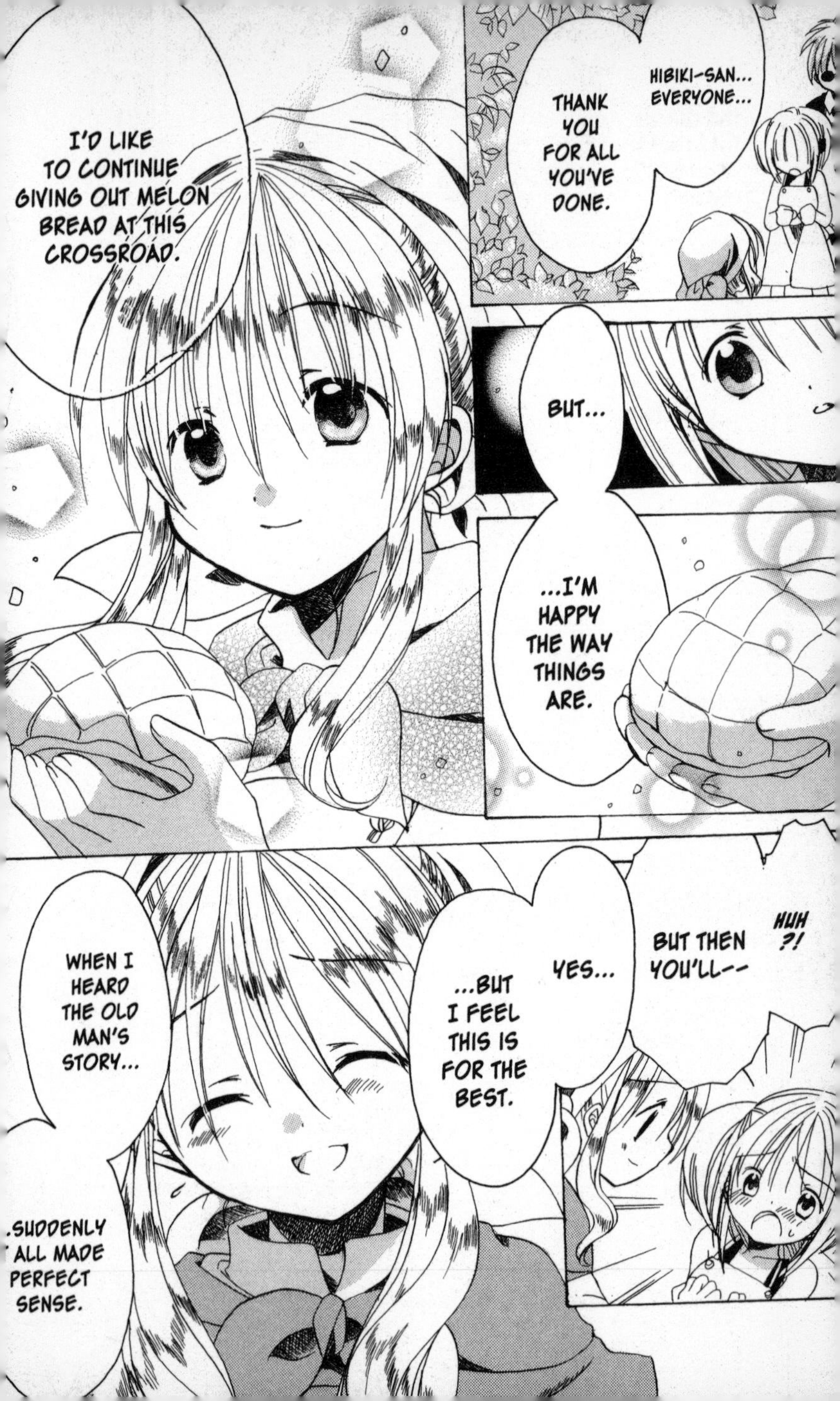
HIBIKI-SAN... EVERYONE...
THANK YOU FOR ALL YOU'VE DONE.
BUT...
...I'M HAPPY THE WAY THINGS ARE.
I'D LIKE TO CONTINUE GIVING OUT MELON BREAD AT THIS CROSSROAD.
HUH ?!
BUT THEN YOU'LL--
YES...
...BUT I FEEL THIS IS FOR THE BEST.
WHEN I HEARD THE OLD MAN'S STORY...
.SUDDENLY ALL MADE PERFECT SENSE.

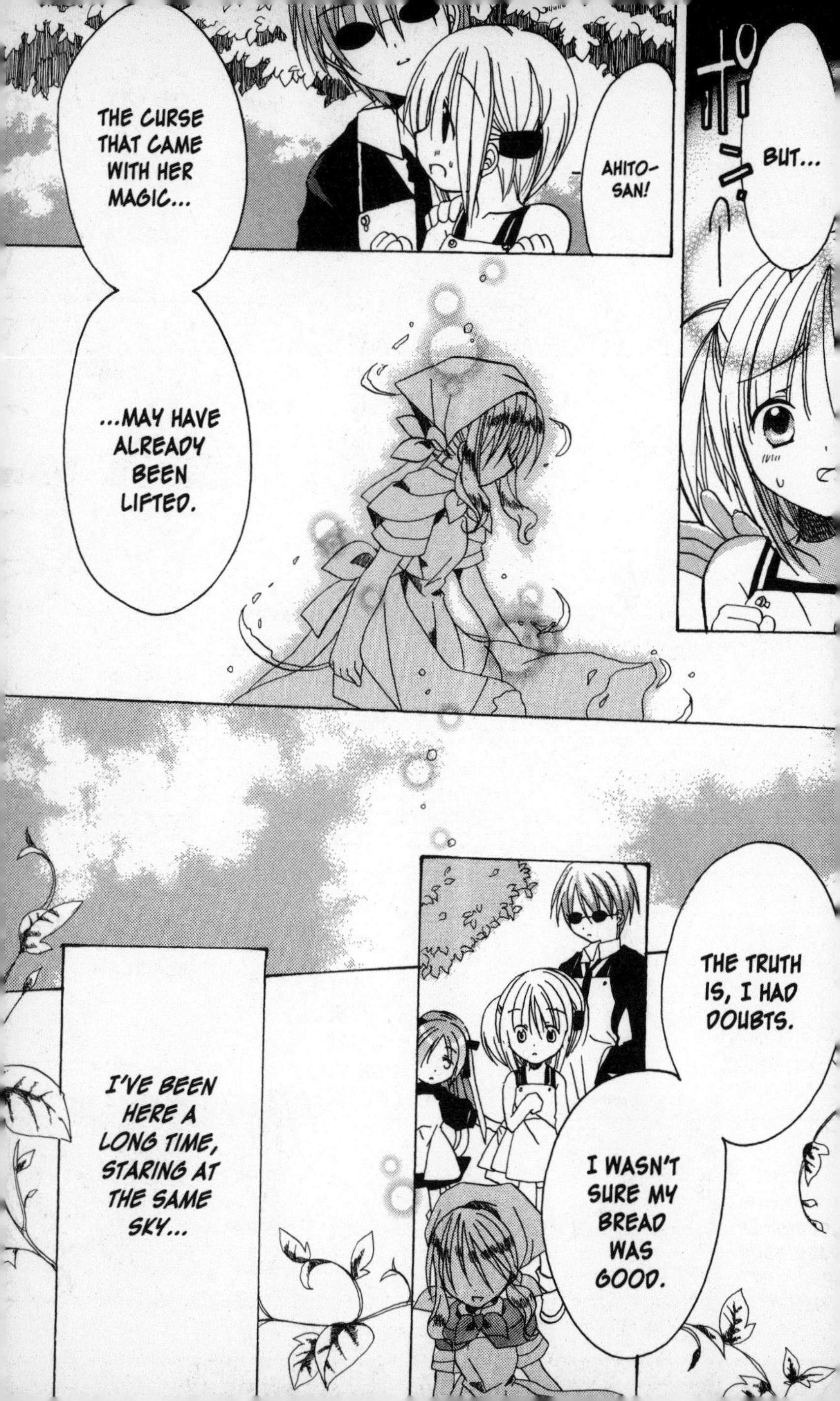
BUT...
AHITO-SAN!
THE CURSE THAT CAME WITH HER MAGIC...
...MAY HAVE ALREADY BEEN LIFTED.
THE TRUTH IS, I HAD DOUBTS.
I WASN'T SURE MY BREAD WAS GOOD.
I'VE BEEN HERE A LONG TIME, STARING AT THE SAME SKY...

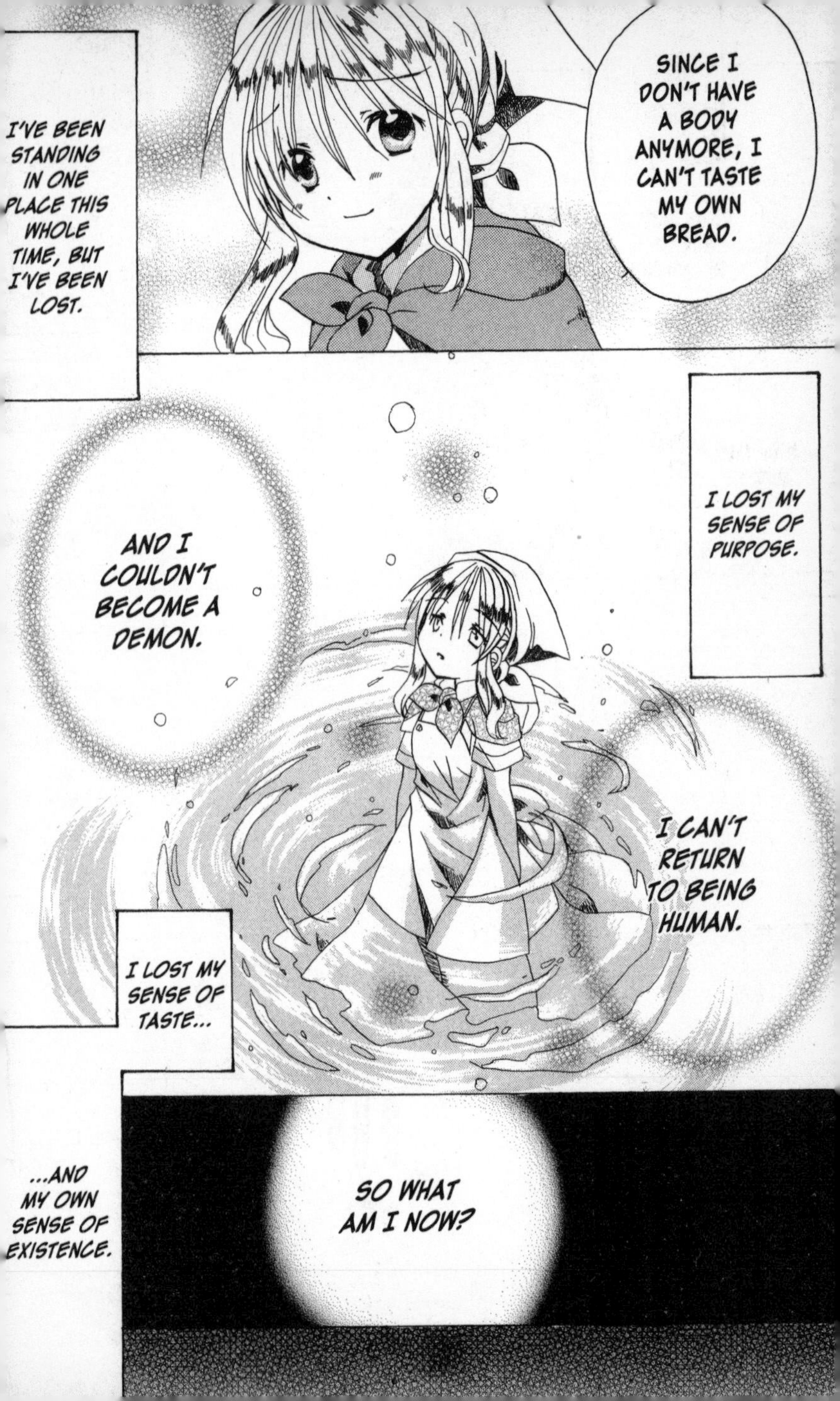
SINCE I DON'T HAVE A BODY ANYMORE, I CAN'T TASTE MY OWN BREAD.
I'VE BEEN STANDING IN ONE PLACE THIS WHOLE TIME, BUT I'VE BEEN LOST.
I LOST MY SENSE OF PURPOSE.
AND I COULDN'T BECOME A DEMON.
I CAN'T RETURN TO BEING HUMAN.
I LOST MY SENSE OF TASTE...
...AND MY OWN SENSE OF EXISTENCE.
SO WHAT AM I NOW?

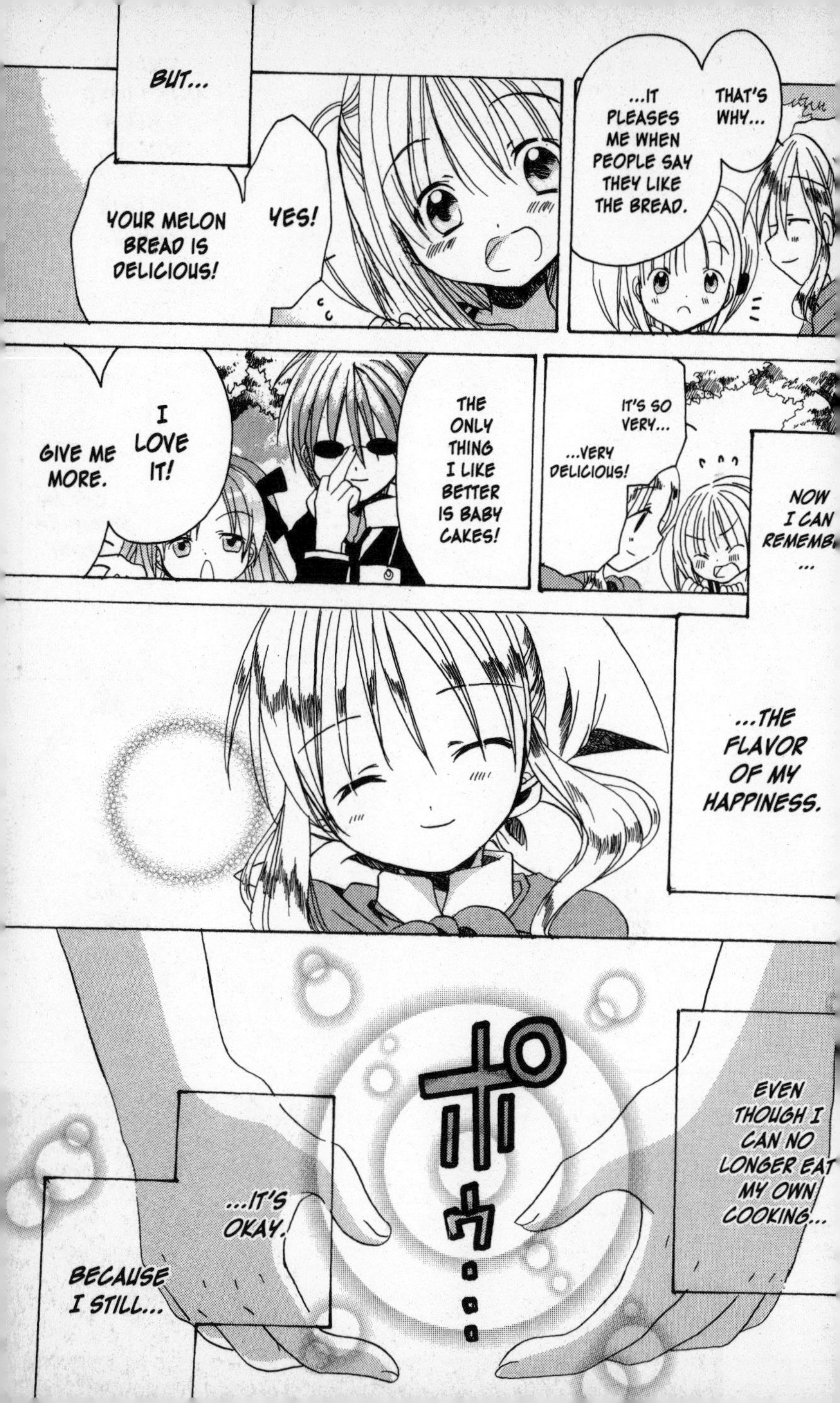
THAT'S WHY...
...IT PLEASES ME WHEN PEOPLE SAY THEY LIKE THE BREAD.
BUT...
YES!
YOUR MELON BREAD IS DELICIOUS!
IT'S SO VERY...
...VERY DELICIOUS!
THE ONLY THING I LIKE BETTER IS BABY CAKES!
I LOVE IT!
GIVE ME MORE.
NOW I CAN REMEMB...
...THE FLAVOR OF MY HAPPINESS.
EVEN THOUGH I CAN NO LONGER EAT MY OWN COOKING...
ポウ...
...IT'S OKAY.
BECAUSE I STILL...

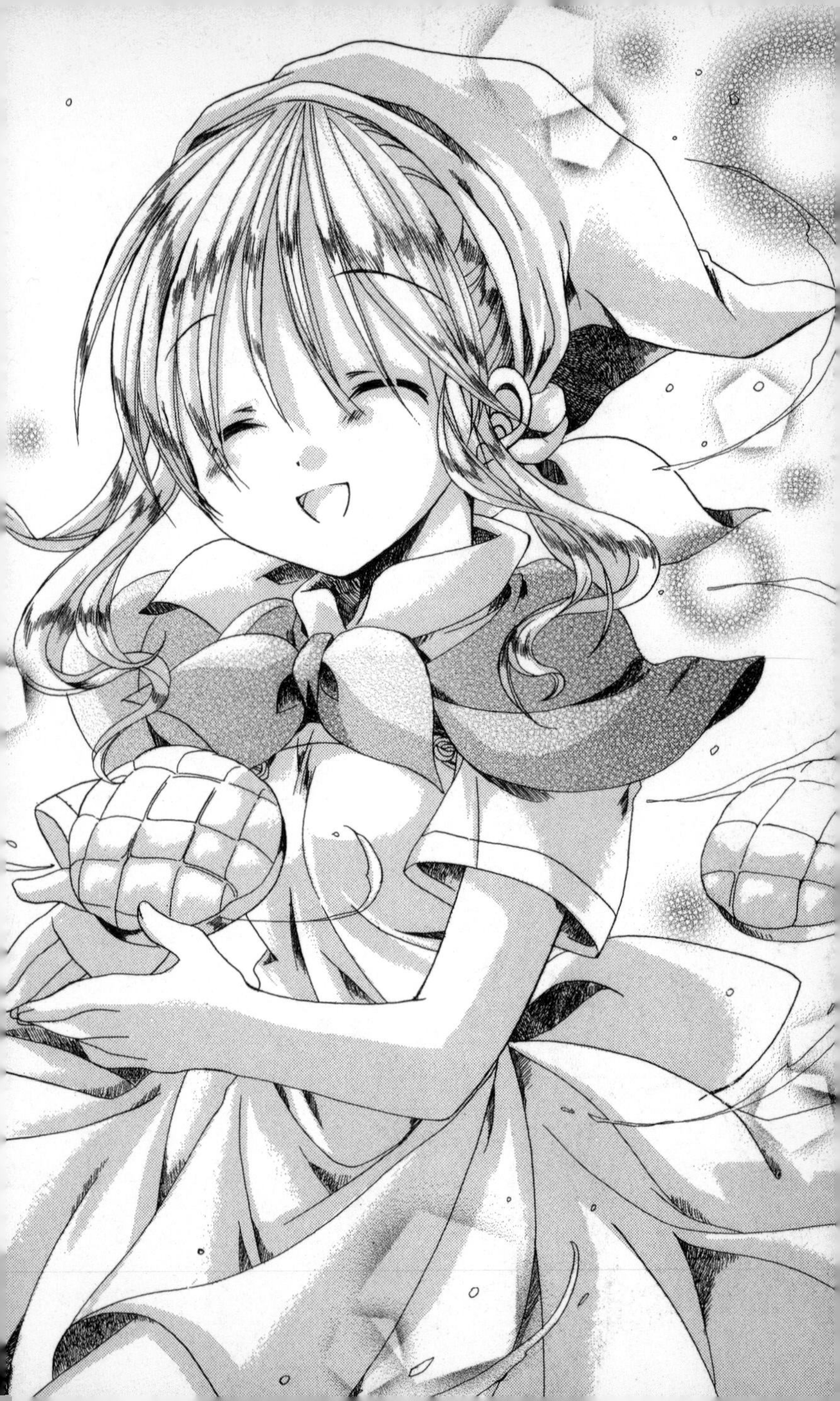

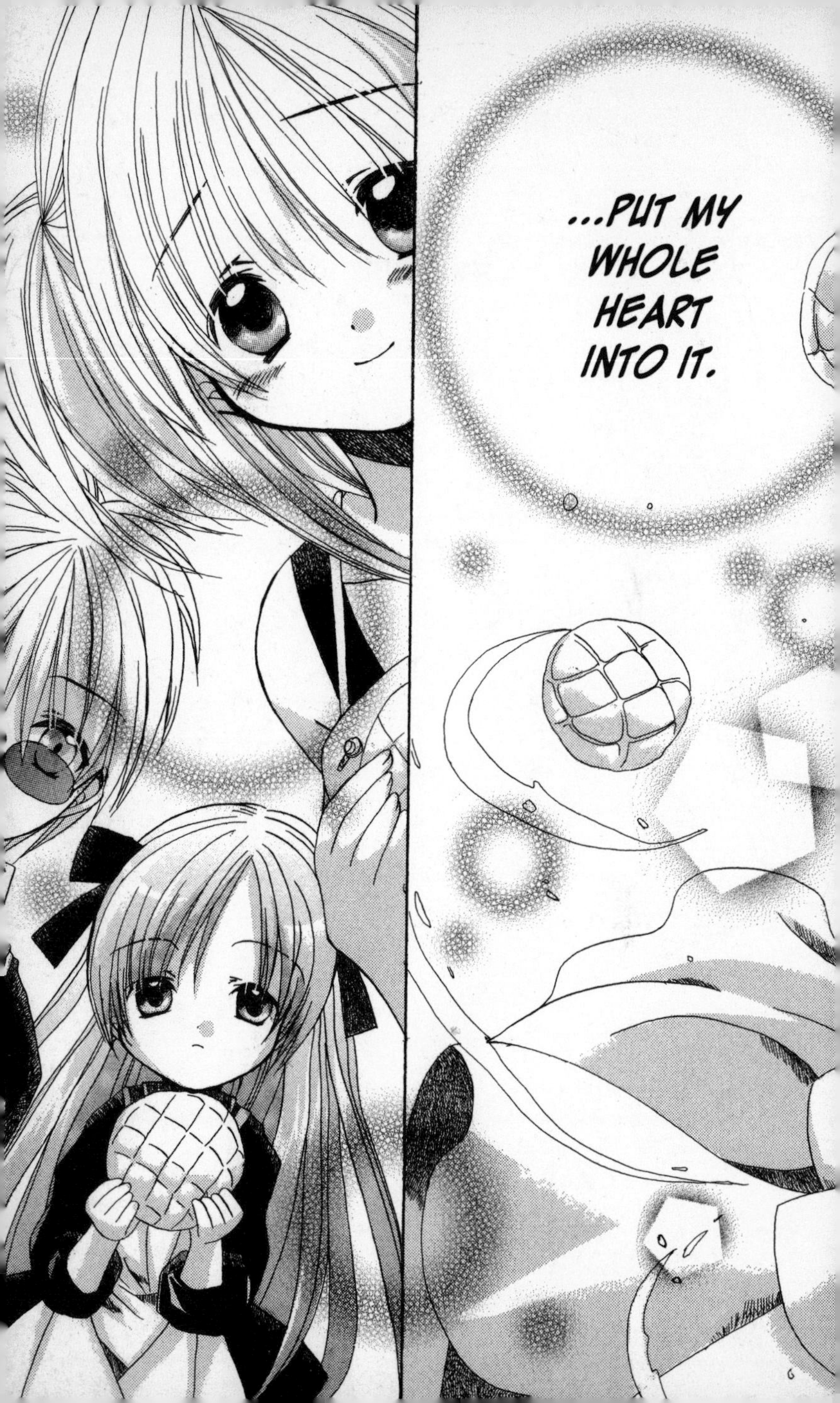
...PUT MY WHOLE HEART INTO IT.

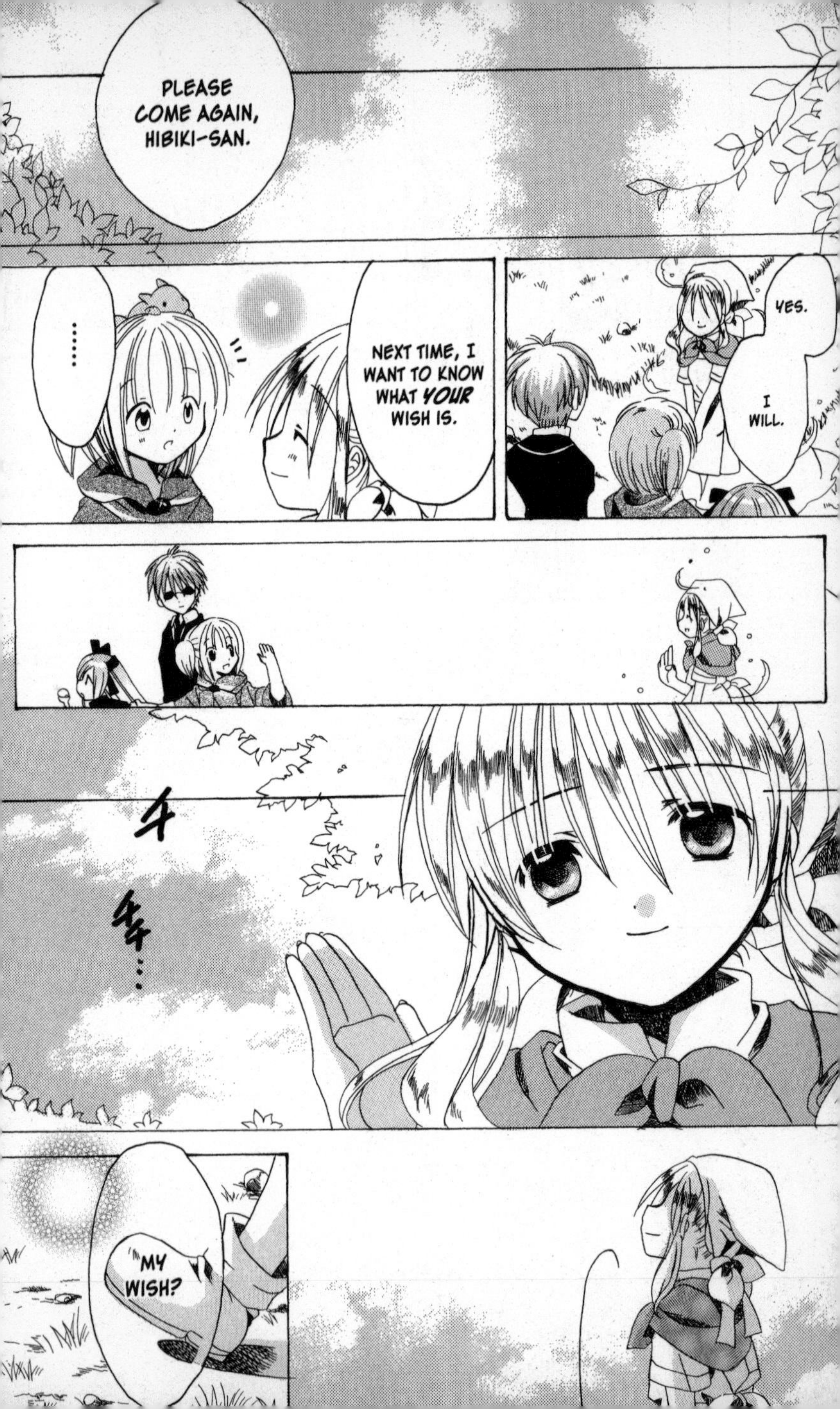
PLEASE COME AGAIN, HIBIKI-SAN.
YES.
I WILL.
NEXT TIME, I WANT TO KNOW WHAT YOUR WISH IS.
......
"MY WISH?"

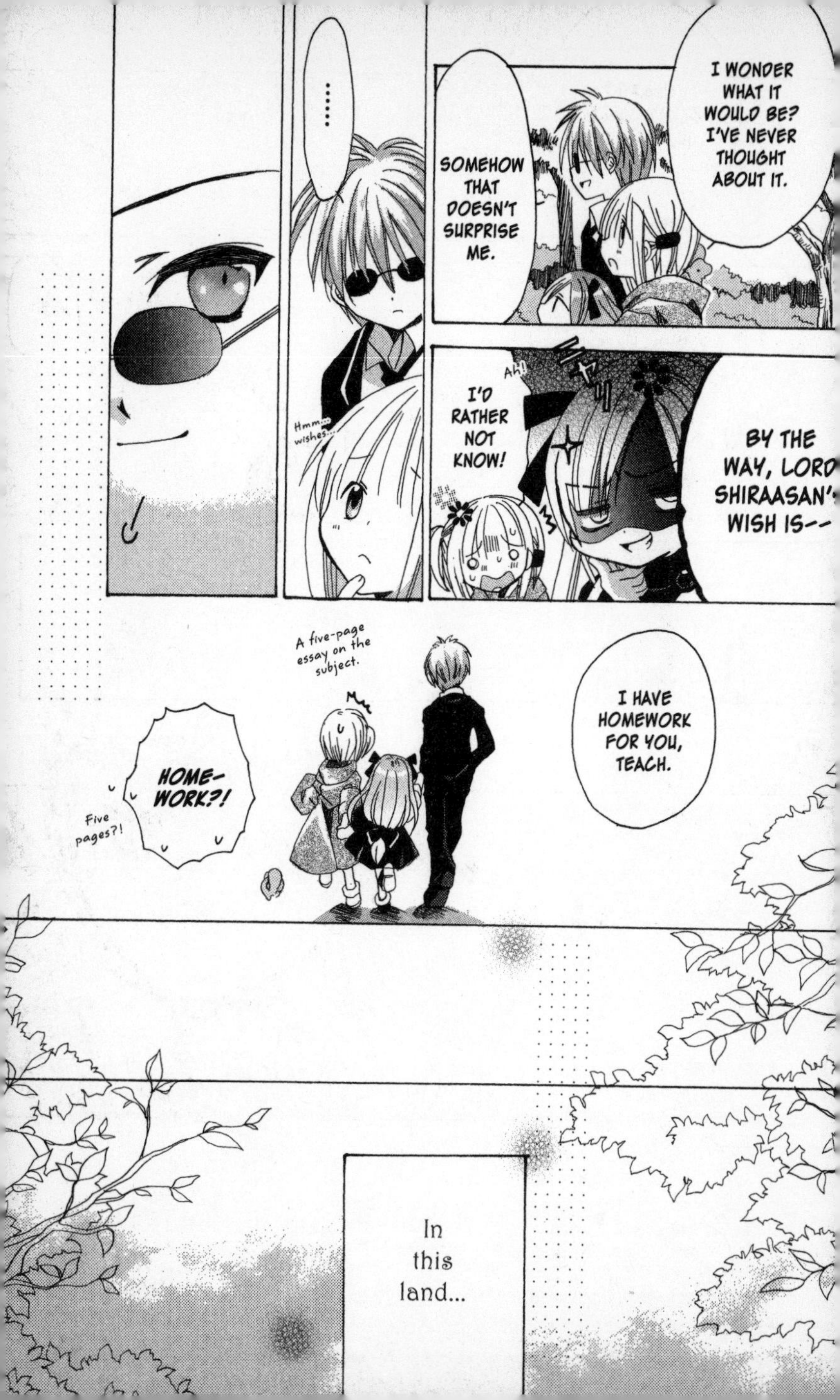

I WONDER WHAT IT WOULD BE? I'VE NEVER THOUGHT ABOUT IT.
SOMEHOW THAT DOESN'T SURPRISE ME.
BY THE WAY, LORD SHIRAASAN' WISH IS--
Ah!
I'D RATHER NOT KNOW!
......
Hmm... wishes...
I HAVE HOMEWORK FOR YOU, TEACH.
A five-page essay on the subject.
HOME-WORK?!
Five pages?!
In this land...

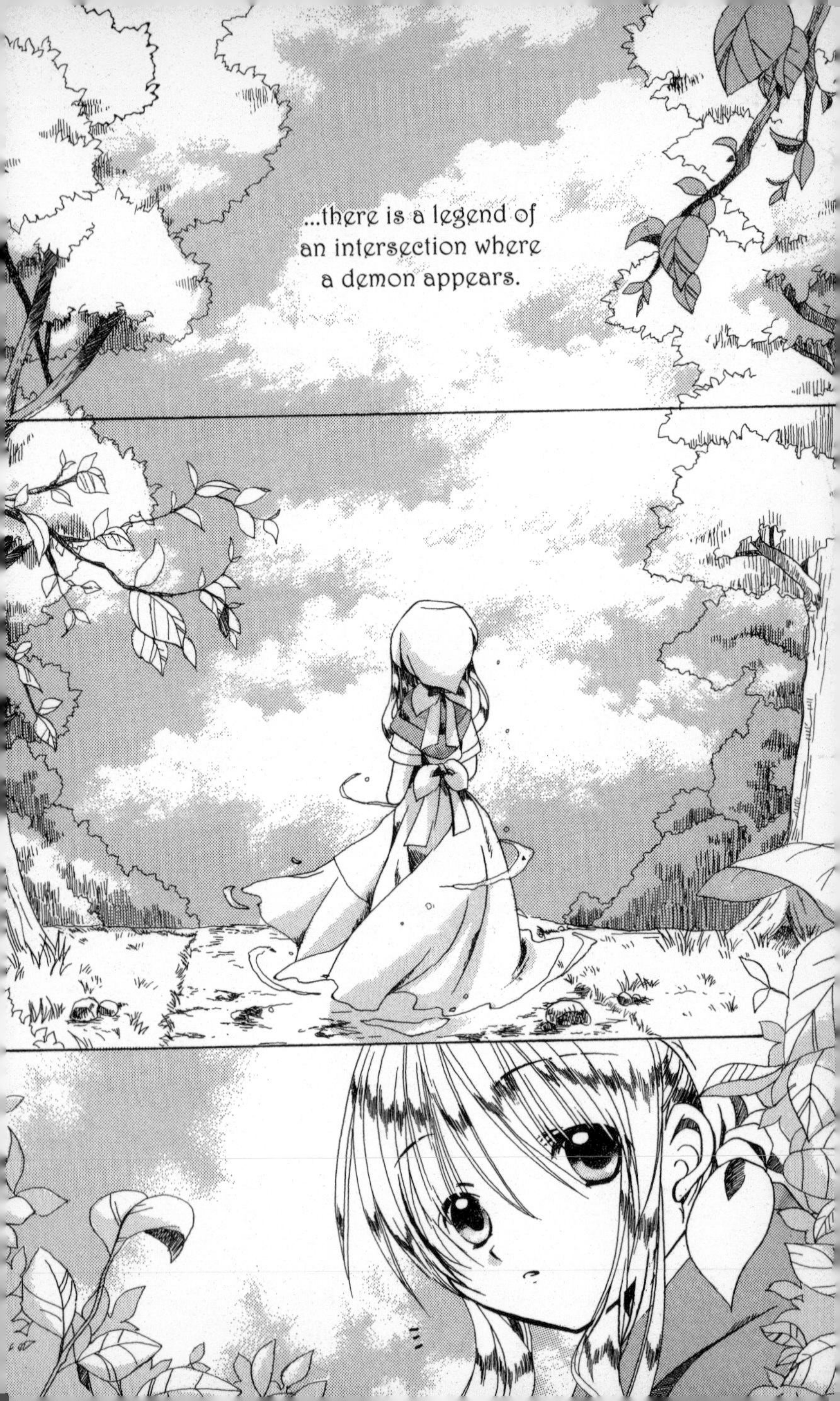
...there is a legend of
an intersection where
a demon appears.

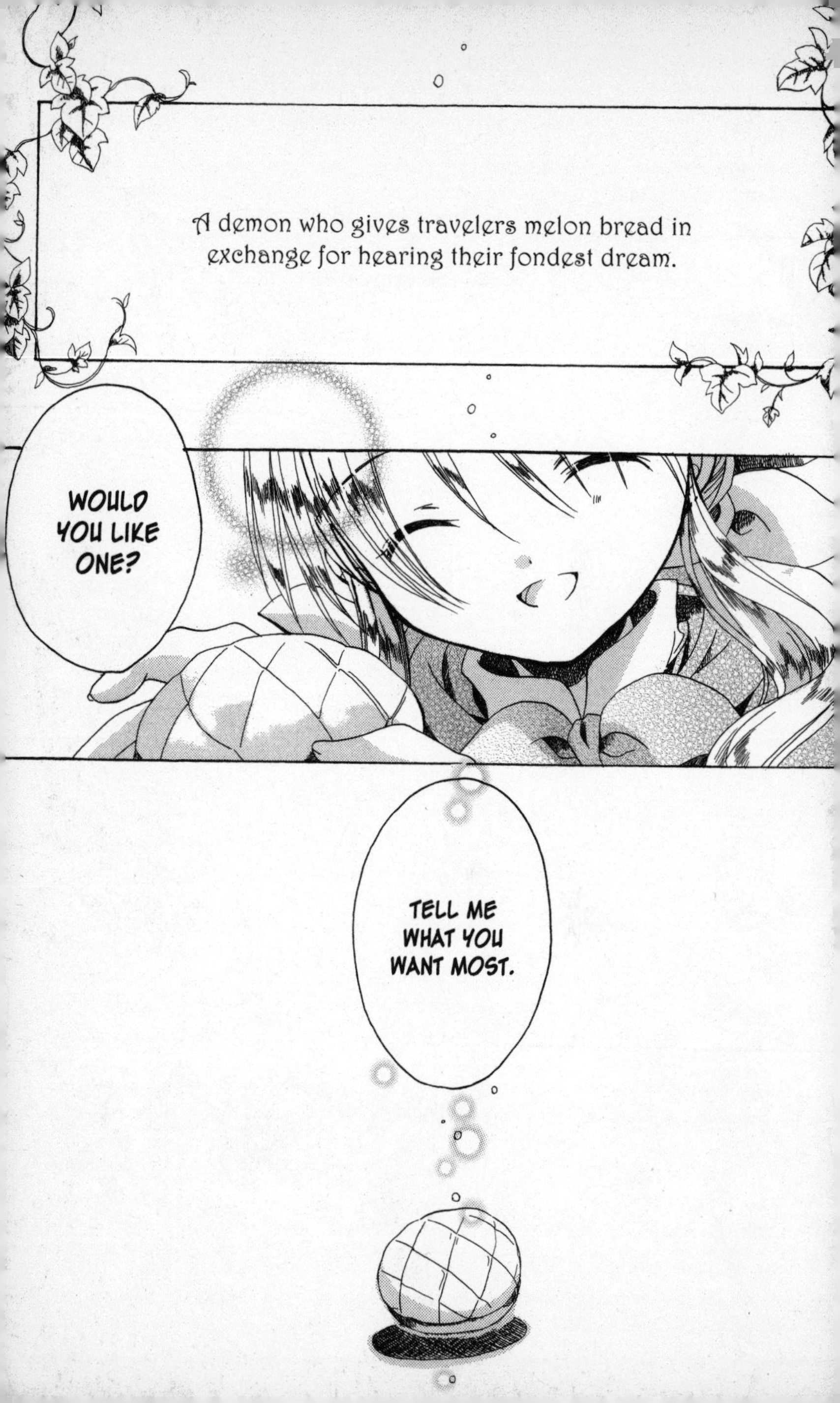
A demon who gives travelers melon bread in exchange for hearing their fondest dream.
WOULD YOU LIKE ONE?
TELL ME WHAT YOU WANT MOST.

HIBIKI'S MAGIC™

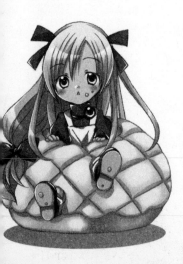

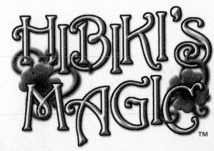

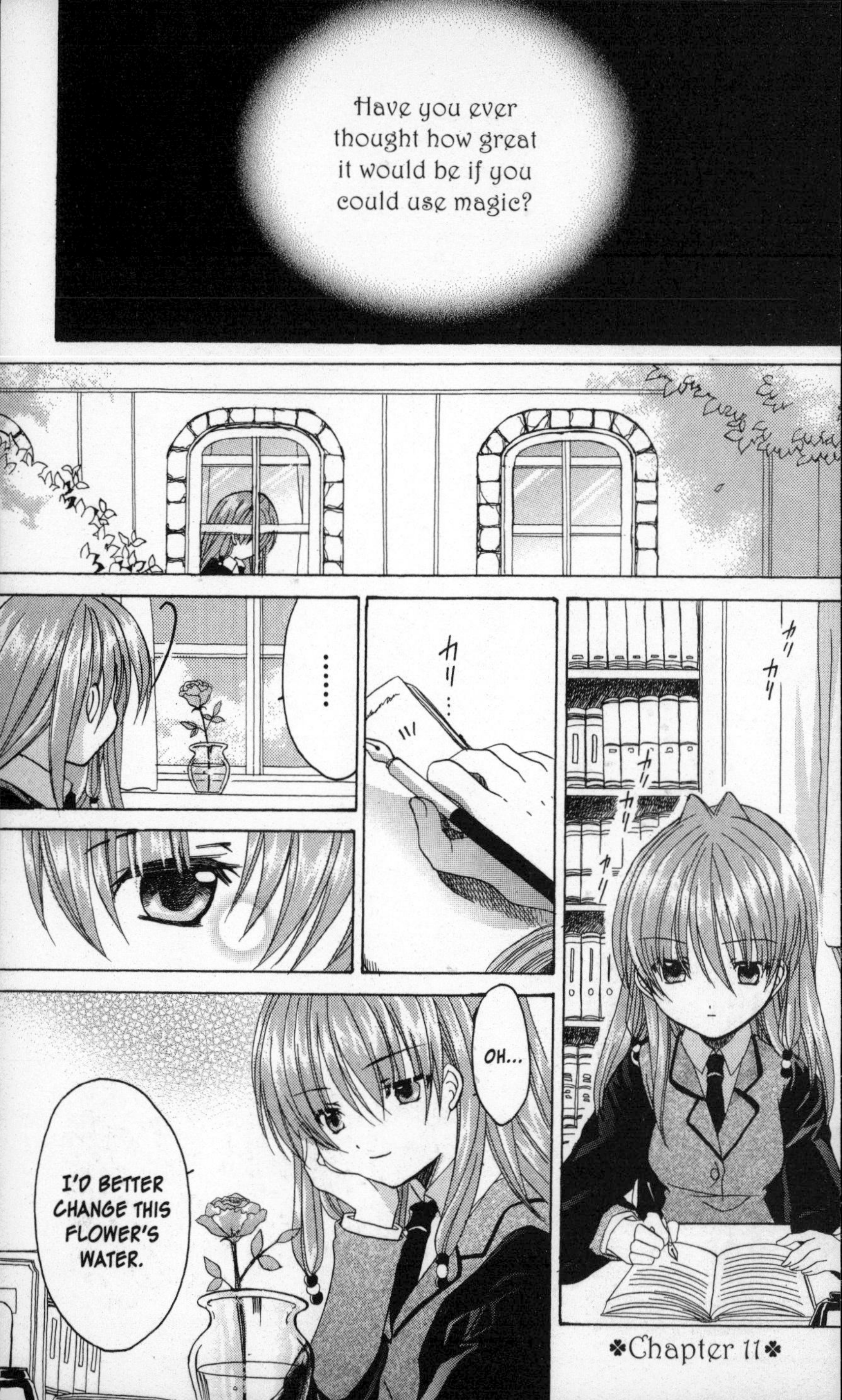
Have you ever thought how great it would be if you could use magic?
カリ カリ
カリ カリ
カリ…
......
OH...
I'D BETTER CHANGE THIS FLOWER'S WATER.

✽Chapter 11✽

THAT WAY...
...IT WILL REMAIN IN BLOOM FOR AS LONG AS POSSIBLE.

✽Chapter 11: The Magic That Saves✽

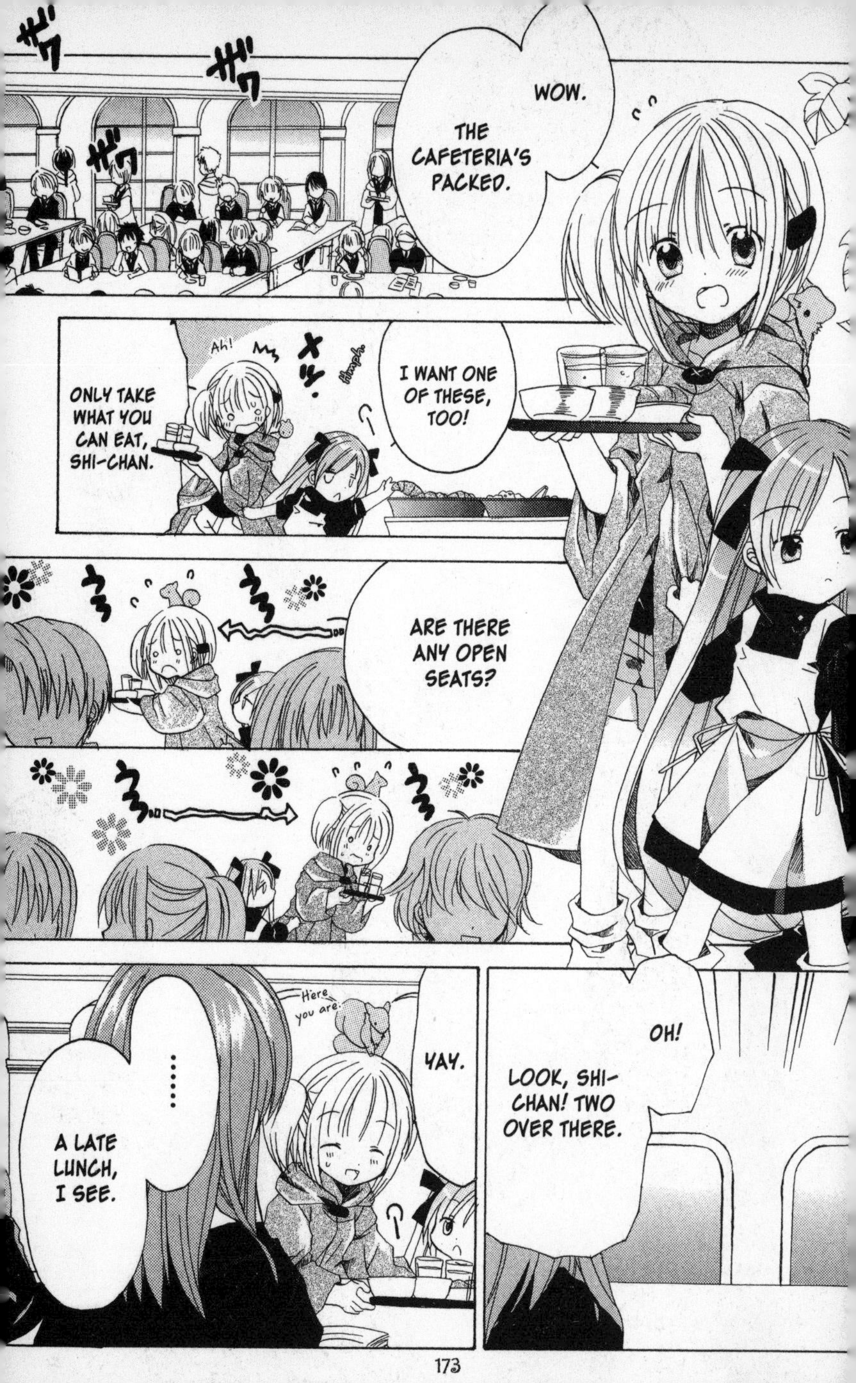
ザワ
ザワ
ザワ
WOW.
THE CAFETERIA'S PACKED.
I WANT ONE OF THESE, TOO!
Hmph.
Ah!
ONLY TAKE WHAT YOU CAN EAT, SHI-CHAN.
ARE THERE ANY OPEN SEATS?
OH!
LOOK, SHI-CHAN! TWO OVER THERE.
YAY.
Here you are.
......
A LATE LUNCH, I SEE.

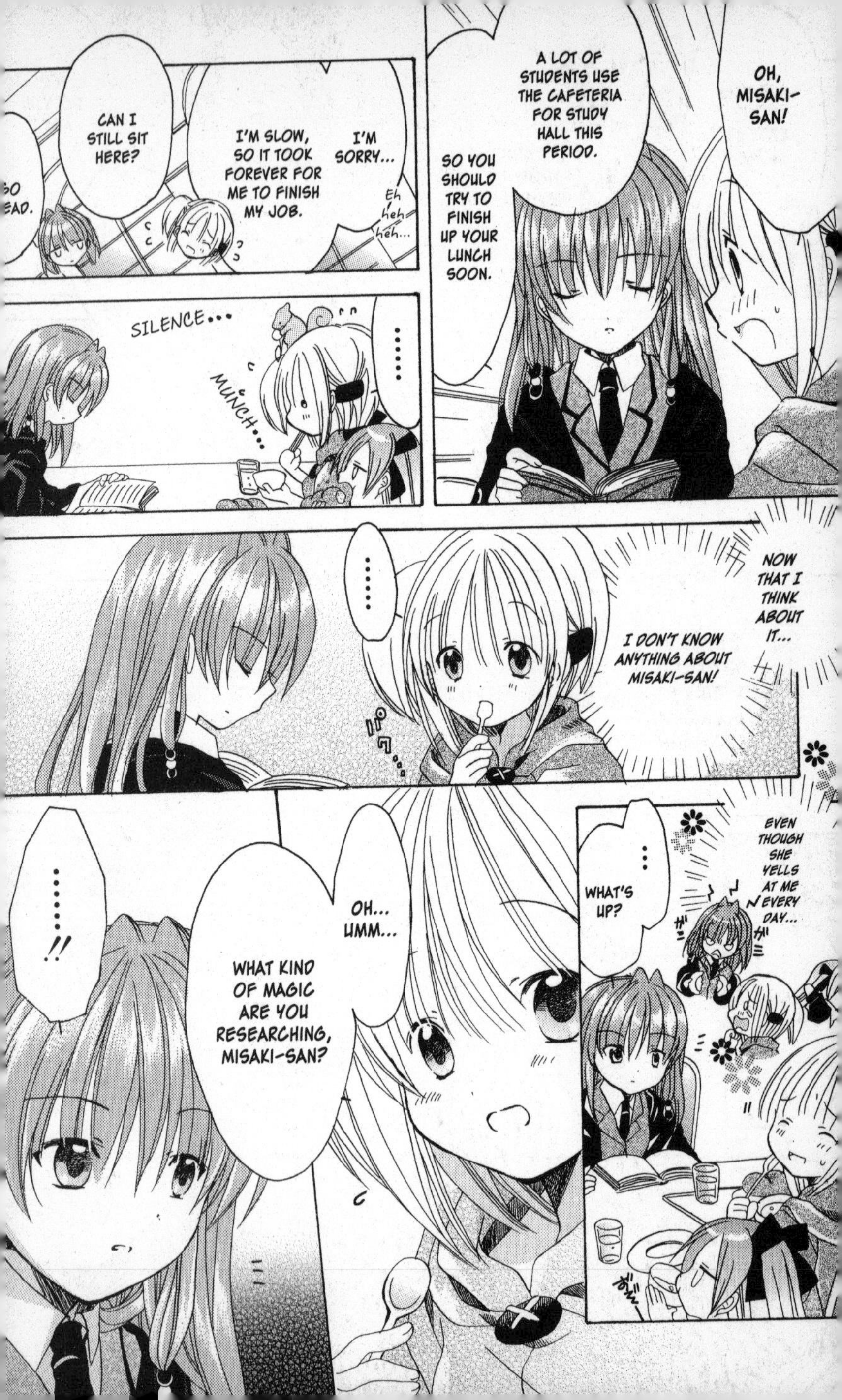
OH, MISAKI-SAN!
A LOT OF STUDENTS USE THE CAFETERIA FOR STUDY HALL THIS PERIOD.
SO YOU SHOULD TRY TO FINISH UP YOUR LUNCH SOON.
I'M SORRY...
I'M SLOW, SO IT TOOK FOREVER FOR ME TO FINISH MY JOB.
Eh heh heh...
CAN I STILL SIT HERE?
GO
EAD.
......
SILENCE...
MUNCH...
NOW THAT I THINK ABOUT IT...
I DON'T KNOW ANYTHING ABOUT MISAKI-SAN!
......
EVEN THOUGH SHE YELLS AT ME EVERY DAY...
...WHAT'S UP?
OH... UMM...
WHAT KIND OF MAGIC ARE YOU RESEARCHING, MISAKI-SAN?
......!!

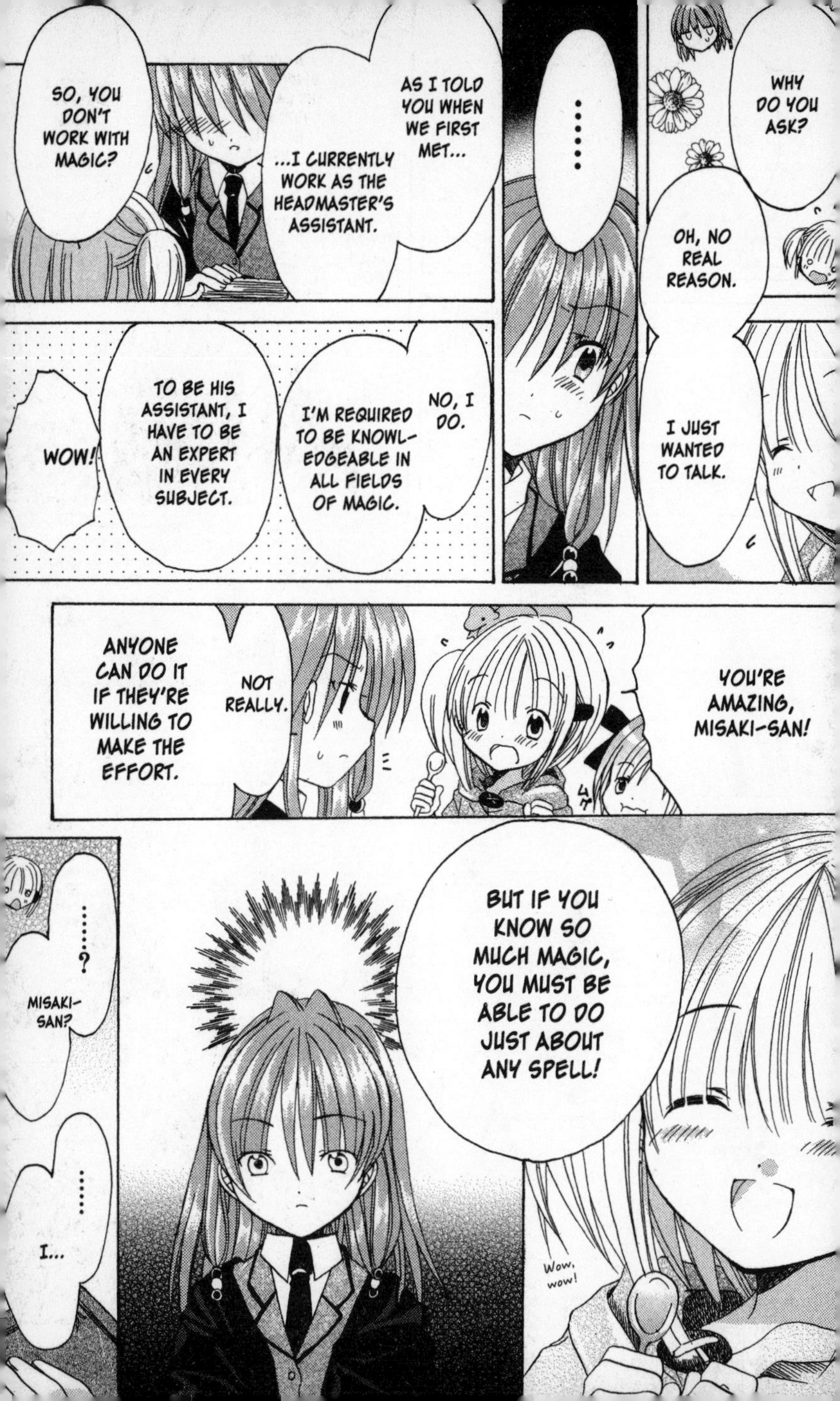
WHY DO YOU ASK?
OH, NO REAL REASON.
I JUST WANTED TO TALK.
......
SO, YOU DON'T WORK WITH MAGIC?
AS I TOLD YOU WHEN WE FIRST MET...
...I CURRENTLY WORK AS THE HEADMASTER'S ASSISTANT.
NO, I DO.
I'M REQUIRED TO BE KNOWLEDGEABLE IN ALL FIELDS OF MAGIC.
TO BE HIS ASSISTANT, I HAVE TO BE AN EXPERT IN EVERY SUBJECT.
WOW!
YOU'RE AMAZING, MISAKI-SAN!
NOT REALLY.
ANYONE CAN DO IT IF THEY'RE WILLING TO MAKE THE EFFORT.
BUT IF YOU KNOW SO MUCH MAGIC, YOU MUST BE ABLE TO DO JUST ABOUT ANY SPELL!
Wow, wow!
......?
MISAKI-SAN?
......
I...

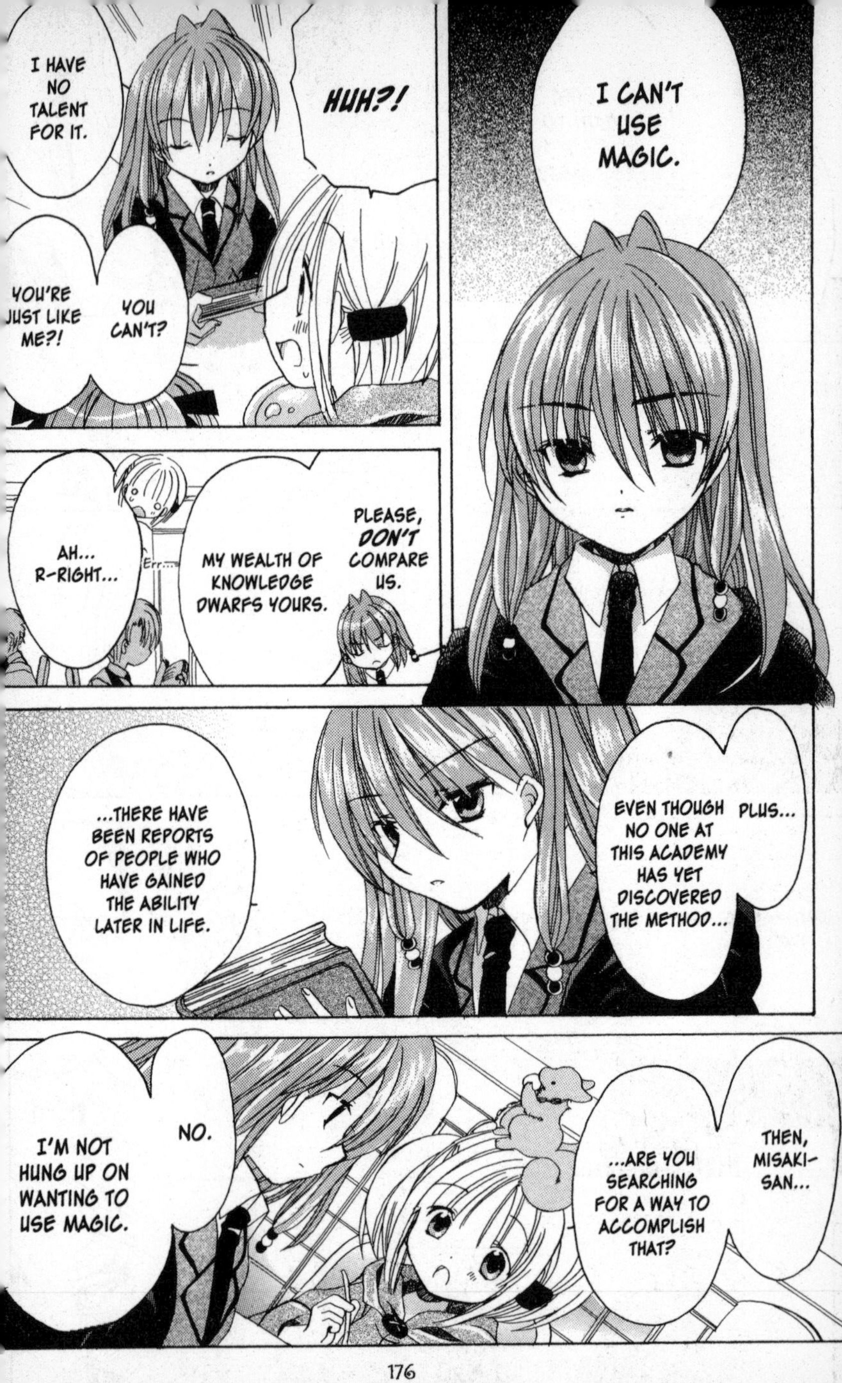
I CAN'T USE MAGIC.
HUH?!
I HAVE NO TALENT FOR IT.
YOU CAN'T?
YOU'RE JUST LIKE ME?!
PLEASE, DON'T COMPARE US.
MY WEALTH OF KNOWLEDGE DWARFS YOURS.
Err...
AH... R-RIGHT...
PLUS...
EVEN THOUGH NO ONE AT THIS ACADEMY HAS YET DISCOVERED THE METHOD...
...THERE HAVE BEEN REPORTS OF PEOPLE WHO HAVE GAINED THE ABILITY LATER IN LIFE.
THEN, MISAKI-SAN...
...ARE YOU SEARCHING FOR A WAY TO ACCOMPLISH THAT?
NO.
I'M NOT HUNG UP ON WANTING TO USE MAGIC.

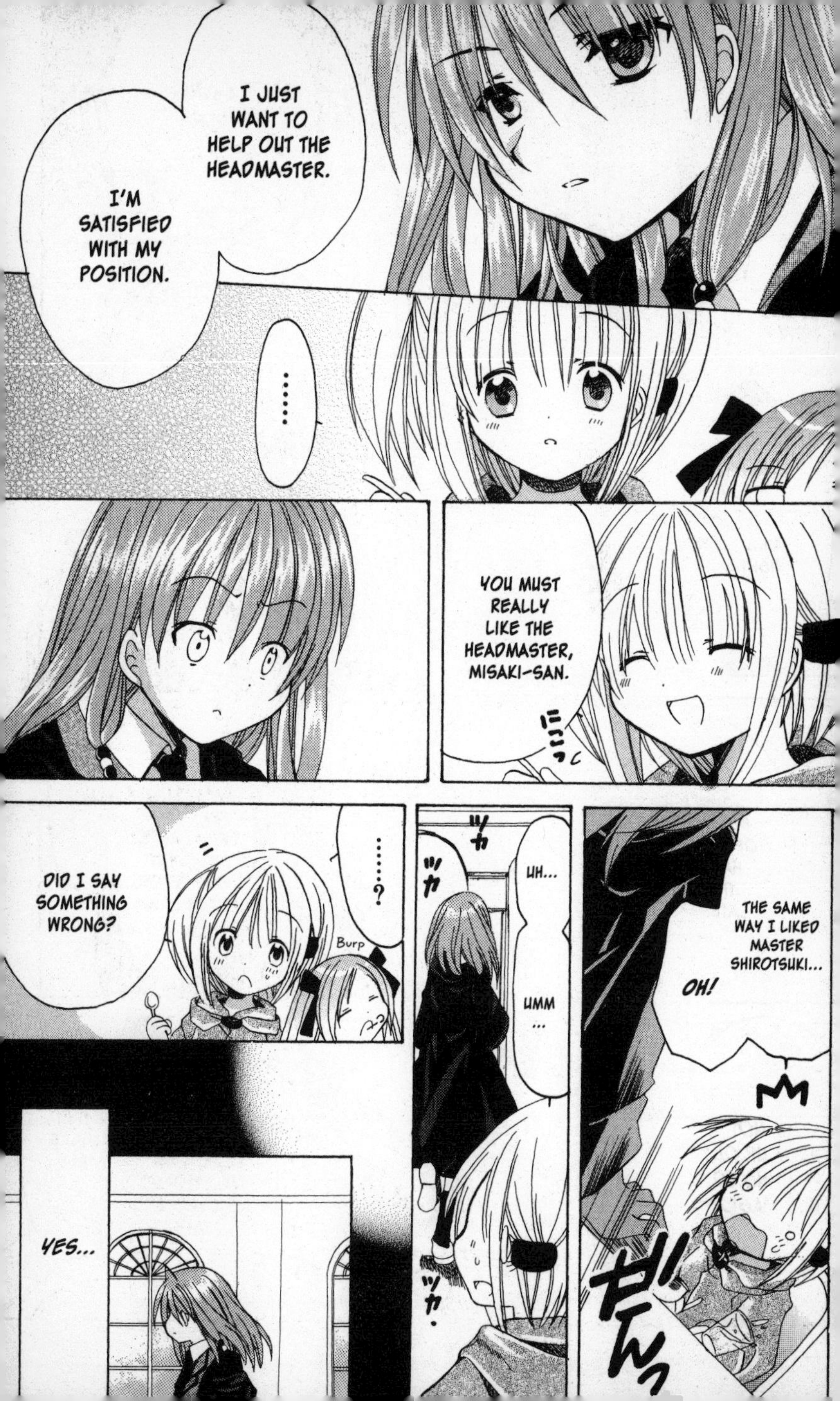
I JUST WANT TO HELP OUT THE HEADMASTER.
I'M SATISFIED WITH MY POSITION.
......
YOU MUST REALLY LIKE THE HEADMASTER, MISAKI-SAN.
ニコッ
THE SAME WAY I LIKED MASTER SHIROTSUKI...
OH!
ツカ
ツカ
UH...
UMM ...
ツカ
......?
DID I SAY SOMETHING WRONG?
Burp
YES...

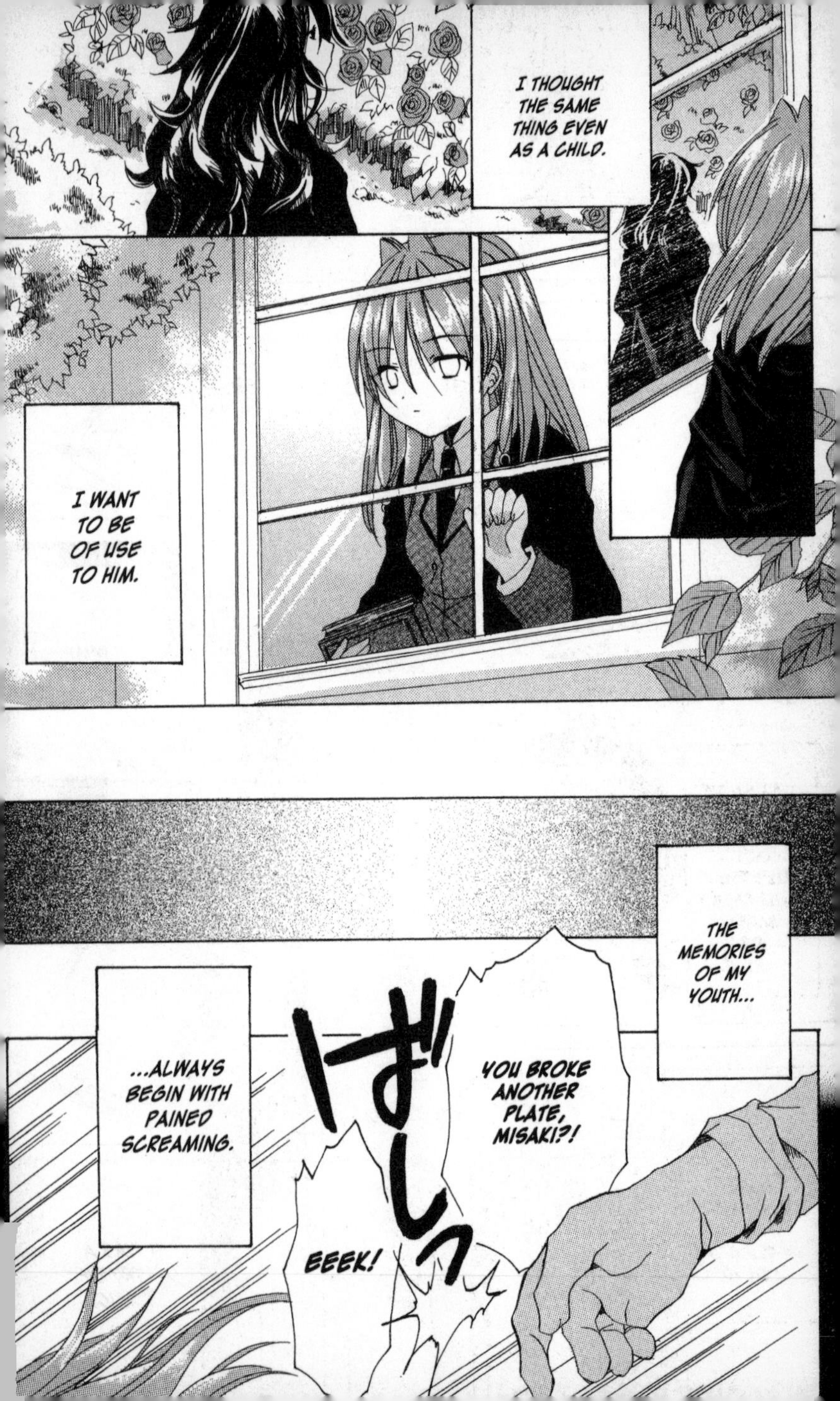
I THOUGHT THE SAME THING EVEN AS A CHILD.
I WANT TO BE OF USE TO HIM.
THE MEMORIES OF MY YOUTH...
YOU BROKE ANOTHER PLATE, MISAKI?!
ばしっ
...ALWAYS BEGIN WITH PAINED SCREAMING.
EEEK!

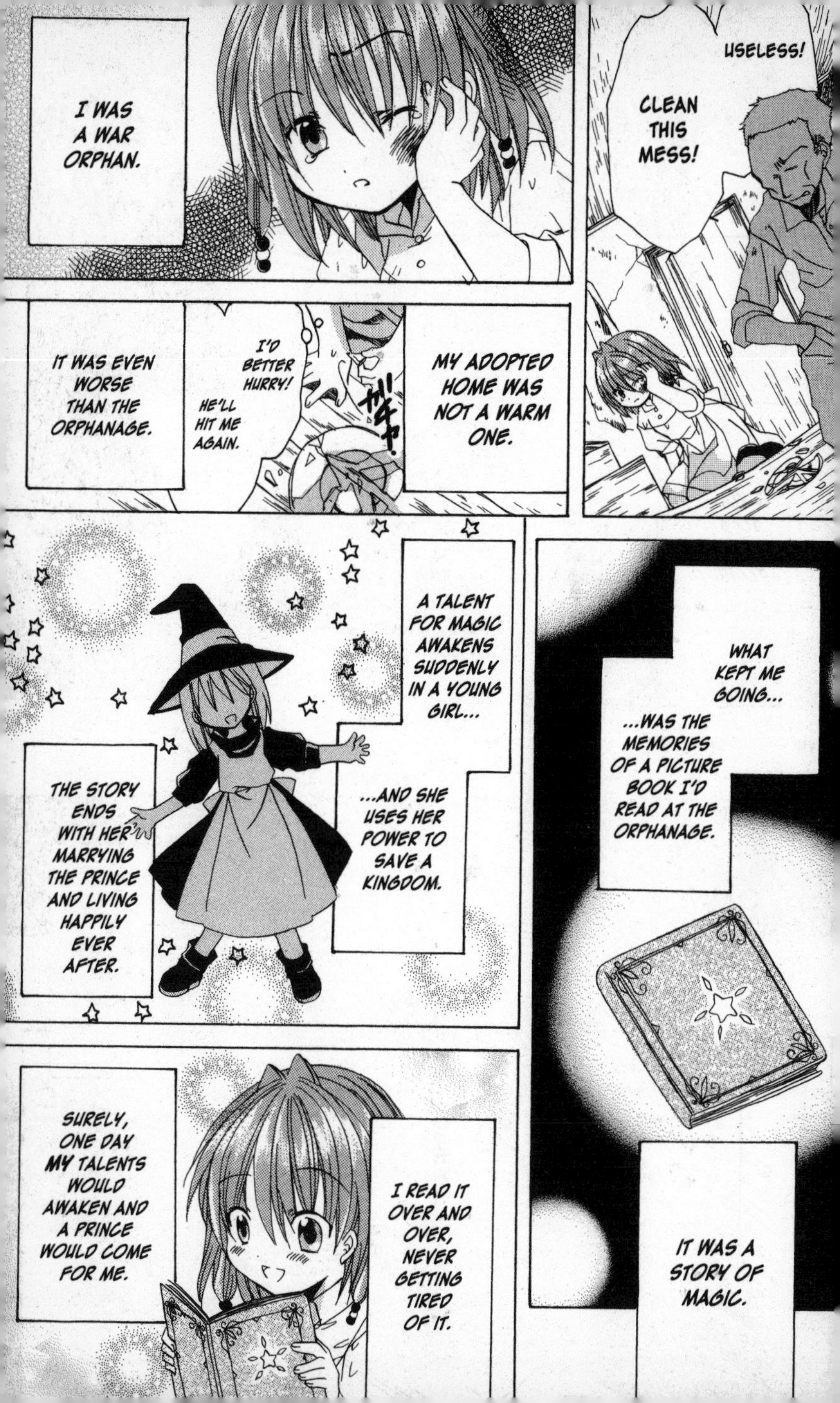
USELESS!
CLEAN THIS MESS!
I WAS A WAR ORPHAN.
MY ADOPTED HOME WAS NOT A WARM ONE.
I'D BETTER HURRY!
HE'LL HIT ME AGAIN.
IT WAS EVEN WORSE THAN THE ORPHANAGE.
WHAT KEPT ME GOING...
...WAS THE MEMORIES OF A PICTURE BOOK I'D READ AT THE ORPHANAGE.
IT WAS A STORY OF MAGIC.
A TALENT FOR MAGIC AWAKENS SUDDENLY IN A YOUNG GIRL...
...AND SHE USES HER POWER TO SAVE A KINGDOM.
THE STORY ENDS WITH HER MARRYING THE PRINCE AND LIVING HAPPILY EVER AFTER.
I READ IT OVER AND OVER, NEVER GETTING TIRED OF IT.
SURELY, ONE DAY MY TALENTS WOULD AWAKEN AND A PRINCE WOULD COME FOR ME.

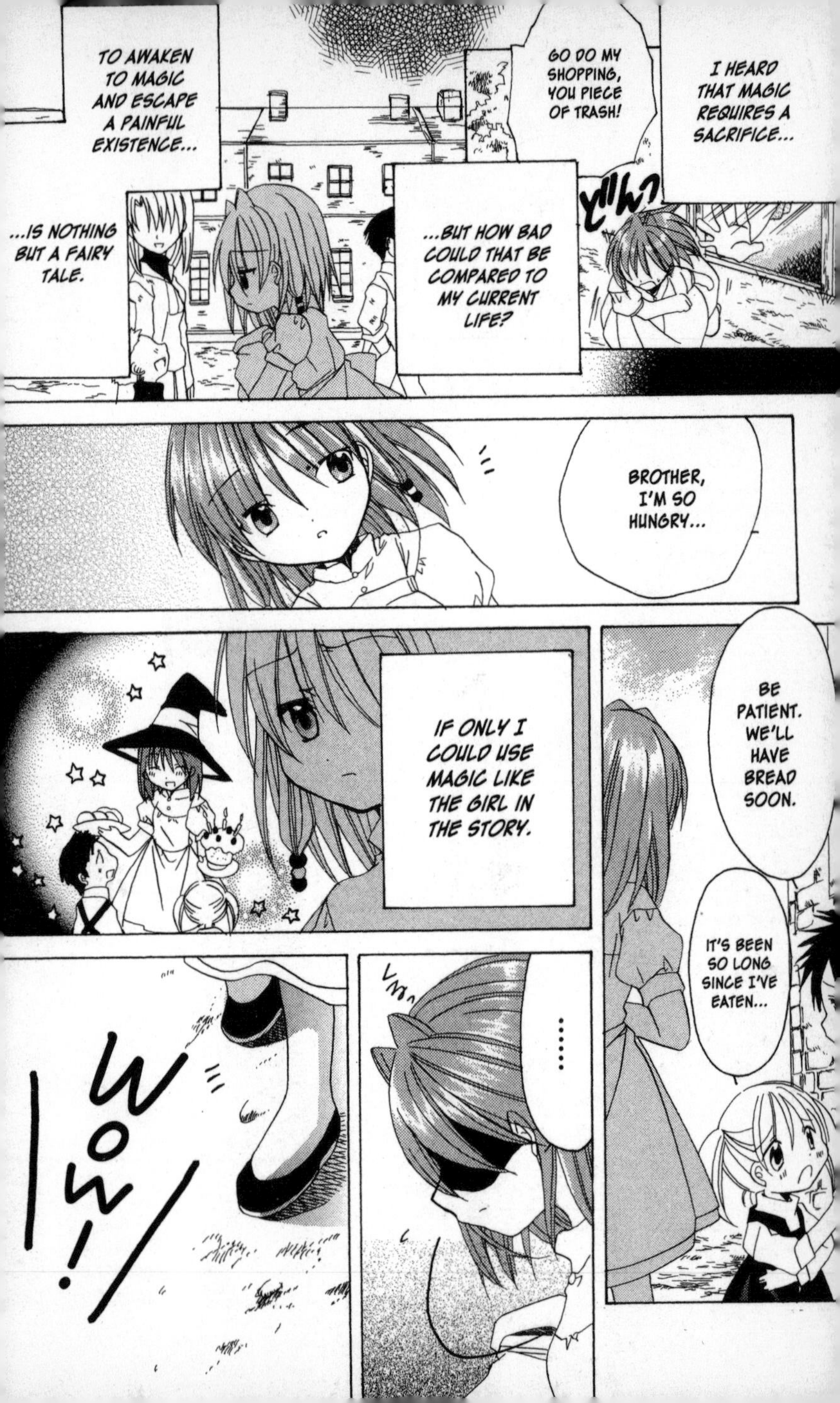
I HEARD THAT MAGIC REQUIRES A SACRIFICE...
GO DO MY SHOPPING, YOU PIECE OF TRASH!
...BUT HOW BAD COULD THAT BE COMPARED TO MY CURRENT LIFE?
TO AWAKEN TO MAGIC AND ESCAPE A PAINFUL EXISTENCE...
...IS NOTHING BUT A FAIRY TALE.
BROTHER, I'M SO HUNGRY...
BE PATIENT. WE'LL HAVE BREAD SOON.
IT'S BEEN SO LONG SINCE I'VE EATEN...
IF ONLY I COULD USE MAGIC LIKE THE GIRL IN THE STORY.
......
WOW!!

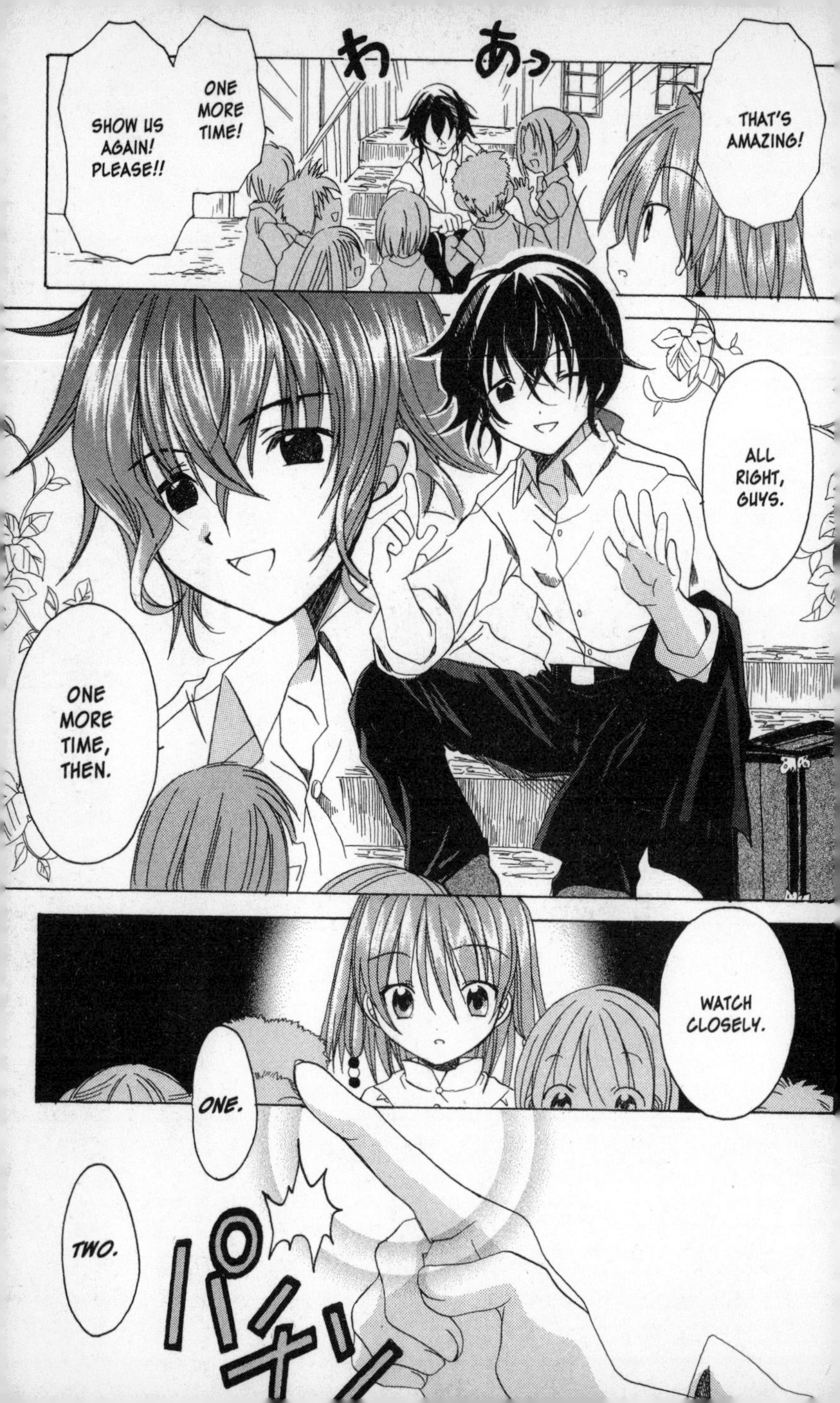
THAT'S AMAZING!
わあっ
ONE MORE TIME!
SHOW US AGAIN! PLEASE!!
ALL RIGHT, GUYS.
ONE MORE TIME, THEN.
WATCH CLOSELY.
ONE.
TWO.
パチン

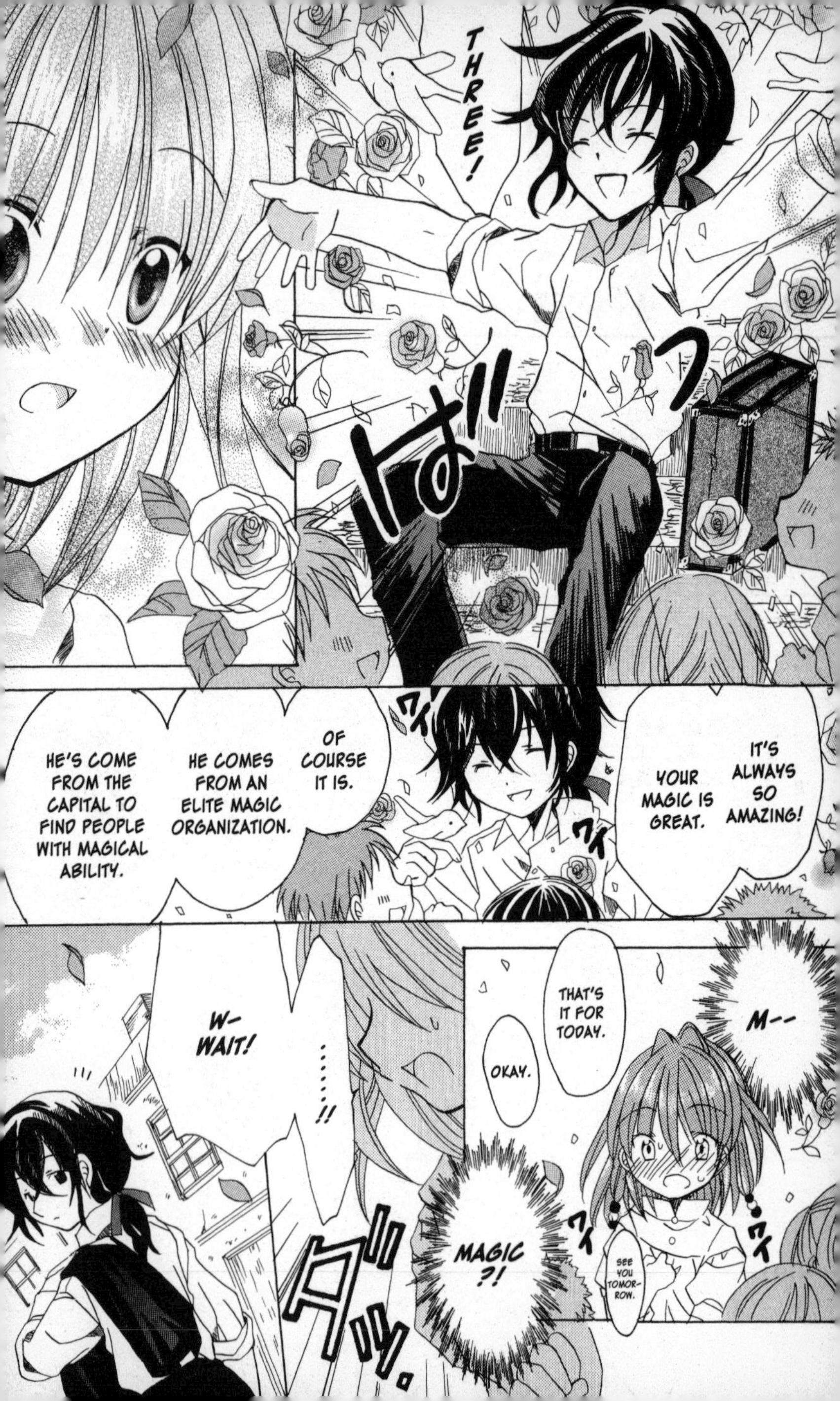
THREE!
IT'S ALWAYS SO AMAZING!
YOUR MAGIC IS GREAT.
OF COURSE IT IS.
HE COMES FROM AN ELITE MAGIC ORGANIZATION.
HE'S COME FROM THE CAPITAL TO FIND PEOPLE WITH MAGICAL ABILITY.
M--
THAT'S IT FOR TODAY.
OKAY.
SEE YOU TOMORROW.
MAGIC?!
W-WAIT!
......!!

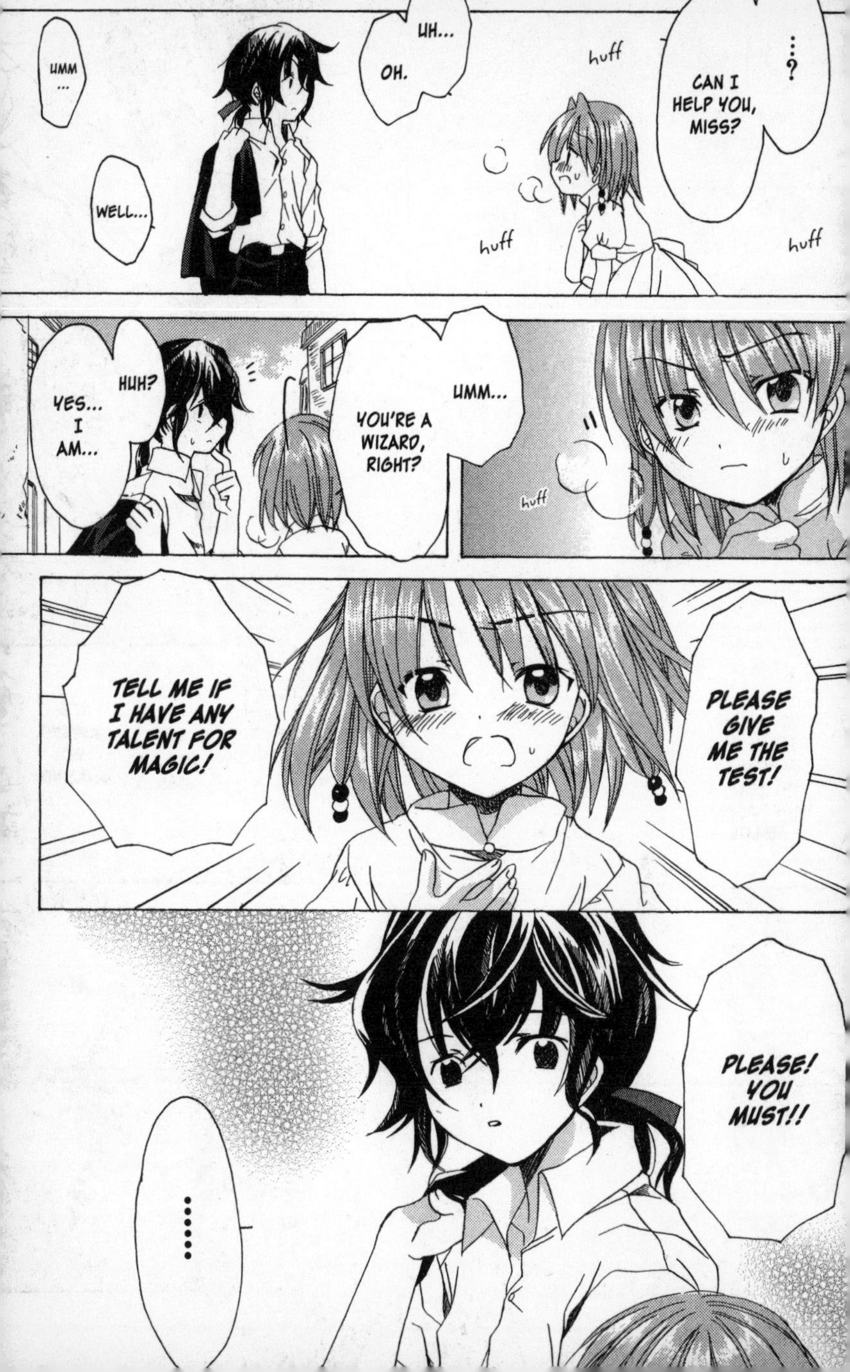
...?
CAN I HELP YOU, MISS?
huff
UH... OH.
UMM ...
huff
huff
WELL...
huff
UMM... YOU'RE A WIZARD, RIGHT?
HUH? YES... I AM...
PLEASE GIVE ME THE TEST!
TELL ME IF I HAVE ANY TALENT FOR MAGIC!
PLEASE! YOU MUST!!
......

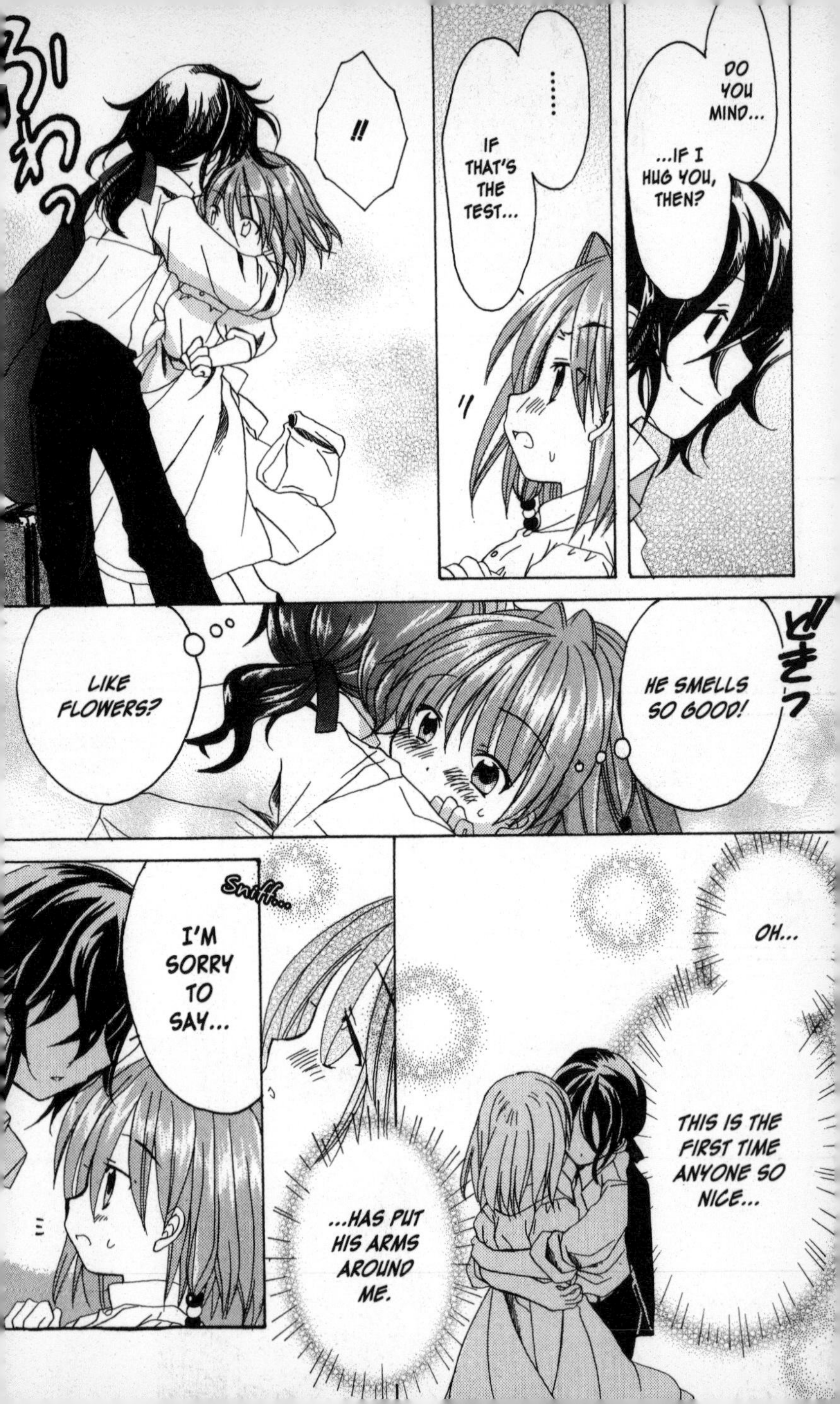
DO YOU MIND...
...IF I HUG YOU, THEN?
......
IF THAT'S THE TEST...
!!
ふわっ
どきっ
HE SMELLS SO GOOD!
LIKE FLOWERS?
OH...
THIS IS THE FIRST TIME ANYONE SO NICE...
...HAS PUT HIS ARMS AROUND ME.
Sniff...
I'M SORRY TO SAY...

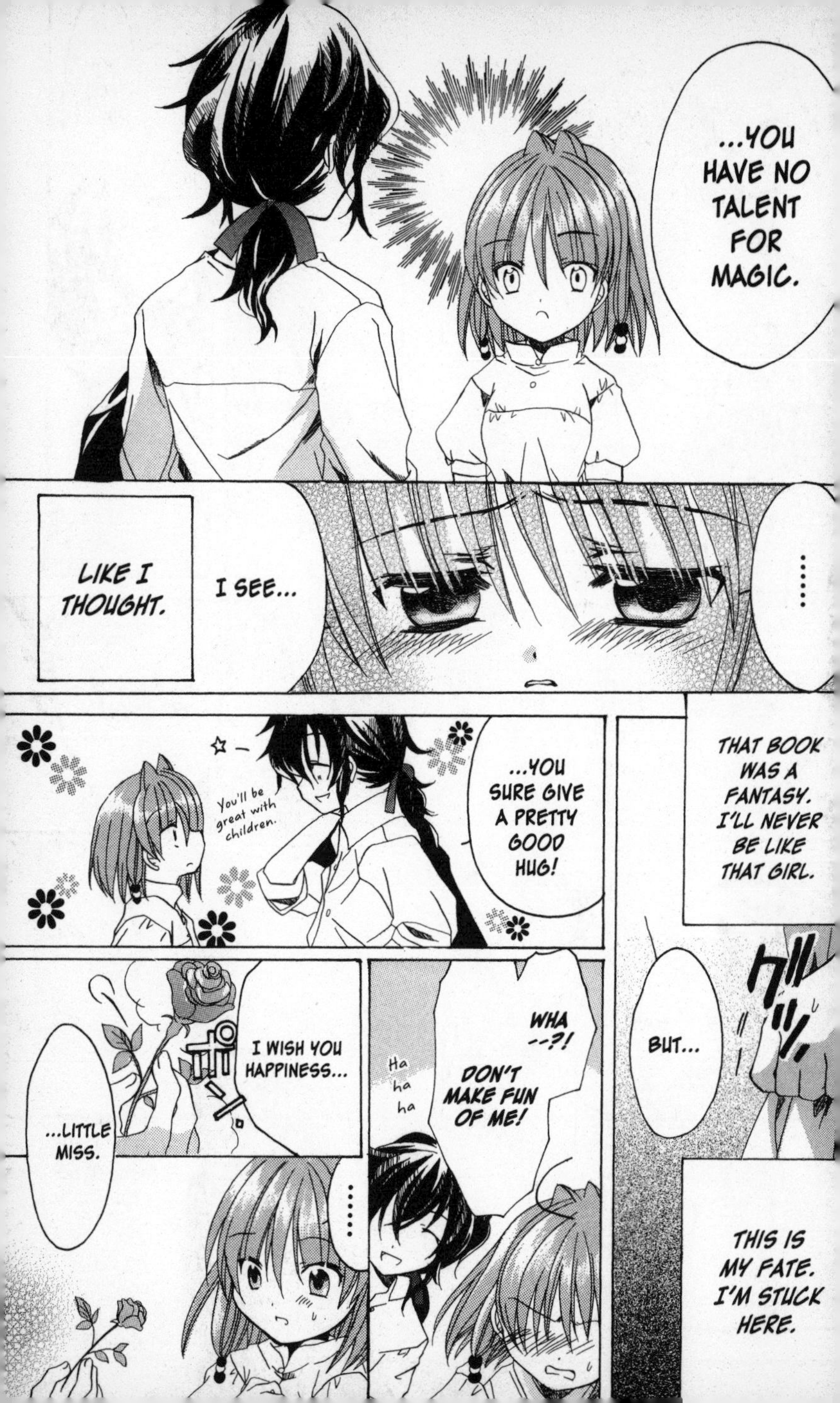
...YOU HAVE NO TALENT FOR MAGIC.
......
I SEE...
LIKE I THOUGHT.
THAT BOOK WAS A FANTASY. I'LL NEVER BE LIKE THAT GIRL.
BUT...
THIS IS MY FATE. I'M STUCK HERE.
...YOU SURE GIVE A PRETTY GOOD HUG!
You'll be great with children.
WHA--?!
DON'T MAKE FUN OF ME!
Ha ha ha
I WISH YOU HAPPINESS...
...LITTLE MISS.
......

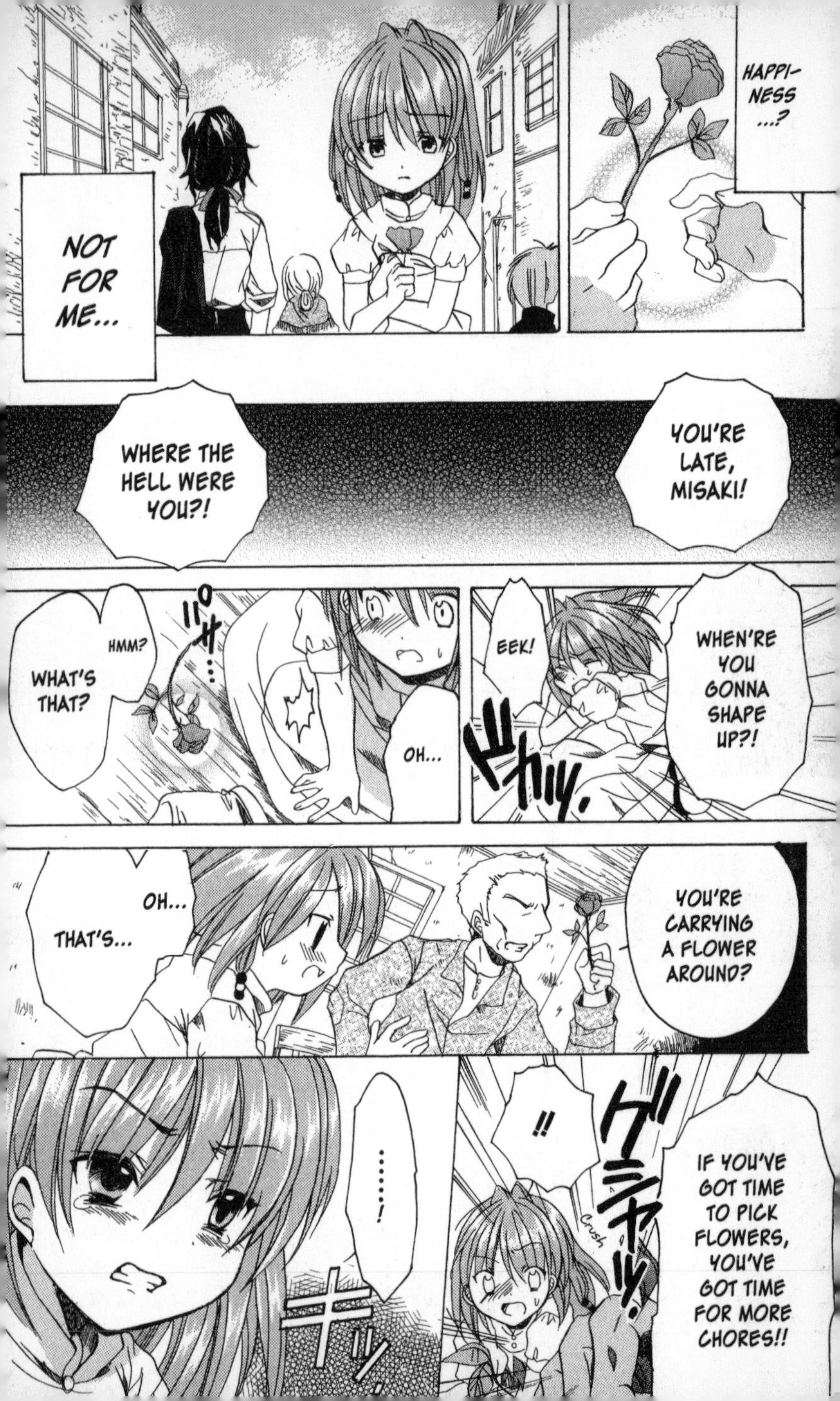

HAPPINESS ...?
NOT FOR ME...
YOU'RE LATE, MISAKI!
WHERE THE HELL WERE YOU?!
WHEN'RE YOU GONNA SHAPE UP?!
EEK!
HMM? WHAT'S THAT?
OH...
YOU'RE CARRYING A FLOWER AROUND?
OH... THAT'S...
IF YOU'VE GOT TIME TO PICK FLOWERS, YOU'VE GOT TIME FOR MORE CHORES!!
!!
Crush
......!

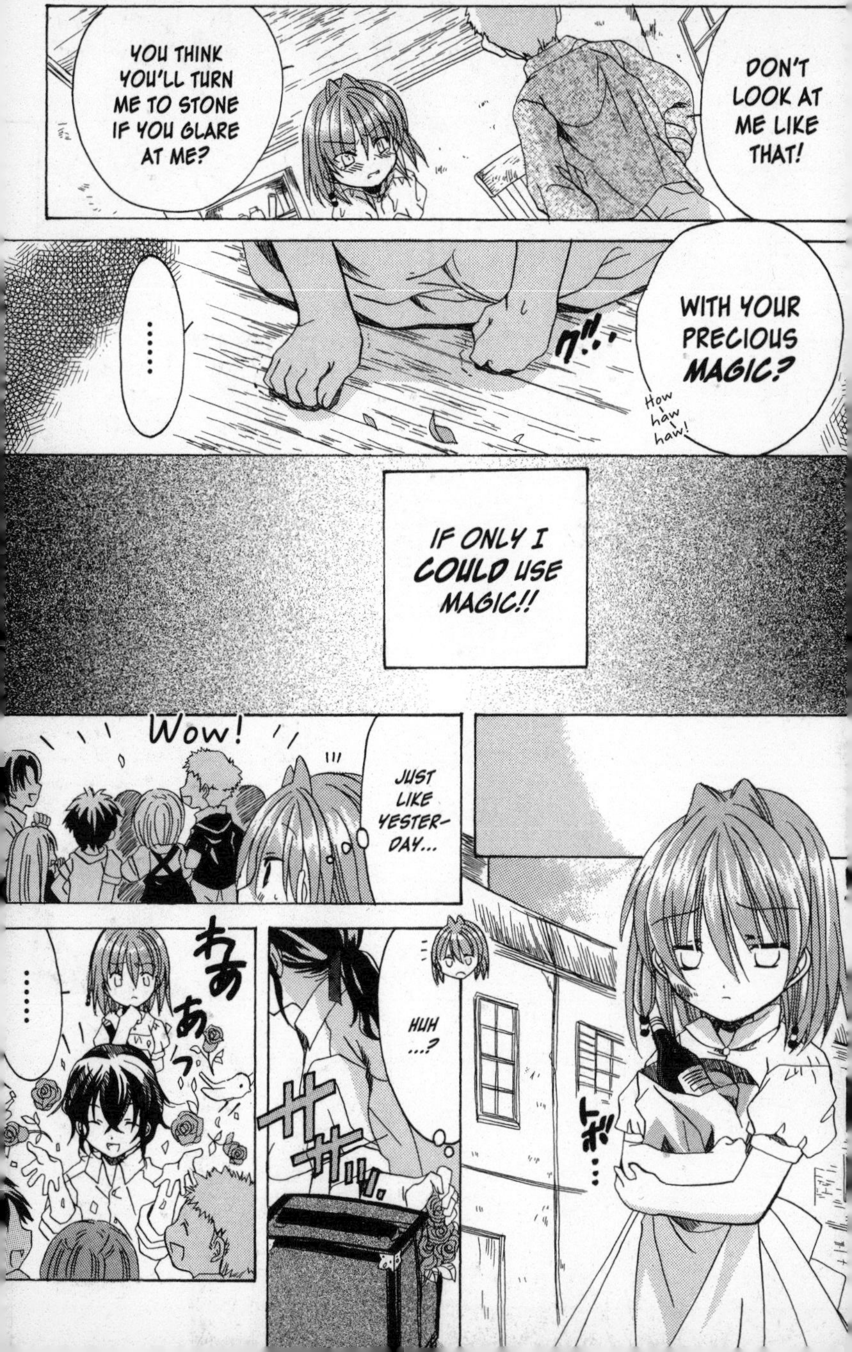
DON'T LOOK AT ME LIKE THAT!
YOU THINK YOU'LL TURN ME TO STONE IF YOU GLARE AT ME?
WITH YOUR PRECIOUS MAGIC?
How haw haw!
......
IF ONLY I COULD USE MAGIC!!
トボ…
JUST LIKE YESTER-DAY...
Wow!
HUH ...?
わあっ
......

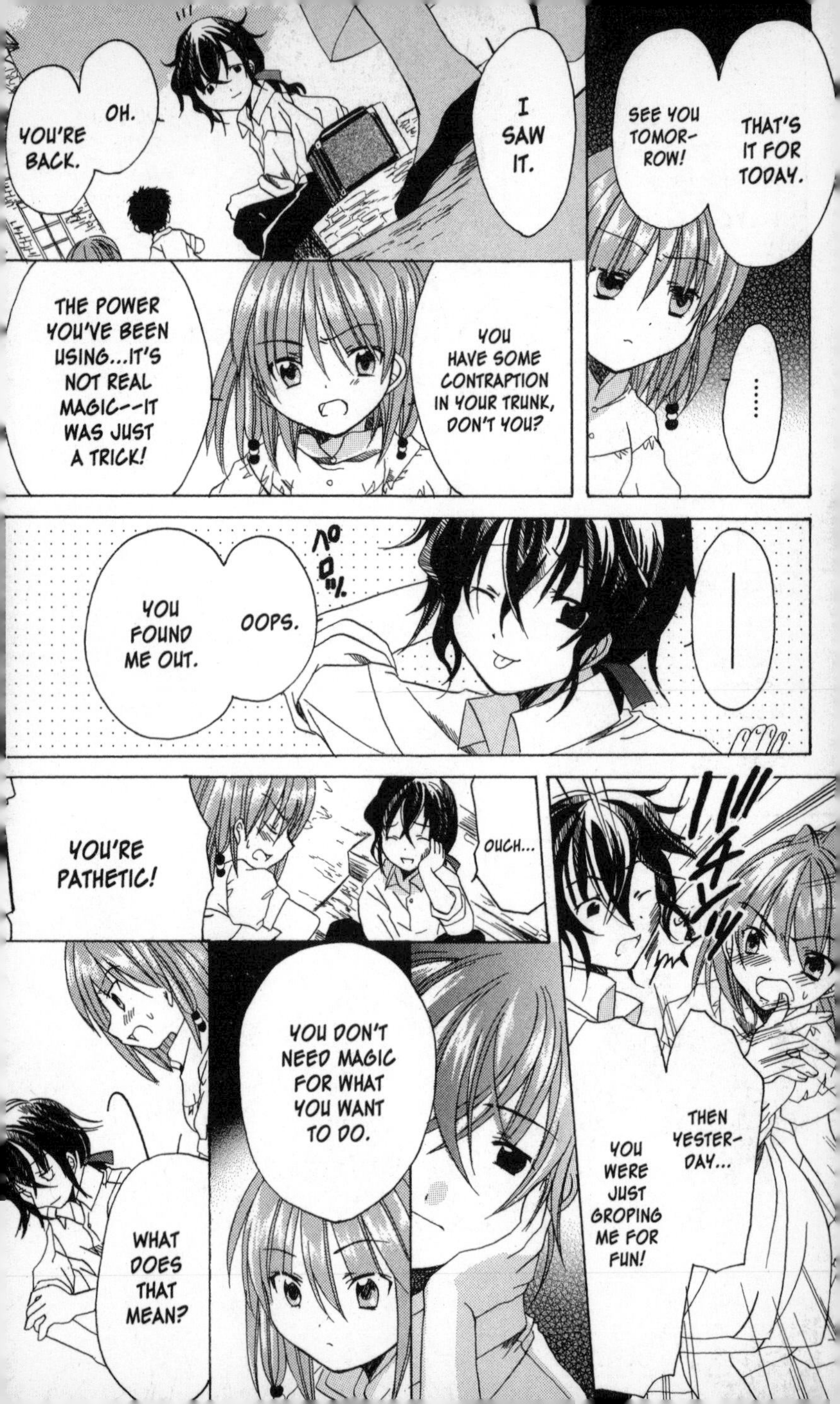
THAT'S IT FOR TODAY.
SEE YOU TOMORROW!
......
I SAW IT.
OH. YOU'RE BACK.
YOU HAVE SOME CONTRAPTION IN YOUR TRUNK, DON'T YOU?
THE POWER YOU'VE BEEN USING...IT'S NOT REAL MAGIC--IT WAS JUST A TRICK!
OOPS.
YOU FOUND ME OUT.
ペロッ
OUCH...
YOU'RE PATHETIC!
THEN YESTERDAY...
YOU WERE JUST GROPING ME FOR FUN!
YOU DON'T NEED MAGIC FOR WHAT YOU WANT TO DO.
WHAT DOES THAT MEAN?

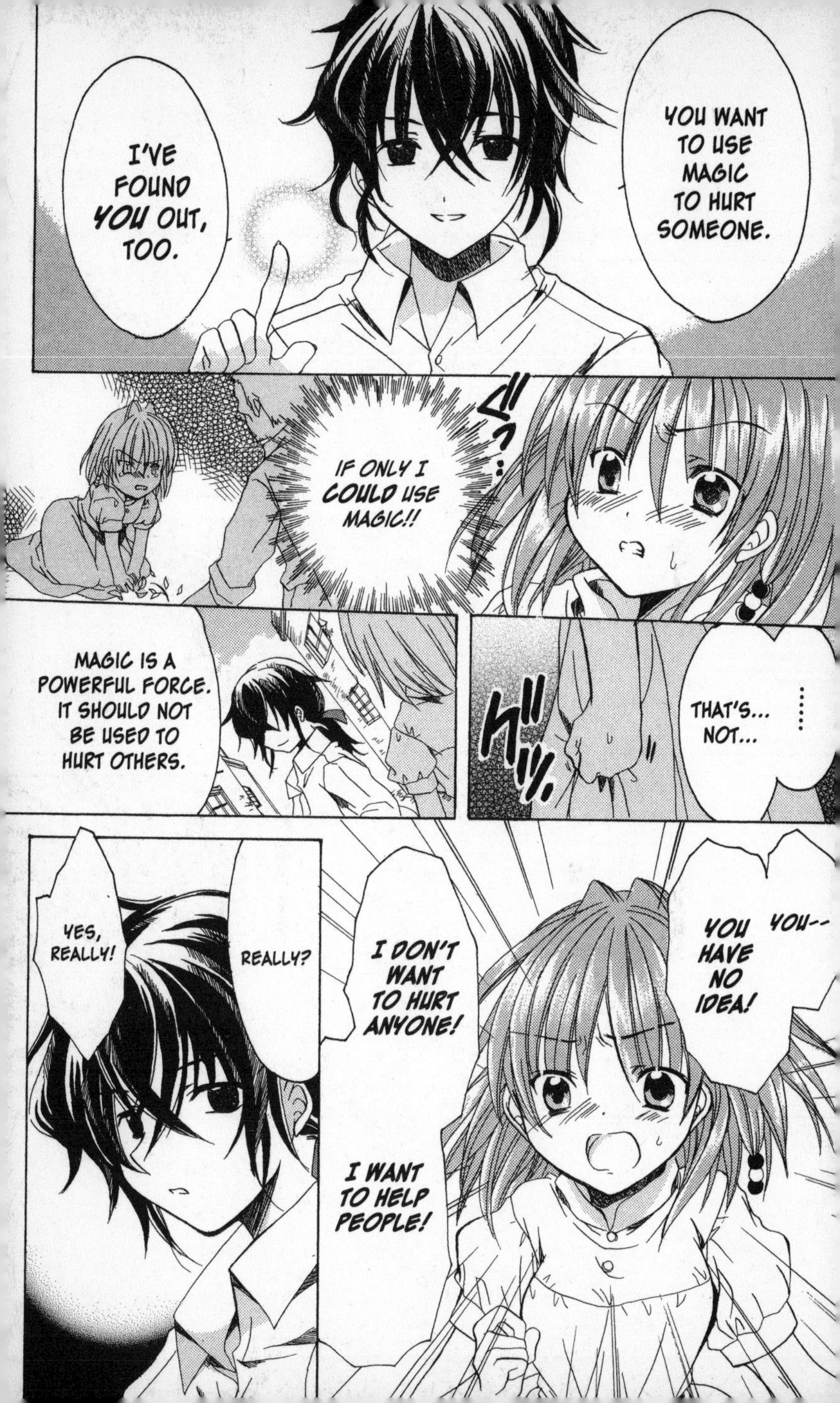

YOU WANT TO USE MAGIC TO HURT SOMEONE.
I'VE FOUND YOU OUT, TOO.
IF ONLY I COULD USE MAGIC!!
......
THAT'S... NOT...
MAGIC IS A POWERFUL FORCE. IT SHOULD NOT BE USED TO HURT OTHERS.
YOU--
YOU HAVE NO IDEA!
I DON'T WANT TO HURT ANYONE!
I WANT TO HELP PEOPLE!
REALLY?
YES, REALLY!

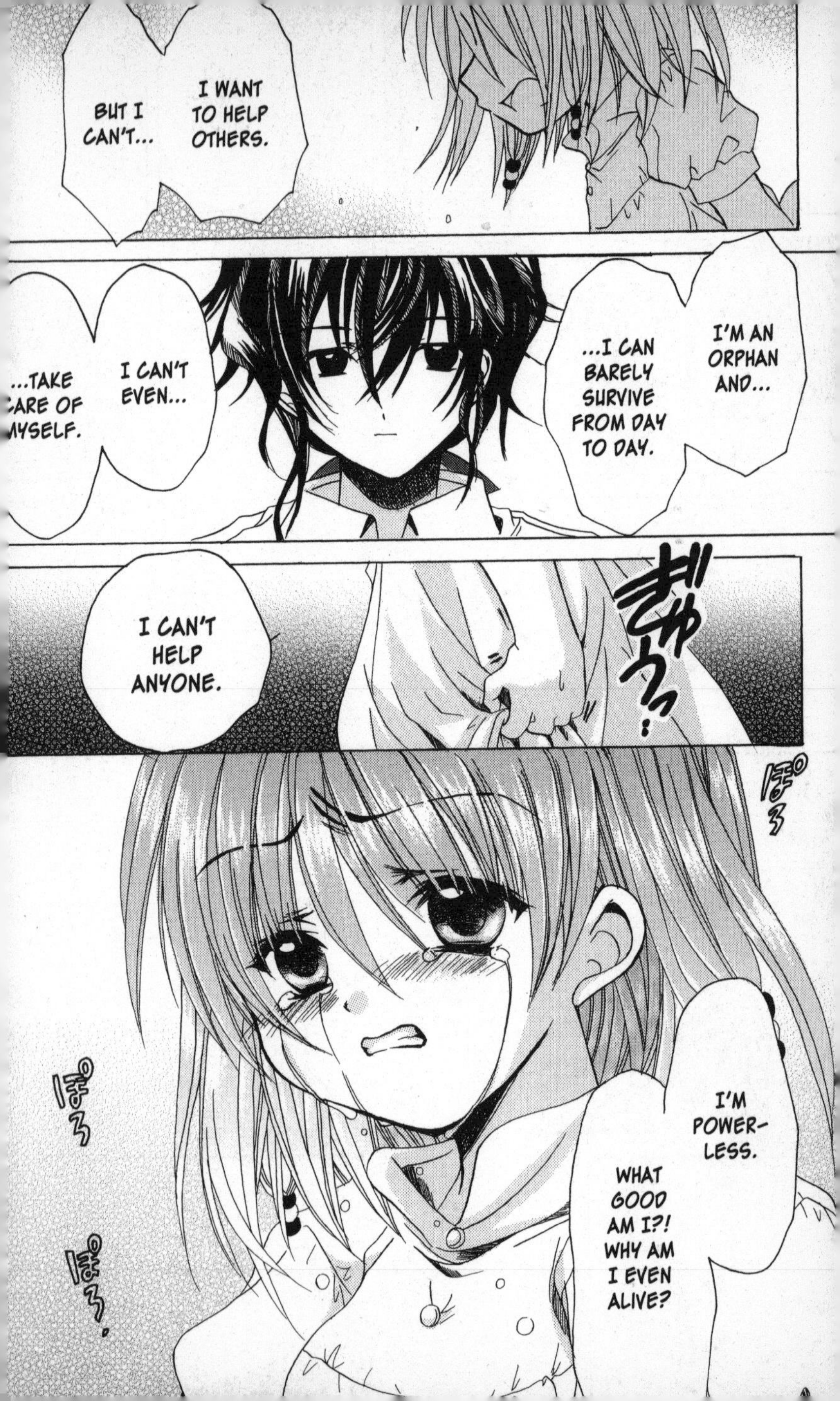

I WANT TO HELP OTHERS.
BUT I CAN'T...
I'M AN ORPHAN AND...
...I CAN BARELY SURVIVE FROM DAY TO DAY.
I CAN'T EVEN...
...TAKE CARE OF MYSELF.
ぎゅうっ
I CAN'T HELP ANYONE.
ぽろ
I'M POWER-LESS.
WHAT GOOD AM I?! WHY AM I EVEN ALIVE?
ぽろ
ぽろ

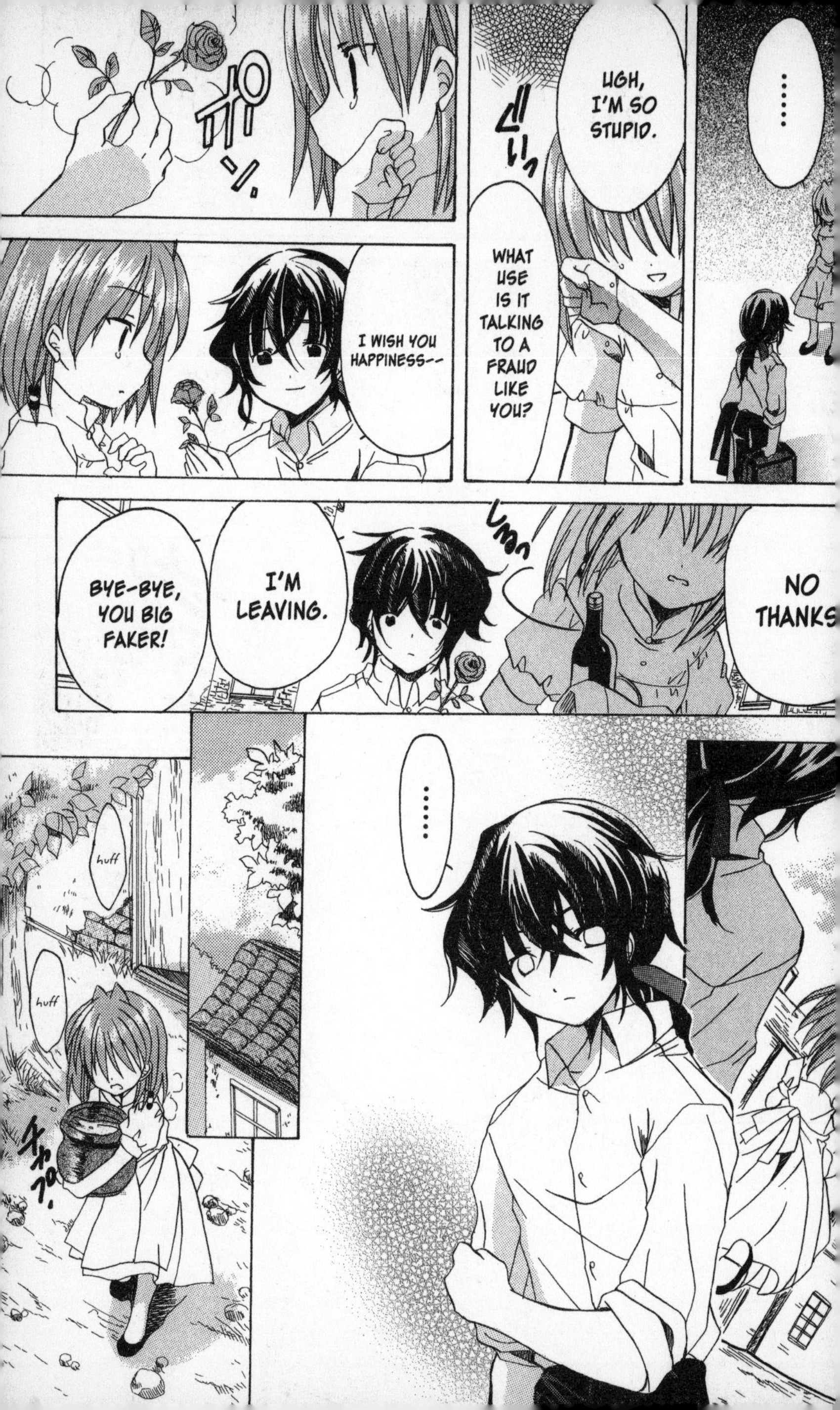

……
UGH, I'M SO STUPID.
WHAT USE IS IT TALKING TO A FRAUD LIKE YOU?
I WISH YOU HAPPINESS--
NO THANKS
I'M LEAVING.
BYE-BYE, YOU BIG FAKER!
……
huff
huff

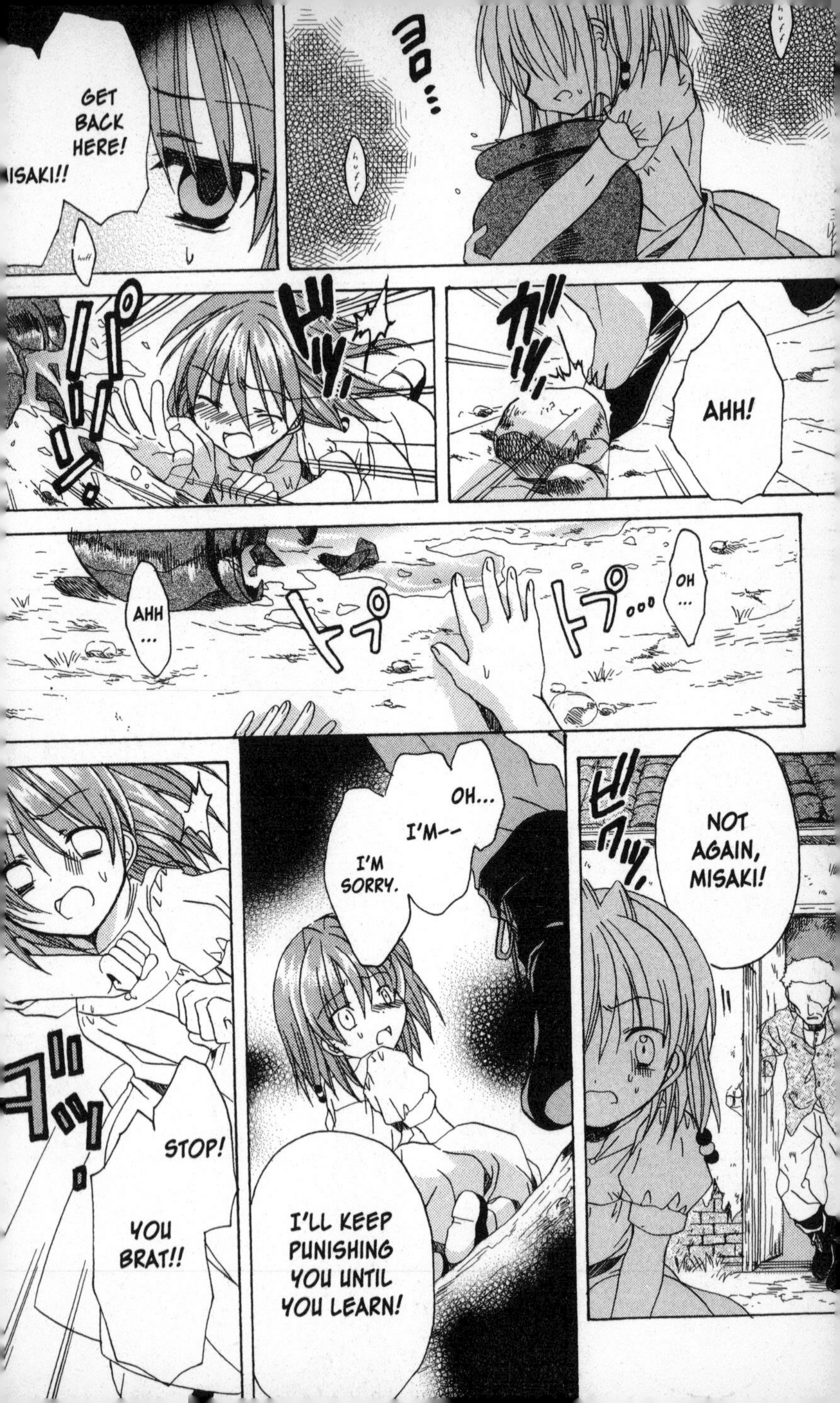
huff
huff
GET BACK HERE!
ISAKI!!
huff
AHH!
OH ...
AHH ...
NOT AGAIN, MISAKI!
OH...
I'M--
I'M SORRY.
I'LL KEEP PUNISHING YOU UNTIL YOU LEARN!
STOP!
YOU BRAT!!

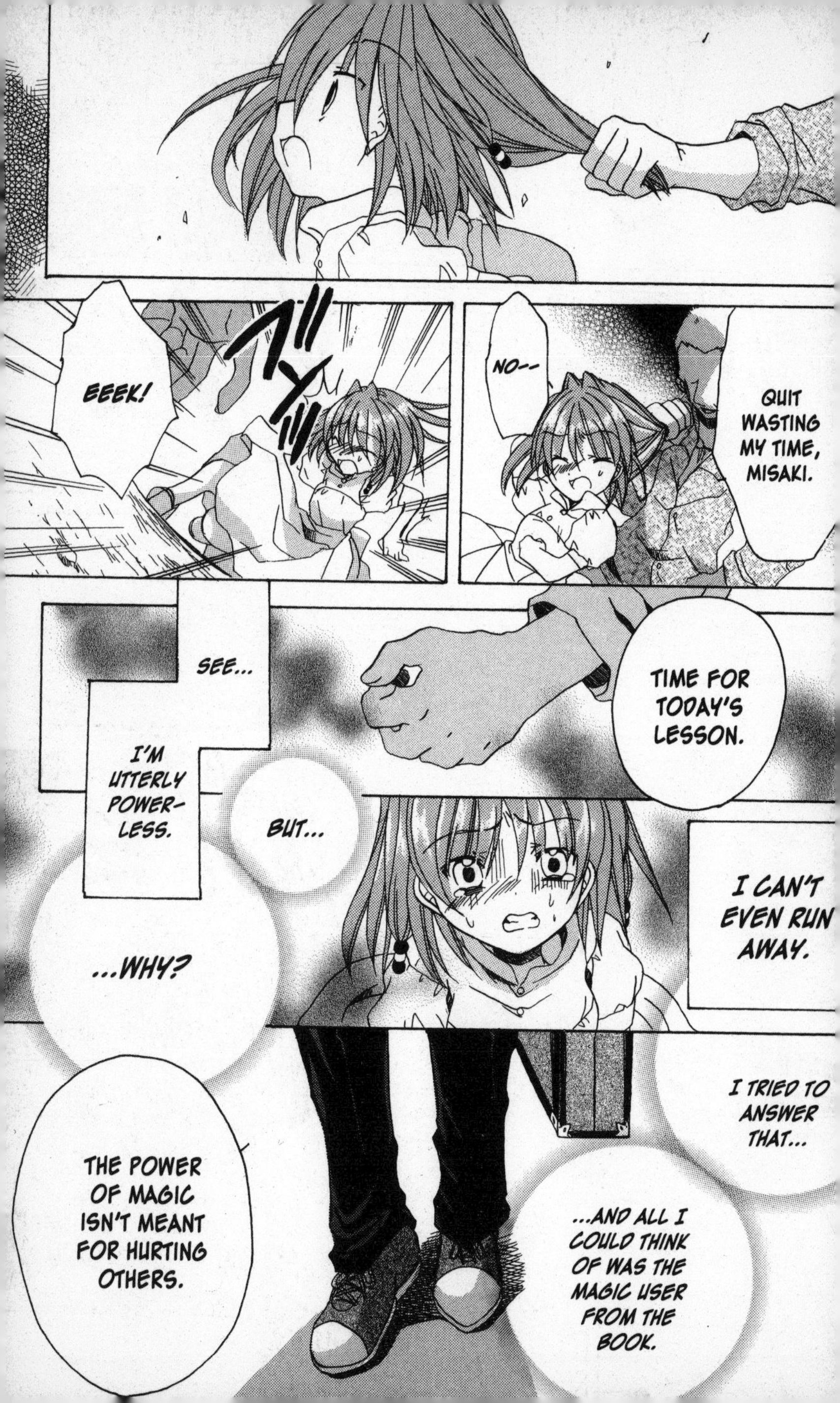
QUIT WASTING MY TIME, MISAKI.
NO--
ズン
EEEK!
TIME FOR TODAY'S LESSON.
SEE...
I'M UTTERLY POWER-LESS.
I CAN'T EVEN RUN AWAY.
BUT...
...WHY?
I TRIED TO ANSWER THAT...
...AND ALL I COULD THINK OF WAS THE MAGIC USER FROM THE BOOK.
THE POWER OF MAGIC ISN'T MEANT FOR HURTING OTHERS.

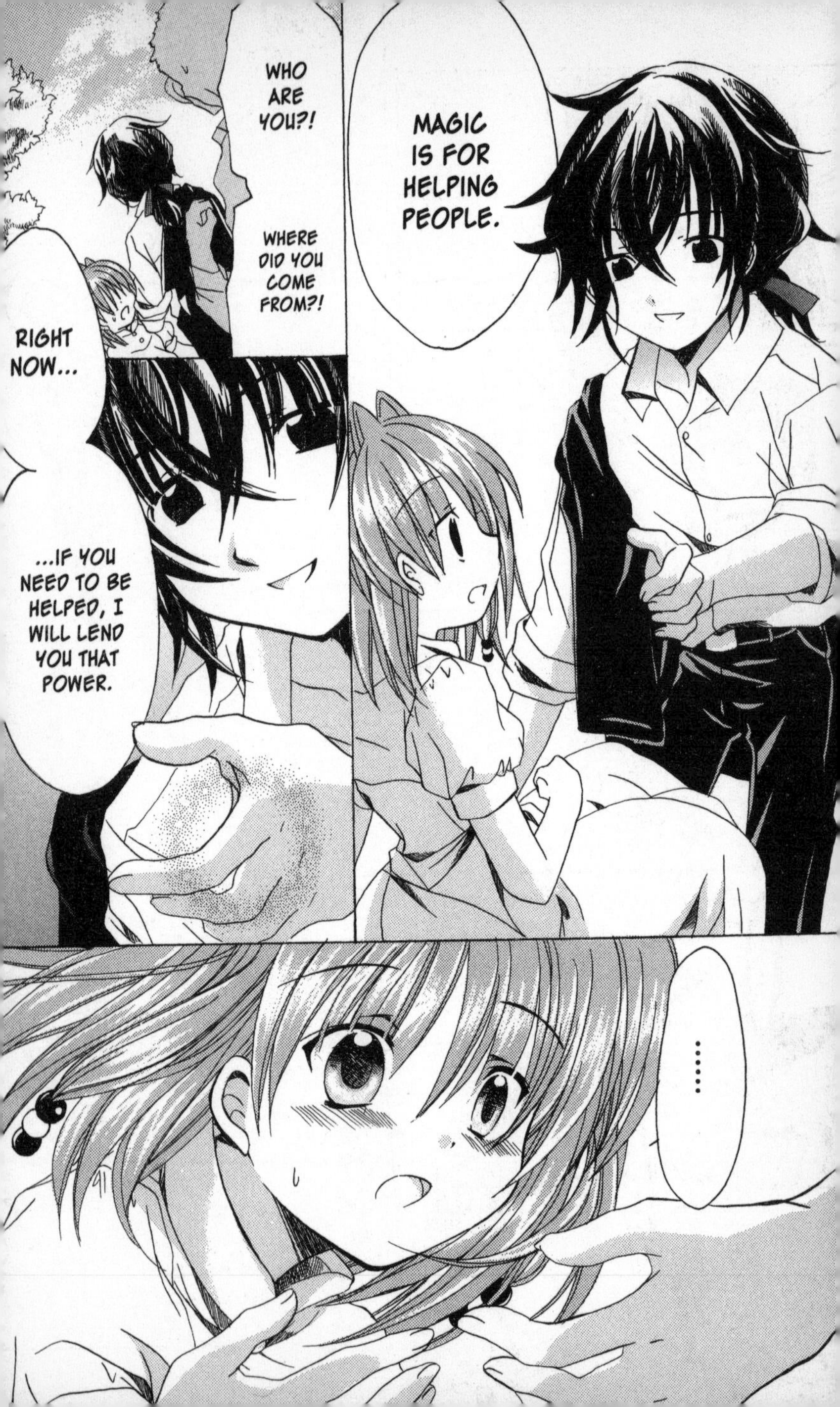
MAGIC IS FOR HELPING PEOPLE.
WHO ARE YOU?!
WHERE DID YOU COME FROM?!
RIGHT NOW...
...IF YOU NEED TO BE HELPED, I WILL LEND YOU THAT POWER.
......

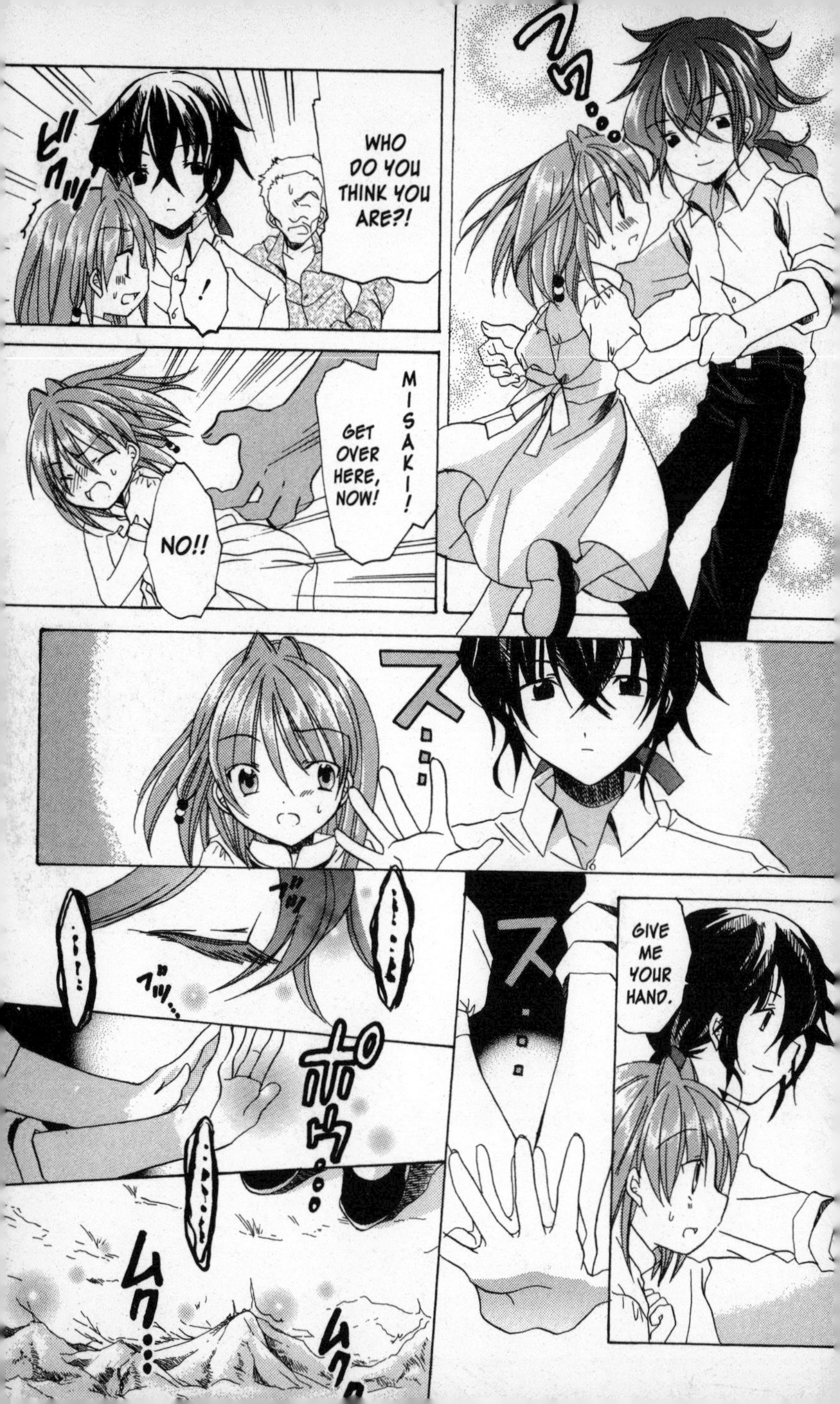
WHO DO YOU THINK YOU ARE?!
!
MISAKI!
GET OVER HERE, NOW!
NO!!
GIVE ME YOUR HAND.

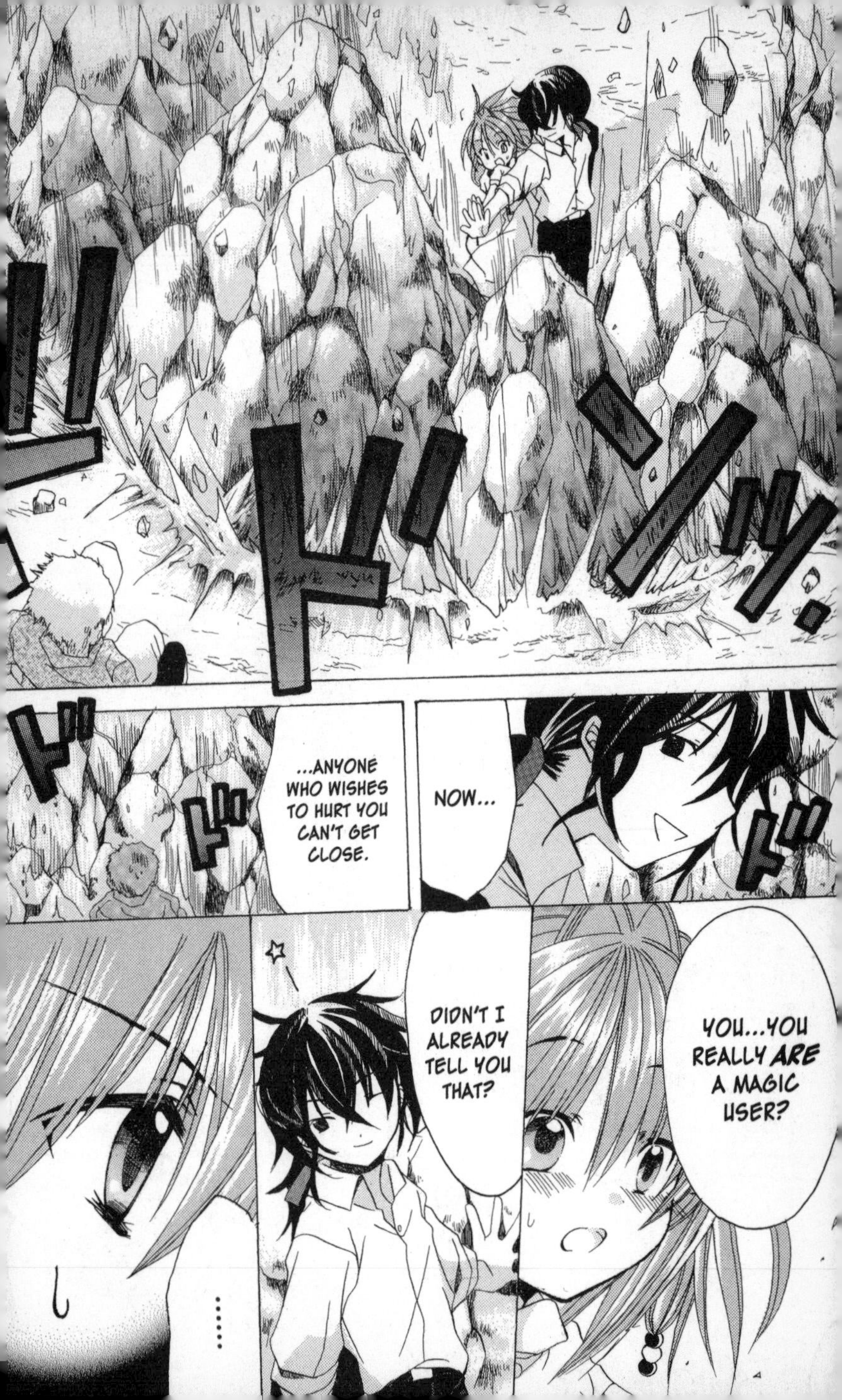
NOW...
...ANYONE WHO WISHES TO HURT YOU CAN'T GET CLOSE.
YOU...YOU REALLY ARE A MAGIC USER?
DIDN'T I ALREADY TELL YOU THAT?
......

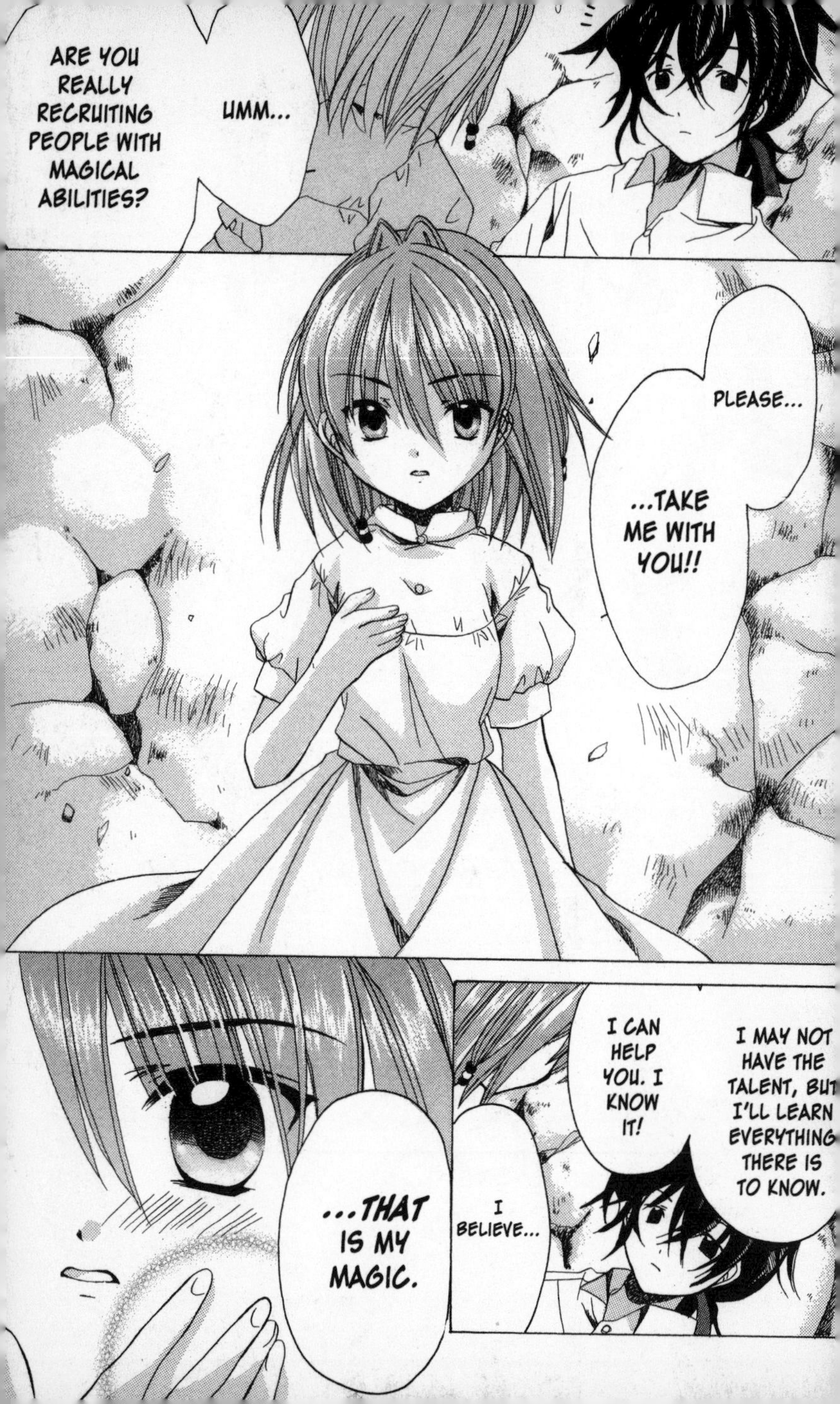
UMM...
ARE YOU REALLY RECRUITING PEOPLE WITH MAGICAL ABILITIES?
PLEASE...
...TAKE ME WITH YOU!!
I MAY NOT HAVE THE TALENT, BUT I'LL LEARN EVERYTHING THERE IS TO KNOW.
I CAN HELP YOU. I KNOW IT!
I BELIEVE...
...THAT IS MY MAGIC.

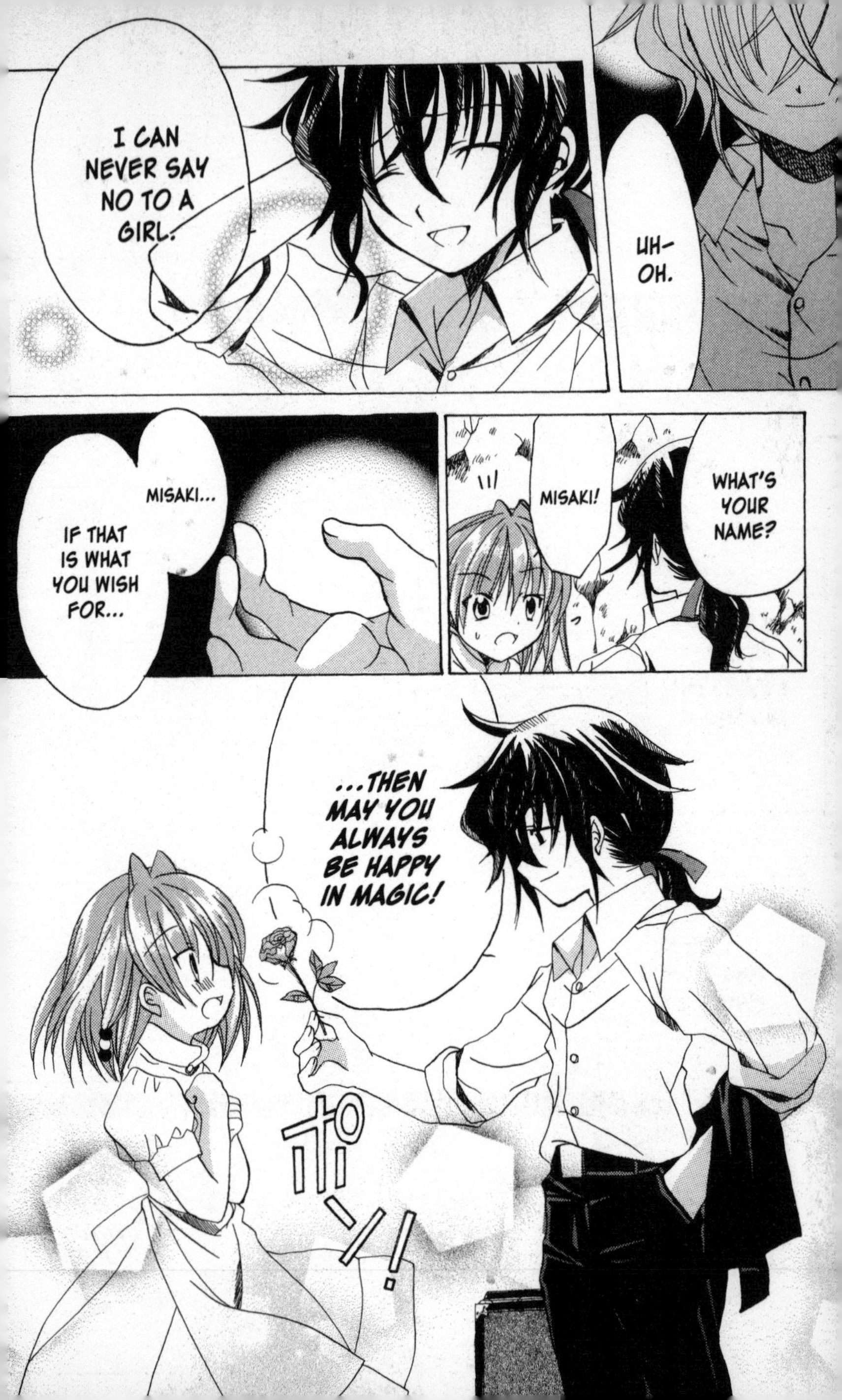
UH-OH.
I CAN NEVER SAY NO TO A GIRL.
WHAT'S YOUR NAME?
MISAKI!
MISAKI...
IF THAT IS WHAT YOU WISH FOR...
...THEN MAY YOU ALWAYS BE HAPPY IN MAGIC!
ポン!!

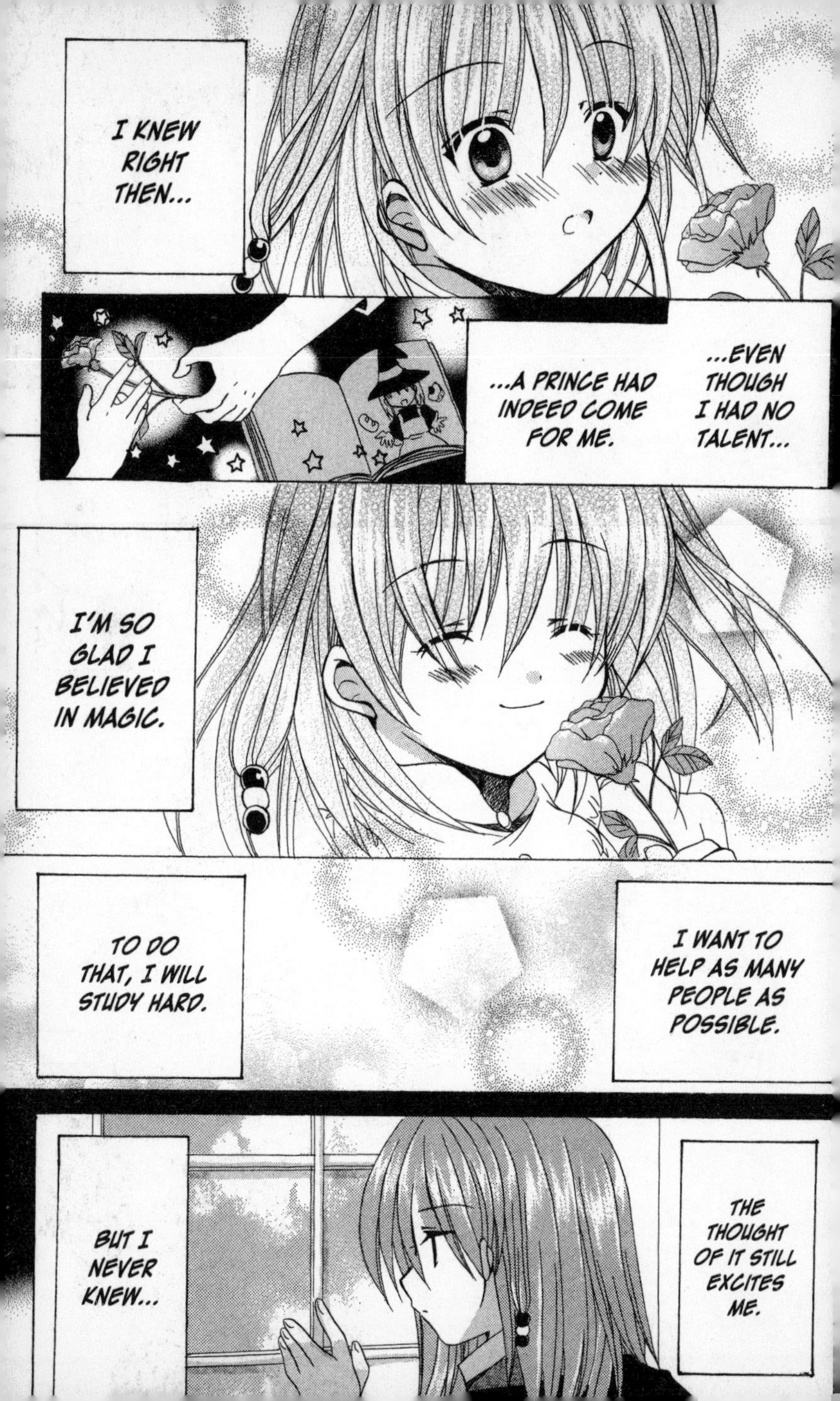

I KNEW RIGHT THEN...
...EVEN THOUGH I HAD NO TALENT...
...A PRINCE HAD INDEED COME FOR ME.
I'M SO GLAD I BELIEVED IN MAGIC.
I WANT TO HELP AS MANY PEOPLE AS POSSIBLE.
TO DO THAT, I WILL STUDY HARD.
THE THOUGHT OF IT STILL EXCITES ME.
BUT I NEVER KNEW...

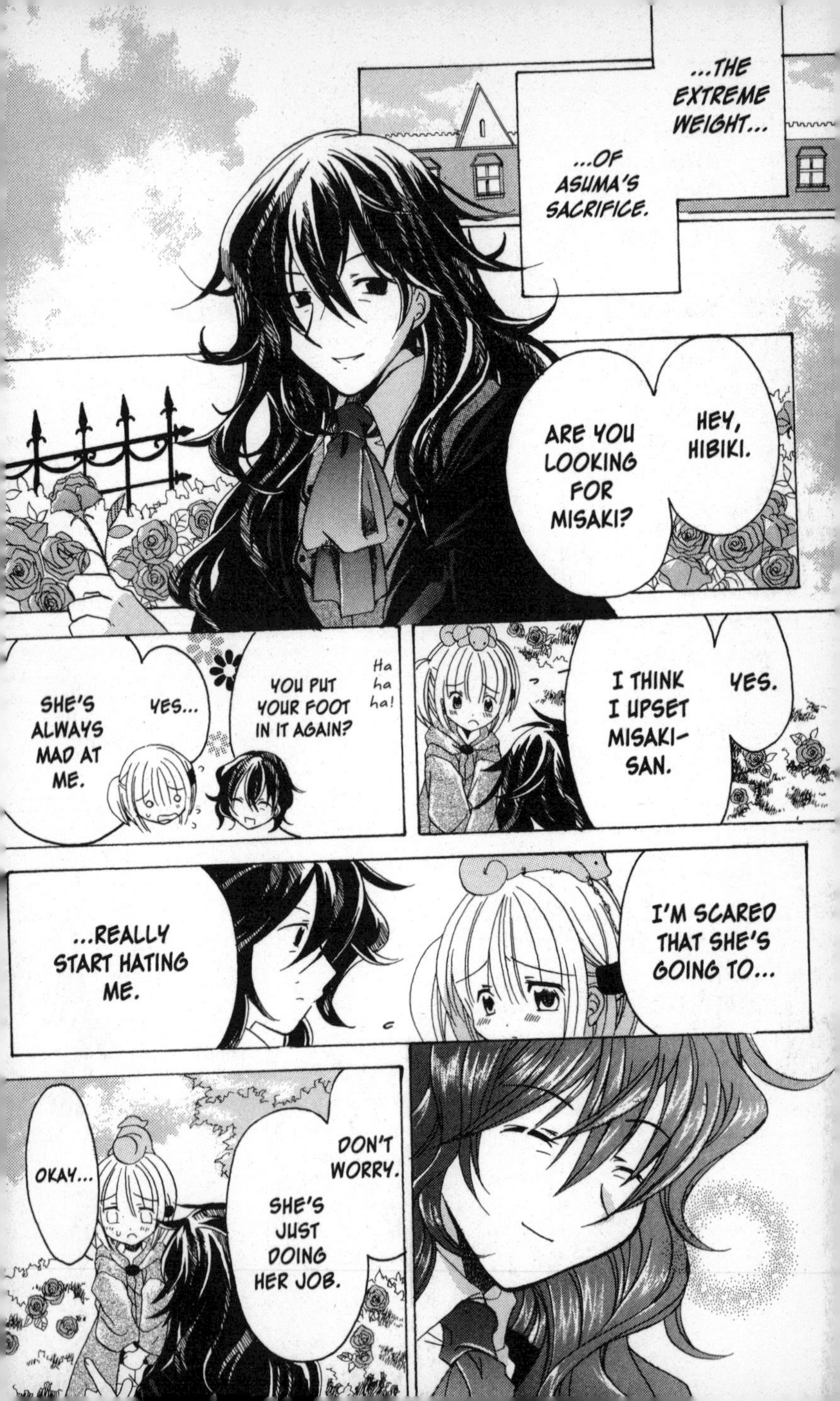
...THE EXTREME WEIGHT...
...OF ASUMA'S SACRIFICE.
HEY, HIBIKI.
ARE YOU LOOKING FOR MISAKI?
YES.
I THINK I UPSET MISAKI-SAN.
YOU PUT YOUR FOOT IN IT AGAIN?
Ha ha ha!
YES...
SHE'S ALWAYS MAD AT ME.
I'M SCARED THAT SHE'S GOING TO...
...REALLY START HATING ME.
DON'T WORRY.
SHE'S JUST DOING HER JOB.
OKAY...

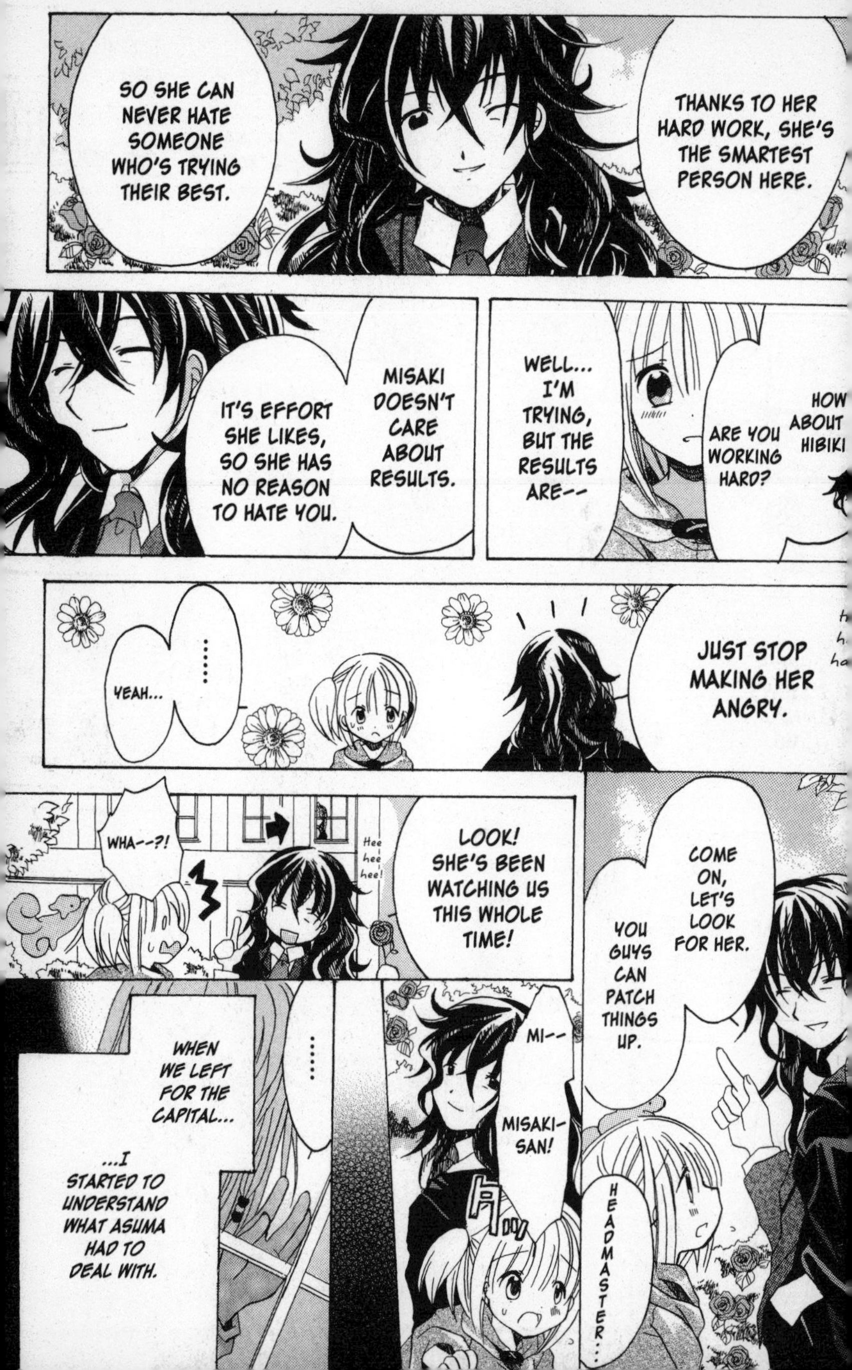
THANKS TO HER HARD WORK, SHE'S THE SMARTEST PERSON HERE.
SO SHE CAN NEVER HATE SOMEONE WHO'S TRYING THEIR BEST.
HOW ABOUT HIBIKI
ARE YOU WORKING HARD?
WELL... I'M TRYING, BUT THE RESULTS ARE--
MISAKI DOESN'T CARE ABOUT RESULTS.
IT'S EFFORT SHE LIKES, SO SHE HAS NO REASON TO HATE YOU.
JUST STOP MAKING HER ANGRY.
......
YEAH...
COME ON, LET'S LOOK FOR HER.
YOU GUYS CAN PATCH THINGS UP.
LOOK! SHE'S BEEN WATCHING US THIS WHOLE TIME!
Hee hee hee!
WHA--?!
HEADMASTER...
MISAKI-SAN!
MI--
......
WHEN WE LEFT FOR THE CAPITAL...
...I STARTED TO UNDERSTAND WHAT ASUMA HAD TO DEAL WITH.

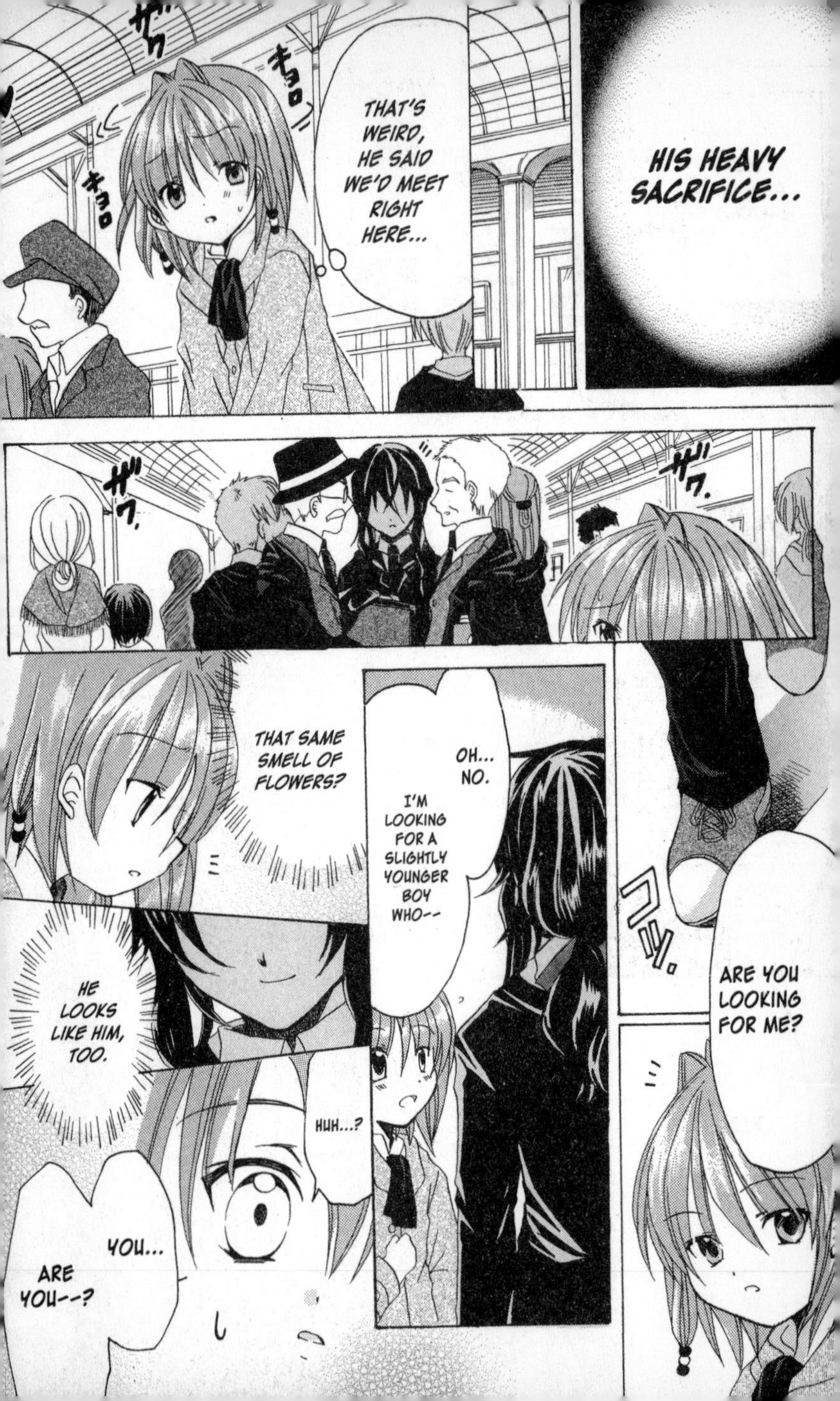

HIS HEAVY SACRIFICE...
THAT'S WEIRD, HE SAID WE'D MEET RIGHT HERE...
ARE YOU LOOKING FOR ME?
OH... NO.
I'M LOOKING FOR A SLIGHTLY YOUNGER BOY WHO--
THAT SAME SMELL OF FLOWERS?
HE LOOKS LIKE HIM, TOO.
HUH...?
YOU...
ARE YOU--?

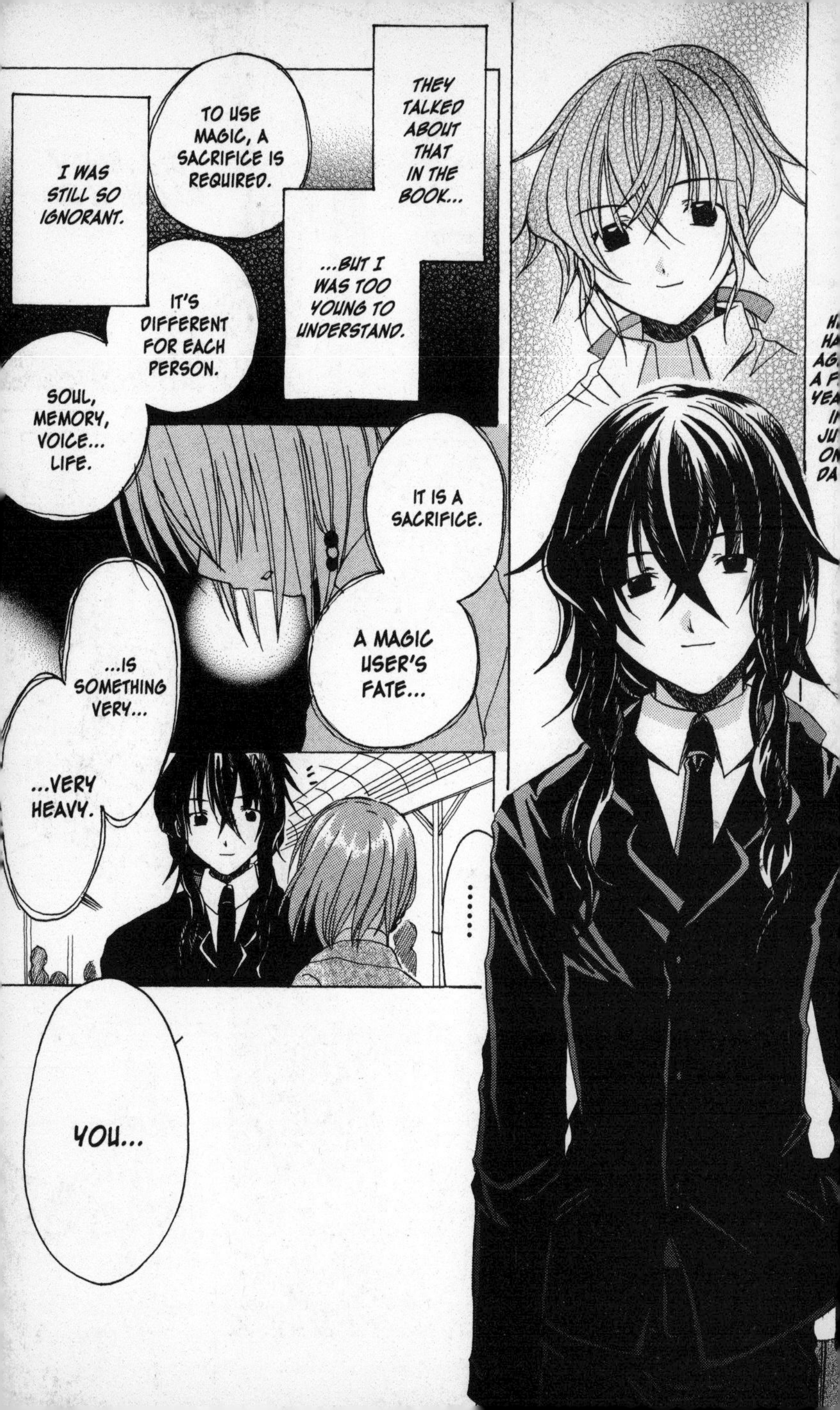
THEY TALKED ABOUT THAT IN THE BOOK...
...BUT I WAS TOO YOUNG TO UNDERSTAND.
TO USE MAGIC, A SACRIFICE IS REQUIRED.
I WAS STILL SO IGNORANT.
IT'S DIFFERENT FOR EACH PERSON.
SOUL, MEMORY, VOICE... LIFE.
IT IS A SACRIFICE.
A MAGIC USER'S FATE...
...IS SOMETHING VERY...
...VERY HEAVY.
......
YOU...

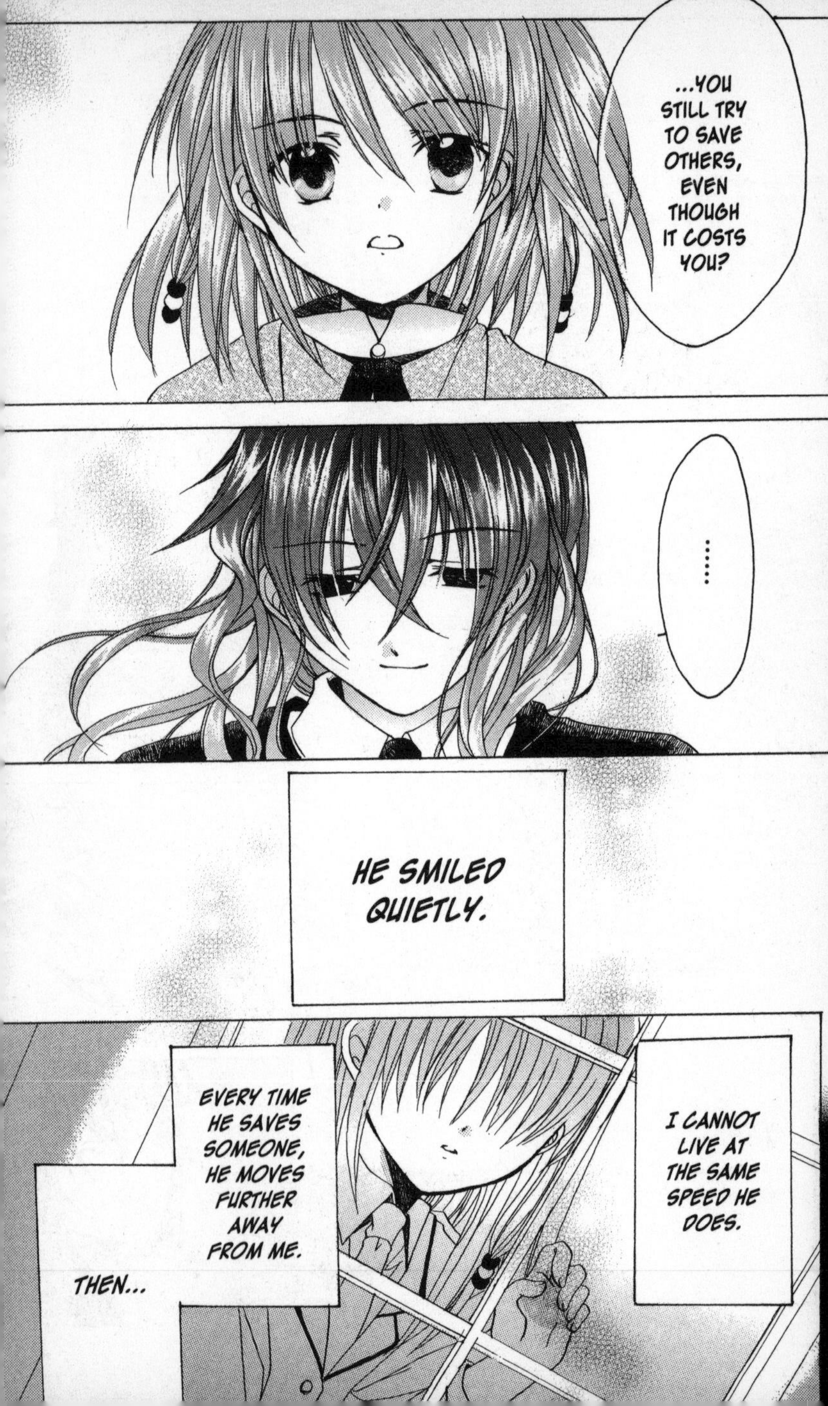
...YOU STILL TRY TO SAVE OTHERS, EVEN THOUGH IT COSTS YOU?
......
HE SMILED QUIETLY.
I CANNOT LIVE AT THE SAME SPEED HE DOES.
EVERY TIME HE SAVES SOMEONE, HE MOVES FURTHER AWAY FROM ME.
THEN...

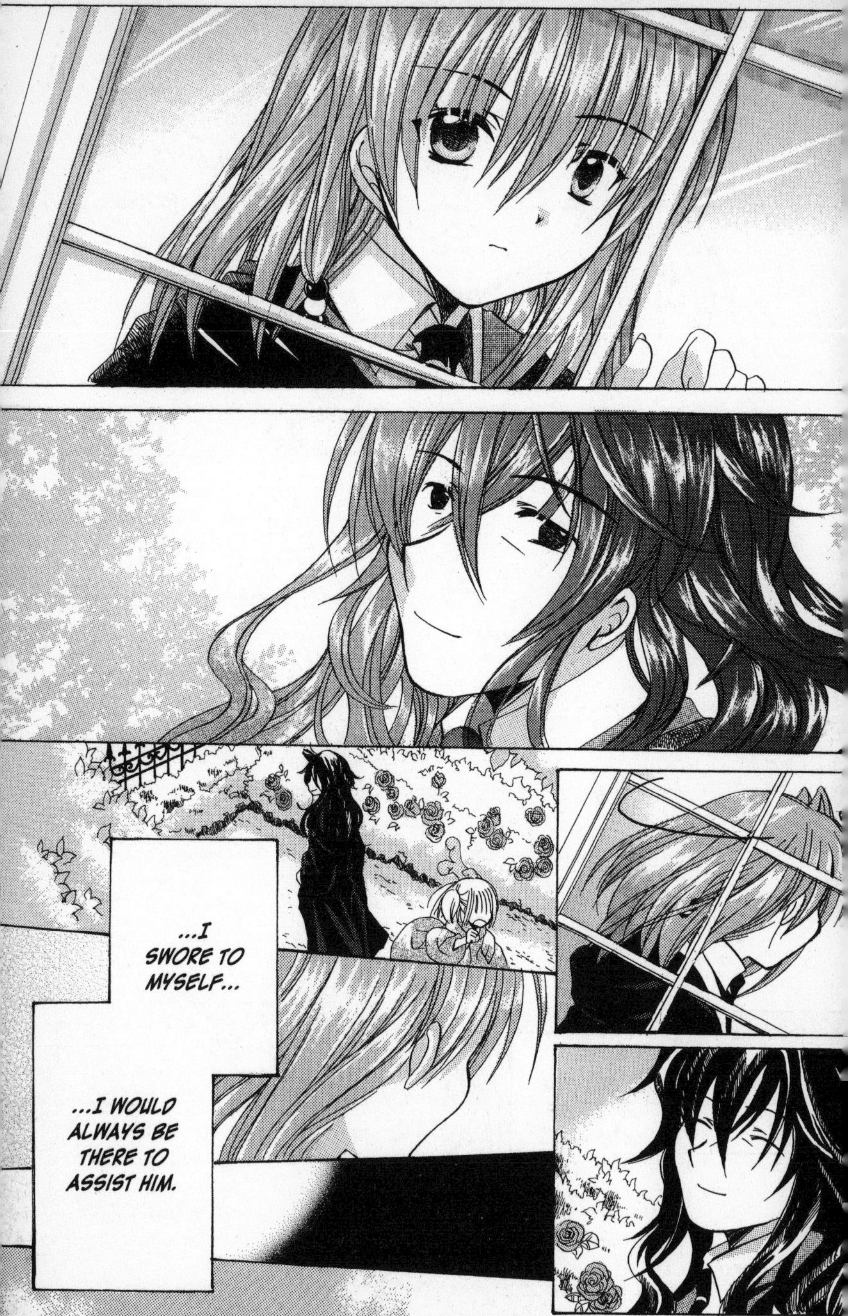
...I SWORE TO MYSELF...
...I WOULD ALWAYS BE THERE TO ASSIST HIM.

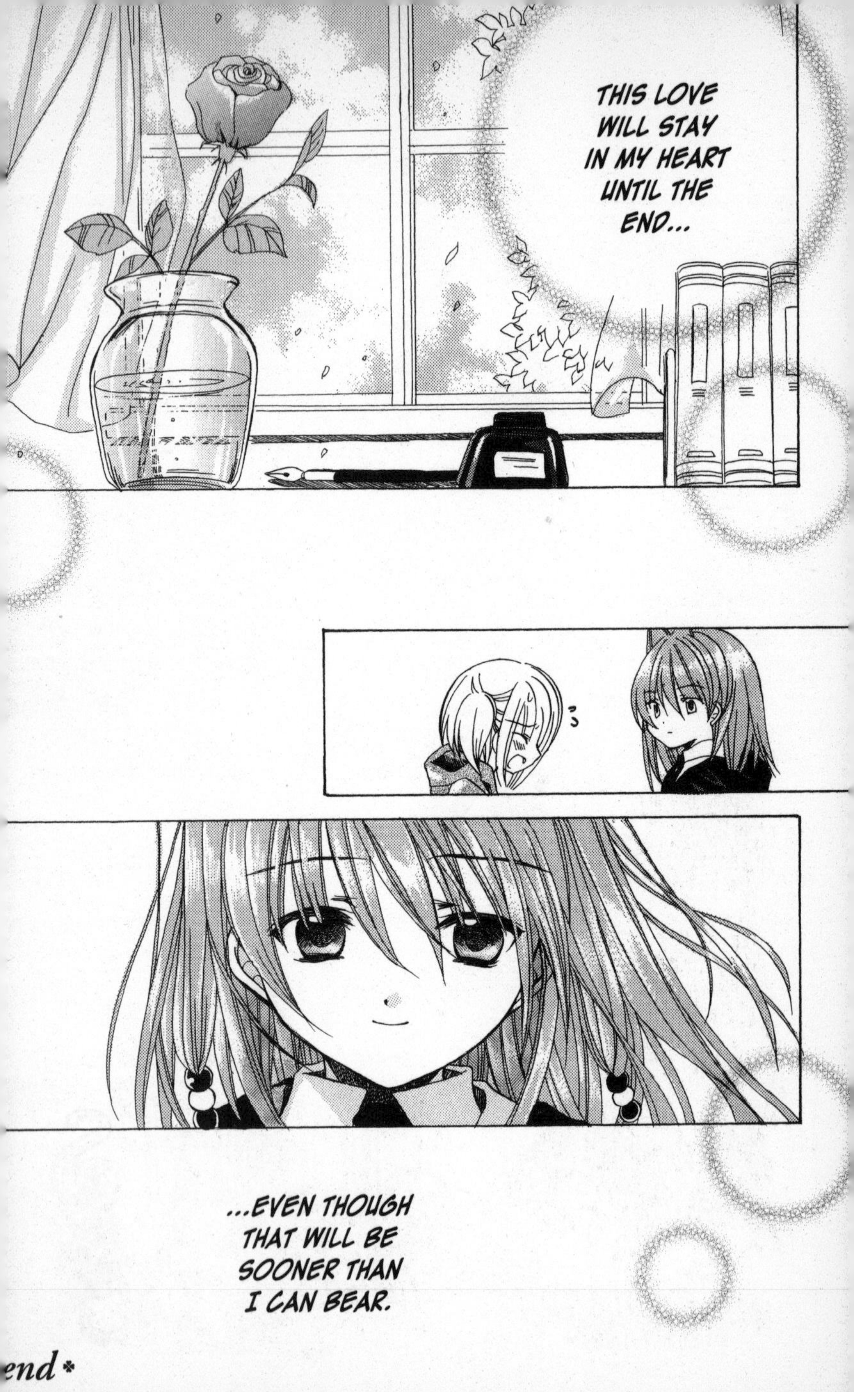
THIS LOVE WILL STAY IN MY HEART UNTIL THE END...
...EVEN THOUGH THAT WILL BE SOONER THAN I CAN BEAR.
end

HIBIKI'S MAGIC™

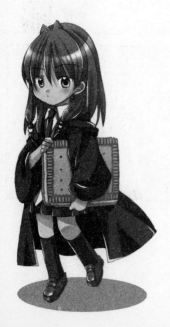

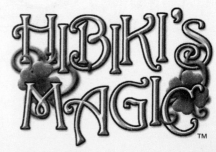

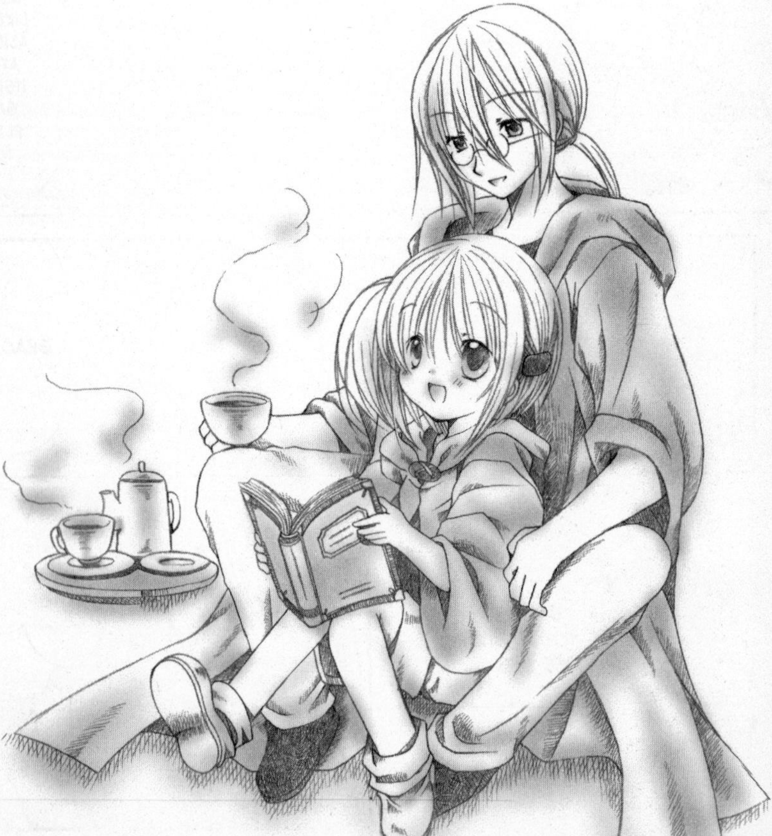

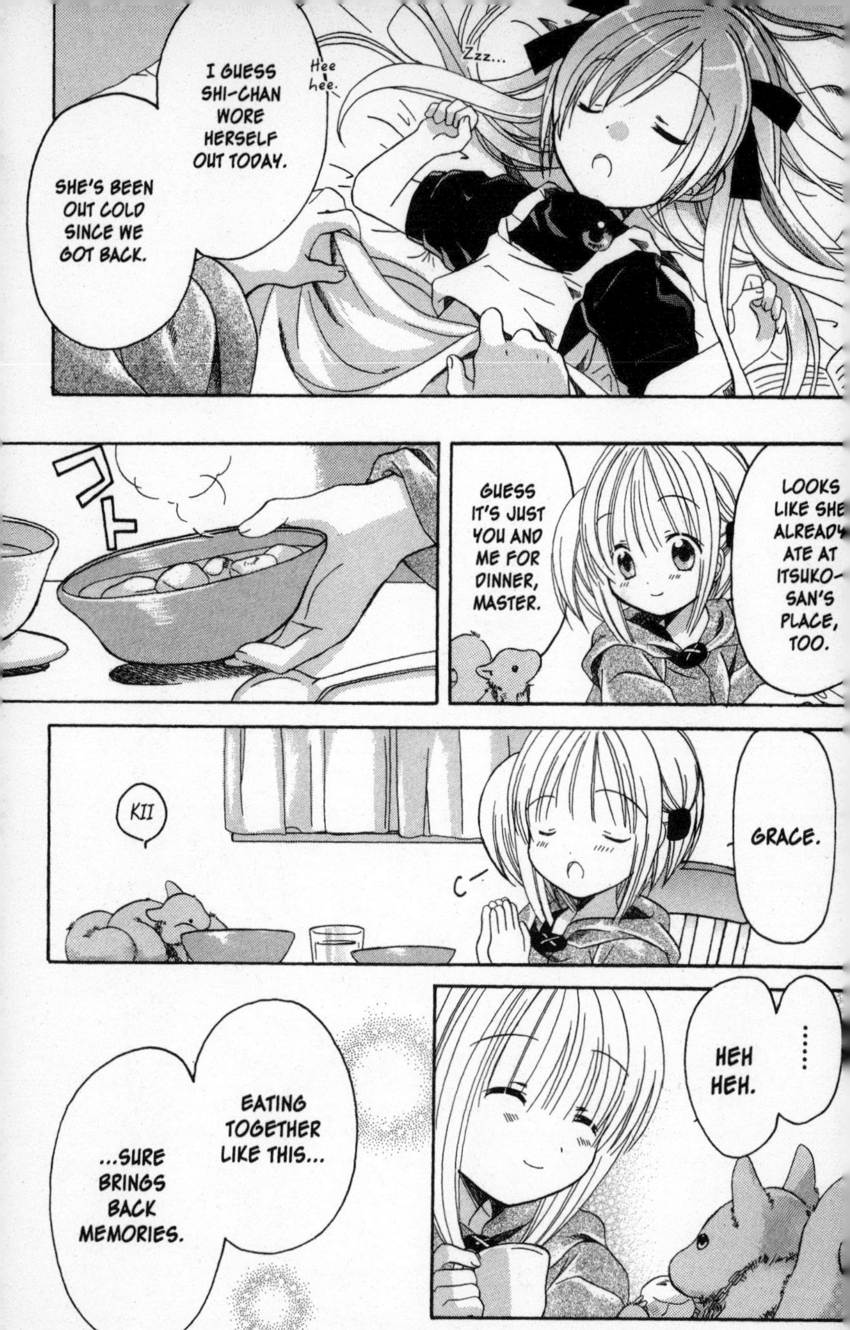
Zzz...
Hee hee.
I GUESS SHI-CHAN WORE HERSELF OUT TODAY.
SHE'S BEEN OUT COLD SINCE WE GOT BACK.
LOOKS LIKE SHE ALREADY ATE AT ITSUKO-SAN'S PLACE, TOO.
GUESS IT'S JUST YOU AND ME FOR DINNER, MASTER.
GRACE.
C—
KII
......
HEH HEH.
EATING TOGETHER LIKE THIS...
...SURE BRINGS BACK MEMORIES.

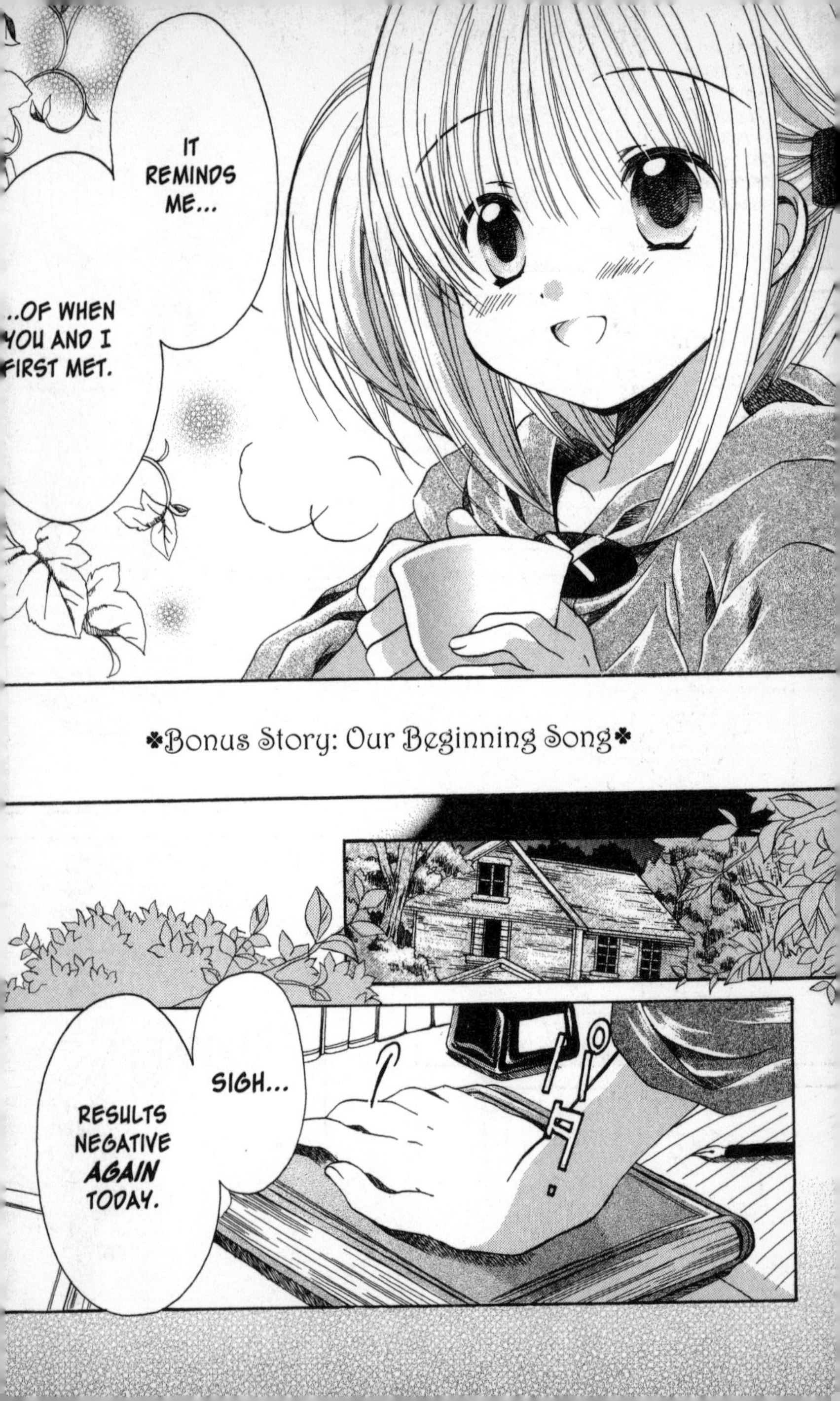
IT REMINDS ME...
...OF WHEN YOU AND I FIRST MET.
✽Bonus Story: Our Beginning Song✽
SIGH...
RESULTS NEGATIVE AGAIN TODAY.

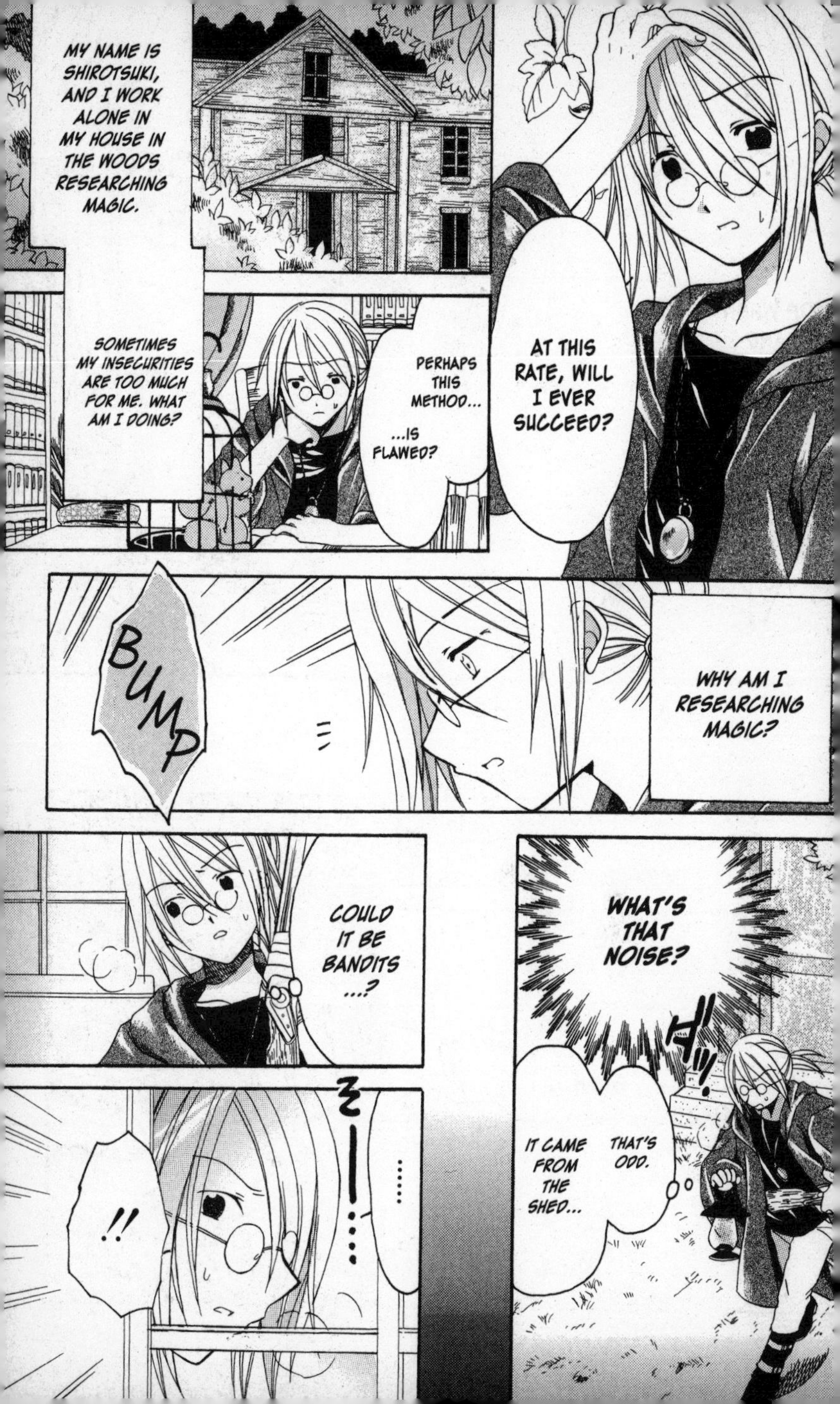
AT THIS RATE, WILL I EVER SUCCEED?
MY NAME IS SHIROTSUKI, AND I WORK ALONE IN MY HOUSE IN THE WOODS RESEARCHING MAGIC.
SOMETIMES MY INSECURITIES ARE TOO MUCH FOR ME. WHAT AM I DOING?
PERHAPS THIS METHOD...
...IS FLAWED?
WHY AM I RESEARCHING MAGIC?
BUMP
WHAT'S THAT NOISE?
THAT'S ODD.
IT CAME FROM THE SHED...
COULD IT BE BANDITS ...?
......
!!

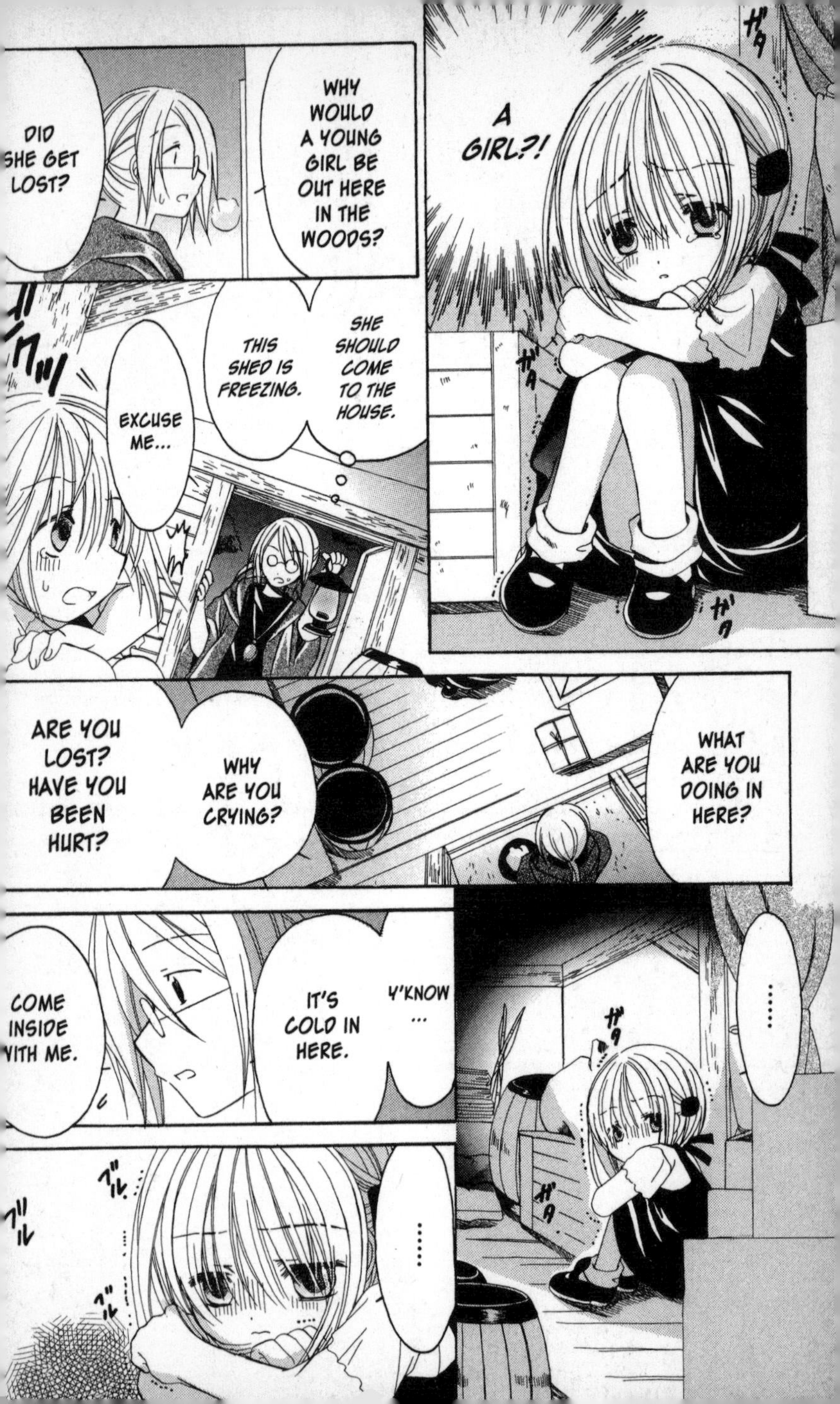

ガタ
A GIRL?!
WHY WOULD A YOUNG GIRL BE OUT HERE IN THE WOODS?
DID SHE GET LOST?
SHE SHOULD COME TO THE HOUSE.
THIS SHED IS FREEZING.
EXCUSE ME...
WHAT ARE YOU DOING IN HERE?
WHY ARE YOU CRYING?
ARE YOU LOST? HAVE YOU BEEN HURT?
......
Y'KNOW ...
IT'S COLD IN HERE.
COME INSIDE WITH ME.
......

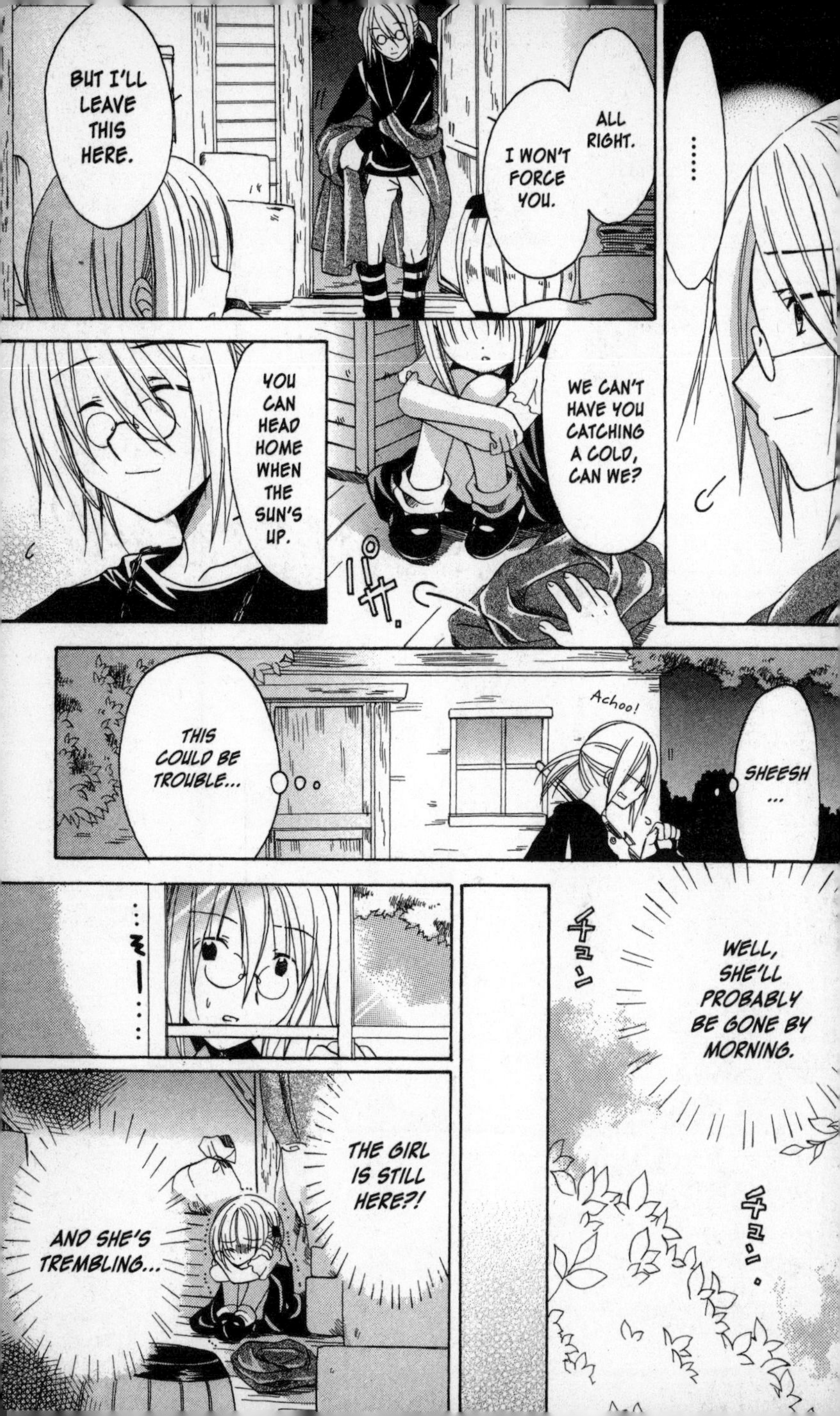
......
ALL RIGHT.
I WON'T FORCE YOU.
BUT I'LL LEAVE THIS HERE.
WE CAN'T HAVE YOU CATCHING A COLD, CAN WE?
パサ。
YOU CAN HEAD HOME WHEN THE SUN'S UP.
SHEESH ...
Achoo!
THIS COULD BE TROUBLE...
WELL, SHE'LL PROBABLY BE GONE BY MORNING.
チュン!
チュン。
...ジー......
THE GIRL IS STILL HERE?!
AND SHE'S TREMBLING...

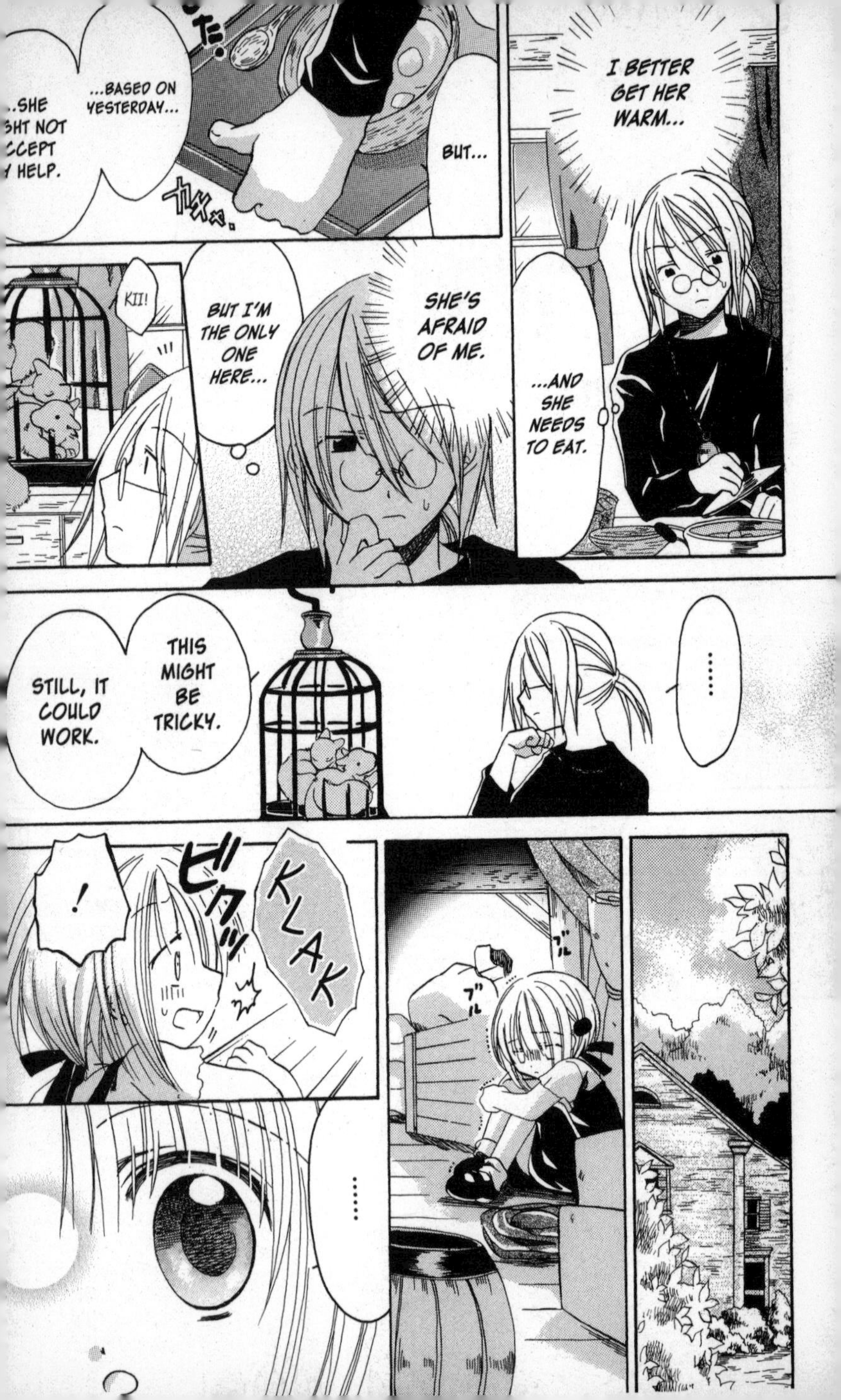
I BETTER GET HER WARM...
...AND SHE NEEDS TO EAT.
BUT...
...BASED ON YESTERDAY...
..SHE GHT NOT CCEPT Y HELP.
SHE'S AFRAID OF ME.
BUT I'M THE ONLY ONE HERE...
KII!
......
THIS MIGHT BE TRICKY.
STILL, IT COULD WORK.
KLAK
!
......

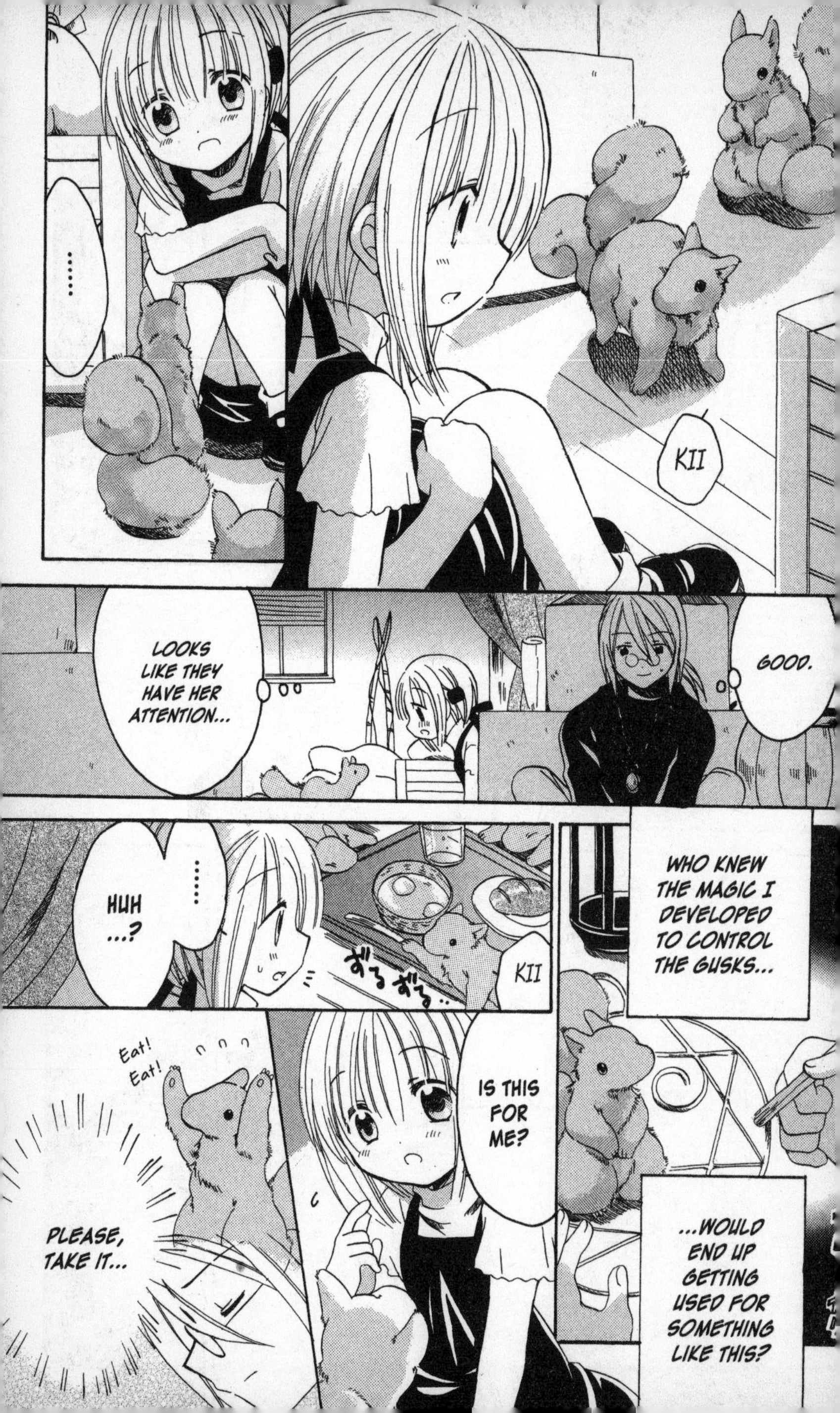
KII
……
GOOD.
LOOKS LIKE THEY HAVE HER ATTENTION...
WHO KNEW THE MAGIC I DEVELOPED TO CONTROL THE GUSKS...
KII
ずるずる…
……
HUH ...?
...WOULD END UP GETTING USED FOR SOMETHING LIKE THIS?
IS THIS FOR ME?
Eat! Eat!
PLEASE, TAKE IT...

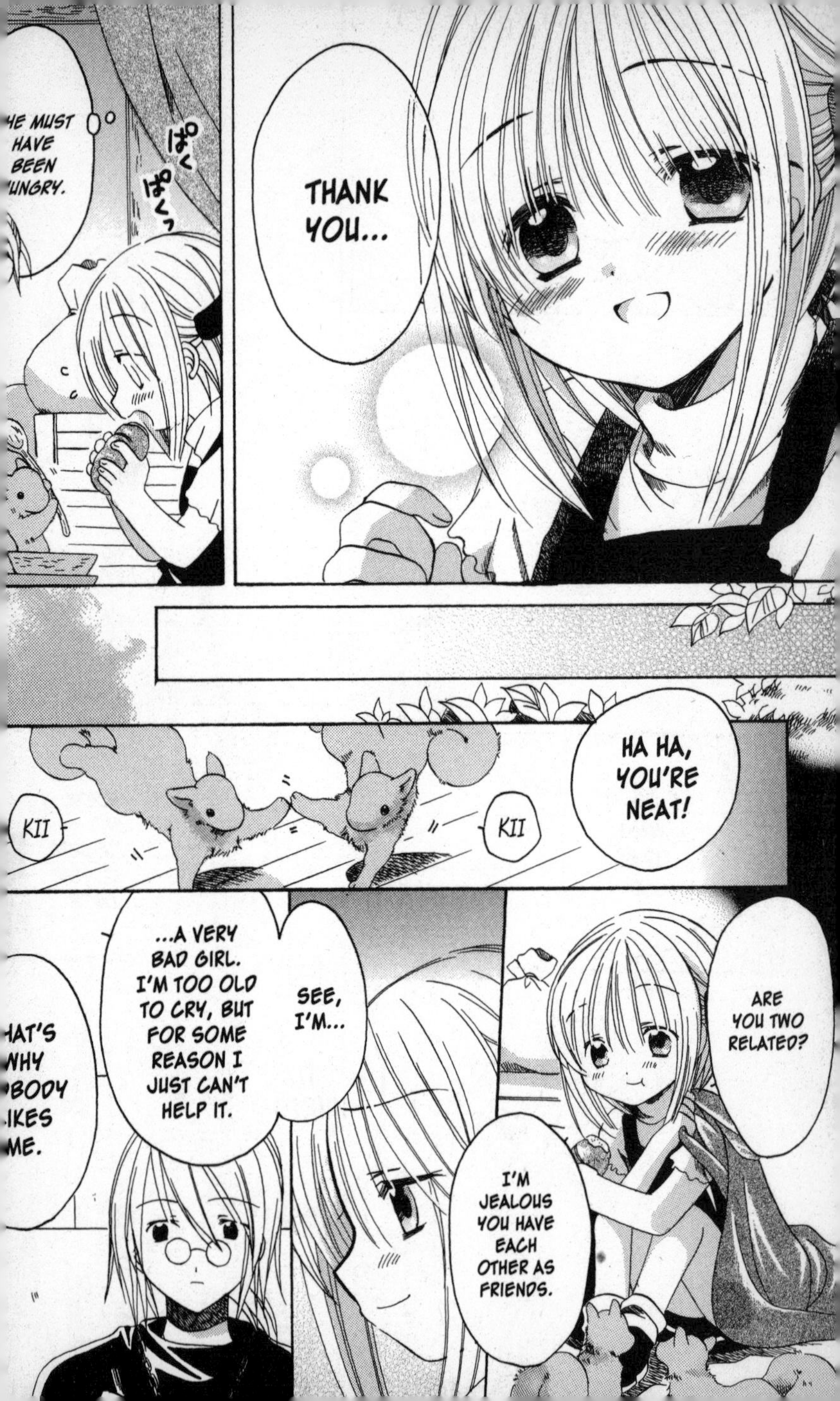
THANK YOU...
HE MUST HAVE BEEN UNGRY.
ぱく ぱくっ
HA HA, YOU'RE NEAT!
KII
KII
ARE YOU TWO RELATED?
I'M JEALOUS YOU HAVE EACH OTHER AS FRIENDS.
SEE, I'M...
...A VERY BAD GIRL. I'M TOO OLD TO CRY, BUT FOR SOME REASON I JUST CAN'T HELP IT.
HAT'S WHY BODY IKES ME.

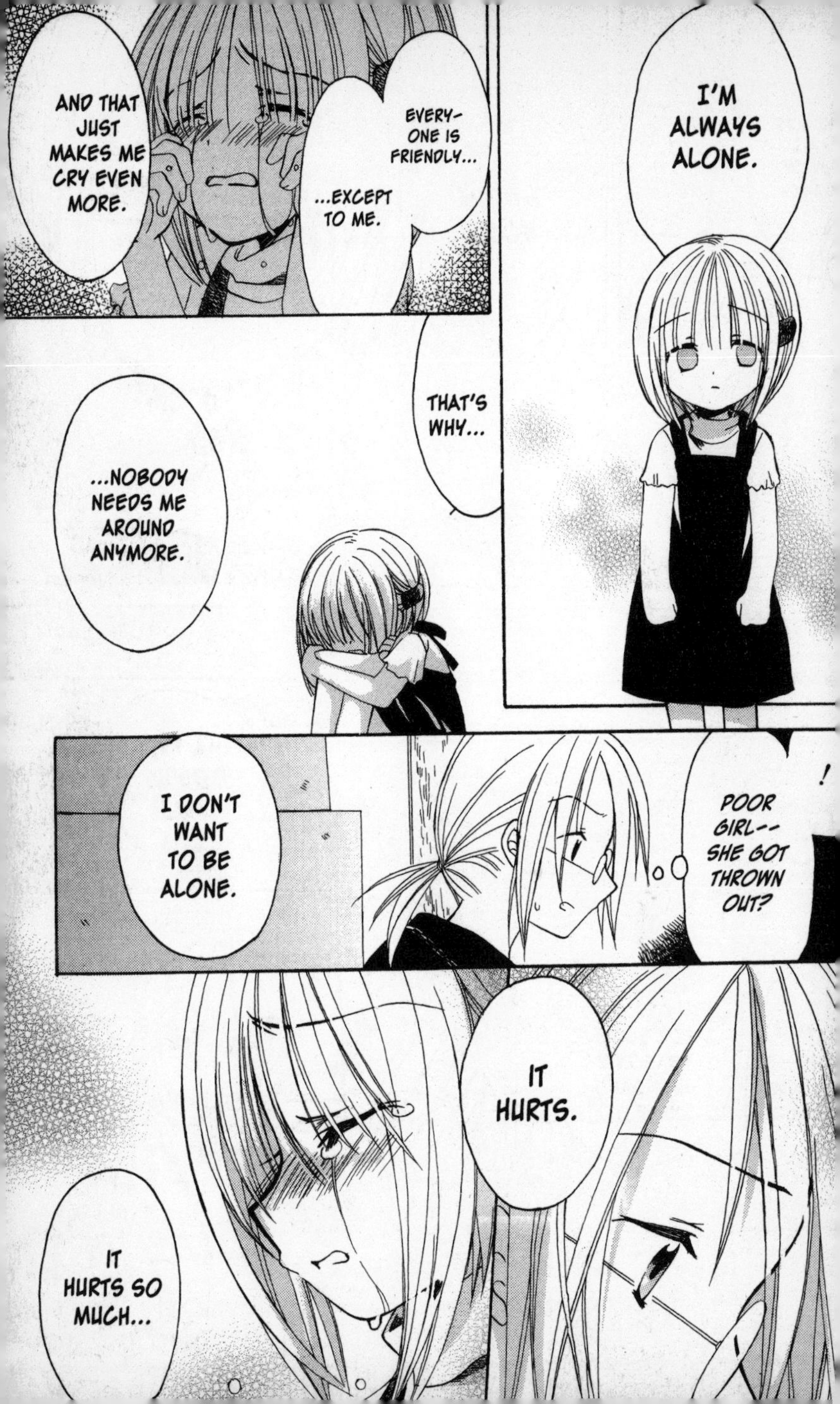

I'M ALWAYS ALONE.
EVERY-ONE IS FRIENDLY...
...EXCEPT TO ME.
AND THAT JUST MAKES ME CRY EVEN MORE.
THAT'S WHY...
...NOBODY NEEDS ME AROUND ANYMORE.
!
POOR GIRL-- SHE GOT THROWN OUT?
I DON'T WANT TO BE ALONE.
IT HURTS.
IT HURTS SO MUCH...

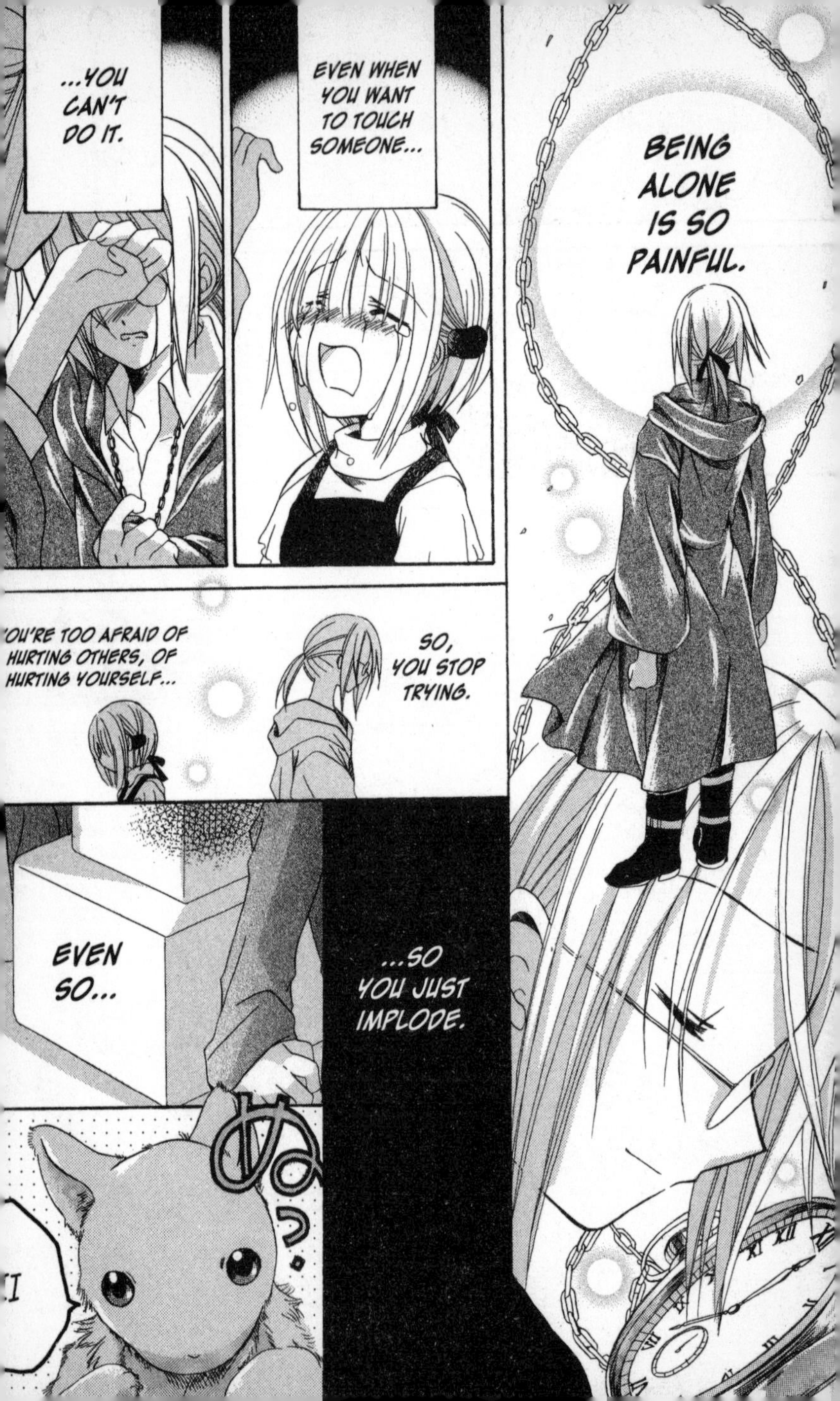
BEING ALONE IS SO PAINFUL.
EVEN WHEN YOU WANT TO TOUCH SOMEONE...
...YOU CAN'T DO IT.
SO, YOU STOP TRYING.
OU'RE TOO AFRAID OF HURTING OTHERS, OF HURTING YOURSELF...
...SO YOU JUST IMPLODE.
EVEN SO...
めっ。

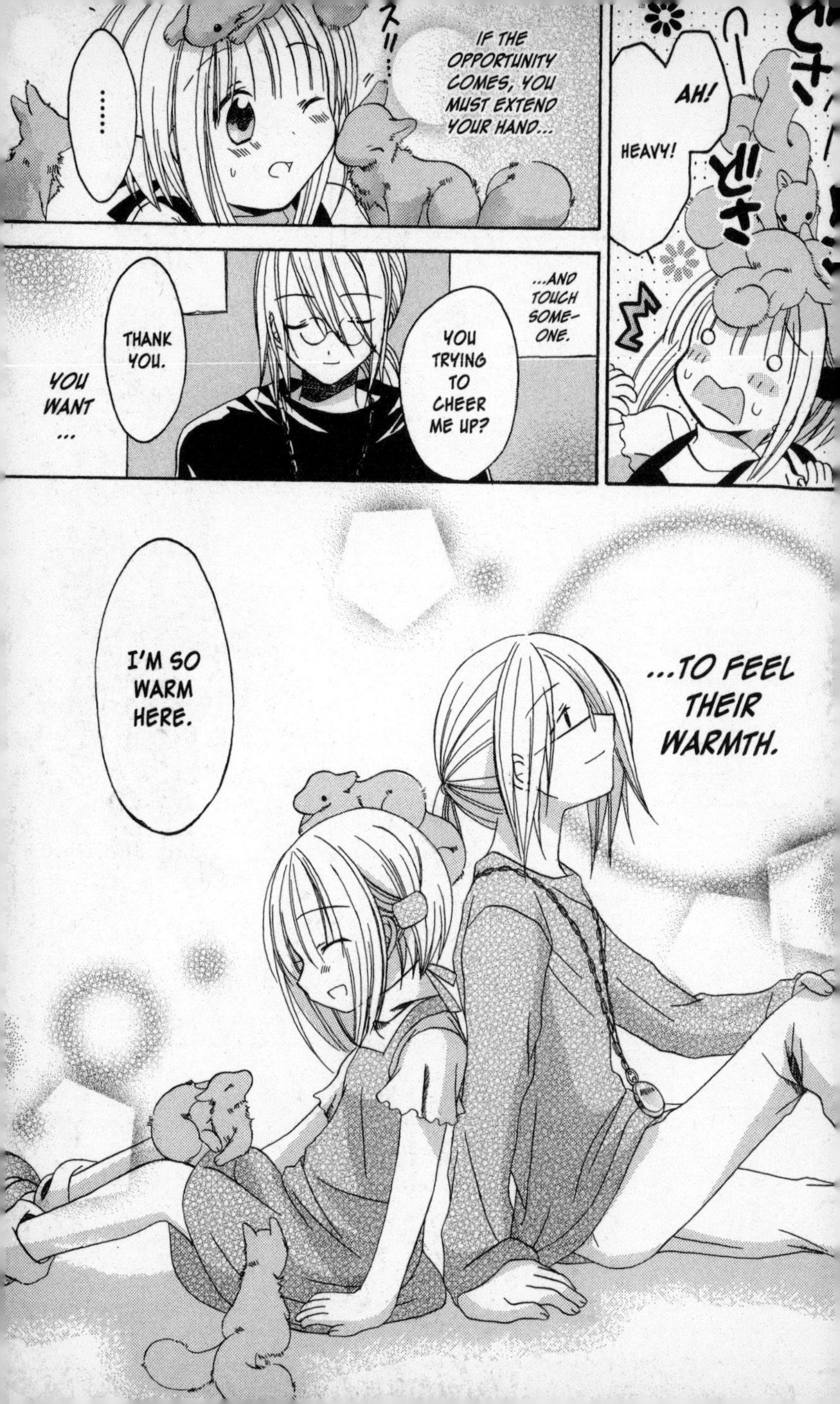

どさー
どさ
AH!
HEAVY!
......
スリ...
IF THE OPPORTUNITY COMES, YOU MUST EXTEND YOUR HAND...
...AND TOUCH SOME-ONE.
YOU TRYING TO CHEER ME UP?
THANK YOU.
YOU WANT ...
...TO FEEL THEIR WARMTH.
I'M SO WARM HERE.

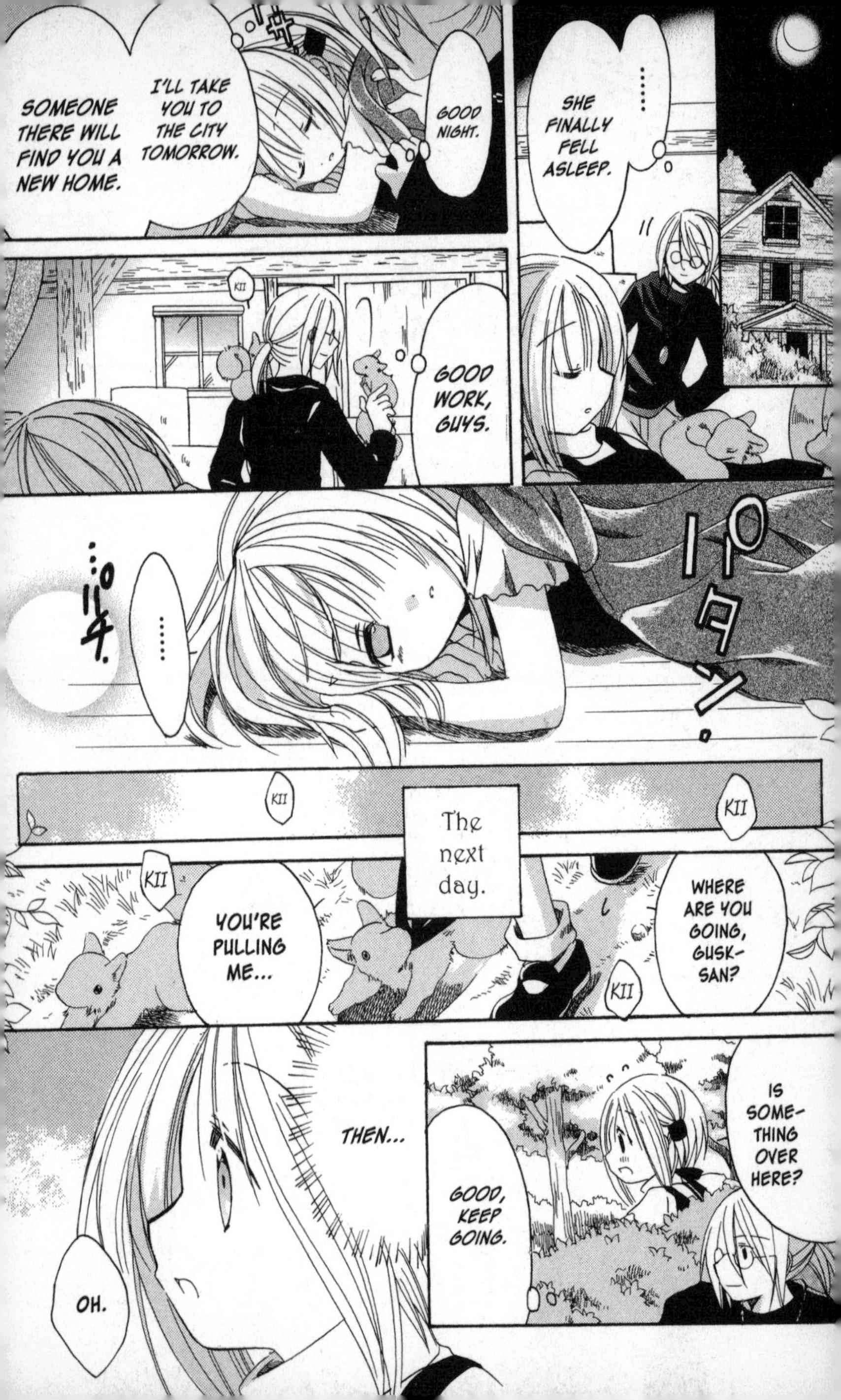
......
SHE FINALLY FELL ASLEEP.
GOOD NIGHT.
I'LL TAKE YOU TO THE CITY TOMORROW.
SOMEONE THERE WILL FIND YOU A NEW HOME.
KII
GOOD WORK, GUYS.
......
KII
KII
The next day.
WHERE ARE YOU GOING, GUSK-SAN?
KII
YOU'RE PULLING ME...
KII
IS SOME-THING OVER HERE?
GOOD, KEEP GOING.
THEN...
OH.

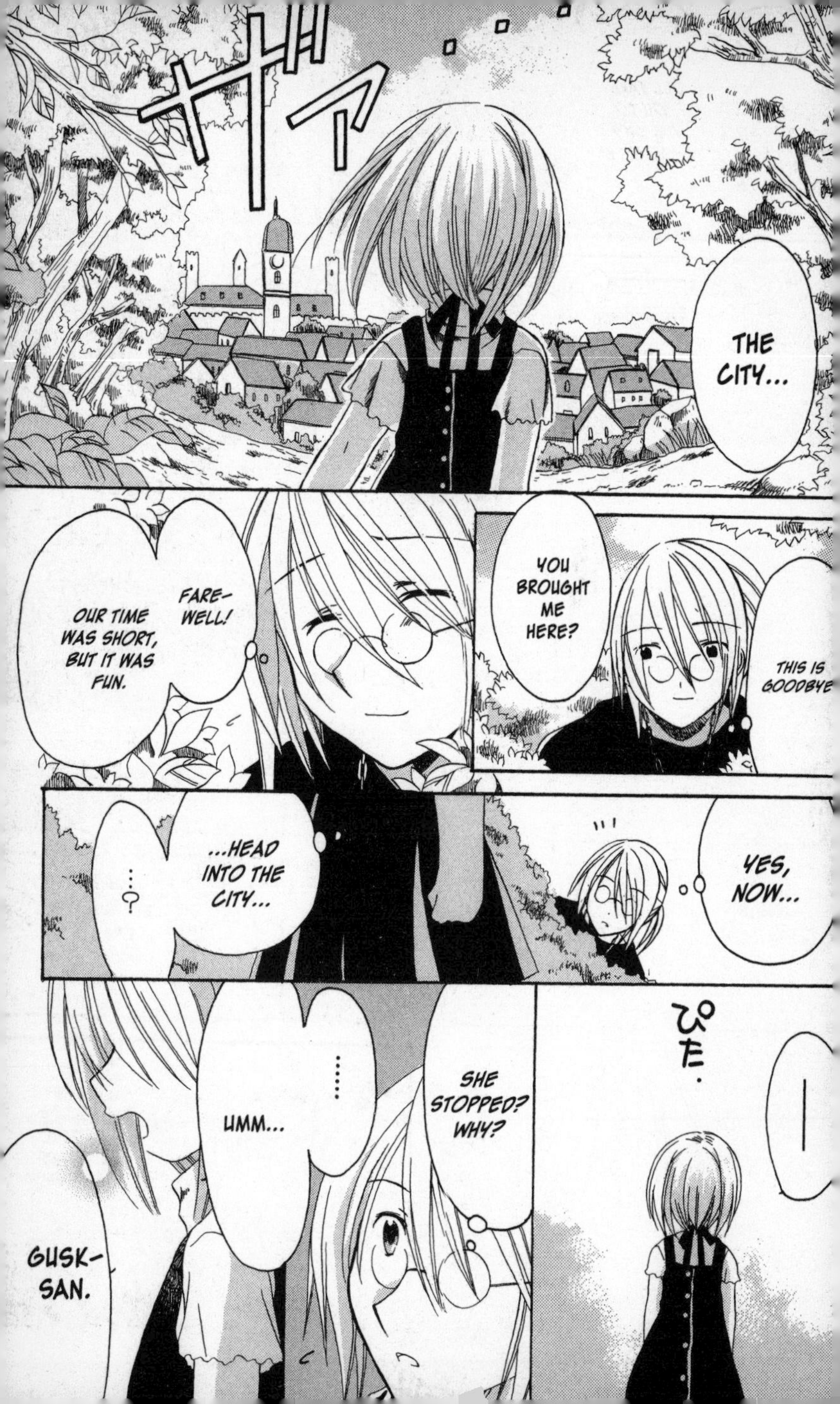

ザァ
THE CITY...
YOU BROUGHT ME HERE?
THIS IS GOODBYE
FAREWELL!
OUR TIME WAS SHORT, BUT IT WAS FUN.
YES, NOW...
...HEAD INTO THE CITY...
...?
ぴた.
—
SHE STOPPED? WHY?
......
UMM...
GUSK-SAN.

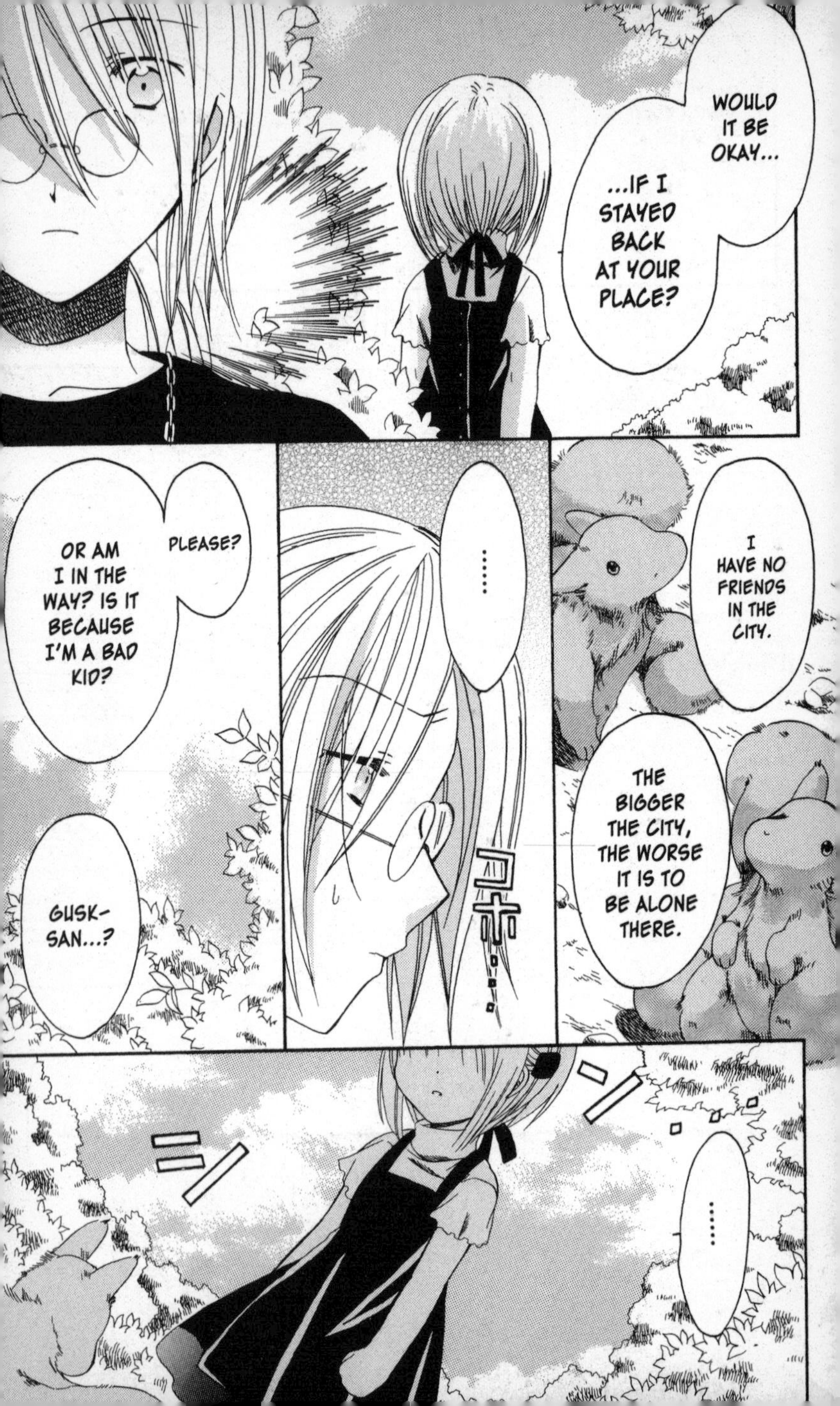
WOULD IT BE OKAY...
...IF I STAYED BACK AT YOUR PLACE?
I HAVE NO FRIENDS IN THE CITY.
THE BIGGER THE CITY, THE WORSE IT IS TO BE ALONE THERE.
......
PLEASE?
OR AM I IN THE WAY? IS IT BECAUSE I'M A BAD KID?
GUSK-SAN...?
......

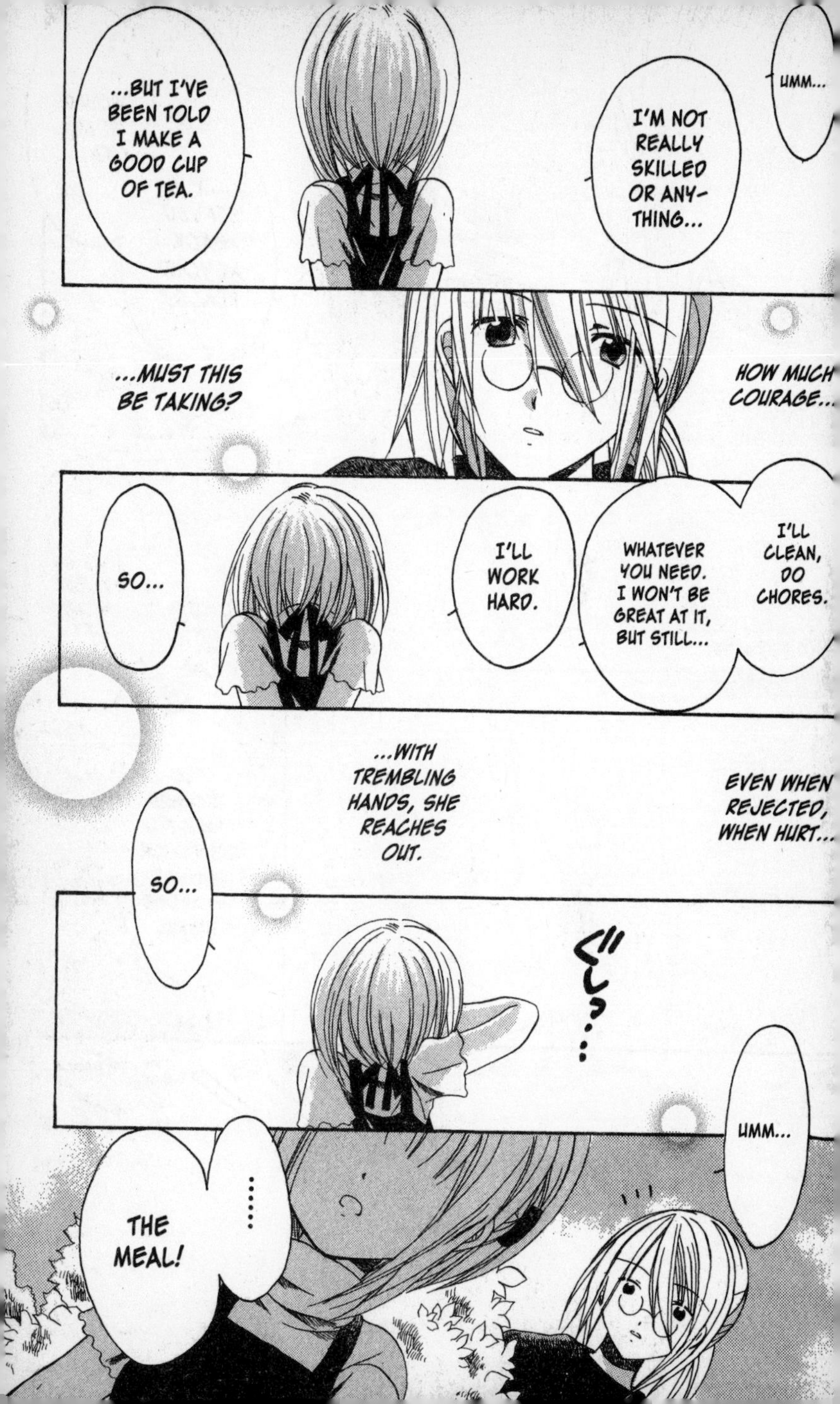
UMM...
I'M NOT REALLY SKILLED OR ANYTHING...
...BUT I'VE BEEN TOLD I MAKE A GOOD CUP OF TEA.
HOW MUCH COURAGE...
...MUST THIS BE TAKING?
I'LL CLEAN, DO CHORES.
WHATEVER YOU NEED. I WON'T BE GREAT AT IT, BUT STILL...
I'LL WORK HARD.
SO...
EVEN WHEN REJECTED, WHEN HURT...
...WITH TREMBLING HANDS, SHE REACHES OUT.
SO...
ぐしっ...
UMM...
......
THE MEAL!

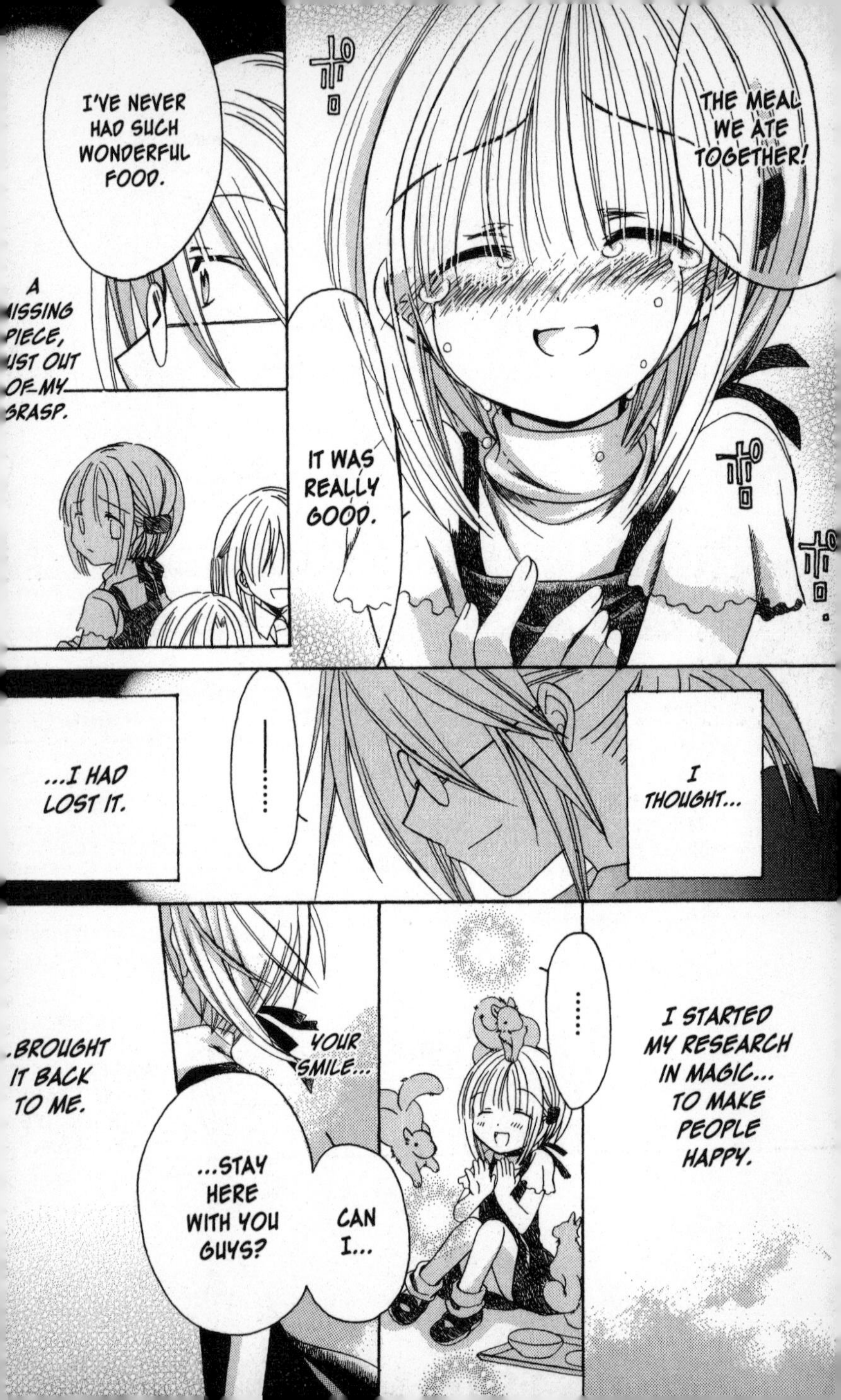

흡
THE MEAL WE ATE TOGETHER!
IT WAS REALLY GOOD.
흡
흡
I'VE NEVER HAD SUCH WONDERFUL FOOD.
A ISSING PIECE, UST OUT OF MY RASP.
I THOUGHT...
......
...I HAD LOST IT.
I STARTED MY RESEARCH IN MAGIC... TO MAKE PEOPLE HAPPY.
......
CAN I...
...STAY HERE WITH YOU GUYS?
YOUR SMILE...
.BROUGHT IT BACK TO ME.

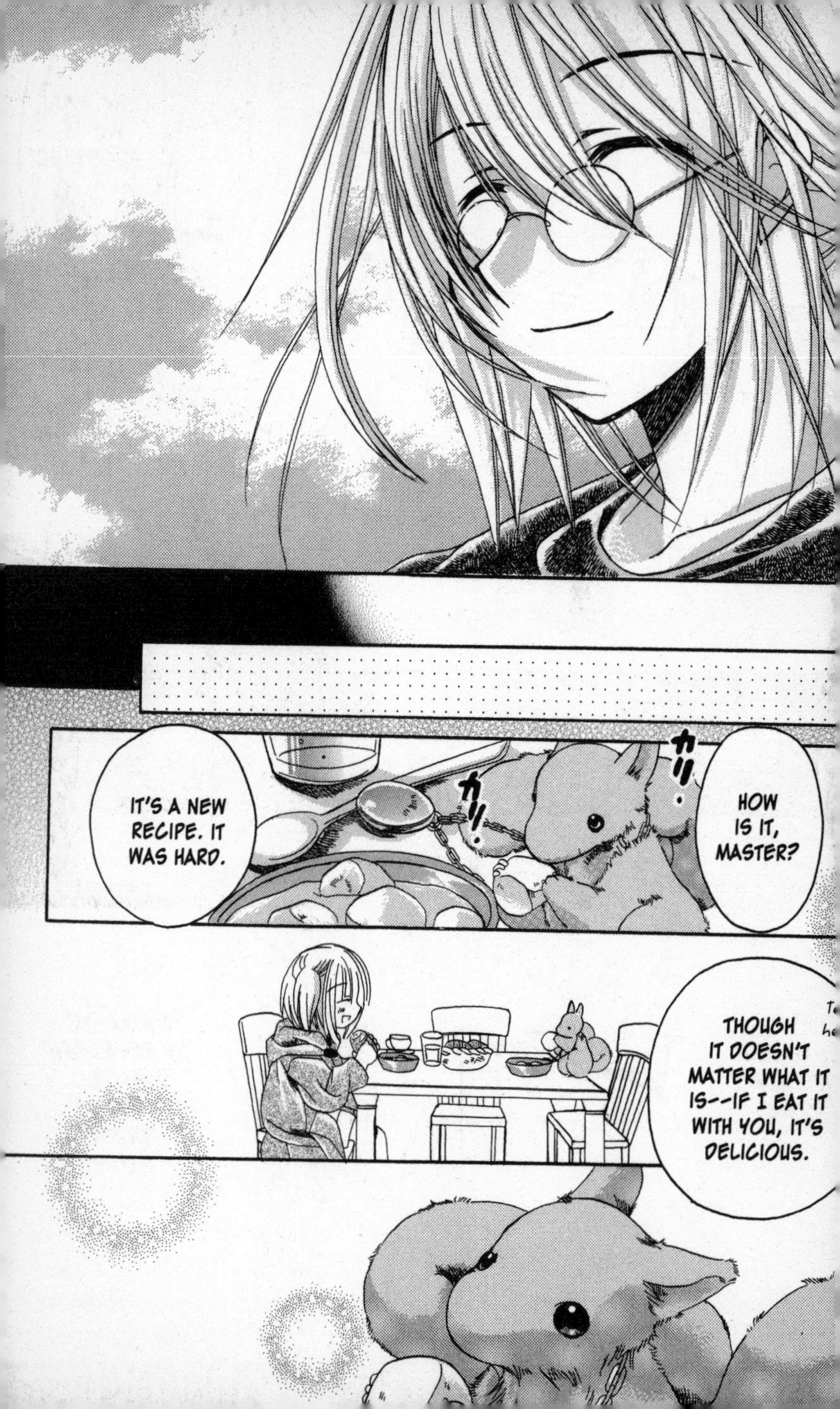

HOW IS IT, MASTER?
IT'S A NEW RECIPE. IT WAS HARD.
THOUGH IT DOESN'T MATTER WHAT IT IS--IF I EAT IT WITH YOU, IT'S DELICIOUS.

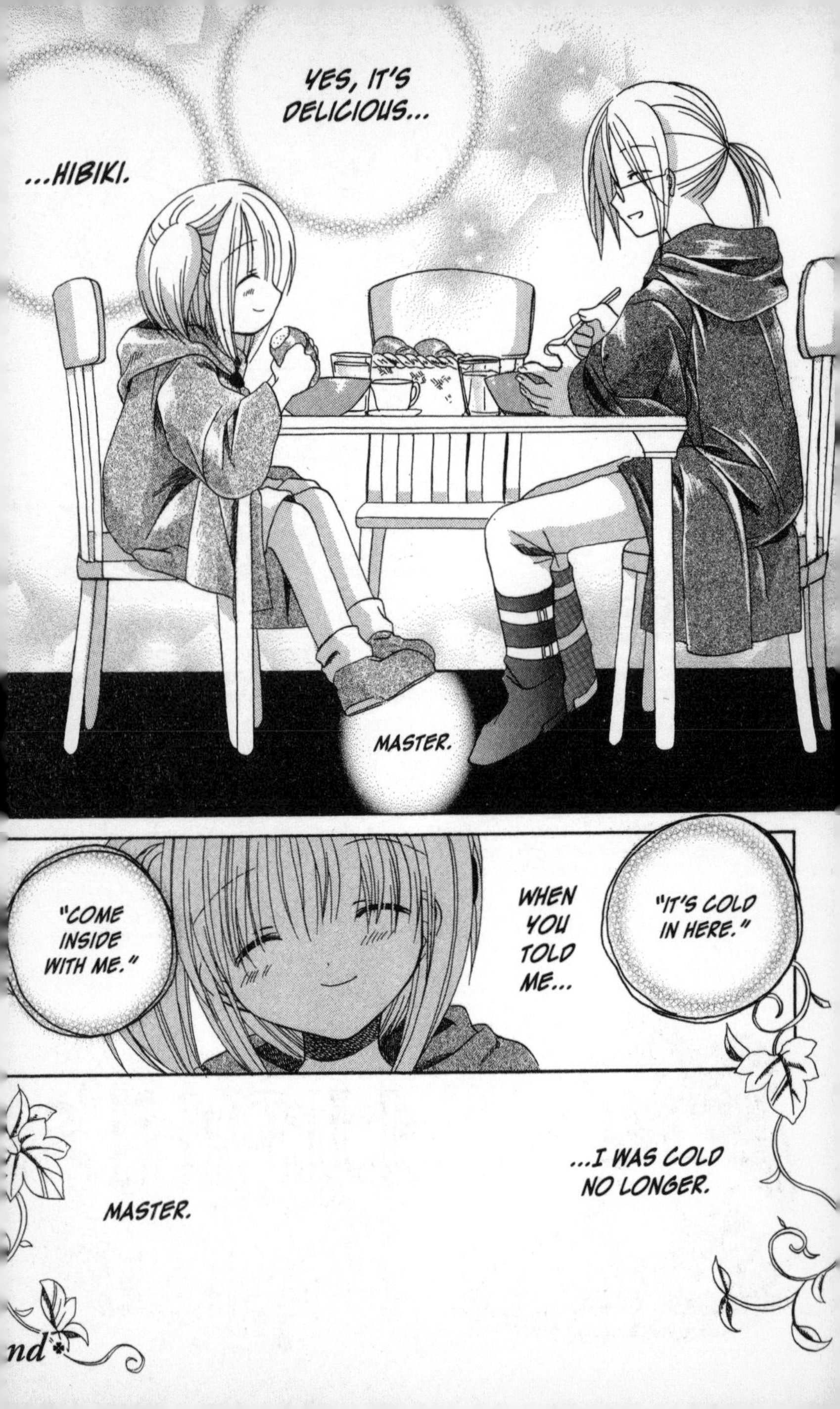
YES, IT'S DELICIOUS...
...HIBIKI.
MASTER.
"IT'S COLD IN HERE."
WHEN YOU TOLD ME...
"COME INSIDE WITH ME."
...I WAS COLD NO LONGER.
MASTER.

HIBIKI'S MAGIC™

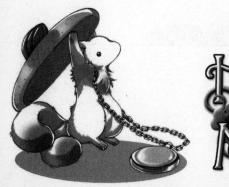

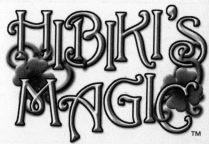

✽ The next volume of *Hibiki's Magic* is going to be huge. Idumi-san and I are working hard on it right now. After that, the turbulent ______ arc will begin, but that seems like a long, long time from now. But I'm already working on the script!

麻枝 准
JUN MAEDA

In regards to CDs...ever since book one, I've been buying more and more. My record is 100 in a single month! I totally blew all my money... The music I listen to doesn't go with *Hibiki's Magic* at all, but I hope you don't mind me listing some of it here.

First is FORDIRELIFESAKE! Their music is destructively beautiful. Their philosophy seems to be "screw melody!" and listening to it makes me feel surrounded, like the end is growing near. I'd like to be listening to their song "Four Letter Lie" when the world ends.

WITH RESISTANCE and TAKEN are two other bands that have the same feel. Both bands have broken up, but they have left behind great music that will survive the grave. TAKEN's last song, "Between Two Unseens," is godly... A painful scream pierces my chest. Amazing guitar playing, as well. What is it with this music?! You rarely find music that can touch you so deeply. This isn't nice-nice melody stuff, so I don't recommend it for everyone. But for fans of out-there music, check it out! See you next volume.

✽ I'm so happy to see you again. Hello, this is Rei Idumi. It's been a long time since volume one, but... (I'm sorry...) volume two is finally here. Thanks to those who stayed so loyal--I really appreciate it. As Maeda-san wrote, the next volume will be very exciting. I know I'm working at a slow pace, but please stick with me! We'll do our best. YEAH! We're just getting started.

依澄れい
REI IDUMI

✽ I thought that maybe I should write about music, too, but...my tastes are so plain. While I draw, I listen to really popular stuff like B'z, Sugamikao, Kenji Otsuki, etc. Of course, I listen to a lot of Key songs as well. Especially when drawing important scenes. The power of music can be amazing. I always have something playing while I work. Oh, and...Maeda-san, you're buying too many CDs!

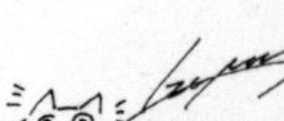

✽ Well, then, I pray I get to see you all in the next volume. Please take care!

Thanks: Rie-san, Nakagawa-san, my first editor Utsumi-san, second editor Sugita-san, the designer, Visual Arts, and everyone else who helped me!

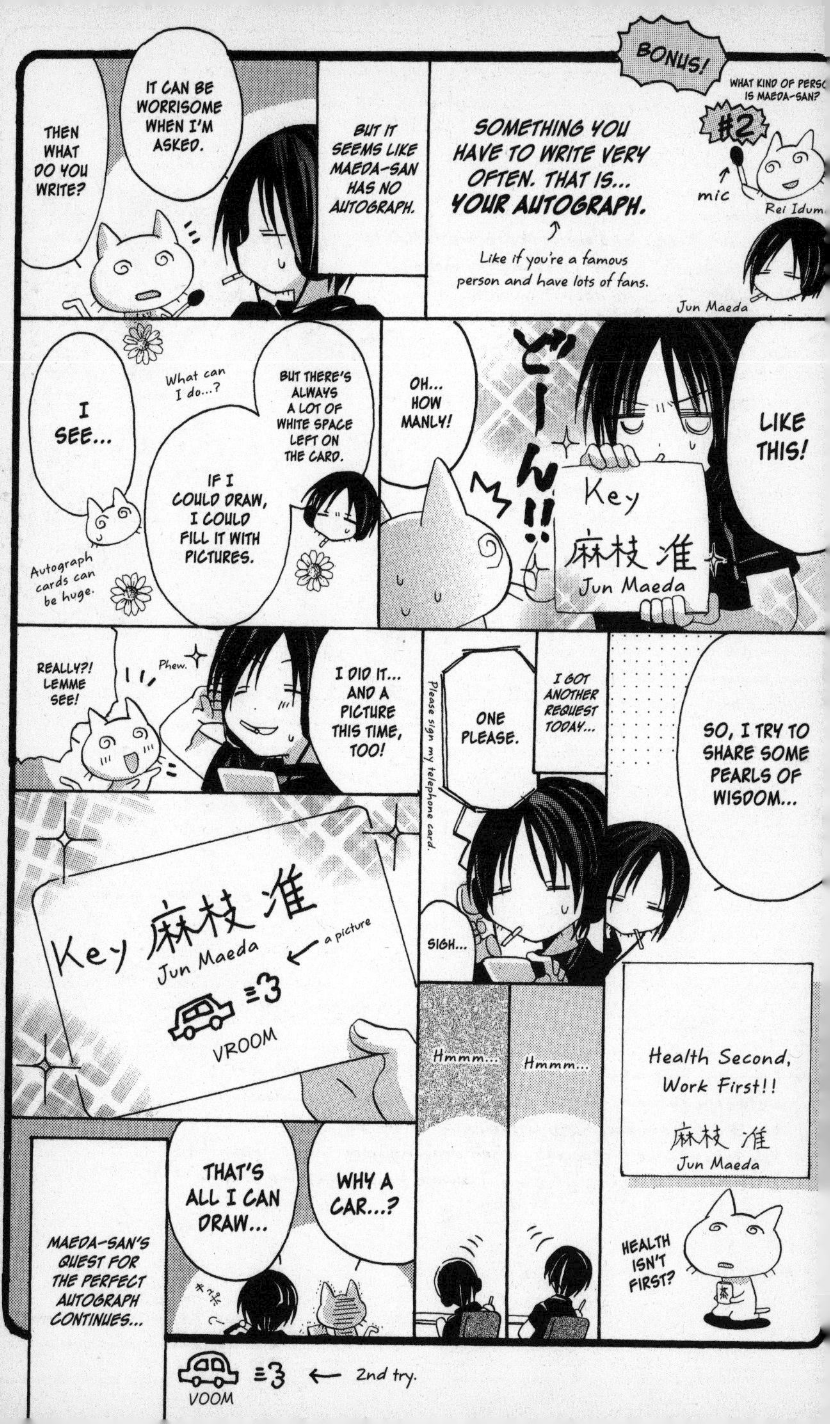
BONUS!
WHAT KIND OF PERSON IS MAEDA-SAN?
#2
mic
Rei Idum
Jun Maeda
SOMETHING YOU HAVE TO WRITE VERY OFTEN. THAT IS... YOUR AUTOGRAPH.
Like if you're a famous person and have lots of fans.
BUT IT SEEMS LIKE MAEDA-SAN HAS NO AUTOGRAPH.
IT CAN BE WORRISOME WHEN I'M ASKED.
THEN WHAT DO YOU WRITE?
LIKE THIS!
どーん!!
Key 麻枝 准 Jun Maeda
OH... HOW MANLY!
BUT THERE'S ALWAYS A LOT OF WHITE SPACE LEFT ON THE CARD.
IF I COULD DRAW, I COULD FILL IT WITH PICTURES.
What can I do...?
I SEE...
Autograph cards can be huge.
SO, I TRY TO SHARE SOME PEARLS OF WISDOM...
I GOT ANOTHER REQUEST TODAY...
ONE PLEASE.
Please sign my telephone card.
SIGH...
I DID IT... AND A PICTURE THIS TIME, TOO!
Phew.
REALLY?! LEMME SEE!
Key 麻枝 准 Jun Maeda
← a picture
≡3
VROOM
Health Second, Work First!! 麻枝 准 Jun Maeda
HEALTH ISN'T FIRST?
Hmmm...
Hmmm...
WHY A CAR...?
THAT'S ALL I CAN DRAW...
MAEDA-SAN'S QUEST FOR THE PERFECT AUTOGRAPH CONTINUES...
≡3 ← 2nd try.
VOOM

New Do #1

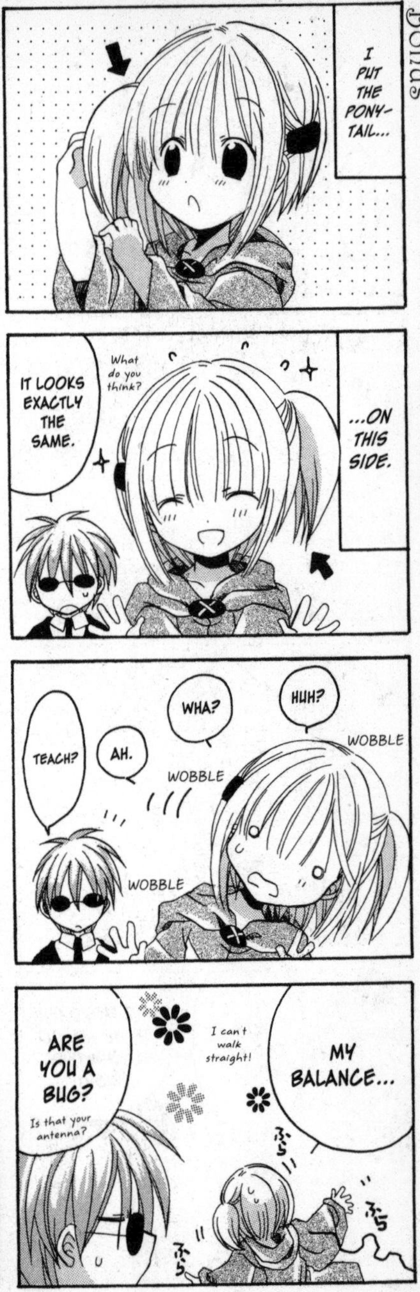
I PUT THE PONY-TAIL...
...ON THIS SIDE.
What do you think?
IT LOOKS EXACTLY THE SAME.
WOBBLE
HUH?
WHA?
WOBBLE
AH.
TEACH?
WOBBLE
MY BALANCE...
I can't walk straight!
ふら
ふら
ふら
ARE YOU A BUG?
Is that your antenna?

New Do #2

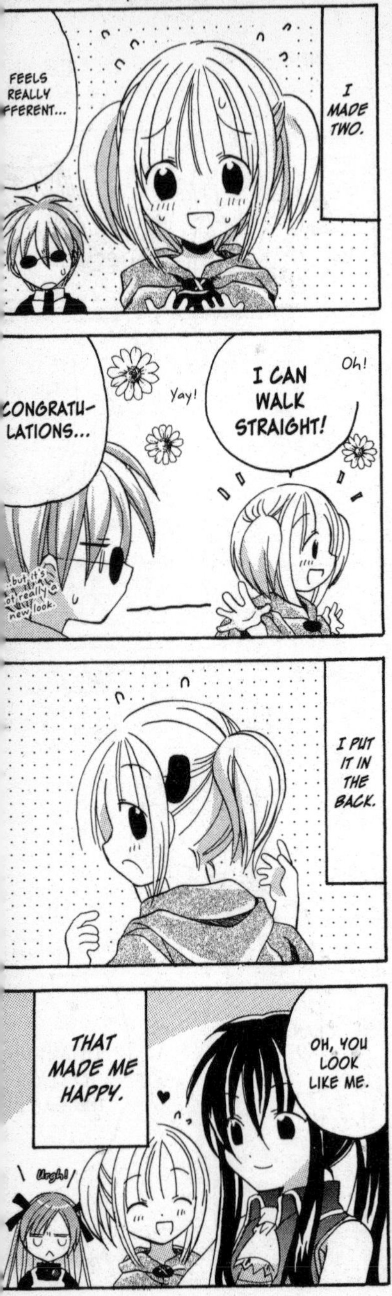
I MADE TWO.
FEELS REALLY FFERENT...
Oh!
I CAN WALK STRAIGHT!
Yay!
CONGRATU-LATIONS...
...but it's not really a new look.
I PUT IT IN THE BACK.
OH, YOU LOOK LIKE ME.
THAT MADE ME HAPPY.
Urgh!

New Do #3

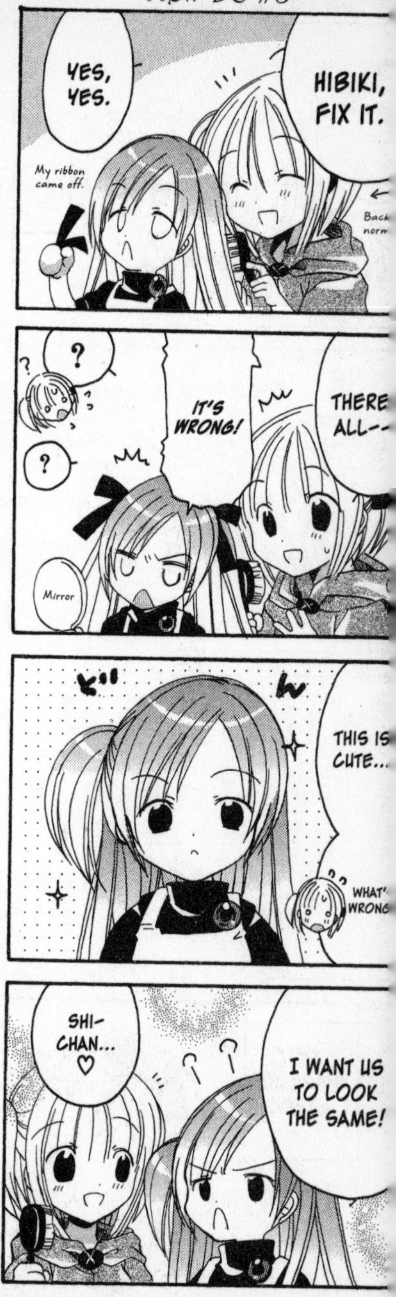
HIBIKI, FIX IT.
YES, YES.
My ribbon came off.
THERE ALL--
IT'S WRONG!
?
?
Mirror
THIS IS CUTE...
I WANT US TO LOOK THE SAME!
SHI-CHAN... ♡

New Do #4

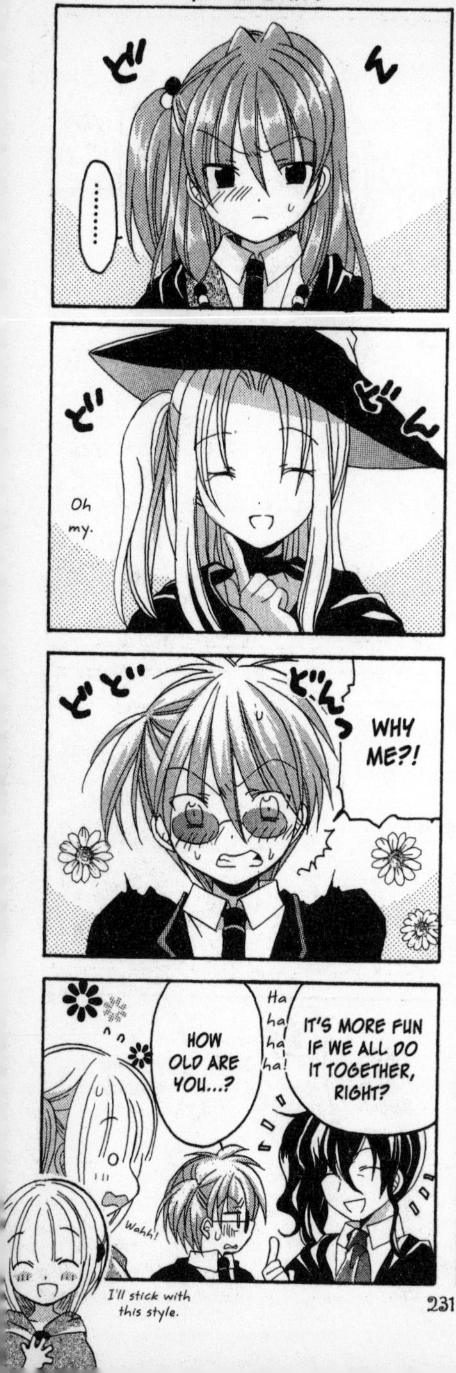
......
Oh my.
WHY ME?!
IT'S MORE FUN IF WE ALL DO IT TOGETHER, RIGHT?
Ha ha ha ha!
HOW OLD ARE YOU...?
Wahh!
I'll stick with this style.

TOKYOPOP.COM

WHERE MANGA LIVES!

JOIN the
TOKYOPOP community:
www.TOKYOPOP.com

LIVE THE MANGA LIFESTYLE!

EXCLUSIVE PREVIEWS...
CREATE...
UPLOAD...
DOWNLOAD...
BLOG...
CHAT...
VOTE...
LIVE!!!!

WWW.TOKYOPOP.COM HAS:

- News
- Columns
- Special Features
- and more...

THE MANGA REVOLUTION • LEADING • 漫画革命 • LEADING THE MANGA REVOLUTION

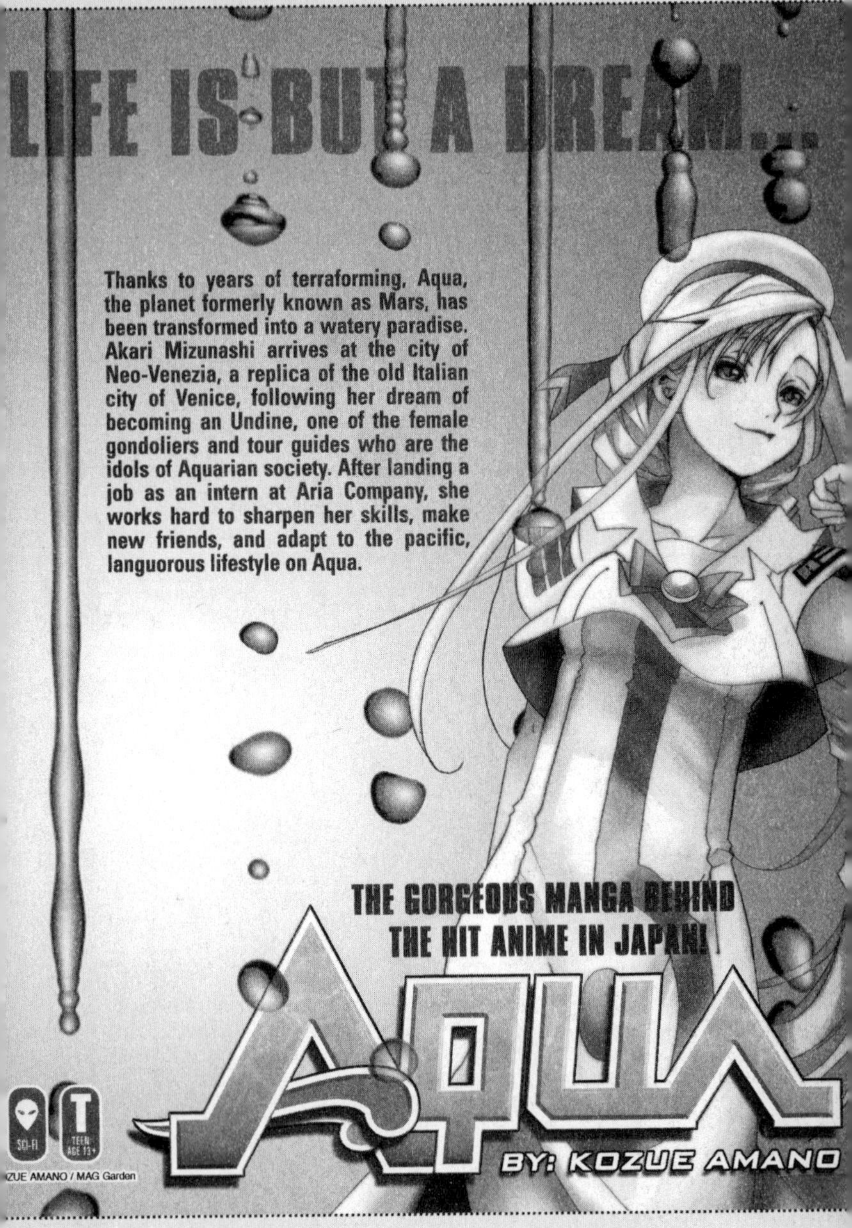
LIFE IS BUT A DREAM...
Thanks to years of terraforming, Aqua, the planet formerly known as Mars, has been transformed into a watery paradise. Akari Mizunashi arrives at the city of Neo-Venezia, a replica of the old Italian city of Venice, following her dream of becoming an Undine, one of the female gondoliers and tour guides who are the idols of Aquarian society. After landing a job as an intern at Aria Company, she works hard to sharpen her skills, make new friends, and adapt to the pacific, languorous lifestyle on Aqua.
THE GORGEOUS MANGA BEHIND THE HIT ANIME IN JAPAN!
AQUA
BY: KOZUE AMANO
SCI-FI
T
TEEN AGE 13+
ZUE AMANO / MAG Garden

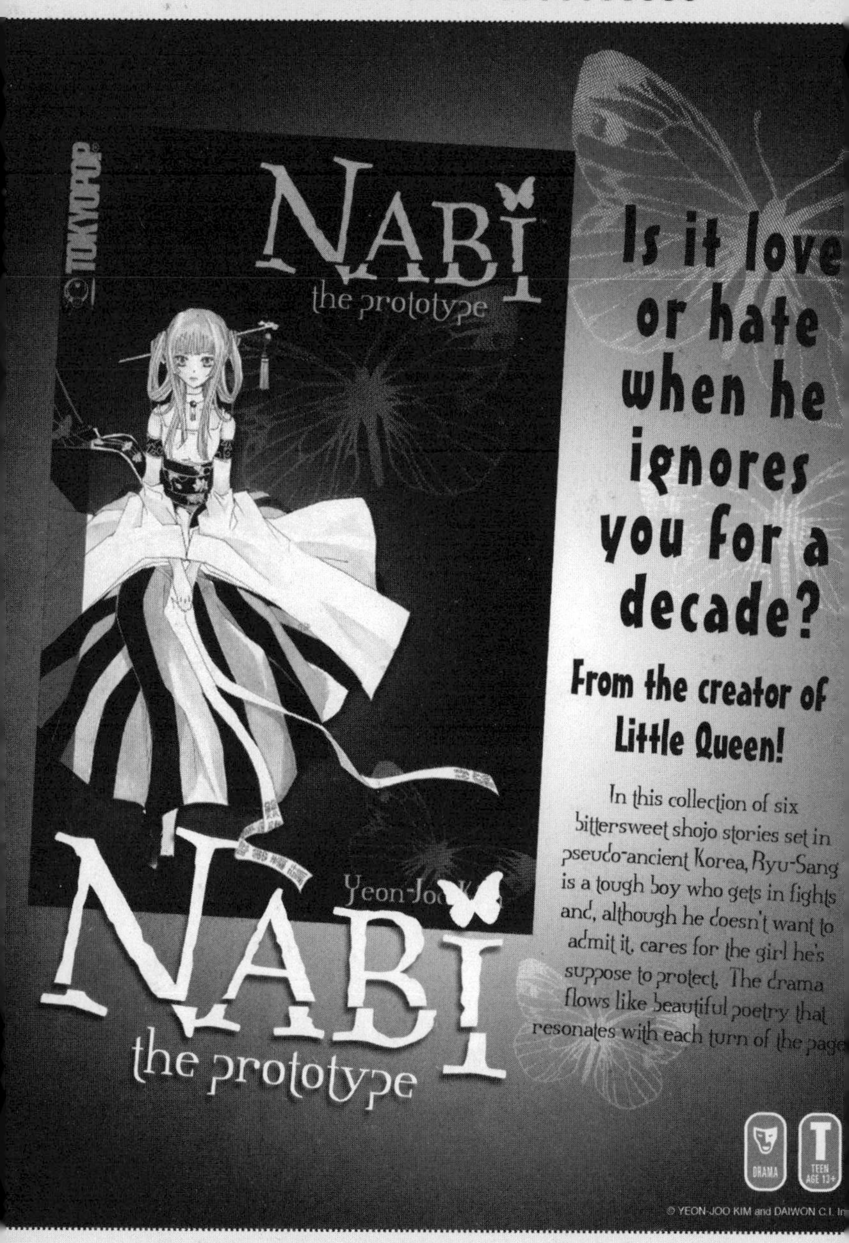
TOKYOPOP
NABI the prototype
Yeon-Joo Kim
NABI the prototype
Is it love or hate when he ignores you for a decade?
From the creator of Little Queen!
In this collection of six bittersweet shojo stories set in pseudo-ancient Korea, Ryu-Sang is a tough boy who gets in fights and, although he doesn't want to admit it, cares for the girl he's suppose to protect. The drama flows like beautiful poetry that resonates with each turn of the page
DRAMA
T TEEN AGE 13+
© YEON-JOO KIM and DAIWON C.I. In

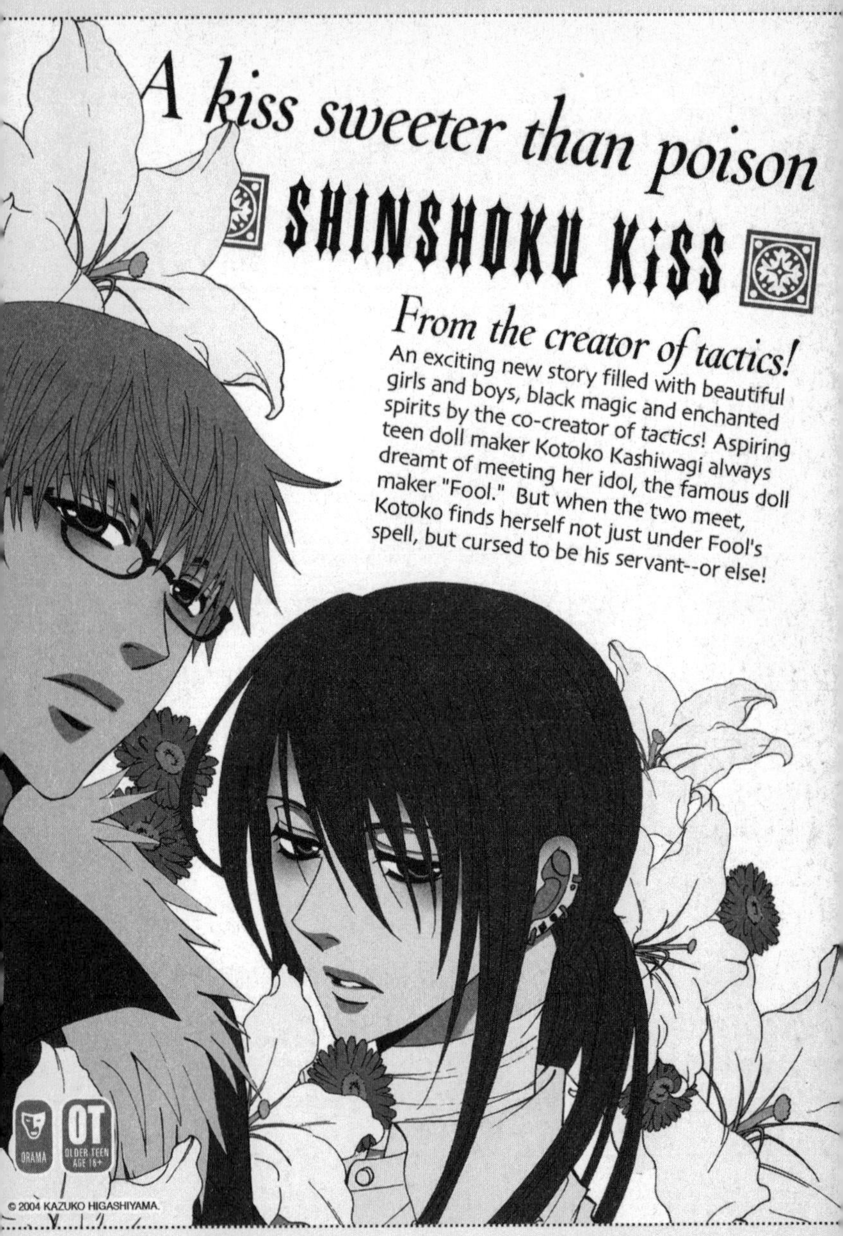
A kiss sweeter than poison
SHINSHOKU KISS
From the creator of tactics!
An exciting new story filled with beautiful girls and boys, black magic and enchanted spirits by the co-creator of tactics! Aspiring teen doll maker Kotoko Kashiwagi always dreamt of meeting her idol, the famous doll maker "Fool." But when the two meet, Kotoko finds herself not just under Fool's spell, but cursed to be his servant--or else!
DRAMA
OT
OLDER TEEN AGE 16+
© 2004 KAZUKO HIGASHIYAMA.

FOR MORE INFORMATION VISIT: WWW.TOKYOPOP.COM

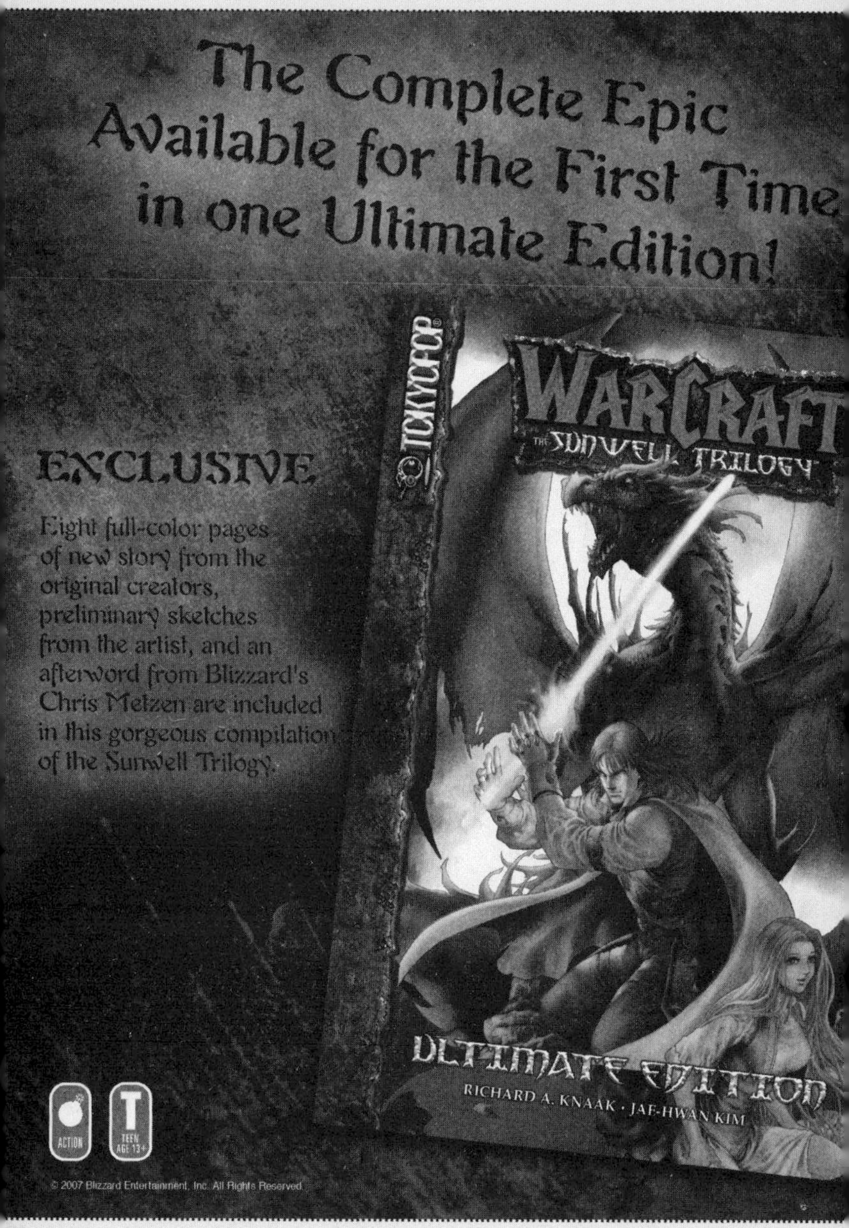
The Complete Epic
Available for the First Time
in one Ultimate Edition!
EXCLUSIVE
Eight full-color pages of new story from the original creators, preliminary sketches from the artist, and an afterword from Blizzard's Chris Metzen are included in this gorgeous compilation of the Sunwell Trilogy.
TOKYOPOP
WARCRAFT
THE SUNWELL TRILOGY
ULTIMATE EDITION
RICHARD A. KNAAK · JAE-HWAN KIM
ACTION
T
TEEN AGE 13+
© 2007 Blizzard Entertainment, Inc. All Rights Reserved.

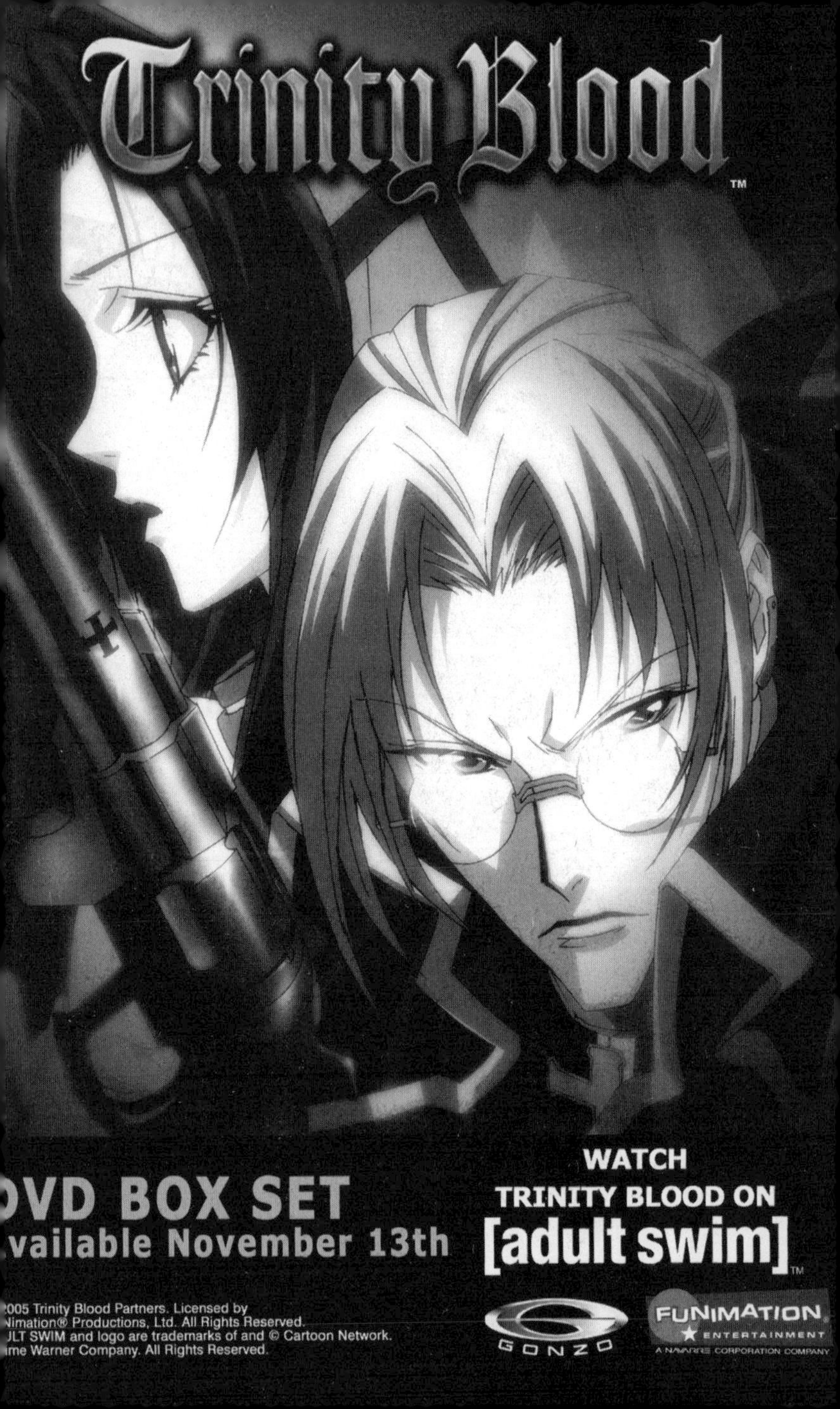
Trinity Blood
™
WATCH
TRINITY BLOOD ON
[adult swim]
™
DVD BOX SET
vailable November 13th
2005 Trinity Blood Partners. Licensed by
Nimation® Productions, Ltd. All Rights Reserved.
JLT SWIM and logo are trademarks of and © Cartoon Network.
me Warner Company. All Rights Reserved.
GONZO
FUNIMATION
ENTERTAINMENT
A NAVARRE CORPORATION COMPANY

SUPER HYPER AUDIOTISTIC SONIC REVOLUTION!!!
www.myspace.com/tokyopop
www.TOKYOPOP.com

Beautiful Color Images from CLAMP's Most Popular Series!

Chobits Art Book

ART NOT FINAL

Your Eyes Only

CLAMP

Luscious, full-color art from the world's most popular manga studio, CLAMP, fills this stunningly gorgeous book. This book is a feast for the eyes of any Chobits fan!

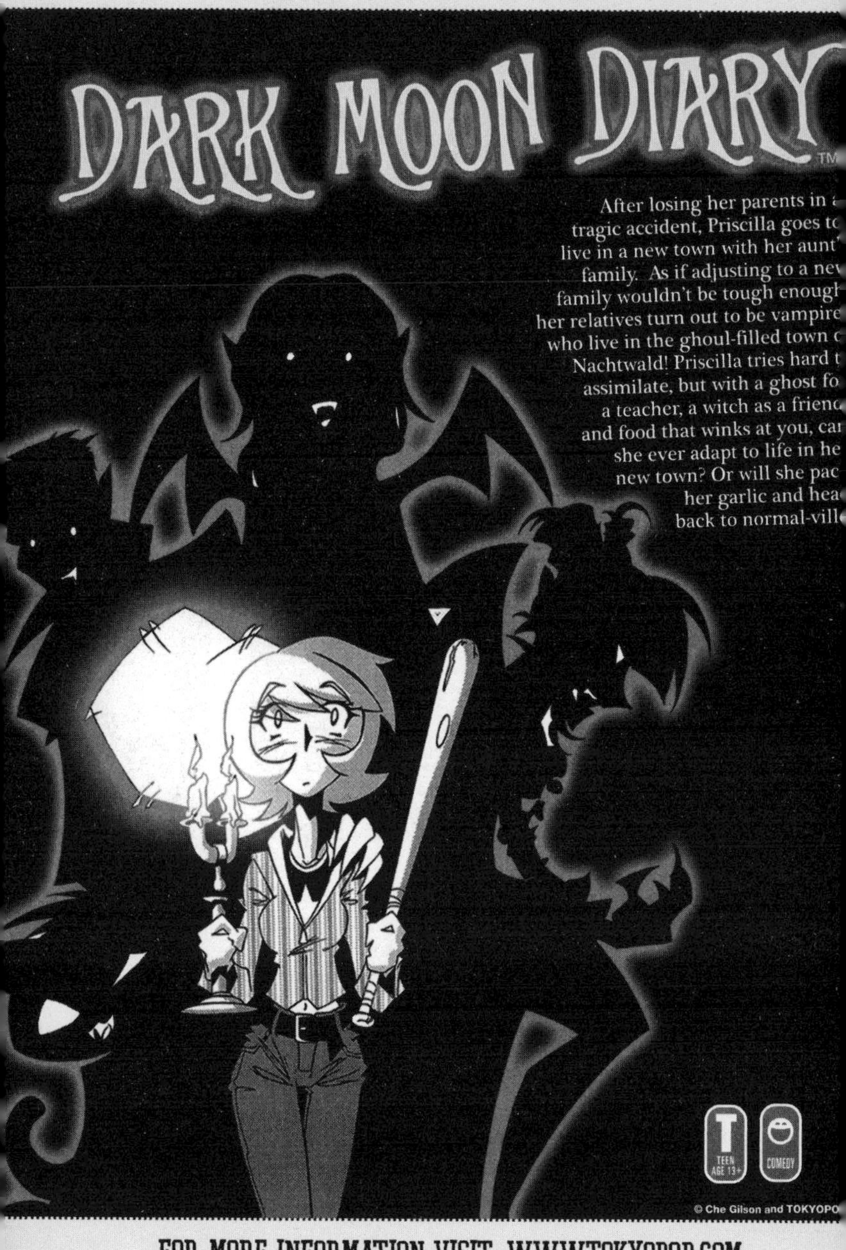
DARK MOON DIARY
TM
After losing her parents in a
tragic accident, Priscilla goes to
live in a new town with her aunt'
family. As if adjusting to a new
family wouldn't be tough enough
her relatives turn out to be vampire
who live in the ghoul-filled town c
Nachtwald! Priscilla tries hard t
assimilate, but with a ghost fo
a teacher, a witch as a frienc
and food that winks at you, car
she ever adapt to life in he
new town? Or will she pac
her garlic and hea
back to normal-vill
T
TEEN AGE 13+
COMEDY
© Che Gilson and TOKYOPO

STOP!

This is the back of the book.
You wouldn't want to spoil a great ending!

This book is printed "manga-style," in the authentic Japanese right-to-left format. Since none of the artwork has been flipped or altered, readers get to experience the story just as the creator intended. You've been asking for it, so TOKYOPOP® delivered: authentic, hot-off-the-press, and far more fun!

DIRECTIONS

If this is your first time reading manga-style, here's a quick guide to help you understand how it works.

It's easy... just start in the top right panel and follow the numbers. Have fun, and look for more 100% authentic manga from TOKYOPOP®!